# THE DETROIT RED WINGS

# THE
# DETROIT
# RED WINGS

## THE ILLUSTRATED HISTORY

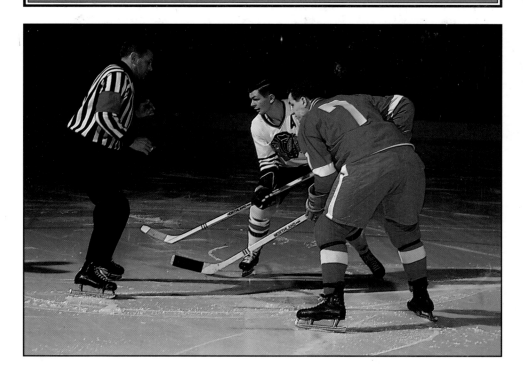

## RICHARD BAK

TAYLOR PUBLISHING COMPANY, DALLAS, TEXAS

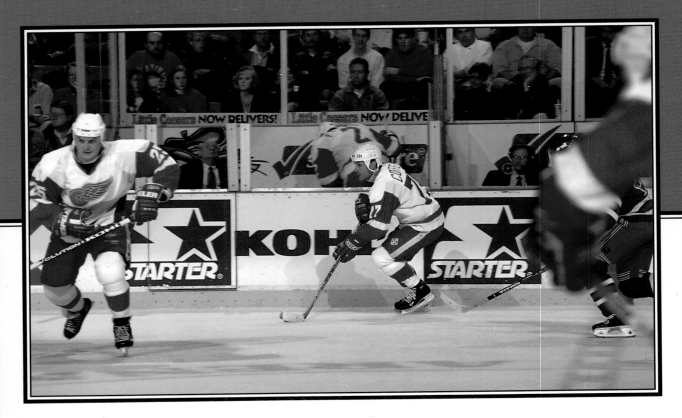

Published by Taylor Publishing Company
1550 West Mockingbird Lane
Dallas, Texas 75235

Book Design by
Bob Moon, SporTradition Publications
798 Linworth Rd. East
Columbus, Ohio 43235

Library of Congress Cataloging-in-Publication Data

Bak, Richard, 1954–
    Detroit Red Wings: the illustrated history / Richard Bak.
        p.   cm.
    Includes bibliographical references.
    ISBN 0–87833–975–2 (cloth)
    1. Detroit Red Wings (Hockey team)—History.   I. Title.
GV848.D47B35  1997
796.96'264'0977434—dc21                    96–23714 CIP

Printed in the United States of America
10 9 8 7 6 5 4 3 2 1

# CONTENTS

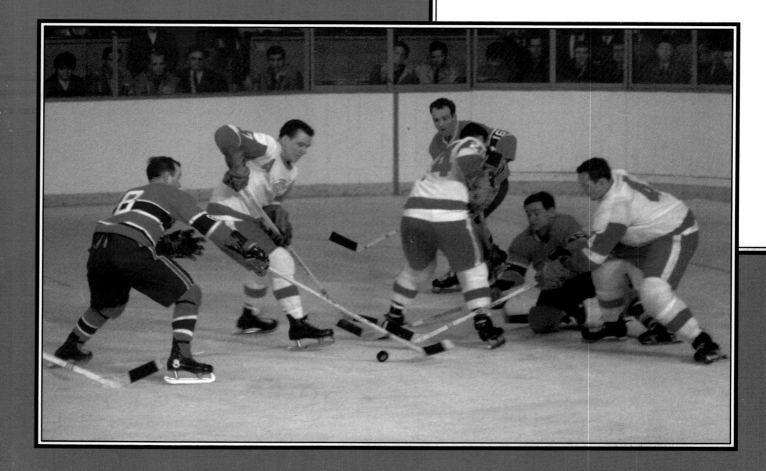

# CHAPTER ONE

**L**ike photographs left too long in the sun, memories of Detroit's first ice age have faded badly over time. There is no one left from the squad of grizzled veterans that traveled from western Canada to form the nucleus of the city's first professional hockey team in 1926. Even the roster of Detroit's first championship team a decade later has dwindled down to one survivor. Come to think of it, there aren't too many *fans* still

# Detroit's First Ice Age

## 1926–1932

around who can hang flesh on the rows of obscure names and numbers that fill the various record books and media guides. Which makes the recollections of pioneer players Stu Evans and Pete Kelly all the more special.

"The game has changed quite a bit since I played," said Evans, who hung up his skates in 1939 after eight NHL seasons. "We weren't as fast as the fellows today. But they're also a lot rougher now. With helmets and expansion, you've got a lot of guys out there who never would have played in my day. In my opinion there's too much fighting, too much stickwork. Good hockey players shouldn't have to resort to that stuff."

Evans never was one to hold anything back. Until his death in 1996, the oldest living ex-Red Wing remained a feisty relic of

**Ebbie Goodfellow in 1928.**

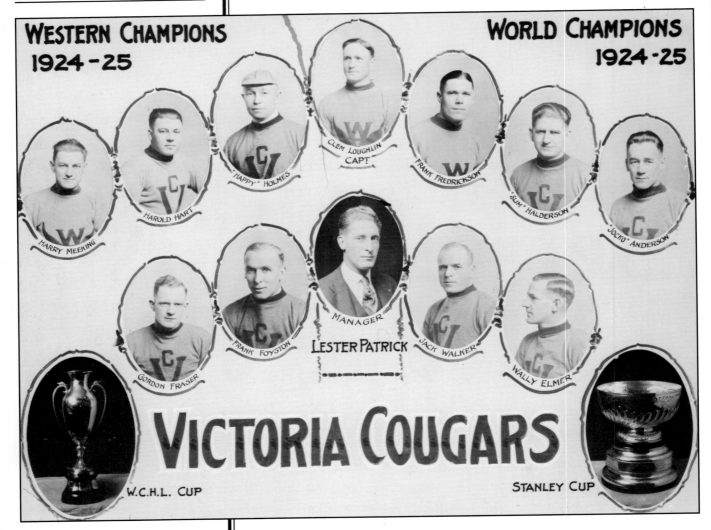

WESTERN CHAMPIONS 1924-25

WORLD CHAMPIONS 1924-25

HARRY MEEKING

HAROLD HART

"HAPPY" HOLMES

CLEM LOUGHLIN CAPT.

FRANK FREDRICKSON

"SLIM" HALDERSON

"JOCKO" ANDERSON

GORDON FRASER

FRANK FOYSTON

MANAGER

LESTER PATRICK

JACK WALKER

WALLY ELMER

# VICTORIA COUGARS

W.C.H.L. CUP

STANLEY CUP

I n 1925 the Victoria Cougars of the Western Canadian Hockey League became the last squad from outside the National Hockey League to win the Stanley Cup, defeating the Montreal Canadiens. The following season they became the last non-NHL team to compete for the Cup, losing to the Montreal Maroons. Shortly afterward, the WCHL disbanded and the Cougars moved practically en masse to Detroit, where they formed the nucleus of the city's first NHL team.

Detroit's rich hockey past, a time when bare-faced goalies, stay-at-home defensemen, and other dinosaurs roamed the earth. Evans, a rugged blueliner from Ottawa, played in Detroit from 1930 to 1934, during which time the franchise evolved in fits and starts from the noncompetitive Cougars to the financially ailing Falcons to, finally, the powerful and prosperous Red Wings.

Pete Kelly was a young right winger for the Wings during their glory days of the mid-1930s. Now in his eighties, the retired athletic director can't always remember what he had for lunch at yesterday's golf outing. But when it comes to re-creating the formative years of hockey in this town, his memories are as vivid as a freshly snapped Polaroid. There was Normie Smith, for instance— the superstitious goalie whose insistence on never changing his underwear during a winning streak probably had some teammates secretly praying for a loss. And an unknown rookie named Modere "Mud" Bruneteau, whose goal one March morning in Montreal put an end to hockey's longest game.

"Playing in the NHL was an early dream of every kid who grew up close to an ice rink," said Kelly. "And it certainly was a good time to join Detroit when I did. There was great harmony on the team. The chemistry was right for a championship."

Evans, who spent the balance of his career in Montreal, wasn't around in the spring of 1936 when the Detroit franchise completed a decade-long turnaround from worst to first by winning its first Stanley Cup. In fact, three years later he did something that would be unthinkable in today's game of multiyear, multi-million-dollar contracts. He quit at the peak of his career to concentrate on a "real" job—working for the Ford Motor Company.

"I had to make a decision, and so I chose the auto business," said Evans, who went on to operate two highly successful Lincoln-Mercury dealerships in the Detroit area. "I didn't see any future in hockey."

Given the NHL's shaky status then, Evans's doubts were legitimate. Who knew if the league was going to last? It was a question asked over and over as professional hockey looked to gain a foothold in the late 1920s and early '30s.

The National Hockey League was founded inside Montreal's Windsor Hotel on November 22, 1917. The circuit, just one of several high-caliber hockey leagues then in existence, included teams in Toronto and Ottawa and two in Montreal, the Wanderers and the Canadiens. Calamity was an early companion. In 1918 the Wanderers were forced to withdraw after their rink burned down. Later, an influenza epidemic forced suspension of the annual Stanley Cup competition, which since 1893, had determined Canada's national champion.

In 1919 the addition of Quebec made the NHL a four-team circuit again. The following season Quebec was replaced by a club in Hamilton, Ontario, after which the league remained a cozy, stable quartet of Canadian cities through the early 1920s.

Then came the American invasion. The first U.S. team, the Boston Bruins, was admitted in 1924, followed by the Pittsburgh Pirates and the New York Americans in 1925. In 1926, a momentous year, three additional franchises—the New York Rangers, Chicago Blackhawks, and Detroit Cougars—joined Boston and Pittsburgh in the new five-team American Division, as the NHL split into two divisions for the first time. The New York Americans and the four Canadian teams comprised the Canadian Division.

The 1926-27 season also was significant in that the Stanley Cup—heretofore competed for by various leagues—became the exclusive domain of the NHL. Even better for the owners of the NHL's three expansion teams, the collapse of the rival Western and Pacific Coast Leagues allowed them to purchase entire rosters of players off the failing clubs. And that is how Charles A. Hughes and a syndicate of 73 local investors—including such heavyweights as industrialist Edsel Ford, department store magnate S. S. Kresge, and newspaper publisher William E. Scripps—stocked the Motor City's first professional hockey team.

Hughes, who is all but forgotten today, was an important man in his time. Born in Grand Ledge, Michigan, in 1881, he graduated from the University of Michigan when he was twenty-one and became a sportswriter for the *Detroit*

The man responsible for bringing pro hockey to Detroit was Charles Hughes, seen standing center in front of the Detroit Athletic Club. Hughes served as president of the team until it was sold during the Depression.

**H**arry "Hap" Holmes was Detroit's regular goatender its first two seasons in the NHL, compiling a 2.11 average, 17 shutouts, and a 30-46-9 record. Before coming to Detroit, Holmes backstopped four different teams to Stanley Cup championships: the 1914 Toronto Blueshirts, 1917 Seattle Metropolitans, 1918 Toronto Arenas, and 1925 Victoria Cougars. No other goalie has ever matched his feat.

*Tribune,* covering the exploits of famous sports figures like Michigan football coach Fielding Yost and the Tigers' fiery superstar, Ty Cobb. He later worked for newspapers in Chicago, then served as Teddy Roosevelt's public relations flack during his African safari. The trip's success revealed Hughes's greatest asset: He was one hell of a schmoozer.

He put that talent to use when he returned to Detroit. In 1912 he helped to organize and publicize an ambitious civic celebration called the Cadillaqua. That venture, designed to be an annual festival honoring Detroit and its founding fathers, died after the first year, but the contacts he made in the burgeoning auto industry proved invaluable. He used his considerable powers of persuasion to convince the city's power brokers to build the magnificent Detroit Athletic Club in 1915 and to hire him as manager. He was also allowed to publish, at his expense, a club magazine. With his contacts in the sports, entertainment, and literary worlds, Hughes was able to persuade a remarkable array of famous and powerful figures to come to the club and to contribute to his publication.

In 1926, he talked several D.A.C. members into backing a bid to bring pro hockey to town. His sales pitch never failed to win over civic boosters. If their

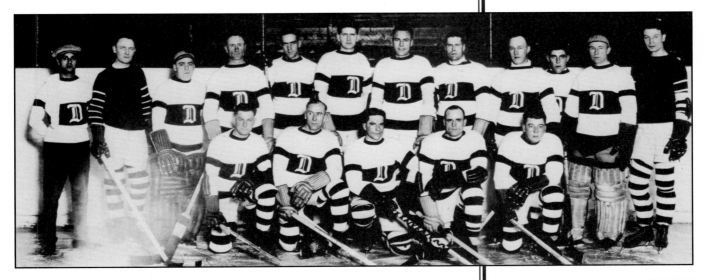

**T**he 1926-27 edition of the Detroit Cougars pose inside Windsor's Border Cities Arena, where the team played while awaiting the completion of Olympia Stadium.

dynamic, emerging city was to be taken seriously, he'd argued, then top-drawer projects like the Cadillaqua, Detroit Athletic Club, and professional sports teams were essential. To demonstrate to potential backers that Detroiters would support a pro hockey team, over the winter of 1925-26 he arranged several exhibitions in Windsor between NHL and western clubs. On one occasion several thousand ticket-seekers had to be turned away at the box office.

The bid was officially accepted on May 15, 1926. According to newspaper reports, Hughes's syndicate paid a $100,000 franchise fee. That didn't include the cost of players. Hughes, who served as president of the new club, was impressed with the Victoria Cougars of the Western Hockey League. In the spring of 1926 the Cougars had just been defeated by the Montreal Maroons, three games to one, for the Stanley Cup. It was a rematch of the previous year's finals, when Victoria defeated Montreal to become the last non-NHL team to win the Cup.

On October 5, 1926, what was officially known as the Detroit Hockey Club, Inc., purchased the rights to fifteen players from the Victoria club for an estimated $100,000. Hughes signed nine of them to contracts and pegged the aggregation the "Detroit Cougars." In addition to maintaining some continuity between what had been one of the sport's finest teams and one of its newest, Hughes reasoned that the feline nickname fit in with that of the only other pro sports franchise in town, the baseball Tigers.

The Detroit club's greatest expense was the million-dollar facility, Olympia Stadium, being planned for the corner of Grand River and McGraw Avenues on the city's west side. This tremendous investment, reported the *Detroit News*, "is based on the assumption that Americans will patronize anything that is spectacular, exciting and thrilling, and because hockey is all of these things the investment has been made."

Traditionally, NHL players had come from Kamsack, Flin Flon, Medicine Hat, and other far-flung Canadian outposts, where the calendar is divided into nine months of winter and three months of rough sledding. The tough game

F rank Foyston was a standout center in the Western Canadian Hockey League from 1916 to 1926 before winding up his career with two seasons for the Cougars. He was one of four former Victoria Cougars to be inducted into the Pro Hockey Hall of Fame, joining teammates Jack Walker, Frank Frederickson, and Hap Holmes.

J ohnny Sheppard led Detroit in scoring with 21 points in 1926-27, its first season in the NHL. The following season, on November 22, 1927, the little forward scored the first-ever goal at Olympia in a 2-1 loss to Ottawa.

has always attracted a certain breed of men. But the first squad to represent Detroit was a particularly worldly lot.

There was defenseman and captain Art Duncan, obtained from Chicago in exchange for the rights to Art Gignac. Duncan, who Hughes appointed coach and general manager, had earned the Military Cross for shooting down twenty-two enemy aircraft during the First World War. Left winger "Wee Johnny" Sheppard was a slick puck handler who spent his summers as a trapper in the Arctic Circle. Six-foot-three, 200-pound defenseman Harold "Slim" Halderson had been a member of the 1920 Canadian Olympic team that won the gold medal in Antwerp. Its captain was the Cougars' square-jawed center, Frank Frederickson, arguably the most colorful player in the league. A pilot during the war, he survived a plane crash only to nearly drown on a torpedoed troop ship in the Mediterranean. "Freddie" turned pro after the 1920 Olympics, amusing a succession of teammates with his skills as an amateur magician and musician.

In essence, the Cougars were a permanent road team during their first NHL season, playing "home" games in the 6,000-seat Border Cities Arena in Windsor while waiting for Olympia Stadium to be built. (The building is still in use today as the home of the Windsor Spitfires of the Ontario Hockey League.) Detroit's debut was November 18, 1926, in Windsor. Shortly before the puck was dropped on that Thursday evening, number-one goaltender Harold "Hap" Holmes announced that he was too sick to play. Herb Stuart was put between the pipes, and the shaky fill-in surrendered goals to Duke Keats and Harry Oliver in the first three minutes as the Boston Bruins skated to a 2-0 victory. Stuart would appear in only two more games during the season before leaving Detroit and the NHL forever.

After a loss in Pittsburgh, the Cougars looked to be back on track when they defeated the Blackhawks in Chicago on November 24, 1-0. Frederickson scored and Holmes turned aside 29 shots to register the franchise's first win and shutout. But reality quickly settled in. Despite having four future Hall of Famers on their 12-man roster—Frederickson, Holmes, center Frank Foyston, and left winger Jack Walker—the Detroit Cougars were not a very good team. These respected but aging veterans would later enter the Hall based on what they had accomplished on other teams, not on what they did in Detroit.

A third of the way into the season, with the team floundering near the bottom of the standings, Duncan made his first significant trade. On January 5, 1927, Frederickson and Harry Meeking were dealt to Boston for Keats and Archie Briden (who had set up both Bruins goals in the Cougars' NHL debut seven weeks earlier). The deal allowed Duncan to give up the responsibilities of coaching to concentrate on those of the blue line and the front office. It was as the Cougars' new player-coach that Keats—a former scoring star with Edmonton in the Pacific Coast League—notched the franchise's first hat trick, putting three pucks past Pittsburgh's "Shrimp" Worters on March 10, 1927. Keats proved to be less capable as a tactician, however. The Cougars only won two and tied two of their final 11 games under their new coach to

finish 12-28-4, the worst record in the league. With 13 goals and 60 penalty minutes, Johnny Sheppard led the team in scoring and penalties, a combination that wouldn't be replicated until the days of Ted Lindsay.

That spring Boston lost in the Cup finals to Ottawa. The Senators' roster included a gritty forward named Jack Adams, who also served as assistant coach. Hughes, smarting from an $84,000 loss in the first year of the Detroit club's operation, decided that the brash thirty-two-year-old Adams was just what the lackluster Cougars needed. He hired Adams as coach and general manager to replace Art Duncan, who had moved on to Toronto.

"I'd been involved in winning the Stanley Cup for Ottawa," Adams later recalled, "so I told Hughes he needed me more than I needed him." Although Hughes was a bust as a hockey man, his hiring of Adams would turn out to be one of the most momentous decisions in franchise history.

Adams had been an avid student of the game since his rink rat days in his hometown of Fort William, Ontario. He'd dropped out of school to work ten-hour days in the local grain elevators for twenty-two cents an hour, with some vague goal of possibly attending medical school. Instead he became a hockey vagabond, hooking up with a professional team in Calumet, Michigan (where one of his teammates was future Notre Dame gridiron legend George Gipp), and then drifting to the Peterborough and Sarnia entries in the rough Ontario

**T**he longtime home of professional hockey in Detroit, Olympia Stadium, goes up in the spring of 1927.

7

Several Cougars line up for a team shot sometime during the 1927-28 season. Standing, from left: Larry Aurie, Carson Cooper, George Hay, Jack Adams, unidentified, and Gordon Fraser. Sitting, from left: Reg Noble, Hap Holmes, Herbie Lewis, and Clem Loughlin.

Reg Noble was one of seven hockey-playing brothers from Collingwood, Ontario. A former high-scoring left winger, he'd already had 10 productive NHL seasons under his belt when Jack Adams acquired him from the Montreal Maroons for $7,500 in 1927. Noble, moved to defense by Adams, shored up Detroit's blueline and served as captain for the first half of his six years with the team. He was elected to the Hockey Hall of Fame in 1962.

Hockey Association. It was while he was playing for Sarnia in 1918 that the Toronto Arenas (as the Maple Leafs were then called) signed him to replace an injured player during their playoff with the Montreal Canadiens for the inaugural NHL crown. The husky forward helped Toronto defeat the Canadiens, despite a half-dozen cuts that required hospitalization. "I must have knocked that kid down a dozen times," one of the Canadiens said admiringly, "but he just kept coming back for more. He's a tough one and a good one, too."

Having survived his NHL baptism by fire, Adams then traveled west with the Arenas as they defeated the Vancouver Millionaires of the Pacific Coast Hockey Association for the Stanley Cup. After a brief stint in the Canadian army, Adams left the failing Toronto franchise for Vancouver. There the short, chunky blonde quickly developed into a perennial All-Star and a fan favorite. On separate occasions the man the local papers dubbed "Jovial Jawn" and "Pudgy Jack" led the PCHA in scoring and penalties, a tribute to his fierce style whether handling the puck or clobbering opponents. He returned to the NHL with Toronto in 1922 and over the next four seasons remained one of the league's top scorers and one of its most respected tacticians. In 1926, Toronto offered him the coach's position, but with the stipulation that he stay behind the bench. Adams thought he still had some life left in his legs, so he left Toronto to sign with Ottawa. It was a fortuitous decision and a fitting way to wrap up his playing career. Nine years after he had broken into the NHL on a Stanley Cup winner, he left the circuit on the same note.

In Adams the Cougars' front office had imported a proven winner, but it would take awhile before the new coach and general manager could turn things around. Among his first moves was to inject fresher, younger blood into the lineup by way of twenty-two-year-old Larry Aurie, who was all of five

and a half feet tall and tipped the scales at 145 pounds. Adams was soon calling the small, combative right wing, whom he had purchased from London of the Canadian Pro League, "the best two-way player in hockey." Adams also opened his wallet to buy forward George Hay and defenseman Percy Traub from Chicago for $15,000 and veteran forward-defenseman Reg Noble from the Montreal Maroons for $7,500. He traded the unremarkable Fred Gordon to Boston for Carson Cooper, who had a demonstrated scoring touch with the Bruins. When the puck dropped to open the 1927-28 season, three-quarters of the previous season's roster had been changed over.

The Adams regime opened on the road with a 6-0 win in Pittsburgh and a 5-2 loss in Boston. After spending their first year in Windsor, the Cougars finally competed on Detroit ice on November 22, 1927, as Olympia Stadium opened its doors to hockey with great fanfare. Designed by C. Howard Crane, whose other local works included the opulent Fox Theatre and Detroit Opera House, Olympia was modeled after New York's new Madison Square Garden, which had opened the previous year. A standing-room-only crowd of more than 10,000 watched Mayor John Smith present Adams with bunches of chrysantheums. The University of Michigan band played, figure skaters entertained between periods, and Foster Hewitt described the entire affair over radio station WGHP.

**B**efore taking over coaching duties in Detroit, Jack Adams made his reputation as a hardboiled player with Toronto (left) and Vancouver. "Adams was an awful slasher," recalled one opponent. "He meant to hurt! On the other hand, he'd take punishment without a murmur. He'd never complain when anyone whacked him. A guy like that you had to admire."

**C**larence "Dolly" Dolson set a franchise record with a 1.43 goals-against average in 44 games his rookie season of 1928-29.

**C**arson Cooper scored 18 goals in 1928-29 to lead Detroit. Ten of them were game winners, a team record that would stand sixty-seven years.

"The side features were pleasing," reported the next day's *News*, "but the result of the game was not." Johnny Sheppard beat Ottawa goalie Alex Connell on a rebound ten minutes into the game to register the first-ever goal at Olympia, but the defending champions scored in the second and third periods to pull out a 2-1 victory. Five days later the Cougars posted their first home win at Olympia, Hap Holmes shutting down the Canadiens, 2-0.

The first few seasons at Olympia were marked by regular outbreaks of fan violence. The majority of patrons were from Canada, and they enjoyed rooting *against* the home team. The rowdyism was particularly bad when one of the league's four Canadian clubs came to town. "I've never seen a place like this in my whole life," said Adams. "There just can't be another city in the world where the home team isn't popular. Even when we win, which I admit isn't too often, we get booed. Things just have to change around here."

The Cougars made significant progress under Adams. At 19-19-6, they finished a .500 club their first winter at Olympia, though they were barely edged out by Pittsburgh for third place and the final playoff spot. George Hay had 22 goals among his 35 points, good for fourth place in the scoring race, while Larry Aurie enjoyed a fine rookie season with 13 goals. Hap Holmes concluded his NHL career with 11 shutouts and a 1.80 goals-against average.

The following year the team improved to 19-16-9. Right winger Carson Cooper led the Cougars with 18 goals, including 10 game-winners—a team record that would stand sixty-seven years. What made Cooper's accomplishment even more noteworthy was that he did it in a forty-four-game schedule. The Cougars' record was good enough for a third-place finish and a postseason berth.

On March 19, 1929, the Cougars played their first-ever Stanley Cup playoff game. They battled the Toronto Maple Leafs, their third-place counterpart in the Canadian Division, in the opener of a two-game, home-and-home series. Under this format the decision would go to the team that scored the most total goals. Toronto won the first game, 3-1, with George Hay accounting for the only Detroit tally. The total-goals format meant that the Cougars not only had to win the second game, they had to win by at least three goals to advance to the next round. Adams's men read the script wrong. Two days later they *lost* by three goals, 4-1—which in 1929 was tantamount to a rout—and went home for the summer.

Despite the abrupt exit, the organization considered the season a success. In addition to making the playoffs for the first time, the Cougars had posted a tidy $175,000 profit. And there was optimism for the future, represented by budding stars like Aurie, left wing Herbie Lewis, and center Ebenezer "Ebbie" Goodfellow.

Goodfellow's story was similar to that of practically every Canadian kid growing up with a passion for his country's national sport. Goodfellow was an Ottawa lad born into a family with too many expenses and not nearly enough money. "My first pair of skates cost twenty-five cents," he told Stan Fischler in *Those Were the Days*:

Detroit Cougars National League Playoffs - 1928-1929

They were called spring skates, the kind you put on right over your shoes, and they had clamps on the back and two clips on the side that you tightened with a key, something like roller skates.

When the snow fell it would get packed down hard on the sidewalks because nobody bothered to shovel them, and we could skate on them and play hockey after school. Those spring skates weren't very steady, but they were good enough to learn on and better than nothing. After that I graduated to tube skates and made my pucks out of hardwood.

I played whenever I could, sometimes three games in one day: morning, afternoon, and evening. When I was 17 I played intermediate hockey and can remember a game at an outdoor rink in minus-30-degree weather and riding home afterward 15 miles in a hay sleigh, pulled by a team of horses.

A year later we traveled to a neighboring town for a game in a blizzard. Drifts were 20 feet high in places, but this time we had cars. Unfortunately, we had to push them practically the whole distance and didn't arrive until after midnight. We started the game at 1 A.M. and finished about 3 or so. But we won.

That kind of tenacity was bound to appeal to Adams, who, in 1928, traded Johnny Sheppard to the New York Americans for the rights to Goodfellow. The new acquisition starred for the Olympics, Detroit's farm team and entry in the International Hockey League, and was named the IHL's top rookie and All-Star center. At the end of the season Adams signed his twenty-two-year-old prospect to a two-year, $6,800 contract, which was "a hell of a lot of money then," Goodfellow recalled.

The 1928-29 Cougars, the first Detroit squad to make the playoffs, included among its ranks Bernie Brophy (second from left). Once, in a game against the New York Rangers, Brophy gathered in a loose puck, picked up a head of steam, barreled past the defense, and fired the puck into the net—his own. The wrong-way goal accounted for the Rangers' 1-0 victory and a new nickname for the red-faced forward: "The Roy Riegels of Hockey."

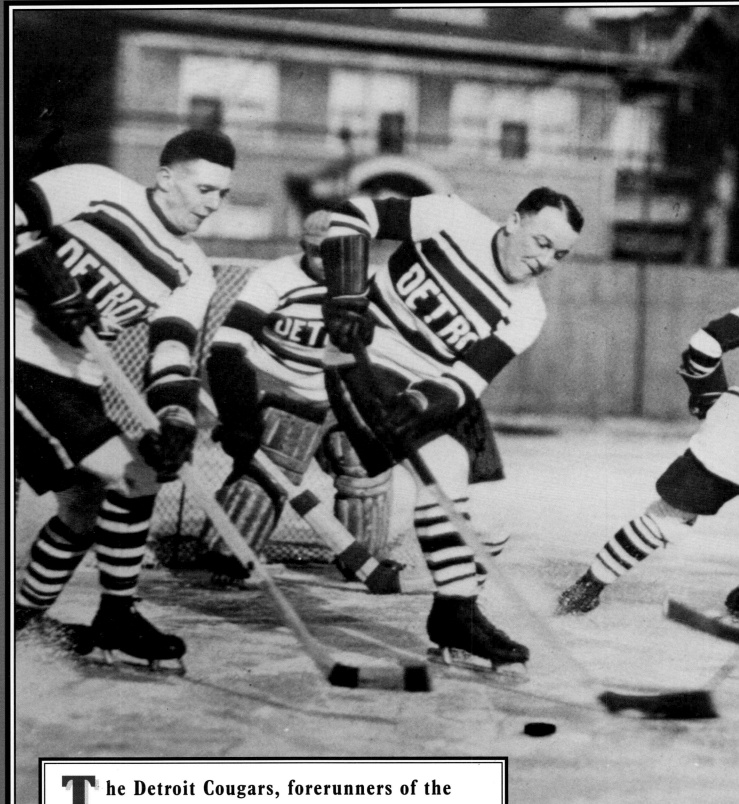

**T**he Detroit Cougars, forerunners of the
Red Wings, scrimmage at Northwestern
Field, across the street from Olympia, in 1928.

Detroit Falcons 1930-31

**L**ooking to change their luck, in 1930 the Detroit Cougars held a newspaper contest to select a new nickname: the Falcons.

By the time Goodfellow started his rookie NHL season in the fall of 1929, the effects of the stock market crash were just beginning to be felt by less prosperous Detroiters. As the Depression deepened over the next three years, auto production dropped from 5.3 million to just 1.3 million, creating unemployment and despair on an unprecedented level. *Detroit Times* reporter Edgar Hayes remembered Adams going door-to-door before and after practice, trying to sell tickets to merchants and people on the street. As the half-filled Olympia stands suggested, he wasn't very successful. While the Motor City sputtered through the dirty '30s, discretionary income dried up. One could get used to lard sandwiches or center-cut bologna. But one couldn't eat hockey tickets.

The Cougars' sad-sack performance matched the economic malaise. In 1929-30, they finished fourth and failed to qualify for the playoffs. Goodfellow was an immediate sensation, scoring 17 goals, while Herbie Lewis and Carson Cooper notched 20 and 18 goals, respectively. The supporting cast, however, wasn't nearly as productive. Before the next season began, the three local dailies sought to change the team's luck by sponsoring a contest to find a new nickname. Of 2,000 entries, 92 chose "Falcons." (The Trojans, Wanderers, and Magnetos were the other top picks.) New uniforms with gold lettering were designed. This marked the first and only time another color besides the traditional red and white has appeared on the team's jerseys. All

A panoramic view of Olympia in 1930. Detroit's farm team, the Olympics, is playing Cleveland.

the hoopla failed to make a difference in 1930-31, as the last-place Falcons once again finished out of the money despite Ebbie Goodfellow's 25 goals (a Detroit record for fourteen years) and 48 points, which were just three behind Howie Morenz's league-leading total. Four of Goodfellow's goals came on Christmas Day, 1930, as Detroit reached double figures for the first time in a game in a 10-1 pasting of Toronto.

The economic situation had reached crisis proportions. Attendance was so poor that one night Adams let a fan into Olympia for five bags of potatoes. In 1930 Philadelphia replaced Pittsburgh, then folded the following season. Ottawa dropped out of the circuit in 1931, came back for a couple of seasons, then went belly-up. It was replaced by St. Louis, which barely lasted the season. Desperate owners trimmed rosters and slashed salaries.

After years of dealing directly with Hughes, Detroit players found themselves negotiating contracts with their general manager. "Adams was a little squeaky about money," Wally Kilrea, a veteran of several Depression-era seasons, including four in Detroit, once reflected. "They told you what you were going to get, and you puckered up. We made just enough to keep us alive. We just wanted to play."

*How* they played would appear slightly foreign to the modern fan. Hockey between the two world wars was a slower, more deliberate affair, though crunching bodychecks and short tempers were as much a part of the action then as they are today. Two blue lines divided the ice into three zones; the red center line would not be introduced until 1943. Players had to carry, not pass, the puck out of their defensive zone. The result was a host of low-scoring games; Detroit played three scoreless ties in the 1927-28 season alone. The following season, a rule change allowed forward passing in all three zones. This opened up play and put more of a premium on stickhandling and speed, though the tempo was still deathly slow compared to today's end-to-end game.

Action typically seesawed, with teams spending several minutes at a time bottlenecked in one zone or the other. Small rosters (a maximum of 11 skaters and one goalie in the 1920s, later expanded to 14 players) meant that coaches usually went with one or two top lines, whose shifts often lasted three or four minutes each. It wasn't unheard of for a top player to play almost the entire sixty minutes. Sometimes they played even more, for games still tied at the end of regulation time continued into a ten-minute overtime period. There were no sudden-death provisions; each team could score as often as possible during the extra half-period. Thus, in one 1934 game against Toronto, Herbie Lewis scored *twice*, part of a club record seven overtime goals he rang up with Detroit.

The slap shot, a staple of the modern game, was still decades away from revolutionizing offensive strategy. Instead, most forwards relied on quick wrists and strong forearms to flick the puck past goalies. Rushing defensemen in the style of Bobby Orr hadn't yet hit the scene, said Stu Evans, a prototype of the big, solid, tend-to-your-knitting rearguard of the period. "Most defensemen didn't carry the puck unless they were in the last five minutes of a game and a goal behind, maybe. But otherwise they stayed at home."

Little Larry Aurie was Jack Adams's all-time favorite player, as respected for his feistiness as for his on-ice intelligence and scoring knack. In a twelve-year Detroit career that began in 1927, the right winger from Sudbury, Ontario, scored 147 goals. A league-leading 23 of them came during the 1936-37 season. Adams thought so highly of Aurie that his jersey number was never issued to another player until Aurie's nephew, Cumming Burton, wore it for a couple of seasons in the late 1950s. Since that time Aurie's number 6 has remained unofficially retired by the Red Wings.

Herbie Lewis played left wing for the Detroit franchise through three different nicknames: the Cougars, Falcons, and Red Wings. A speedy skater and excellent two-way winger, Lewis scored 148 goals between 1928 and 1939 for Detroit. He also played in the first NHL All-Star game, a 1934 benefit to aid injured Toronto defenseman Ace Bailey. He was elected to the Hall of Fame in 1989.

LAURIE AURIE

BERT McINENLY

A pair of trading cards from the early thirties featured right wing Larry Aurie and defenseman Bert McInenly.

The facilities and equipment were primitive by today's standards. "You wouldn't believe the dressing room at Olympia then," said Mark Beltaire, who covered the team for the *Detroit News* in the 1930s. "These long wooden benches, with uniforms hanging on a nail. There was one tiny shower room with maybe two or three showerheads."

At Olympia and all other NHL rinks, the concrete floor beneath the unpainted ice made the playing surface appear gray, making it hard for skaters and fans to follow the puck. The ice wasn't resurfaced between periods, only swept with a broom, so that by the end of the game it resembled a mushy moonscape. Rough ice not only greatly reduced scoring opportunities, it also indirectly led to the untimely death of the game's greatest star of the 1920s and '30s. One evening Howie Morenz of the Montreal Canadiens, the Wayne Gretzky of his day, caught his skate in a rut, broke his leg, and subsequently died of a blood clot in the hospital.

It was Morenz, incidentally, who was responsible for the first facemask. A shot off his stick broke the nose of Montreal Maroons goalie Clint Benedict during the 1928-29 season. Benedict donned the leather mask—which was little more than a noseguard—for just one game before abandoning it. It would be another thirty years until a goaltender started wearing a mask on a regular basis. Despite the ever-present danger of serious head and eye injuries, only a handful of players wore leather helmets, and none of those had the plastic face shields so familiar today. Some, including most goalies, liked to wear a small cloth cap. Although it didn't offer any protection, it helped to keep a player's head warm. It was considered great sport to swat the cap off an opponent's head while play was going on.

The Depression did have a positive effect on the Falcons' fortunes. With Ottawa sitting out the 1930-31 season, several Senators were loaned to other NHL clubs. Detroit picked up five players, the most notable of whom was netminder Alex Connell.

Connell had backstopped Ottawa to the 1927 Stanley Cup and would repeat the feat eight years later with the Montreal Canadiens. One of the finest netminders ever, Connell still holds the record for the longest scoreless sequence, once registering six consecutive shutouts for the Senators. In 1931-32, Detroit's lend-lease goalie compiled an 18-20-10 record. Although Detroit averaged just two goals per game and didn't place a scorer in the top ten, its defense was superb. Only one team allowed fewer goals than the 108 that managed to get by Connell.

The thirty-year-old goalie was utterly unflappable, as he proved one night late in the season at Madison Square Garden. That March evening the Falcons were playing the New York Americans in an important contest that would decide whether or not the Americans would make the playoffs. The game was in overtime, tied 1-1, when the Americans' Red Dutton blasted a shot that appeared to blow past Connell and ricochet in and out of the Detroit net. While the goal judge set off the red light and New York players started celebrating, the referee disallowed the goal. It never went in, he stated emphatically. During the

## Detroit's First Ice Age

commotion the goal judge directed a few choice words at Connell, who reacted by skating behind the net and punching his antagonist squarely in the nose.

This was immediately recognized by arena officials as a serious offense. The Americans were owned by a notorious bootlegger named Big Bill Dwyer, and the fellow Connell had bloodied was known to be one of Dwyer's trigger-men. "Evidently his fingers on the red light switch were as fast as his fingers on the trigger," Connell later said.

The game ended in a draw. As the Detroit goalie trundled toward the locker room, he noticed an unusual number of policemen pushing back the crowd. It wasn't until two detectives came up to him in the dressing room that he realized that his life could be in danger.

Connell was given a police escort back to his hotel and told to stay in his room until Detroit left town the next day. However, that evening an old friend of Connell's was in town, and so the two decided to make a quick run for some sandwiches. Several men followed them as they walked out the hotel lobby door and into a nearby diner.

"Aren't you Alex Connell, goalkeeper for the Detroit Falcons?" one of the heavies demanded. Connell assured them that not only was he not the man in question, he had never even *heard* of the Detroit Falcons. The men let him go. That evening, policemen stood guard outside Connell's hotel room to assure his safety. A few years later, a New York reporter told the quick-thinking goalie that both of the gangsters he had encountered had met untimely ends. When Connell asked how, the reporter replied, "Bang! Bang!"

That spring the Falcons were gunned down in the opening week of Stanley Cup action by the Montreal Maroons, who edged them, 3-2, in a two-game, total-goals playoff. Not long afterward, the Detroit Hockey Club defaulted on its mortgage and the franchise along with its property were put into receivership. After seven seasons of slipping and sliding in the standings and at the box office, the future of professional hockey in Detroit was in serious jeopardy. But a big shooter by the name of James Norris was on his way to town, and he would revive the team and give it its first taste of glory.

The Detroit Olympics were a farm club that operated out of Olympia for a decade until being sold to Pittsburgh magnate John Harris during the Depression. Players like Stan McCabe (top) and Rusty Hughes (above) were typical of the players who conveniently bounced back and forth from the parent club to the Olympics during this period.

# CHAPTER TWO

**B**y the end of the 1931-32 season, the Detroit Hockey Club didn't have enough money in its coffers to buy its goalie a baseball cap. Investors in Charles Hughes's syndicate, many connected in some way to the practically comatose auto industry, kept their hands in their pockets. Some, like team vice president John Townsend, a real estate developer, had gone bankrupt. "If the greatest star in the game

# Rolling Out the Winged Wheel

## 1932–1942

was made available to us for $1.98," Jack Adams lamented, "we couldn't have afforded him."

While Adams grumbled over his inability to buy and sign talent, the club flirted with bankruptcy, Olympia Stadium was padlocked, and players nervously considered their options. It was at this point that the proverbial man on horseback galloped into town.

James Norris, a fifty-three-year-old Chicago millionaire who made his fortune in the grain business, had tired of operating the semipro Chicago Shamrocks. A former member of the famed amateur Winged Wheelers during his youth in Montreal, he was anxious to buy an NHL franchise—if not in the Windy City

Wilfred "Bucko" McDonald, Detroit's barrel-chested blueliner for five seasons during the thirties, sports the winged-wheel insignia that new owner James Norris introduced when he bought the team in 1932.

The James Norris regime instantly restored some badly needed harmony. The team finished in second place in the NHL's American Division in 1932-33, the franchise's first as the newly christened Red Wings.

(where he already owned a big chunk of Chicago Stadium, home of the Blackhawks), then anywhere. In the summer of 1932, Norris purchased the floundering Falcons, Olympia Stadium, and the Detroit Olympics farm team for the bargain-basement price of $100,000.

The senior Norris was known as "Pops" to distinguish him from his oldest son, James D. Norris. Junior, a handsome man-about-town who loved running with the sporting crowd, was destined to become a co-owner of the Blackhawks in 1946 and a major figure in the prizefighting scandals that nearly ruined boxing in the 1950s. During the 1930s, he served as a kind of assistant general manager, providing a conduit between the players and the boss. The genial young man evidently did a good job, for the local press often commented favorably upon the team's "harmony"—a key ingredient in any championship clubhouse.

Pops Norris was a brash, no-nonsense type used to getting his way. In an attempt to control costs, he and other owners enforced a salary cap for the 1932-33 season. Detroit's Reg Noble and Hap Emms were among several players who balked at signing. But this was a time when a factory hand was happy to make forty cents an hour and hungry Detroiters were resorting to stealing dog biscuits from the city pound. The $7,500 per-man limit (lowered to $7,000 two years later) seemed more than generous to the average Joe. Threatened with suspension, the dissidents finally signed. Norris paid better than most other owners anyway, with a seasoned regular like Stu Evans, for example, making $4,000 a year.

Norris was firm with Adams. "I'll give you a year on probation," he told him after taking over, "with no contract."

Spurred by Norris's mandate to improve the team, and aided immeasurably by the new owner's open-wallet policy, Adams quickly went about turning the franchise into a winner. "Pops was the bankroll and the boss," he said, "and after he took over Detroit hockey never looked back."

Adams already had several developing young forwards in Ebbie Goodfellow, Larry Aurie, Herbie Lewis, and Johnny Sorrell. Doug Young, a sophomore defenseman, continued to deliver bone-crushing checks on the blueline; during the season he was joined by John Gallagher, a veteran rearguard acquired from the Montreal Maroons. A more important acquisition was John Ross Roach, an eleven-year veteran that Adams spirited from the New York Rangers.

At 5-foot-5 and 130 pounds, Roach wasn't the smallest goalie in the league (Shrimp Worters was two inches shorter), but the balding thirty-two-year-old reigned as its most unemotional. He bravely planted his deadpanned face in front of flying pucks for the full schedule of 48 games, registering 10 shutouts

## Rolling Out the Winged Wheel

and a stingy 1.94 goals-against average. That year Roach became the first Detroit player to make the official First All-Star Team.

Adams also looked to the Rangers for a young center named Carl Voss. The twenty-five-year-old American-born Voss was a sweet playmaker, tallying 8 goals among his 25 points to win the inaugural Rookie-of-the-Year Award. The cost to Norris for Roach and Voss was a combined $16,500, a worthwhile investment. The team made it back in receipts from a late-season New York-Detroit contest that saw some 5,000 people turned away from Olympia. Roach shut out his former teammates, 2-0, in front of 14,402 rabid fans. It was the first time the Rangers had been blanked in 77 tries, a tremendous run in those low-scoring days.

The 1932-33 season was the first in which Detroit players took the ice in their now-famous blood-red uniforms with the winged-wheel crest. Norris, a man who always knew his own mind, didn't need a newspaper contest to arrive at a new name for his franchise. In a bow to the Montreal Winged Wheelers, he renamed the Detroit Falcons the "Red Wings" and borrowed their emblem, figuring it fit in perfectly with Detroit's image as the Motor City. The Wings' red jerseys caused confusion when they visited the Montreal Canadiens, who wore similarly colored game sweaters at home. The league solved the problem by ruling that the Wings had to wear white pullovers over their sweaters; eventually Norris had white jerseys issued for road games.

Norris was nothing if not innovative. Recognizing hard times, he instituted the league's first season-ticket plan, whereby fans were allowed to pay for their tickets in five monthly installments. He also experimented with the idea

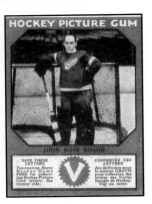

## THE DETROIT RED WINGS

Three stars of the Wings' resurgence in 1932-33. Left wing Hap Emms and center Ebbie Goodfellow had 21 goals and 42 points between them. Goalie John Ross Roach posted 10 shutouts and a 1.94 goals-against average, playing the full 48-game schedule. For that, he became the first Detroit player named to the first All-Star team.

The Wings' defense in 1933. From left: Walter Buswell, Stu Evans, John Ross Roach, Doug Young, and John Gallagher.

of playing games during the day; heretofore, all NHL games were evening affairs that typically began at 8:15 or 8:30 P.M. On March 19, 1933, the Wings and Blackhawks played the league's first matinee game at Chicago Stadium. Face-off was at 3:30 P.M. Detroit won, 4-2. The season-ending win climaxed a stretch drive that aroused public interest and contributed to a final record of 25-15-8. The Red Wings' remarkable turnaround left them tied with Boston for the top spot in the American Division. However, the Bruins were awarded first place by virtue of having scored more goals.

The Wings' opponent in the opening round of the playoffs was the Montreal Maroons, runner-up in the Canadian Division. The favored Maroons were a formidable foe, fielding three of the league's top scorers, but Roach blanked them in their own rink, 2-0. The Wings returned to Detroit for the home half of the two-game, total-goals playoff to discover that the town had become hockey mad. An estimated 50,000 people tried to get through Olympia's doors. Those that succeeded included Edsel Ford, mayor Frank Murphy, city council president James Couzens, Michigan football coach Harry Kipke, and a host of other luminaries who only a couple of years earlier wouldn't have entered Olympia on a bet. After years of half-filled houses and hostile fans, the Wings were suddenly the city's darlings. Certainly they had little competition in attracting the sports-mad section of the populace. All three experiments in professional football during the 1920s had ended in failure, there was no pro basketball to speak of, and the Tigers were perennial second-division cats who had not won an American League pennant in a quarter-century. The city was hungry for a winner, if for no other reason than to temporarily get its mind off of the Depression.

Duly inspired, the Wings roared back from a two-goal deficit to win, 3-2, propelling them into the second round against the New York Rangers. After the game thousands of people hung around Olympia to cheer the city's newest sport heroes.

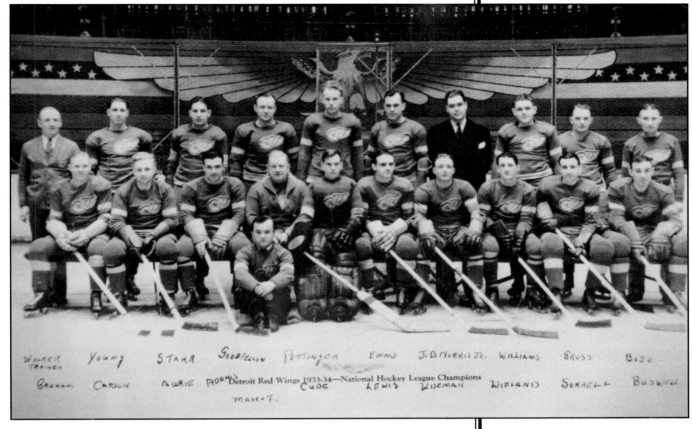

WALKER TRAINER    YOUNG    STARR    GOODFELLOW    PETTINGER    EMMS    J.D. NORRIS JR.    WILLIAMS    GROSS    BOZO

GRAHAM    CARSON    AURIE    ROACH    CUDE    LEWIS    WISEMAN    WIELAND    SORRELL    BUSWELL

MASCOT

Detroit Red Wings 1933-34—National Hockey League Champions

"There isn't a man on that team who should make any All-Star team," observed Rangers coach Lester Patrick. "But, as a group, they are almost unbeatable. It only goes to show what harmony, loyalty, pep and cohesion can accomplish when linked together and wisely directed." The Rangers ended the Wings' Cinderella season with 2-0 and 4-3 victories. But few doubted that, thanks to Pops Norris and Jack Adams, hockey had found a permanent home in Detroit.

During the 1933-34 season Adams added to his reputation of being a good judge of horseflesh by trading Carl Voss to Ottawa for center Ralph "Cooney" Weiland, a former scoring champion. The following year Weiland would become the first Detroit forward to be named an All-Star. When John Ross Roach went down with an injury, Adams gained permission to borrow Wilf Cude from the Canadiens to tend net. Changing sweaters for a few months could hardly have bothered the worldly twenty-three-year-old Cude, who had been born in England on the Fourth of July before emigrating to Canada. He was outstanding in a Detroit uniform, posting a 1.62 average in 29 games. Although Detroit really didn't have any superstars to speak of, it finished on top of the American Division with 58 points, seven ahead of preseason favorite Chicago.

The playoff format was in a state of flux then. This time the formula called for the two first-place teams, after drawing a bye in the opening round, to slug

The Wings won their first divisional crown in 1933-34 and played in their first Stanley Cup finals that year, losing to Chicago three games to one. Wilf Cude, on loan from the Montreal Canadiens to replace the injured John Ross Roach, was brilliant all season in goal.

JOHN SORRELL

ohnny Sorrell was known as the "Frail Falcon" because of his slight build. The left winger, who played eight seasons in Detroit, topped the club with 20 goals in 1933-34. He was the first Detroit player to score on a penalty shot, beating Boston's Cecil "Tiny" Thompson on February 7, 1937 at Olympia.

it out in a semifinal match. So the Wings would have to get past Toronto, a powerful aggregation whose stars included the loop's top two scorers, Charlie Conacher and Joe Primeau. It was a daunting task for the unheralded Wings, but the underdogs from Detroit seized a quick two-game advantage with 2-1 (overtime) and 6-3 victories at Olympia. However, the champions of the Canadian Division seemed to have regained the momentum by smashing the Wings twice in Toronto, 3-1 and 5-1.

The rubber game was played in Detroit on an electric Friday night before a packed house. The winner would go on to challenge Chicago for the Stanley Cup. After Goodfellow scored at 15:03 of the first period, Cude turned back every Toronto rush for the rest of the evening to preserve the 1-0 victory to secure a spot in the Stanley Cup finals for the very first time. Detroit players tried to hoist Cude onto their shoulders, but the crush of fans rushing onto the ice wouldn't allow it. "One of the first to reach Cude was big Charlie Conacher, the same Toronto forward who had been firing deadly pucks on him all night," reported the next day's *Free Press*. "Conacher shook his hand, patted him and grinned as though Cude had done him a favor by turning off his shots instead of ending the dearest hopes of the Toronto team."

In Chicago was another popular netminder, Charles Gardiner, who not only would dash the dearest hopes of Detroit fans, but also would be the center of a tragic subplot that made the Wings' failed bid for the Stanley Cup seem minor in retrospect.

Gardiner, who had just won the second Vezina Trophy of his career, was so highly thought of by his teammates that they had unanimously elected him captain, a rare honor for a goalie. He had played most of the season in intermittent pain, the result of an infection that he had been battling since suffering a bout of tonsillitis the previous year. Wilf Cude knew the All-Star goalie well; they had grown up together in Winnipeg, where Gardiner was revered for his good humor and charitable acts.

In the first game of the Cup final, played April 3, 1934 at Olympia, the opposing netminders were at the top of their game. Each allowed just one goal as the game clock ticked off regulation time and then twenty minutes of the first overtime period. Finally, two minutes into the second overtime, the Blackhawks won it when Paul Thompson put the rubber past Cude.

Two days later the Hawks followed up their thrilling overtime win by scoring three third-period goals on Cude to break a 1-1 deadlock. Chicago left Detroit with a two-game series edge and one sick goalie. Despite suffering from severe pain in the region of his kidneys, Gardiner insisted on suiting up for game three at Chicago Stadium. The Wings blitzed the pain-wracked goalie for five goals; at the other end of the rink, Cude allowed but one.

This set the stage for what would turn out to be the last games Gardiner and Cude would ever play for their respective teams. Both were brilliant, Cude with his smashed nose beating back Chicago rushes, and Gardiner playing over near-constant pain to repel Detroit's attacks. The game remained scoreless through regulation and the first overtime.

The turning point came eight minutes into the second extra period. "Clint Smith of the Blackhawks came skating down at me and I jabbed my stick out for a pokecheck," recalled Ebbie Goodfellow. "I missed the puck, he stepped on my stick and more or less fell down while I came up with the puck. Now, anybody would say in fairness that I didn't deliberately trip him, but I was still given a two-minute penalty." Goodfellow sweated out the two minutes. Just as he was leaving the penalty box, Harold "Mush" March unleashed a forty-footer that Cude should have handled—but didn't. The puck slid into the net to give Chicago a 1-0 victory and its first Stanley Cup. Afterward Cude went back to Montreal, where he played out the rest of his career. Gardiner returned to Winnipeg a hero. The glory was short-lived. Eight weeks after defeating Detroit he was rushed to the hospital, where he died of a brain hemorrhage brought on by the infection he was never able to beat.

In the first two years of the Norris regime the Wings had racked up a combined 116 points, better than any other team in that period. However, there were still some observers who considered the Wings over-achievers who were bound to find their true level—a belief seemingly vindicated by the results of the 1934-35 campaign. That year Detroit dropped to last place in the American Division, though their 45 points would have been good enough for third in the Canadian Division. The irony was that, after years of not having a top-ten scorer, the basement-dwelling Wings placed three men in the top six. Herbie Lewis had 16 goals and 43 points to place sixth on the scoring charts, while linemate Larry Aurie accumulated 17 goals and 46 points to finish third. This was one behind 22-goal scorer Syd Howe, who Adams had acquired from St. Louis, along with defenseman Scotty Bowman, for an eye-popping $50,000. Adams, although never a patient loser, knew that this maturing trio of scorers, when added to an already capable crew of blueliners and forwards, portended great things for the future.

The most important acquisition was center Marty Barry, who Boston sent over when it reacquired Cooney Weiland prior to the start of the 1935-36 season. Barry, a superb playmaker, would wind up leading the team in goals his first season, in assists the next three, and in scoring three out of four years. Also added to the mix were forward Hec Kilrea, obtained from Toronto; Bucko McDonald, a free-spirited defenseman who was noted for throwing his considerable weight around the ice; and Normie Smith, a roly-poly pick-up from St. Louis who had replaced John Ross Roach as the number-one netminder.

**S**tick work was as big a problem in the 1930s as it is today. Here the Red Wings' Syd Howe prepares to defend himself from the Canadiens' Toe Blake, who is looking for an opening to lower the lumber.

Normie Smith tended goal for parts of seven seasons in Detroit, but he was never better than in the 1936 playoffs when he blanked the Montreal Maroons for 248 minutes and 32 seconds—a record shutout sequence for Stanley Cup play. He's seen here stonewalling the defending Cup champions during that series, which the Wings won to advance to the finals against Toronto.

"We had great balance," recalled Pete Kelly, another Adams acquisition. "We had a good scoring line in Aurie, Lewis, and Barry. Normie Smith had come along a year earlier, and Normie was a great goalie. There were some games that he'd let a few slip by. But when the game was the toughest, he'd come through."

That was evident in the second-from-last game of the 1935-36 season, when Chicago invaded Olympia with first place on the line. The Wings had led the division most of the way, then run into a rough stretch of seven winless games that allowed the Blackhawks back into the race. Smith put on a display that had the 13,519 fans on hand alternately cheering and grimacing. He knocked aside shot after shot from Chicago, including a rocket from Mush March in the second period that caught him square in the groin. Time was called for several minutes while Smith recovered his breath and tried to remember why he had ever wanted to be a goalie in the first place. The game and the drama resumed, with the Wings prevailing in a wide-open but cleanly fought game, 5-3. Captain Doug Young celebrated the American Division championship by flinging a puck into the stands, while Smith waddled gingerly off the ice.

Smith's true test came four days later, when the Red Wings faced off against the Montreal Maroons in the opener of a best-of-five semifinal. Detroit's 56 points had been tops in the league, but many experts were picking the Maroons—first-place finishers in the Canadian Division and defending Stanley Cup champions—to once again go all the way.

None of the 10,000 fans who filed into the Montreal Forum the night of March 24, 1936 could have predicted that, come the following calendar day, he or she would still be watching these two teams battling each other for the first goal of the game. But that's exactly what happened, as Detroit and Montreal skated through three regulation periods and then *five* overtime periods without either side scoring.

"When I went into the game, I had some butterflies," Smith recalled on the golden anniversary of what would turn out to be hockey's longest game. "Of course, I had no idea how long the game would eventually last. But as it got longer and longer into the game, I seemed to settle down."

Which was more than could be said of the puck. There were no Zambonis then to smooth the ice between periods, Pete Kelly reminds us. "They only swept the ice, so it was quite rough with a lot of skate marks. The longer the game went on, the more difficult the puck was to control."

It was two o'clock in the morning when the two teams wearily trudged from the clubhouse and back onto the ice for the start of the sixth overtime period. The Maroons had been fortified by sips of coffee and brandy between

periods, while the Wings had used up two gallons of rubbing alcohol. The play continued as before, sluggish and cautious, as both goalies' pads grew heavy with water and sweat.

It was a shy twenty-one-year-old forward named Modere "Mud" Bruneteau who finally brought a halt to the marathon. The rookie right winger had played sparingly during the season, scoring just two goals. But with about eight minutes left in the period, Adams sent him over the boards for his first shift of the night. His fresh legs were the difference. He trailed Hec Kilrea on a rush across the Maroons' blue line, zoomed around the defense, and took a pass in front of the net. The clock read 2:25 A.M. when the rookie's shot—Detroit's 66th of the game—sailed past Lorne Chabot to give the Wings a 1-0 victory.

"Thank God that Chabot fell down as I drove the puck toward the net," said Bruneteau, who struggled to the locker room as some appreciative fans jammed dollar bills into his gloves and jersey. "It was the funniest thing. The puck just stuck there in the twine and didn't fall on the ice."

Maybe it was too exhausted, like everybody else in the building. To this day, no game has ever lasted as long. It was officially clocked at 176:30, the equivalent of nearly three regulation games. The unprecedented triple-header left everyone from the referees to the wire-service operators spent. Smith, who had made an incredible 90 saves in suffocating pressure, was the most bone-tired of the lot. "I really found out how tired I was afterwards when we went to the Lumberjacks Club in Montreal and I had one bottle of ale," he said. "That set me right back on my heels."

Remarkably, the second game of the series looked to be a repeat of the first. It was scoreless until midway through the third period, when Syd Howe hit

**M**odere "Mud" Bruneteau looks on in retirement on the man he used to be. In the early hours of March 25, 1936, his goal beat the Maroons, 1-0, and ended hockey's longest game.

The Red Wings and Maple Leafs battle it out in the 1936 Stanley Cup finals.

paydirt on the power play. Goals by Lewis and Aurie sealed the 3-0 decision. A key to Detroit's rock-hard defense was Adams's decision to switch Ebbie Goodfellow from center to the blueline. Goodfellow was selected a second team All-Star at his new position and would graduate to the first team the following season.

The frustrated Maroons finally scored on Smith in the opening frame of game three, Gus Marker snapping his streak of 248 minutes and 32 seconds without surrendering a goal. It remains the longest shutout sequence in playoff history. A second-period goal by Johnny Sorrell tied the score and a third-period tally by Scotty Bowman wrapped up a 2-1 win and the series. Playing the equivalent of five games in less than a week, Smith had allowed just one shot to get by him—a performance that had even the Maroons clapping him on the back after the match ended.

It didn't seem that anything could stop Wings now, certainly not the Maple Leafs. The best-of-five Cup finals began April 5 in Detroit, with the Wings slamming the Leafs, 3-1. Two days later the hometown boys really got Olympia rocking, blasting Toronto, 9-4. The nine goals were the most scored in a Cup final since the league expanded a decade earlier.

The Wings were on the verge of sweeping through the postseason, something no team had ever done before. They held a 3-0 lead going into the final

period of the third game at Maple Leaf Garden. Facing extinction, Toronto stormed back with three goals in the last seven minutes to tie it. Then, 31 seconds into overtime, Frank "Buzz" Boll completed a stirring comeback by putting the puck past Normie Smith. It was the quickest overtime game ever in Stanley Cup play and had the Leafs thinking upset.

Detroit put an end to those thoughts two nights later. In the second period, the Wings wiped out a one-goal deficit when Goodfellow and Barry scored 44 seconds apart. "We started patting each other on the back again like we did the previous game, then remembered what happened," said Pete Kelly, who scored what proved to be the Cup-clinching goal at 9:45 of the third period. The shot ricocheted off the support bar in the back of the net—so quickly that the goal judge didn't have time to turn on the light. For a few anxious moments Kelly feared the goal wouldn't count, but then referee Bill Stewart skated over and signaled that he had seen it go in.

Just 72 seconds later, Toronto's Bill Thoms scored, shaving the margin to 3-2. "It was touch-and-go after that," Kelly said. "It was pins and needles just to hang on." But the vaunted Detroit defense shut down the high-powered Toronto attack for the final nine minutes to preserve the victory and give the Motor City another trophy to put on its mantel.

"There were no TV cameras then," said Kelly. "We didn't parade around the ice with the Cup. It was presented to us later, at the Royal York Hotel. There were quite a few fans from Detroit crowded in there, I remember. In fact, the whole scene remains very vivid in my mind. April 11, 1936—it was quite a moment."

"When we got back to Detroit after the game," said Goodfellow, "the town had gone wild. There seemed to be thousands of people at the railway station and we were driven in a procession to Olympia, where another celebration took place."

**A**pril 11, 1936: Pete Kelly beats Toronto's George Hainsworth to seal Detroit's first Stanley Cup. "The Holy Grail at last," reported the next day's *Detroit Times*.

A half-dozen champions lather up in the visitor's clubhouse at Maple Leaf Gardens after winning Detroit's first Stanley Cup. The sud-busters, from left to right, are Herbie Lewis, Bucko McDonald, Scotty Bowman, Marty Barry, Pete Kelly, and John Gallagher.

Marty Barry's reputation as a quiet strongman kept opponents at bay and his penalty minutes low, resulting in his winning the Lady Byng Trophy in 1937 for combining sportsmanship and ability. "I don't want to be a gentleman," he protested. "I want to be the guy who scores the most goals." That year the Montreal native finished third in regular-season scoring and led all playoff performers with 11 points in 10 games.

The Red Wings' drive to the Cup capped a remarkable sweep of major sports titles. The previous October the Tigers had won their first championship, beating the Chicago Cubs in the World Series. A few weeks later the Lions had demolished the New York Giants to win their first National Football League title. And Joe Louis, a young Negro boxer who had won the city's Golden Gloves championship at Olympia, had become an international celebrity with his devastating knockouts of former heavyweight champions Primo Carnera and Max Baer. Sportswriters dubbed Detroit "the City of Champions," a shot of pride for an economically wounded community now on the rebound. "It seemed that all you had to do was throw on a Detroit jersey and you'd win," Kelly said of those days.

It would be several more years before the Tigers and Lions would win a second championship, but Wings fans didn't have to wait nearly as long. Adams's express train roared to another American Division title in 1936-37, leading the NHL in points, scoring, and defense. Detroit players dominated the All-Star selections, grabbing four of six spots. In addition to Goodfellow, the postseason squad included Normie Smith, who won the Vezina Trophy as the loop's stingiest goalie; Marty Barry, who missed winning the scoring title by three points and was awarded the Lady Byng Trophy for his gentlemanly play; and Larry Aurie, whose 23 goals made him the first Red Wing to lead the league in that category.

The Wings had a tougher road to travel in 1937 than they did the previous spring. They opened semifinal play against the Montreal Canadiens without Doug Young. The team's captain, a top-flight defenseman, had broken his leg. Adams called up Rollie Roulston to replace him, but then Roulston broke his leg, too. Adding to Adams's misery was Aurie's broken ankle, which kept him out of postseason play. Nonetheless, the Wings rolled over Montreal in the first two games, 4-0 and 5-1, in front of record crowds at Olympia.

## Rolling Out the Winged Wheel

Injuries soon turned what appeared to be the makings of a rout into a long and drawn-out struggle. Halfway through the third game, Normie Smith took a wicked shot off his elbow and collapsed onto the ice, unable to continue. Adams had no choice but to substitute Jimmie Franks, a young and inexperienced goalie from the Hornets, the former Detroit Olympics farm team now operating in Pittsburgh. The Canadiens solved the nervous twenty-two-year-old rookie for two goals to pull out a 3-1 win. Smith recovered in time to play the fourth game, but Montreal won again by the same score to force the series to a fifth and final game.

The sore-armed Smith and his counterpart in the Montreal net, Wilf Cude, turned in a goaltending classic at Montreal's Forum. Ebbie Goodfellow's goal gave Detroit a 1-0 lead, but Bill McKenzie later tied the affair. That was all the scoring until 11:49 of the third overtime period, when Hec Kilrea finally blasted one past Cude. The draining 2-1 victory put the Wings in the Cup finals against the New York Rangers.

The Rangers were rested and eager to tackle the injury-depleted Wings. They had swept past the Maple Leafs and the Maroons in the minimum amount of games, Davey Kerr allowing just one goal in four games. Kerr was magnificent again in the opener, played April 6 at Madison Square Garden. He allowed but a single goal while Smith and his replacement, Earl Robertson, let five New York shots elude them.

Robertson, another call-up from the Hornets, had been pressed into service in the first period after Smith, his sore arm throbbing with pain, declared he could no longer continue. Robertson would later develop into a steady number-one goaltender for the Rangers' crosstown rivals, the Americans. But in the spring of 1937, with Detroit's hopes of another Stanley Cup resting on his shoulders, the twenty-six-year-old rookie was judged by many in the press to be lacking. His inexperience, coupled to the Wings' injury-riddled lineup, made the Rangers heavy favorites to grab game two and to probably sweep the series.

The Wings got some help from an unlikely source—the Ringling Brothers Circus. Every April Madison Square Garden booked "The Greatest Show on Earth," a scheduling conflict in which the Rangers always came out second-best. This meant the rest of the series would have to be played in Detroit. Robertson's confidence soared inside the friendly confines of Olympia Stadium, and as a result the Wings skated off with an impressive 4-2 victory to knot the series.

Fights were the order of the day when the Maroons and Red Wings met on January 24, 1937, in a rematch of the previous year's hotly contested playoff. In the top photograph, Larry Aurie dukes it out with Lionel Conacher while an unidentified Wing rushes to his rescue with upraised stick. In the bottom shot, officials try to restrain Marty Barry from wading into a free-for-all that already includes half of the players on the ice.

Larry Aurie, the league's leading goal scorer in 1936-37, was kept out of postseason play by a fractured left leg. During the playoffs Bud Shaver of the *Detroit Times* presented the game little winger with the newspaper's "Hero Award," a watch. He played one more season before retiring to manage the Pittsburgh Hornets farm club.

Another valuable member of the injury-depleted Red Wings was captain Doug Young, who was sidelined for most of the 1936-37 season with a broken leg. The otherwise durable defenseman, who'd only missed one game in the previous five seasons, later worked for many years as the official scorer at Olympia.

Detroit forward Hec Kilrea joins a scrum along the board during the 1937 Stanley Cup finals between the Wings and Rangers. Note that the boards are just that, made of wood instead of plastic, and that there is no glass to prevent pucks or bodies from flying into the stands.

"I don't know how they hang in there against us," said Lester Patrick. "It's Jack Adams. Even with such a hobbled team in there he manages to keep his same disciplined offense and defense."

Robertson was even stingier in game three, permitting just one goal, but it was enough for New York to take the affair, 1-0, and the series' lead. To make a bad situation even worse, Goodfellow was sidelined by an injured knee. The Wings were down to nine healthy bodies, and even these were suffering from an assortment of ailments. The Rangers denied the Wings permission to add players to their depleted roster—an example of poor sportsmanship that riled the Detroit organization. Game four was touch-and-go for the full 60 minutes, but Robertson and the rest of the underdog Wings built a stone wall in front of the net while Marty Barry settled the affair with a third-period goal. Their 1-0 victory stunned the Rangers, delighted the crowd, and set up the conclusion to one of the most spirited title defenses ever in hockey. In the deciding game, played April 15, 1937, Barry scored twice and Johnny Sorrell added

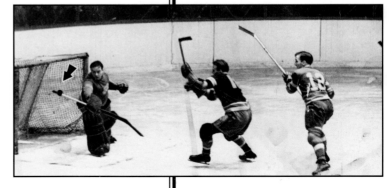

another as the Wings clinched a second straight Cup in true championship style, 3-0. Adams was so overwhelmed he fainted in the locker room.

**B**efore the next season started the Wings' coach spoke to reporters in Fort William, Ontario, where he was attending his parents' golden anniversary celebration. Adams tried to remain on an even keel as he discussed his team's chances for a three-peat.

"On paper, we should run away with it again," he said. "We won last year with five of our leaders on the sidelines and they'll all be back this year and in fine fettle. But a lot of strange things can happen to a hockey team over a season and there are seven other good clubs playing in the NHL who want the championship and the Cup as much as we do."

**N**ew York's Ching Johnson keeps his body between Bucko McDonald and the net as the opposing defensemen eye the action up ice. Dave Kerr is the goalie in this scene from the opener of the 1937 finals, won by the Rangers, 5-1.

**R**ookie Earl Robertson, called up from Pittsburgh to replace the injured Normie Smith during the '37 finals, bats out Lyn Patrick's hard shot. "We figured that we had two strikes on us when we lost Normie, who was a very good goalkeeper," remembered Pete Kelly. "But Robertson came through in the clutch and did a great job."

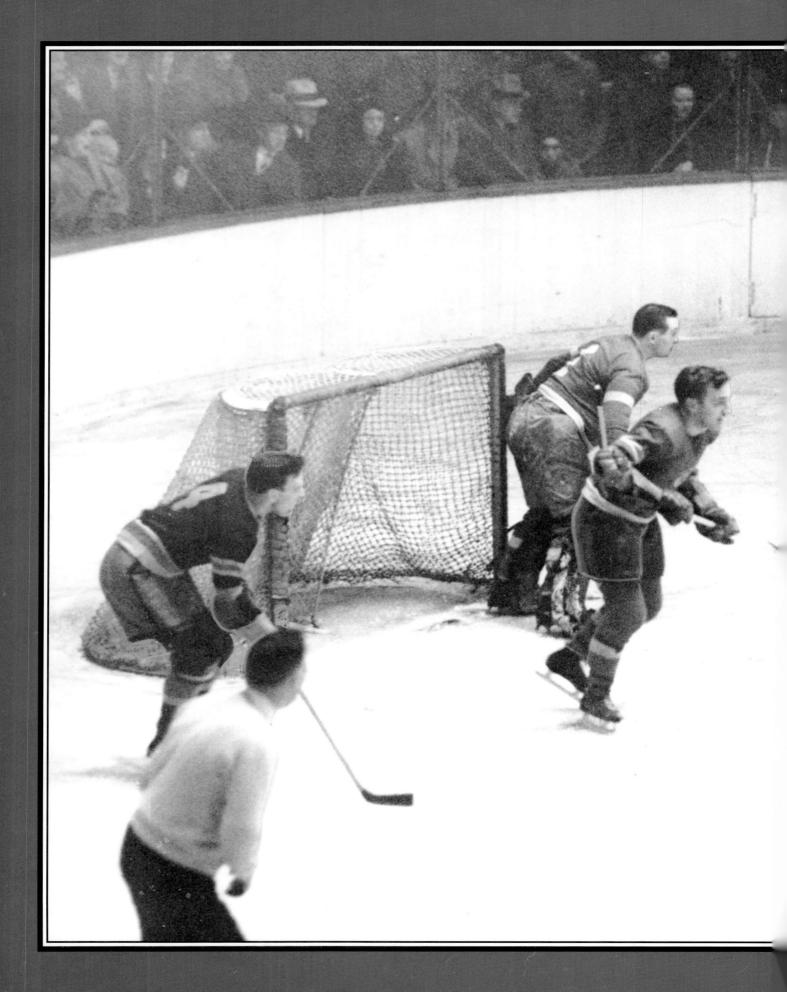

The Red Wings' defense smothers another New York charge in the fifth and decisive game of the 1937 Cup finals. The Wings won, 3-0, as Earl Robertson posted his second straight shutout. They were the last two games the rookie goaltender would ever play for Detroit.

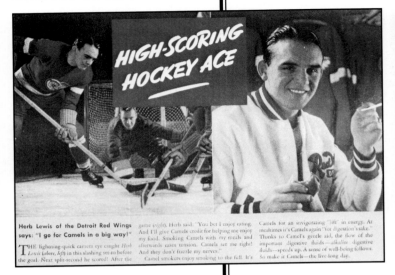

Cigar-chomping Herbie Lewis was a major contributor to Detroit's back-to-back Stanley Cups, though in this advertisement he credited Camel cigarettes for giving him "an invigorating 'lift' in energy."

The team started out slowly, and even a $75-per-man bonus from Pops Norris at Christmastime couldn't inspire the shopworn veterans out of their lethargy. The same players who had flashed and slashed their way to two straight Stanley Cups seemed to have grown old—or worse, complacent—overnight. The Barry-Lewis-Aurie line posted only 32 goals, roughly half of what it had been producing in the past. The Wings shocked everybody by becoming the first defending Stanley Cup champion to drop to the basement. It was a humiliating lesson, said sportswriter Mark Beltaire. "Jack made up his mind then that he would never again stand pat with a winning team."

As Adams himself explained: "I'll never again make the mistake of hanging onto players for too long. When it comes to dealing with my teams I'm going to have ice water in my veins." It was a cold-hearted philosophy that would restore the franchise as a perennial contender—but, taken to its extreme, would also wreck a great team two decades later.

A bright spot was Carl Liscombe. The twenty-two-year-old left winger out of Galt, Ontario, became the first rookie to lead the team in goals, scoring 14. That included three in a span of one minute and 52 seconds in a 5-1 win over Chicago on March 13, 1938. Liscombe's lightning like hat trick would remain an NHL record until 1952.

With the financially ailing Montreal Maroons forced to suspend operations, the league reverted to a single division at the start of the 1938-39 campaign. The playoff format was changed, with six of the remaining seven teams qualifying for the postseason.

It was a historic season, travelwise. Normally, teams moved from city to city by train, a mode of transportation that was not nearly as romantic as memory's rosy overglow often makes it out to be. "If you wanted to get any sleep on the train, you had to drink a couple of beers," said Liscombe. "Otherwise, that *clickety-clack, clickety-clack* would keep you awake all night. The three or four kids who didn't drink would be up until six in the morning reading comic books."

## Rolling Out the Winged Wheel

A noisy train suddenly looked awfully good on December 21, 1938, the day the Red Wings became the first major sports team to take a scheduled flight. Adams chartered a DC-3 to fly from New York to Chicago. The genesis was bad weather, which had made train travel impossible. "The players were upset," said Mark Beltaire. "They looked out and there was snow on the wings. I thought there was going to be a revolt."

"We were in the airport and Jack Adams started handing out quarters to all of the players," remembered Liscombe. "They had life insurance policies in machines and he made each player buy four and make them all out to the Detroit Red Wings. That way if the plane went down, the team would at least get some money back on their investment."

The white-knuckled Wings landed without incident and went on to finish fifth. They squeaked past the sixth-place Canadiens in the best-of-three quarterfinal when Marty Barry's overtime goal produced a 1-0 verdict in the final game. Then they were bounced out of the playoffs by Toronto. This series also went the limit, the Leafs winning the finale in Toronto, 5-4.

That series was a last hurrah for many of the old Detroit heroes. Before the next season started several favorites retired or were sent packing, including Barry, Larry Aurie, Herbie Lewis, Doug Young, Normie Smith, and Hec Kilrea. Wally Kilrea (Hec's younger brother), Johnny Sorrell, and Bucko McDonald had preceded them. The team was in the process of rebuilding

After the defending two-time Cup champions plummeted to last place in 1937-38, Jack Adams took the Wings on a transatlantic cruise to Europe, where they played a series of exhibitions with the Montreal Canadiens.

Adams rebuilt the Wings around players like defenseman "Black Jack" Stewart, seen here in an intrasquad scrimmage prior to the start of the 1938-39 season. Stewart, wearing the white jersey, launched his Hall-of-Fame career that year. His trademarks were his teeth-rattling bodychecks and thick, heavy stick. "It's not for shooting," the five-time All-Star would explain. "It's for breaking arms."

with the likes of Liscombe, tough-guy defensemen Jimmy Orlando and Jack Stewart, and forwards Sid Abel and Don "The Count" Grosso.

New in the nets was Cecil "Tiny" Thompson, who had spent the last decade in Boston before being sold to Detroit for $15,000 during the '38-39 campaign. The four-time winner of the Vezina Trophy had to be good the following season, as the Wings netted fewer goals than any team in the league. Despite Thompson's sterling play, it was Goodfellow who was given the Hart Trophy. The thirty-four-year-old Goodfellow had led all defensemen in scoring and had jolted his usual quota of forwards off of the puck. But the award still came as a bit of a surprise, considering that his club had won only 16 games and finished fifth.

That was still good enough to get the Wings into the best-of-three quarterfinals against the New York Americans. Detroit won in three games, but then lost two straight to Toronto in the semifinals. The second game, played on March 28, 1940, at Olympia, featured one of the ugliest and prolonged battles ever to disgrace an NHL rink. It began in the final minute of play, as a frustrated Don Grosso first high-sticked Nick Metz, then lowered the lumber on Syl Apps. Suddenly the entire ice was filled with swinging, swearing skaters.

"Jimmy Orlando and Syl Apps went at it like heavyweights," recalled Mark Beltaire. "I remember Ebbie Goodfellow mixing it up with several guys. He'd skate around, pick up a Toronto player, then haul off and hit him. I've never seen anything like it." At its peak the fifteen-minute brawl involved all 12 players on the ice, 17 more who jumped the boards to join in the fray, and an incensed female fan who leaned out of the stands to pummel the Leafs' Red Horner with her purse.

"I'll tell you, we were just lucky to be getting out of here with our lives," exclaimed Toronto president Conn Smythe, whose wisecracks and mocking gestures had always irritated Adams. "Those Red Wings are nothing more than just a gang of hoodlums." When informed of his remarks, Adams shot back, "Smythe's a baby! We're just sorry we can't play the Leafs seven nights in a row."

It was a hell of a way to end a season, but an equally riotous playoff encounter with Toronto awaited Adams two years down the road.

By now Adams was an institution, not only in Detroit but also in the entire NHL. Practically through the sheer force of his personality he had made the franchise a winner, and in the process turned Detroit into a hockey town. There was little need for him to go up and down Grand River selling tickets, as he once had, but he rarely passed up a chance to address a service group or

banquet crowd, where he could talk up the Red Wings and charm the audience. He brooked no criticism of his team, often chastising writers for what had appeared in that morning's paper: "How dare you write something like that. Aren't you a loyal Detroiter?"

"Adams thought hockey was the greatest thing on God's green earth," said Mark Beltaire. "He hated anyone who'd dare denigrate it." Beltaire recalled that Adams wanted him to be a "homer" instead of an objective reporter. "'For God's sake, Jack,' I'd tell him. 'They're a bunch of Canadians owned by a guy in Chicago.' We'd go around and around about that."

Although the public usually saw a rotund "Happy Jack," in the clubhouse Adams could be bombastic, dictatorial, and even cruel. In an era where kids from small-town Canada didn't dare question a coach's authority, Adams's tactics worked, although there were some casualties along the way. One was Stu Evans, a strong-willed type who chafed under Adams's biting sarcasm and iron rule.

"He was a tough guy to get along with," said Evans. "One night against Boston we played poorly. He came in the locker room and really bawled the hell out of us. He could be very sarcastic, very insulting." Adams liked to motivate his players by hurling slices of fruit at them between periods and

Cecil "Tiny" Thompson came to Detroit during the 1938-39 season after spending an illustrious ten and a half years in Boston.

41

**A**bout 1940, Joseph Golinkin captured the beauty of a Detroit-New York game at Madison Square Garden in one of his watercolor works.

walking around with one-way tickets to minor-league towns sticking conspicuously out of his back pocket. He dealt Evans to Montreal because they couldn't get along. "I was glad to go," said Evans.

Adams didn't drink or smoke, and he expected his players to follow suit. He cringed when he opened a magazine and saw that a Red Wing had picked up an extra hundred dollars endorsing cigarettes. He was livid whenever he caught a player drinking or running around after hours.

Ebbie Goodfellow remembered a nocturnal escapade in Montreal in the 1930s, when Adams caught a fleeting glimpse of some players sneaking through the back entrance of the Windsor Hotel. Adams leaped out of his chair in the lobby and ran up the stairs in hot pursuit.

"When he got to our floor he arrived just in time to hear one of the doors slam shut," said Goodfellow. "He figured it must have been one of his players so he dashed to the door and barged in. Eddie Wiseman, the rookie, was there lying peacefully in bed, snoring to beat the band with his blanket pulled up to his neck. Adams didn't care. He walked right up to him, pulled the blanket off, and there was Wiseman with all his clothes on, even an overcoat. Before Adams could say anything, Eddie looked up, rubbed his eyes, and said, 'Geez, coach, it's awfully cold in here!'"

According to Carl Liscombe, there was an up side to the lack of a chummy relationship between coach and players: It helped create a good deal of the clubhouse harmony that the Red Wings had become famous for. "There was no dissension among the players," he said. "We all hated Jack Adams."

There was, however, no denying Jolly Jack's genius in getting the most out of his men. This was evident in 1941 and '42, when each April an ordinary Detroit squad found itself in the position of being one series win from capturing an unexpected Cup.

The Wings came in third in 1940-41, largely on the strength of Syd Howe's 44 points (which tied him with four others for the second-highest point total in the league) and Johnny Mowers's goaltending. The rookie lost the Vezina to Toronto's Turk Broda on the last night of the season, but it was the Wings, not the second-place Maple Leafs, who advanced to the final round against league champion Boston. Detroit got there by beating the Rangers, two games to one, in the quarterfinals, then erasing Chicago two straight in the semifinals.

The powerful Bruins, coached by former Wing Cooney Weiland and featuring the stellar goaltending of ex-Detroit farmhand Frank "Mr. Zero" Brimsek, exposed the Wings as pretenders to the throne. Detroit's offense, anemic all season, could muster only six goals in the final round. Meanwhile, Boston center Milt Schmidt scored three goals and had four assists all by himself.

**B**y the early forties, all of the players who had delivered back-to-back Stanley Cups a few years earlier were gone, including old favorites Ebbie Goodfellow (right) and Larry Aurie.

Goodfellow, who filled in for Jack Adams for the last three games of the '42 finals after the coach was suspended for slugging an official, returned for his fourteenth season as a part-time player and assistant coach. His last game was Christmas day, 1942.

Aurie retired after the 1937-38 season to work in the Wings' farm system. But the following season, when a rash of injuries forced Adams to look for help, he came out of retirement for one game.

On January 10, 1939, Aurie scored in the Wings' 3-0 victory over Montreal, then promptly hung up his skates again, this time for keeps.

A raging Jack Adams, infuriated by a series of penalties, attacked official Mel Harwood at the end of the fourth game of the 1942 finals against Toronto. The Wings wound up losing the game, their coach, and the series, as the Maple Leafs made history by coming back to win the last four games after dropping the first three.

Right wing Eddie Wiseman, who had broken in with Detroit in 1932 and was traded just before the Wings captured their first Cup, also had a big series against his old teammates. Boston won the first two games by a goal each, 3-2 and 2-1. The Bruins then captured the next two at Olympia, 4-2 and 3-1, to complete the first finals sweep since the best-of-seven format began.

A sweep was tough to take, but it wasn't nearly as bitter a pill to swallow as what happened the following spring. The Canadian press would one day select Toronto's shocking return from the grave in the '42 finals as the comeback of the century. Detroiters have always remembered it as the collapse of the century. In either case, Adams's men never get any credit for being the overachieving crew that they were. After compiling a mediocre 19-25-4 record, they upset Montreal, then Boston, in the first two rounds. Their appearance in the championship round astonished many. No fourth-place team had ever won a Stanley Cup before, so what chance did a fifth-place team like Detroit really have against the second-place Leafs, who had eliminated the league-champion Rangers in the opening round? The concensus in the press box was that the Wings would once again be beaten four straight in their bid for the Cup.

The Wings' crafty coach never cared for naysayers. Adams devised a strategy to take advantage of Bucko McDonald, the former Wing now playing defense for the Leafs. He knew that McDonald covered a lot of ice, but that owed more to his wildly fluctuating weight than to any speed. Instead of carrying or passing the puck across the blueline, Adams had his players shoot it past the defensemen, then skate like mad after it. Dumping and chasing has long been an accepted offensive strategy, but in 1942 it was still brand new. The result was Detroit skating out of Maple Leaf Gardens with 3-2 and 4-2 victories, Don Grosso netting a pair of goals in each.

It was more of the same in the third game, as the upstart Detroiters blitzed Toronto, 5-2, to the joy of a full house at Olympia. Adams had predicted after the first game that his team would beat the Leafs in six. Now it looked like it was going to be a sweep—a monumental achievement, and doubly sweet since it would come at the expense of his most bitter rival. Later, in a hotel lobby, Leafs forward Billy Taylor joked with reporters. "Don't worry about us," he said, "we'll beat them four straight."

Which they did, but not before a desperate gambit by Toronto coach Hap Day and some fireworks from Jack Adams. The Wings built a 2-0 lead in game four on goals by Mud Bruneteau and Sid Abel, then were stunned when the Leafs rallied to tie late in the second period. Day had benched McDonald and Gordie Drillon, the team's leading scorer during the regular season, and inserted seldom-used forward Don Metz and rookie defenseman Ernie Dickens into the lineup. Carl Liscombe put Detroit ahead when he beat Turk Broda at 4:18 of the third period. With the champagne on ice inside Olympia and 13,694 fans ready to bust loose, the Leafs methodically fought back, captain Syl Apps scoring the equalizer two minutes later. Then, with a little more than seven minutes left to play, Apps and Metz set up Metz's brother, Nick, for what turned out to be the game-winner.

Adams's frustration over the impending loss built into an explosion that contributed mightily to Detroit's downfall. With the clock winding down, referee Mel Harwood whistled Eddie Wares for a misconduct penalty. When Wares objected too vigorously, Harwood added a $50 fine. A few seconds later, the Wings were called for having too many men on the ice. Don Grosso threw his gloves and stick at Harwood's feet, earning himself a $25 fine.

This kind of officiating was all too much for Adams, whose face was beet-red with anger. At the conclusion of Toronto's 4-3 victory, he ran across the ice and took several swings at Harwood. The linesmen and players finally broke up the scuffle, but Adams later broke into the officials' dressing room and again had to be restrained. League president Frank Calder announced that Adams had been suspended indefinitely and that Wares and Grosso had been fined an additional $100. Ebbie Goodfellow would take over the coaching duties for the duration of the series.

In stark contrast to the bombastic Adams, the Leafs remained unflappable, even as they added another rookie, eighteen-year-old forward Gaye Stewart, to the lineup. They bombed Detroit, with Don Metz scoring three goals and setting up two others. "The 9-3 win in Toronto was the turning point in the series," said Stewart, who lated played a season with the Wings. "Up until then, we had some doubts, but after that win, going to Detroit didn't bother us at all. From the fifth game on, nobody on our club thought we were going to lose."

The sky-high Leafs blanked the Red Wings at Olympia, 3-0, then returned home to complete the most amazing turnaround in hockey history. After Syd Howe's goal and Johnny Mowers's inspired goalkeeping had produced a 1-0 Detroit lead, they rallied for three third-period goals in a rousing 3-1 victory. As the disconsolate Wings mumbled into their beer and wondered what in the world had happened to them, the jubilant Leafs gathered inside the Royal York Hotel to celebrate their first Stanley Cup in a decade. Thus ended another tumultuous chapter in a rivalry that, many years after the memorable evening when Jolly Jack went ballistic, still retains its blowtorch intensity.

Eddie Bush had a very limited NHL career, scoring 10 points in 27 games for the Wings over two seasons. But on April 9, 1942, the big defenseman established the club's single-game scoring mark for the postseason when he had a goal and four assists in the second game of the finals against Toronto. Bush's five-point effort has since been matched by Norm Ullman and Steve Yzerman.

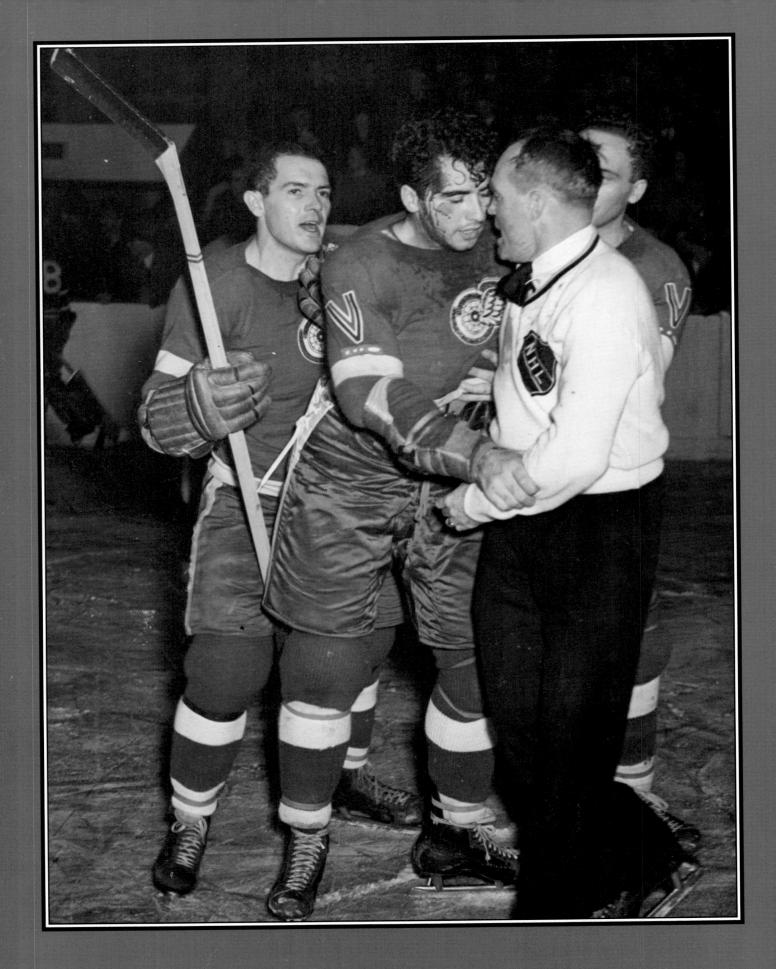

# CHAPTER THREE

No hockey rivalry, not even one as supercharged as the one between Detroit and Toronto, could compare to the real war that engulfed the world for six years. Great Britain's entry into the conflict in 1939 involved all citizens of the British Commonwealth, including Canadians, and it wasn't long before the war's effects were felt in a variety of ways. By the time Detroit played Boston in the '41 finals, for instance, the Bruins'

# And Then There Were Six

## 1942–1948

famous "Kraut Line" of Milt Schmidt, Woody Dumart, and Bobby Bauer had been renamed the more politically correct "Kitchener Kids," and most of the Maple Leafs had volunteered for military training with the Toronto Scottish Reserve. Conversely, it was business as usual on Pearl Harbor Sunday—December 7, 1941—as the Wings beat Montreal, 3-2, at Olympia and the rest of the league's teams also played their regularly scheduled games. In fact, the NHL would go through the entire war without a single interruption in its schedule. In the spring of 1945, when the Red Wings asked that a playoff game be postponed in honor of President Franklin Roosevelt's death, the league said absolutely not. The show must go on.

On November 7, 1942, in the first meeting between Detroit and Toronto since the Leafs' unprecedented comeback in the '42 finals, Wings defenseman Jimmy Orlando was bloodied in a vicious stick-swinging fight with Gaye Stewart.

Center Murray Armstrong was one of three players Detroit purchased for $35,000 from the New York Americans after that team folded during the war. Notice the patch on Armstrong's sleeve: "EVERYBODY AT LEAST 10% IN WAR BONDS." Players wore that and the "V" (for victory) patches on their jerseys throughout World War II.

Black Jack Stewart. "Naturally, he was not a favorite of out-of-town fans," teammate Max McNab said. "When we would go play in Toronto, Montreal, New York, Boston or Chicago, Jack would be the last one to step on the ice for us. At the very last minute this unbelievable booing would start. I would look up into the stands and be thinking, 'What the hell is that all about?' Then I'd realize that the booing was because Black Jack had just stepped on the ice."

Which is not to say that there weren't some significant changes in the game. Many players were forced to put their careers on hold while they served their country. "Hockey was something you just forgot about," said Sid Abel, who lost nearly three full seasons when he went overseas with the Royal Canadian Air Force. Some never returned to the game that they loved. Joe Turner, a Windsor kid who impressed Adams during his brief trial as an NHL netminder, was working under coach Herbie Lewis at Detroit's farm team in Indianapolis when he decided to join the Marine Corps. He was later reported killed in action somewhere in the Pacific.

Railroad timetables were rigidly followed, forcing the league to abandon regular-season overtime. When the Blackhawks and Red Wings skated to a 3-3 tie on November 8, 1942, it marked the last regular-season game to go into an extra session until the practice was reinstated in 1983. Fans were understanding of delays. They knew there was a war on. One night in 1945, nearly 8,000 fans patiently waited three hours at Olympia for the New York Rangers to straggle in. The game finally started at 11:13 P.M. and didn't end until nearly one o'clock the next morning.

The war years also coincided with the NHL's shrinking from a seven-team league to a circuit of six clubs. The financially floundering New York Americans shifted to Brooklyn in 1941 before finally drowning in a pool of red ink the following year. This left Detroit, Chicago, Boston, Toronto, Montreal, and New York to begin the 1942-43 season. This solid six-pack—fondly (if disingenuously) characterized today as the "Original Six" franchises—would remain intact for the next quarter-century, until expansion doubled the size of the league in 1967. The schedule was expanded from 48 to 50 games, with each club facing every other team five times on home ice and five times on the road.

On November 1, 1942, the Red Wings kicked off a new season in red, white, and blue fashion, as 30 aviation cadets were sworn in at center ice prior to their game with the Bruins. Boston lost, 3-0, and would wind up the year in second place, four points behind the Wings, who set a new team record with 61 points. Key contributors to the Wings' 25-14-11 record were Johnny Mowers, whose six shutouts were one more than the rest of the league *combined*; and Jack Stewart, whose bone-crushing hits had earned him the sobriquet "Black Jack" and a spot on the First All-Star Team. "Jack was a guy who gave it his all, every minute of every game," remembered reporter Mark Beltaire. "At the end of every season I'd see him on the end of the bench, totally exhausted. He'd tell me, 'Mark, this is my last game. No more.' Next year he'd be back." Mowers received the Vezina Trophy and a first-team selection, as well.

The NHL's newly formatted "second season" called for best-of-seven series between the first- and third-place clubs and the second- and fourth-place finishers. The winners of this semifinal round would then meet for the championship in another best-of-seven series. The playoff structure would stay the same throughout the entire six-team era. To Adams's delight, the Wings whipped the third-place Leafs in six games in their semifinal matchup. It was the first time Detroit had gotten past Toronto in the playoffs since 1936.

The Wings give themselves a few loud cheers for clinching the regular season championship in 1943. A few weeks later they would be celebrating a Stanley Cup win over the Bruins.

Johnny Mowers won the Vezina Trophy in 1942-43 while accounting for six of the league's 11 shutouts that year. He lost his skills after serving three years in the service and played just seven more games after his discharge.

The finals began on April Fool's Day in Detroit, the Wings rolling over the Bruins by a 6-2 score. Mud Bruneteau, the team leader with 23 goals, notched the second playoff hat trick in the franchise's history. Three days later Adams's men won again, 4-3, before moving on to Boston, where Mowers put the clamps on the Bruins. He pushed aside every puck fired his way as the Red Wings broomed the Bruins with 4-0 and 2-0 victories.

Afterwards the new champions "had to run like hell to catch the train," recalled Carl Liscombe, who had led all playoff scorers with 14 points. "We barely had time to stop and buy sandwiches before we got to the station. There were some Red Wing fans on the train, too, so we set up the Stanley Cup in the men's room on the train, filled it with beer and served it to everyone in paper cups. I know none of us went to bed that night."

The convincing manner in which the Wings copped their third Stanley Cup helped to take some of the sting out of the memory of the previous April's collapse against Toronto. But it couldn't ease Adams's pain. The "King Wing" returned to Detroit to find that his mother had suffered a heart attack while listening to the broadcast of the final game. Ironically, it came less than a year after Adams's eighty-year-old father had passed away, shortly after listening to a radio tribute to his son. Adams's answer to this double dose of tragedy was to throw himself even more into his work.

The 1943-44 season promised to be a challenge, with stars like Mowers, Stewart, and Abel gone into the service and others trying to juggle defense jobs with the comparatively nonessential work of defending a Stanley Cup championship. Syd Howe and Mud Bruneteau, for instance, worked at the Ford Rouge plant, while defenseman Alex Motter and center Connie Brown repaired dies with Mowers at the Hancock Tool and Die Plant before all three entered the Canadian armed forces. Motter and Brown would never play another NHL game after the '43 playoffs; Mowers, his prime years spent in the army, would play just seven ineffective games after his return from duty.

Not everybody was so patriotic. Jimmy Orlando had earned a reputation as a battling blueliner, leading the league in penalty minutes three consecutive seasons. However, he appeared to be in no hurry to donate his pugilistic skills to combat fascism. Three months after he had helped Detroit win the Cup, a U.S. judge convicted him of draft evasion and sentenced him to serve four years in a federal penitentiary. Adams had posted the $4,000 bond that allowed Orlando to remain free, then was left with egg on his face when his player refused to leave his native Canada and give himself up to American authorities. The sentence was remitted when Orlando joined the Canadian army. He returned safely from the war, but not to the NHL.

All told, Adams lost nine starters from his '42-43 squad. He wasn't alone; most owners found themselves patching holes in their lineup the best way they could. This meant dressing has-beens, never-weres, draft-board rejects, returning war veterans, and draft-resistant teenagers. This rainbow of choices could be found in the four goalies Adams was forced to go with during the '43-44 campaign. He brought back thirty-five-year-old Normie Smith, who hadn't faced an NHL shot in five years, and Jimmy Franks, who'd been a bust replacing Smith in the '37 playoffs, before settling on the diminutive Connie Dion.

Dion's lack of size (5-foot-4, 130 pounds) was compensated by the fact that he had served his time in the military and thus could be expected to stick around. "The Asbestos Kid" became the number-one goaltender, but Adams still found room to work in a promising farmhand, Harry Lumley. On December 22, 1943, the seventeen-year-old Lumley started his first NHL game, losing to Chicago, 7-1. He wasn't the youngest player to be trotted out during the war years. The previous season Armand "Bep" Guidolin was sixteen when he

Carl Liscombe led the team with 14 goals as a rookie in 1937-38, then set new club marks with 36 goals, 37 assists, and 73 points six years later. All told, the left wing scored 137 goals in nine Detroit seasons, plus 22 more in 59 postseason contests.

cracked Boston's starting lineup. (The stocky left winger later played two seasons in Detroit.)

Lumley, destined to be Detroit's goalie of the future, was limited to just three appearances his rookie season. One, oddly enough, was when New York borrowed him in a game against Detroit after their goalie, Ken "Tubby" McAuley, was injured. Although the league had allowed teams to expand their active game roster from 12 to 13 players because of the war, most still carried just one goaltender. If he was hurt, he had up to ten minutes to recover and return to the game. If not, a substitute had to be brought in. Usually this meant suiting up

a trainer (who often doubled as a practice goalie), pulling a local semipro out of the stands, or borrowing someone from the other team. On this occasion Lumley dutifully filled in for the Rangers, who should have awarded all their goalies combat pay for the number of shots they allowed each game.

The once-proud Rangers, who finished last in each of the four seasons that America was at war, were an example of how the conflict could ravage rosters. They hit rock-bottom in 1943-44, when they allowed 310 goals—a record 6.2 a game. A good chunk of those came on January 23, 1944, when the Wings bombed them, 15-0, at Olympia in the most lopsided game ever played in the NHL. The Wings poured in a record eight goals in the third period alone, Joe Carveth assisting on half of them. Shell-shocked Tubby McAuley had to face 58 shots—about an average night's work for him. Everybody but defenseman Cully Simon had a hand in the scoring, including Syd Howe, who registered his seventh career hat trick as a Wing.

Howe would double his output when the two teams met again at Olympia two weeks later. On February 3, 1944, the Wings once again blew the Rangers off the ice, this time by a 12-2 score. Howe put two past McAuley in the first period just 18 seconds apart, then scored two more within a 62-second span in the second period. He lit the lamp for a fifth time in the third period, then 57 seconds later banged in his sixth and final goal. He fell one short of the record seven goals Quebec's Joe Malone had scored in a 1920 game against Toronto. Amazingly, Howe was not even the leading scorer that night, because Don Grosso had a goal and six assists for seven points. This tied a league mark held by several players, including Carl Liscombe, who the previous season had piled up three goals and four assists in a game against—who else?—the Rangers.

The reasons for this outbreak of scoring were twofold: watered-down rosters and—more significantly—the introduction of the red line, which opened

Left wing Don "The Count" Grosso leaves a sprawled Jack McDonald of the Rangers in his wake in a 1944 game at Madison Square Garden. In 1941-42, Grosso topped the club with 23 goals and 53 points, then led all postseason performers with eight goals and 14 points.

The "other" Howe, Syd, retired as the NHL's all-time scorer in 1946 with 528 points in 17 seasons. Of his 237 goals, a record six came in one game against the New York Rangers on February 3, 1944, at Olympia.

In 1944-45, Bill "Flash" Hollett became the first defenseman ever to score 20 goals. His output helped put the Wings in the Cup finals, where they lost to Toronto in the lowest-scoring seven-game series in history.

up the game to speed and passing. The beginning of hockey's modern era was ushered in by a flurry of 30-goal scorers, including Detroit's first two: Carl Liscombe (36) and Syd Howe (32). The Wings, one of four teams to break the 200-goal barrier for the first time, finished in second place in 1943-44 at 26-18-6, a record 25 points behind the Canadiens. Montreal had lost fewer players to the service than any other team, a fact borne out by its 38-5-7 record. In the playoffs Detroit lost to Chicago in five games, and the Blackhawks in turn were swept by Montreal for the Cup.

The league's new emphasis on offense was custom-made for a player like Montreal's Maurice "Rocket" Richard. The fiery, slashing right wing had scored a record dozen goals in the '44 playoffs. The following year, 1944-45, he ripped through the NHL's last wartime season in similar style, scoring 50 goals in 50 games as Montreal once again outdistanced second-place Detroit. On December 28, 1944, he had what he later considered his greatest game, scoring five goals and assisting on three others as the Canadiens demolished Detroit, 9-1. It was the first time an NHL player had scored eight points in a single game.

Performances like that made Richard the darling of French-speaking Canadians, who had always considered themselves second-class citizens to their English-speaking countrymen. This feeling of cultural and socioeconomic oppression was particularly keen in Quebec, where the Rocket hailed from. They loved it when Richard, who had the added advantage of being ambidextrous, took the puck on an end-to-end rush, picked up speed as he barreled his way through the opposition, then ended his cometlike journey by using either a forehand or backhand shot to put it in the bank. "What I remember most about the Rocket were his eyes," said Detroit's Glenn Hall, who first faced Richard's bull-like rushes in the mid-fifties. "When he came flying toward you with the puck on his stick, his eyes were all lit up, flashing and gleaming like a pinball machine. It was terrifying."

By the spring of 1945, Adams's makeshift squad of regulars, retreads, and rookies had solidified nicely. The youthful Harry Lumley, dubbed "Apple Cheeks" for his rosy countenance, had taken over fulltime goaltending duties from Connie Dion. "Fortunately, most of my older teammates took me under their wings," he recalled. "Old-timers such as Flash Hollett and Earl Seibert treated me as if they were my father and I was their son."

Such paternalism also was extended to rookie Ted Lindsay, a tough-as-nails nineteen-year-old who had jumped directly from the junior ranks, where he had helped the Oshawa Generals win the Canadian junior championship, to the NHL. Lindsay, a 5-foot-8, 160-pound left wing, hailed from Renfrew, Ontario.

His father, Bert Lindsay, had been an outstanding goalie in the early years of the century, backstopping the famed Renfrew Millionaires and also the Victoria Cougars. "Terrible Ted" was an accomplished two-way operative and a Jack Adams favorite. When he wasn't using his stick to work over opposing forwards, he was using it to put the puck into the net: 17 times his first year as a Red Wing.

"Two guys I'll always remember and be grateful to are Joe Carveth and Murray Armstrong," said Lindsay. "Two of the finest gentlemen I ever knew in hockey. Murray wound up being my centerman and Carveth was my right winger in training camp. They made me feel so comfortable and so at home. Murray would give me a pass that I should've had in my back pocket and put in the net, but I'd goof it up or something. He'd say, 'Don't worry about that, kid. I'll try to make that pass better next time.'"

Hollett and Seibert, the two defenseman, had been acquired from Boston and Chicago, respectively. Hollett not only managed to break the Canadiens' stranglehold on the First All-Star Team, being the only non-Montreal player named to the starting six, he also used his speed to score 20 goals—an unthinkable achievement for a defenseman before the advent of the red line. It would remain a record until Bobby Orr broke it a quarter-century later.

The most significant record to fall that season was the all-time scoring mark. On March 8, 1945, in a 7-3 victory over the Rangers at Olympia, Syd Howe notched his 515th career point to overtake Nels Stewart, the former scoring great for the Montreal Maroons, Boston Bruins, and New York Americans. The thirty-three-year-old Howe, then in his sixteenth NHL campaign (11 as a Red Wing), would extend his record to 528 points before retiring at the end of the following season.

All of these milestones were satisfying in their own ways, but of course they paled in importance to winning the Stanley Cup. To everybody's surprise, the powerful Canadiens were upended in the semifinals by Toronto. The Red Wings spotted the Bruins the first two games in the other semifinal matchup, then roared back to win the next three by identical 3-2 scores, the last one in overtime. Boston got the equalizer with a 5-3 win on its home ice, but Detroit returned the favor with a 5-3, seventh-game victory at Olympia that thrust it into the final round against the Maple Leafs.

After three games Toronto appeared to have the Cup locked up, as Frank McCool posted an unprecedented three straight postseason shutouts, 1-0, 2-0, and 1-0. The Wings finally broke through at 8:35 of the first period in game four, snapping McCool's streak at 188 minutes and 35 seconds while rolling to a 5-3 victory. Lumley blanked the Leafs in game five in Detroit, 2-0, and again in game six in Toronto, as Mud Bruneteau, hero of the famous overtime victory against the Maroons nine years earlier, struck again. This time he scored

That's my boys! Jack Adams gives Harry Lumley (left) and Ed Bruneteau a hearty embrace after the two starred in a 1-0 overtime win over Toronto in the sixth game of the 1945 Stanley Cup finals. Lumley threw the shutout while Bruneteau scored after 14 minutes of overtime. The Maple Leafs came back to win the seventh game and the Cup, however, 2-1.

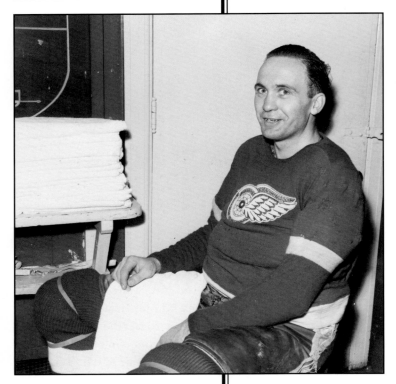

W hen it came to uniforms, NHL owners stressed durability over comfort. Check out the heavy wool jersey worn by Alex Motter during the war years, which has been mended in several spots and is still unravelling in others. It wasn't until the late 1950s that the large, hot, overhead lights needed for television coverage caused teams to begin switching to lightweight jerseys.

fourteen minutes into the first extra session for a 1-0 win that knotted the series.

The Red Wings not only had momentum going for them as both teams boarded the overnight train for Detroit, they also had recent history. Three years earlier, they had blown the Cup after winning the first three games; now it looked as if Toronto was going to do the same. But the crowd that filled Olympia the evening of April 22, 1945, went home dejected. At 12:14 of the third period, defenseman Walter "Babe" Pratt banged in a rebound from five feet in front of Lumley to give the Leafs the victory and the Cup, 2-1.

"It's their system that beat us," explained Bill Quackenbush, the mild-mannered defenseman then in his third year with the Wings. "They'd score a goal and then try to hang on. They played that system to perfection. They played only two lines against us in the whole series. We faced guys like Gus Bodnar, Lorne Carr, Nick Metz, and Teeder Kennedy. They played for the one-goal advantage and then they'd check, check, check." The two teams concluded a season of record-breaking offense by combining for a paltry 18 goals, still the lowest-scoring seven-game series ever played.

Sid Abel and Jack Stewart returned to the Red Wings the following season, their rusty skates contributing to a fourth-place finish and a first-round loss to Boston. The 1946-47 campaign was a virtual repeat—another fourth-place finish followed by a blowout loss in the semifinals, this time to Toronto. Detroit's immediate postwar teams didn't appear to be anything to shout about, especially in comparison to those in Toronto and Montreal, which seemed destined to monopolize Lord Stanley's silver chalice for the forseeable future. But there was one major difference in the composition of the Red Wings team that got bounced out of the '46 playoffs and the squad that went home early in the spring of 1947: a shy, slope-shouldered prairie kid with Popeye arms named Gordie Howe.

H ockey's greatest player was born March 31, 1928, in Floral, Saskatchewan, a nondescript town nine miles east of Saskatoon, where he grew up, and about 1,600 miles northwest of Detroit, where he would gain his fame. "That place is so flat," somebody once said of Saskatoon, "you can sit on your front porch and watch your dog run away for three straight days."

The family would grow to include nine children. It was a hardscrabble life of deprivation, poverty, and daily struggle. The family drank powdered milk and often ate oatmeal three times a day. The house, which Gordie's father had bought for $650, had coal-burning stoves and little else. Insulation consisted of wrapping the drafty windows with plastic and stuffing felt into the cracks. There was no running water; instead the family used a forty-five-gallon drum of water that was kept on the porch and brought inside when it was cold. The children usually bathed at school instead of at home.

"The biggest fear I had when I joined the Red Wings," Howe later said, "was that somebody would come and see where I lived."

In Saskatoon the mercury often dipped to minus 30 or 40 degrees. Snowstorms sometimes blocked the entire front of the house. "We'd have to go out the back and try to dig through to the front door," he remembered in his autobiography.

"You'd kick out about seven or eight feet of snow. It was amazing. You know, I look back and I think, those were hardy people who established their homes out there. People used to walk to work in a blizzard. You know it's cold when you come out of the house and you see the smoke from the wood fires going straight up in the air, like two-by-four columns, right on up into the sky. It was so damn cold even the smoke was trying to get out of town as fast as it could."

Gordie got his first skates when he was four. A neighbor lady, destitute and desperate, came by the house with a sack filled with odds and ends that she was selling in hopes of feeding her baby. "I didn't have much to offer," recalled Gordie's mother, Katherine, "but I reached into my milk money and gave her a dollar and a half. We dumped the contents of the sack onto the floor. Out fell a pair of skates. Of course Gord pounced on them."

Unfortunately, his sister Edna also pounced on them. Each emerged with one skate, several sizes too big. They put on several stockings until they fit, then went outside to try out their new treasure. One-legged skating soon lost its appeal to Edna, who after a week finally surrendered her skate to her brother for a dime.

Gordie got his even temperament and charitable disposition from his mother (who had given him the dime) and inherited his looks and dry humor from his father. Ab Howe, a hard-bitten sort of few words, went through life with a flask in his pocket. "He said it was in case of snakebite," Gordie explained. "So, every once in a while, he'd yell 'Snakebite!' and take a snort." Once his father went fishing with a friend, had a few belts, then managed to capsize the boat. While the friend swam away to get help, the senior Howe hung onto the boat for all he was worth. After a half-hour he finally let go—only to have his feet hit bottom. The boat had capsized in three feet of water.

Howe could skate for miles on the frozen roads and gullies around his house. Although hard times forced him to wear discarded equipment that had been fished out of the garbage and repaired (including his jockstrap and cup), he felt "like a million dollars" whenever he jumped on the ice. "We could play hockey all day. Imagine a twelve-hour game. You'd play all day, go home and eat, come back and say, 'Who's winning?'"

Growing up in the middle of the Great Depression helped develop self-reliance. He trapped gophers for a penny a tail, delivered groceries, caddied at

**F**ormer Boston star Roy Conacher dusted off four years of inactivity because of military service and scored a team-best 30 goals for Detroit in 1946-47. But when the left wing couldn't come to terms, Adams sent him to Chicago, where two years later he won a scoring title.

**B**illy Taylor, acquired from Toronto in 1946, entered the NHL record book when he piled up seven assists in a 10-6 victory over Chicago on March 16, 1947. The following year Taylor, now playing in New York, was suspended for life by league president Clarence Campbell for betting on games.

**G**ordie Howe as a 17-year-old member of the Omaha Knights, the Detroit farm club for which he turned pro in 1945.

the city golf course, and caught fish and sold them for a nickel or dime apiece to the local Chinese restaurant. As a teenager he went to work pouring concrete sidewalks with his dad. He could lift five ninety-five-pound bags of cement at once, grabbing them kitty-corner from a bended-knee position, then swinging around and throwing them onto a wagon. "My dad would always brag about how much I could lift," he said, "so I could never embarrass him by dropping the bags." Gordie's pride resulted in a hernia operation when he was still young, but the strenuous work accounted for the Herculean strength in his hands, wrists, shoulders, and arms.

By the time he was fifteen, Howe was making a reputation for himself as an all-around athlete at King George School. He was already six feet tall and close to 200 pounds. He never grew after that, playing most of his professional career between 196 and 205 pounds. He wasn't much of a student, handicapped by what was later diagnosed as dyslexia. Some boys teased him by calling him "doughhead." None of this prevented him from carefully practicing his penmanship; he was certain that someday he would be asked for his autograph, and he wanted to make sure that when he signed his name it would be neat and legible.

He was fifteen when he was invited to a New York Rangers tryout in Winnipeg; homesick and shy, he turned down an offer to attend Notre Dame College in Wilcox, Saskatchewan, on a scholarship. The following year a Detroit scout, Fred Pinckney, invited him to a Red Wings camp in Windsor. Pinckney bought him his first suit of clothes for the trip. Jack Adams was impressed with what he saw and arranged for him to work out with the junior club in Galt, Ontario. As part of the bargain Adams promised to get him a Wings jacket.

"I wanted that jacket so bad all the time I was in Galt," recalled Howe. "I remember that quite a few times I walked down to the railroad station by myself. I knew when the Red Wings' train would be coming through town traveling to games. I'd just wait there for them. I figured that if they stopped for anything, I'd go aboard and see if I could ask Adams about my jacket, but the train never stopped. They went rolling on through every time. I'd just walk back home."

Howe never entered high school in Galt, as was originally planned. Instead he found work in a defense plant. In September 1945, he was invited to camp with the Wings. The wartime housing shortage forced him to bunk at

Olympia, where he amused himself by killing rats with his stick. After scoring two goals in an exhibition in Akron, Ohio, he signed his first professional contract to play for the Wings' farm club in Omaha, Nebraska. There he scored 22 goals and saved $1,700 of his $2,700 salary.

The following September he reported to the parent club's training camp. After learning that he would stay with the Wings, he cautiously approached the King Wing about some unfinished business. "Mr. Adams," he said, "it has been two years now and I haven't got my jacket yet." Adams had had more important things on his mind, but he wasn't about to lose a top gun over a seventeen-dollar jacket. He sent Howe to a sporting goods store downtown and told him to sign for it. Ted Lindsay and Marty Pavelich accompanied the youngster. "It was smooth like satin on the outside," Howe said, "with leather sleeves and an alpaca lining. It had a big 'D' with 'Red Wings' written on it. It looked like the most beautiful jacket in the world."

Howe made his NHL debut on October 16, 1946, in the season opener against Toronto. Adams put him on a line with Syd Howe and Adam Brown. Here was irony. A few years earlier Gordie had fished Beehive Corn Syrup labels out of his neighbors' garbage and mailed them to the manufacturer in return for pictures of NHL players. His favorite, because of the name, was Syd Howe. Unfortunately, Gordie got stuck with far more pictures of Toronto goalie Turk Broda.

Lo and behold, who should be in the nets that evening at Olympia but Broda, who in the second period earned the distinction of surrendering the first of Howe's 801 regular-season NHL goals. After Howe scored, he thought to himself, "Okay, now I'm registered in the record books." Then Brown skated over and deadpanned, "You didn't get that, I got it." The two argued until Brown started laughing. "Oh geez," the relieved rookie said. "I was gonna go to the president of the league! That was my goal!"

The goal gave Detroit a 2-1 lead. In the final period, Howe got the crowd going again with a bodycheck that knocked Leafs captain Syl Apps out of the game with a twisted knee. Abel's late goal produced a 3-3 tie. "Gordon Howe is the squad's baby, eighteen years old," observed the following day's *Detroit News*. "But he was one of Detroit's most valuable men last night. In his first major-league game, he scored a goal, skated tirelessly and had perfect poise."

Howe's burning ambition was to stay with the varsity. Like most untested players, he had a two-way contract that called for a substantial pay cut should he be farmed out—from $7,500 to $3,500. This was incentive enough to do well. The problem was getting ice time. He was used sparingly and didn't pot his second goal until nine games later. It took another 11 games before he scored his third. Joe Carveth gave the anxious youngster some advice. Carveth "warned me not to be surprised if I didn't do too well the first half of the season, that things would work out better in the second half, when I settled down. He was right." Howe finished his first year in the league with seven goals and 15 assists for 22 points, then went scoreless in the five games he played in the '47 playoffs.

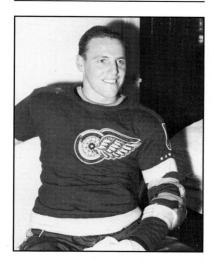

Adam Brown scored 24 goals in 1943-44 and 20 in 1945-46, his only two full seasons with Detroit. Before being traded to Chicago, the left winger assisted on a historic goal: Gordie Howe's first, scored October 16, 1946 against Toronto's Turk Broda.

An early photo of the Production Line. Captain Sid Abel centers his two young wingers, Howe and Lindsay. "Those boys could score goals in their sleep," insisted Jack Adams.

After the season Adams made a momentous decision. After 21 seasons at the helm of the Wings, still the longest stretch of any coach with one team in the annals of the NHL, he was stepping aside to concentrate on his duties as general manager. Tommy Ivan, who had coached Howe at Omaha in 1945 before taking over the farm club in Indianapolis, was to move behind the Wings bench starting with the 1947-48 season.

Ivan, a small, dapper man who had first joined the Detroit organization as a scout in 1938, also made a momentous decision. He put the rangy right wing on a line with Ted Lindsay and Sid Abel. The three clicked right from the get-go. "He got on the line with Lindsay and Abel," said Bill Quackenbush, "and it sure made my job easier. The way those guys forechecked and backchecked was a big help to all the defensemen. They were a great two-way line." On game nights they meshed together like perfectly calibrated gears. By the end of their

first season together the newspapers had dubbed them "The Production Line." Obviously inspired by the city's famous assembly lines, this was as much a bow to their blue-collar work ethic as to their prolific point production.

Abel, who was married, a war veteran, and captain of the team, was a mentor to his younger and less worldly linemates.

"Sid taught us so much," Howe recalled. "We used to sit up in the trains for hours after the game, and he'd go over everything. He'd take us through the whole game, pointing out what we did right and what we did wrong. I think I learned more on the trains than I did on the ice." The favorite meeting place was the "smoker" at one end of the car. "I guess you'd call it a bathroom these days, but they had only one john and about six sinks," said Lindsay. "They had benches against three of the walls, and we'd just sit there and listen to him."

Howe's gifts were subtle. He appeared almost laconic as he glided down the ice in long, powerful strides, shrugging off opponents as he moved the puck from his forehand to his backhand. His greatest weapon was a blistering wrist shot, which was most deadly within 15 to 20 feet of the net. Abel had only one complaint. It was the way in which Howe would often take the puck and hold onto it for what seemed minutes. "I don't mind his great stickhandling," he said. "But why stickhandle around the same player three times?"

Although he was still a teenager, Gordie was a major physical force on the ice. In his very first NHL game he had lost three teeth—strangely, the only teeth he would ever spill in league competition. "After that," he said, "someone had to come through lumber to get me." Ten years later a hockey maga-

The 1947-48 Red Wings, the first Detroit squad in twenty years to be coached by someone other than Jack Adams. The roster included forward Armond "Bep" Guidolin, second from left in the back row, who was only twenty-two years old but already starting his fifth NHL season. He had broken into the league with Boston as a sixteen-year-old in 1942, the youngest NHLer ever.

**B**ill Quackenbush, Ted Lindsay, and Jack Stewart were the Red Wings' representatives in the first NHL All-Star Game, played October 13, 1947 in Toronto. The game's original format pitted the defending Stanley Cup champions against a squad composed of all-stars from the other five teams, as selected by a vote of writers and broadcasters. Detroit's Olympia Stadium hosted the game, created to benefit the players' pension fund, in 1950, 1952, 1954, and 1955. The biggest rout in the series was October 8, 1950, when Lindsay's hat trick paced a thrashing of the All-Stars, 7-1.

zine would poll NHL managers to get their opinion of who the toughest player in the league was. Howe won. "He is not only a great player," said one, "but he is tough and mean, too."

"Gordie was a hard-nosed kid," agreed Ivan. "He used to get me some foolish penalties but appeared determined to prove early that he was no patsy."

One night Howe drew a call for attempting to knock an opponent into the next county. "What's the matter?" Ivan asked him afterwards. "Don't you like him?"

"I don't like anybody," replied Howe.

That wasn't true, of course. But through neccesity his on-ice persona in the dog-eat-dog world of professional hockey bordered on "being a little crazy," he admitted. In his first playoff series, the '47 semifinals, he had almost started a riot at Olympia when he and the Leafs' Gus Mortson started brawling inside the penalty box, which in those days was shared by the guilty from both teams. Fans joined in. The police finally restored order, but not before the fighting had spilled over into the aisle and one spectator had pitched a chair at Mortson. In the hubbub it was easy to overlook that the whole fracas had started when Howe had come to the aid of his antagonistic buddy, Lindsay.

Lindsay, three years older than Howe, was a disciple of Black Jack Stewart's school of charm. Like the Wings' All-Star defenseman, who explained that he used his clublike stick not to score but "to break arms," he was an instigator who was always among the league leaders in penalties and stitches. Away from Olympia, the brash, cocky Lindsay and socially inept Howe were close friends, eventually sharing a house in Detroit. Howe had his share of altercations, but he would always be slower to anger than his mercurial linemate. Said Howe: "Lindsay was so concerned about me, he used to tell me, 'Spear that son of a bitch.' He got me in more trouble. He'd be yapping like hell at their left winger, then the guy would nail me. And I'd say, 'Oh, here we go again.' Ted's mouth got me in more fights than any other factor. And Ted got his stick in everybody."

Encouraged by Abel and Ivan to shoot more often, Howe responded with 16 goals in his sophomore season, 1947-48. Only Lindsay, whose 33 goals led the league, and center Jim McFadden, whose 24 goals earned him the Calder Trophy, lit the lamp more often that year for Detroit. With Harry Lumley tossing a league-high seven shutouts and rookie Leonard "Red" Kelly added to the league's best blueline corps, the Red Wings bolted back into contention with a 30-18-12 record. Because the league had expanded to a 60-game schedule the previous year, they were able to set a new team standard with 72 points while finishing second. Five points ahead were the Maple Leafs, who decided a nip-and-tuck race by sweeping a season-ending home-and-home series against the Wings.

The Wings rolled over the Rangers in six games in the opening round of the playoffs, Howe scoring his first postseason goal. This earned them the right to meet Toronto in the finals. Howe was in there battling all the way, at one point earning an easy decision over little Howie Meeker. "Howie swung once and buried his head in Howe's midriff," reported the *Toronto Star*. "Gord promptly hit him with three on top of the noggin, raising a set of goose eggs." The Wings raised the biggest goose egg—a big fat zero in the win column. They were routed, 5-3, 4-2, 2-0, and 7-2, as the Production Line was held to a single point, a goal by Lindsay.

Adams, enduring his first season away from the bench, was characteristically upset by the sweep. At times he felt helpless, though he always sat in the first row of seats, where he could second-guess Ivan and harangue officials to his heart's content. However, he could also look out his office window, through the haze that floated above Detroit's booming auto factories, and note with satisfaction that several talented youngsters were either already dressing at or making their way to Olympia. Better days, he predicted, were on the horizon.

**T**ed Lindsay may have gotten his stick into a Maple Leaf on this occasion, but it was Detroit that took the pratfall in the 1948 Stanley Cup finals. Toronto swept the Wings, allowing the Production Line just one goal.

**T**rophy night in 1948 saw Jim McFadden (right) win the Calder Trophy as top rookie, largely on the strength of his 24 goals and 24 assists.

# CHAPTER FOUR

**I**n the mid-fifties, by which time the Red Wings were winning one regular-season title after another and lifting hockey's silver mug with alarming regularity, observers often compared them to the other great sports dynasty of the decade. The Red Wings, it was said, were the New York Yankees of hockey. "No, no," Jack Adams would always argue. "The Yankees are the Detroit Red Wings of baseball."

The cornerstone of the Red Wings' continuing success was a farm system of unparalleled breadth and depth. During Adams's thirty-five-year tenure he would establish working arrangements with clubs throughout Canada (Hamilton, Edmonton,

# Silver Streak

## 1948–1955

Flin Flon, Galt, Guelph, Sudbury, and Windsor) and the United States (New Haven, Omaha, Fort Worth, Pittsburgh, and Indianapolis). At one point the Detroit organization had 110 minor-leaguers under contract—enough players to stock the entire NHL. No matter what the player's position or skill level, he was drilled in the Red Wing way of doing things, a uniformity and quality of instruction that paid dividends when Adams decided to promote a youngster to the big club in Detroit.

The farm system was particularly fertile in the 1940s and '50s, producing such future Hall of Famers as Ted Lindsay, Gordie Howe, Bill Quackenbush, Harry Lumley, Red Kelly, Terry Sawchuk, Marcel Pronovost, Alex Delvecchio, Glenn Hall, Johnny

---

**Terry Sawchuk and Sid Abel plant a kiss on the Stanley Cup in 1952, one of four that the Red Wings won during the fifties.**

**B**ill Quackenbush was a first-team All-Star twice during his seven seasons with Detroit, including 1949, when he became the first blueliner to go through an entire season without drawing a penalty and the first to be awarded the Lady Byng Trophy.

Bucyk, and Norm Ullman. Adams had an eye for talent. His penchant for spotting, signing, and developing prospects at an early age was reflected by the fact that Detroit's rookies often were two or three years younger than their counterparts on other clubs. Adams's philosophy was that his players should expend as much of their youthful prime as possible in the NHL, where the games counted most. This also insured that there wouldn't be too many miles on a player's odometer when it came time for him to be traded—which, due to the general manager's impatience, petulance, ego, and irrationality, was in many cases almost inevitable.

The one person Adams never had thoughts of trading was Number 9, Howe. As a rookie, Adams's golden teenager had actually worn 17 on the back of his jersey until somebody pointed out to him that train berths were assigned by uniform numbers. By this formula, players with single digits got the more comfortable lower berths. So, after Roy Conacher was traded prior to the start of the 1947-48 season, Howe requested and received Conacher's number 9. That it happened to be the same number that his chief rival, Rocket Richard, wore, interested Howe not a bit. He simply wanted a good night's sleep on the long train rides back from Montreal, Boston, and other NHL outposts.

"Gordie Howe is the greatest young player I've ever seen," Adams gushed in 1948-49, a season that marked the start of the Wings' unmatched seven-year stay at the top of the standings. "There is not enough money in the NHL to buy him. I just love the kid." That year Detroit set new team highs in victories (34) and points (75) as it finished first, nine points ahead of the Bruins. Knee surgery caused Howe to miss 20 games, but he still managed to score 37 points, only one behind Richard, who had played the entire schedule. In voting for the postseason All-Star teams Howe also finished behind his Montreal counterpart. However, his second-team selection was the beginning of an unfathomable 21 consecutive All-Star berths, a string that would last through the Truman, Eisenhower, Kennedy, Johnson, and Nixon administrations.

Howe's was not the only standout performance on the '48-49 Wings. Sid Abel led the loop with 28 goals, finished third in scoring with 54 points, and was awarded the Hart Trophy and a spot on the First All-Star Team. Ted Lindsay's badly separated shoulder caused him to miss one-sixth of the schedule and probably prevented him from grabbing league honors in goals and points; as it was, he still notched 26 goals and 28 assists to match the captain's 54 points. Jack Stewart and Bill Quackenbush, both reknowned for their robustly delivered bodychecks, remained virtually impenetrable on defense and

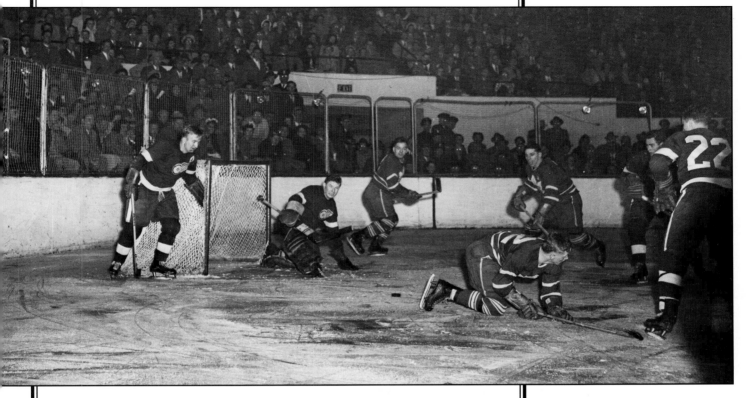

were named first-team All-Stars. In contrast to the heavily penalized Black Jack, the poke-checking Quackenbush became the first defender to go through the entire season without spending a single second in the sin bin and the first blueliner to be awarded the Lady Byng Trophy.

Detroit got past Montreal in the semifinals, the Production Line scoring 12 goals (eight by Howe) in a seven-game series that was decided by a 3-1 win in Detroit. But fourth-place Toronto, bidding to become the first team to win three consecutive Stanley Cups, once again spoiled the Wings' party. Detroit could dent Toronto's air-tight defense for only five goals, as for the second straight April the Maple Leafs swept Adams's men in the finals.

If getting past Toronto in the postseason had become a major problem—the Leafs had now won four Stanley Cups at the Wings' expense in the last seven seasons—finishing first was on the road to becoming routine. The final standings in March of 1950 again showed Detroit on top, its stellar defense unaffected by a surprising offseason trade that had moved Quackenbush to Boston for four players, including winger Pete Babando. The schedule had been expanded to 70 games, reflecting postwar prosperity and the increased demand for sports entertainment on both sides of the border. This gave the still maturing Detroit squad the opportunity to establish new team records with 37 victories and 88 points, placing it 11 points in front of the Canadiens. Thanks to the Production Line, it again led the circuit in goals.

Hockey's top line was a marvel to watch, recalled Joe Falls, then a young wire service reporter on his way to making a name for himself in Detroit

**H**arry Lumley kicks away a Toronto shot during the 1949 finals. The Maple Leafs swept the Wings to win their third Stanley Cup in a row.

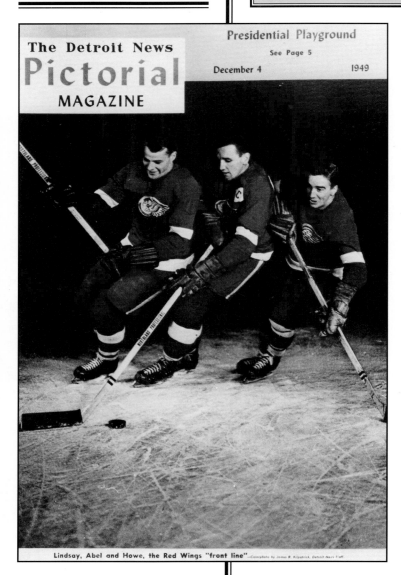

The Detroit News
**Pictorial**
MAGAZINE

Presidential Playground
See Page 5

December 4     1949

Lindsay, Abel and Howe, the Red Wings "front line" —Colorphoto by James R. Kilpatrick, Detroit News Staff.

**T**he Production Line finished 1-2-3 in scoring in 1949-50. Lindsay led the league with 78 points, followed by Abel (69) and Howe (68).

sports journalism. "Bootnose, Scarface, and Blinky," Falls fondly reminisced when Abel's number 12 was retired to the rafters of Joe Louis Arena in 1995:

> Sid Abel, Ted Lindsay, and Gordie Howe.
> The Production Line.
> They would start the game and play shifts of two and three minutes. None of these 45-second bursts. They control the puck, crossing and criss-crossing in front of each other, working it up the ice, relentlessly, until one of them lets a shot go on net.
> You would watch them closely and marvel at their skills: Lindsay, with the perfectly combed hair, running into everyone, stick high, an assassin who looked like an altar boy; Howe, with those sloping shoulders and thick neck, keeping the puck away from everyone, even his teammates, making one amazing move after another; and No. 12, the one in the shoulder pads, weaving around the ice, taking the puck when it came to him and looking for an opening to get it closer to the goal.

Abel was nicknamed "Bootnose" because of a severely hooked proboscis; Lindsay was dubbed "Scarface" for the sewing that was always holding his features together; and Howe earned his moniker, "Blinky," because of a facial tic that occasionally caused his eye to twitch uncontrollably. In 1949-50 the trio of teammates finished 1-2-3 in scoring, only the fourth time that that had happened in NHL history. Lindsay had 23 goals and 55 assists for 78 points, followed by Abel (34-35-69) and Howe (35-33-68). Their collective 92 goals and 215 points caused Adams to marvel, "Those boys could score in their sleep."

A favorite play was to expertly blast the puck off a certain spot on the end boards at Olympia so that the ricochet produced an unexpected scoring chance. The trio practiced this over and over, taking care to mark the exact spot at each end of the rink every time the boards were painted. "Gordie would lead the charge down the right wing," said teammate Murray Costello, "and just after he crossed center ice he'd fire the puck between the defensemen. If he hit that spot just right, and he was uncanny about hitting it, the puck came right out to the top of the left circle, and Lindsay would scoot in behind the defensemen and get a point-blank shot on goal."

## Silver Streak

Howe and the man villified for sending him into his near-fatal crash into the boards, Leafs captain Ted "Teeder" Kennedy, size each other up sometime in the early fifties.

Howe, who'd led all scorers in the '49 postseason, didn't have much of an opportunity to strut his stuff when the Wings faced off with their old nemesis, Toronto, in the opener of the 1950 playoffs. In fact, he almost lost his life. In the second period, with the Leafs up 3-0, Howe came charging towards Ted "Teeder" Kennedy as the Toronto captain led a rush across center ice. Seeing out of the corner of his eye that he was about to be hammered into the boards—the referee already had his arm up to signal a charging penalty—Kennedy suddenly pulled up. Howe, hurtling like a runaway locomotive, stumbled, glanced off his intended target, and plowed head-first into the top of the boards right in front of the Detroit bench. Jack Stewart, who'd also had Kennedy in his sights, couldn't check his momentum and fell over his unconscious, bleeding teammate. As the full house at Olympia watched in stunned silence, Howe was placed on a stretcher, taken into the dressing room for assessment, then rushed by ambulance to Harper Hospital.

He had broken his nose, shattered his cheekbone, seriously scratched his right eye, and—worst of all—possibly fractured his skull. The young star, whose brain was hemorrhaging, was in critical condition. At 1 A.M., about four hours after the accident occurred, neurosurgeon Dr. Frederic Shreiber started a very delicate, life-saving operation. He drilled an opening in the skull, then drained fluid to relieve pressure on the brain. After the ninety-minute operation the patient was put in an oxygen tent. Meanwhile, all of Detroit and Saskatoon listened to radio updates of Howe's condition.

The news came in the morning and was good: The patient was stabilized and his condition upgraded to serious. He would pull through. The fourth graders at a local Catholic school concluded that they'd had a hand in his recovery. Their teacher was Ted Lindsay's sister, and she had asked them to pray for a special friend of hers.

Charges and threats flew between the teams as they prepared for game two. A league inquiry would later clear Kennedy of any blame in the accident. He

Howe and Lindsay were inseparable their first few years together, sharing everything from a showerhead at Olympia to a house in Detroit. When Lindsay married, Howe moved in with the newlyweds.

Defenseman Leo Reise Jr. was the hero of the 1950 semifinals with two overtime goals against Toronto—half of his regular-season total. "I shot one forehand and one backhanded," the unlikely hero later said of his two clutch goals. "They weren't that well-executed. One bounced off another player. One went straight in." Reise, whose father played in the NHL with Hamilton and New York, spent five and a half of his nine seasons in Detroit.

always maintained that the only thing he was guilty of was getting out of the way. It was a view privately held by some Wings. Publicly, however, the organization expressed outrage at what had happened, claiming that Kennedy had hit Howe in the eye with the butt end of his stick, causing him to pitch forward into the boards. The controversy gave Detroit a clear rallying point—one desperately needed since Toronto's 5-0 first-game victory meant that the Wings had dropped 12 straight postseason contests to their bitterest rivals.

To no one's surprise, the next game turned into a body-slamming, stick-swinging grudge match. The game exploded into open warfare when Lindsay was taken off his feet by Leafs defenseman Gus Mortson.

"Everybody in the rink saw it, except the referee," Red Kelly told Stan Fischler. "There was no call but a few seconds later our defenseman, Lee Fogolin, hit somebody on the Leafs and he got two minutes. Before you knew it, everybody was fighting. Vic Lynn, a big Toronto left wing, and I ended up fighting down in the corner of the rink. One of my defense partners, Leo Reise, had been nicked with a stick and started bleeding. Reise went a little berserk. He came around with his stick and caught Jimmy Thomson of Toronto on the shoulder. He was fortunate he didn't get it in the head. Soon the two goaltenders, our Harry Lumley and Turk Broda of Toronto, met at center ice and with all their equipment on went at it, rolling around on the ice. By now everyone was on the ice and people were throwing chairs from the stands at Olympia. It was almost a riot."

Katherine Howe, who had flown in from Saskatoon to stand watch over her son, was attending her first NHL game as a guest of Wings management. The violence moved her to tears. "If this is hockey," she cried, "I hope my son has to quit." To the satisfaction of everybody else jammed into Olympia that night, the wild-eyed Wings finally snapped their streak of futility with a 3-1 victory.

Back in Toronto, the Leafs pounded out a 2-0 decision to pull ahead in the series. In game four the two teams played just 38 seconds of overtime before Leo Reise attempted a pass from the Leafs' blueline. "I wanted to put it in front of the net," explained the Wings' tall, blonde defenseman. Instead the puck slid past Turk Broda for a 2-1 Detroit victory that squared the series.

The teams continued to exchange victories, Broda posting his third shutout, 2-0, at Olympia, and then Lumley returning the favor with a 4-0 whitewash at Maple Leaf Gardens. The league's two top goalies maintained their outstanding netminding in game seven, played on Easter Sunday in Detroit. At the end of regulation neither had allowed a puck to get past. Then, for the second time in five nights, Reise settled matters. The twenty-seven-year-old defensive specialist, who would never score more than five goals in any of his nine NHL seasons, again tried to throw the puck in front of the net. "I can still see the puck going in," recalled Red Kelly. "Leo backhanded it at Broda and it bounced once and it bounced twice and at the second bounce, Broda kicked it and it went over the top and into the net, eight and a half minutes into the first sudden death." The 1-0 nail-biter avenged Howe's injury and squashed Toronto's bid to win four straight Cups.

## Silver Streak

Reise's heroics put the Wings in the finals against the New York Rangers, upset winners over Montreal. With Madison Square Garden booked for its annual circus, the Rangers were forced to open in Detroit, followed by two "home" games on neutral ice in Toronto. As if that wasn't enough, before the finals began Black Jack Stewart read the riot act to all the younger Wings inside Max McNab's hotel room.

"You fellows are going to be around for another ten or twelve years," he told them. "Me and Sid have to win it this year, so I don't want to see you guys screwing around. And if anybody has a bad night because he isn't ready or isn't working, just remember one thing. When the game is over and you come into the dressing room, I'll be the first guy you'll meet. And I don't care what Mr. Adams says tomorrow or what Mr. Ivan says tomorrow; that doesn't mean anything. Just listen to what I'm saying or you'll meet me after the game."

"That was the strongest pep talk I ever heard in all my years in hockey," marveled McNab. "And let me tell you something: Black Jack Stewart was the last guy in the world you would want to mess around with. The last!"

Despite the scheduling difficulties and Black Jack's impassioned threats, the fourth-place New Yorkers gave the favored Wings all they could handle. With Gerry "Doc" Couture (a 24-goal scorer during the season) and veteran Joe Carveth (recently reacquired from Montreal) ably filling in for Howe, the Wings administered a 4-1 thumping in the curtain-raiser. However, Toronto fans adopted the boys in blue and white as their own. Of course, they didn't really like the Rangers; they simply hated the Red Wings. Their lusty cheering helped New York to a 3-1 decision in game two. The Wings regrouped, blocked out the booing and catcalls from Toronto fans, and zipped past the Rangers in game three, 4-0.

Detroit fans were confidently expecting their team to make short work of the Rangers as the games moved to the friendly confines of Olympia. Thanks to a beanpole center named Don "Bones" Raleigh, however, the Wings instead found themselves on the brink of an unthinkable collapse. In game four Raleigh banged the puck off the post and into the net at 8:34 of sudden death, giving the underdog Rangers a 4-3 win and fresh life. And then in game five he let loose a 10-footer that—shades of Leo Reise—whistled through Lumley's legs for his second overtime winner in a row. Raleigh, described by one New York paper as "a toothless, frail-looking 150-pounder, who casts no shadow when he stands sideway," became the first man to score overtime goals in back-to-back playoff games. Thanks to Bones, New York's orphans now were just one more victory away from an improbable Stanley Cup championship.

Game six had originally been scheduled for the Rangers' home ice; that is, Toronto. But a league rule prohibited the potentially decisive game of a series to be played at a neutral site, which is what the Maple Leaf Gardens, for all its purported New York partisanship, technically was. Therefore, the league office ruled, the Rangers must stay in Detroit for the duration of play.

The fired-up Rangers barged out to a 3-1 lead, but Abel and Couture countered for Detroit. The Rangers' Tony Leswick scored early in the third period

Gerry "Doc" Couture played center for the Wings from 1945 to 1951, though he also filled in at right wing when Howe was injured in the 1950 playoffs. Couture scored 19 goals in 1948-49 and 24 the following season. Many observers contend that Couture actually scored the goal that won the '50 Stanley Cup, tipping in Pete Babando's shot past Chuck Rayner.

Joe Carveth was not an exceptionally gifted skater or shooter, but he made the most of his opportunities. With many of hockey's stars in the service during World War II, the right wing from Regina, Saskatchewan, emerged as the Wings' top scorer in 1944-45 and 1945-46. He also led all playoff performers with 11 points in the 1945 postseason. He spent the rest of the forties with Boston and Montreal but returned to help Detroit win the Stanley Cup in 1950.

A Rangers attacker is hip-checked off the puck in action from the 1950 Stanley Cup finals between Detroit and New York. "That series gave my kind of player a chance to shine," said Jack Adams. "I mean guys like Abel. Sid had bad legs but lots of heart. He was clearly played out in the last game, but he still managed to score a goal on his knees. That's what kept us alive!" Abel's third-period goal won the sixth game of the finals, 5-4, and set the stage for Pete Babando's Cup-winner in the finale.

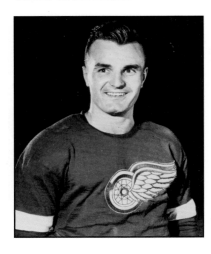

Pete Babando decided the first Stanley Cup seventh game to go into overtime. Not long after his historic goal he was traded to the Chicago Blackhawks.

for a 4-3 lead; however, Lindsay restored the tie at the 4:13 mark. Then, six minutes later, Abel scored what proved to be the game winner on one of the most acrobatic plays ever seen in Stanley Cup competition. He rushed the New York net, tripped over goalie Chuck Rayner's pads, and while in flight still managed to steer the puck around the fallen goalie and into the yawning yarn. Old Bootnose's miraculous maneuver set up the finale on April 23 at Olympia.

The tired, displaced, but still overachieving Rangers, who had now been on the road for three weeks, had enough steam left in them to race out to a 2-0 lead. Power-play goals by Pete Babando and Abel, spaced 21 seconds apart in the second period, wiped out that advantage. Buddy O'Connor restored the Rangers' lead midway through the period, but Jim McFadden responded with a goal of his own. With the scoreboard reading three goals apiece, both teams then fought through 52 minutes of suffocating scoreless hockey until a winner was determined.

The decisive moment was engineered by George Gee, a clever center Adams had acquired from Chicago the previous season. A little over eight minutes into the second overtime session, Gee took a pass from Babando and sailed in on Rayner. The Rangers' goalie moved 15 feet out of his cage to smother the shot. Before taking the ensuing faceoff to the left of the New York net, Gee skated over to Babando. "Move over behind me," he instructed. "You're too far to the left."

Babando did as he was told, moving over about 18 inches to his right. Gee won the draw, whipped the rubber to Babando, who in turn wristed a backhander towards the scramble in front of the net. From 15 feet away the puck hummed through a tangle of arms and legs and past the screened Rayner into the far righthand corner of the net.

Goal! For the first time ever, an overtime goal in the seventh game of the finals had determined the Stanley Cup champion. The draining, dramatic 4-3

## Silver Streak

win ended years of postseason frustration and created pandemonium at the old red barn. Against a backdrop of ear-splitting cheering and chants of "We want Howe!", Detroit players threw their gloves into the air, lifted Tommy Ivan onto their shoulders, and grinned from ear to ear as Sid Abel skated around the far reaches of the Olympia ice pushing a little wooden table holding the Stanley Cup. When Howe made his way from the stands to participate in the celebration, Lindsay deliriously grabbed the fedora off his shaved head and tossed it into the seats. Then he launched a Stanley Cup tradition by hoisting the trophy high over his head and skating around the rink with it. Television cameras caught that moment—one that generations of hockey-mad youngsters have grown up emulating with trash cans and old tires.

"Our team was on top of the hockey world and the sky was the limit for us," said Max McNab, who that evening joined his teammates in a rowdy champagne party at the Book-Cadillac Hotel. "As long as Gordie could return in good shape, the team figured to be a winner for years."

While Detroiters savored their Cup victory during the summer of 1950, Jack Adams went about partially disassembling the team that had won it. In July he swung one of the biggest trades in NHL history, sending Lumley, Stewart, Babando, and two others to Chicago in return for four players. The principals were defenseman Bob Goldham, a shot-blocking specialist who'd been a rookie on the Toronto team that had shocked Detroit in the '42 finals, and center Metro Prystai, whose 29 goals the previous season had been surpassed by only Howe, Lindsay, and Rocket Richard. Forced to labor in the shadow of Detroit's many marquee performers, the relatively unheralded Goldham and Prystai nonetheless would be key contributors to the Wings' dynasty-in-the-making.

Terry Sawchuk's unique "gorilla" style of goaltending is on display here as he prepares to stop Montreal's Tom Johnson. "During the course of a game you probably get 10 great shots where you have to make spectacular saves," recalled teammate Johnny Wilson, "and Sawchuk was always making the spectacular save."

That Adams was able to deal players of the magnitude of Lumley and Stewart and not have the team skip a beat was a testament to the farm system, which, thanks to his efforts and those of chief scout Carson Cooper, remained deeper than a well-digger's shoes. By 1950 checking forwards Marty Pavelich and Glen Skov, defensemen Marcel Pronovost and Benny Woit, left winger Johnny Wilson, center Alex Delvecchio, and goaltender Terry Sawchuk were either already in the big club or just a year away from being promoted.

Sawchuk had the greatest immediate impact. In 1950-51 the twenty-year-old wunderkind from Winnipeg had a league-best 11 shutouts and compiled a 1.98 goals-against average, losing the Vezina by a single goal but winning the Calder Trophy as top rookie. That year the Wings became the first club to crack the century barrier in points, compiling 101 on a record of 44-13-13 to finish on top, six points ahead of Toronto. Howe became the first player in nearly a quarter-century to lead the NHL in goals (43), assists (43), and points (86). The latter broke Herb Cain's record of 82 points, set seven years earlier with Boston. Sid Abel was fourth on the scoring list with 23 goals and 61 points, two more than Lindsay. Red Kelly, who at age twenty-three had already established himself as the best rushing defenseman in the league, set a new record for blueliners with 54 points, which included 17 goals. He also became the second Detroit blueliner in three seasons to receive the Lady Byng Trophy. Kelly would go on to win the award again in 1953 and 1954, the last defenseman to be so honored.

Howe and Lindsay had by now emerged as the greatest one-two force in hockey. On January 25, 1951, the truculent twenty-five-year-old Lindsay got into a fight with Boston's "Wild Bill" Ezinicki that old-timers recall as one of the most vicious battles ever seen at Olympia. It began with some innocent-looking pushing and shoving, then quickly degenerated into a no-holds-barred brawl employing sticks and fists. It ended with Ezinicki falling backwards, knocking himself out, while Lindsay continued to punch away. Ezinicki had his nose broken, lost a tooth, suffered two black eyes, and needed 11 stitches to close a stick cut in his forehead. He required several more to repair his torn mouth and to take care of the hole in the back of his head where he'd hit the ice. Both players were fined $300 and suspended for three games by league president Clarence Campbell, which gave Terrible Ted a chance to mend his badly swollen knuckles.

While Lindsay was increasingly being painted as a thug by the out-of-town press, his twenty-two-year-old buddy was being favorably compared everywhere to Rocket Richard—everywhere but in Montreal, of course. When a leading expert in sports science released a study that showed Howe to be superior to Richard in 16 of 17 different categories, Montreal's bellicose coach vigorously defended his man. "It's obvious," claimed Dick Irvin, "that this is an

attempt to rob Richard of the right he deserves as the greatest right wing in hockey today." The broadcasters and sportswriters who picked the postseason All-Star squads made their feelings known when they selected Howe for the first team in 1951, ending Richard's six-year reign.

Which Number 9 was greater? It was a delicious debate, one that throughout the fifties fueled countless bar-stool arguments, led to numerous schoolyard spats, and inspired endless reams of copy. As was his style, Howe let his playing speak for him. On February 17, 1951, he scored his 100th career goal—a game-winner against the Canadiens. That it happened to be on "Rocket Richard Night" in front of a record crowd at The Forum embarrassed the Rocket's supporters but made the milestone that much sweeter for Gordie's many admirers.

Although he was loath to say it while he was still competing, Richard himself considered Howe the better player. "He was stronger, more fluid, better with the puck," he admitted years after both had retired. There was one significant difference, however, one often commented upon at the time by those who preferred spikes of passion to steady, understated brilliance. Recalled Richard: "I used to say to him, 'Gordie, you're much better than I am, but you don't have the drive to win games like I do.'"

The Rocket's red glare never burned more intensely than in the 1951 semifinals. Montreal, which had won only four of its 14 regular-season meetings with Detroit and finished 36 points behind the defending Stanley Cup champions, stole the first two games at Olympia on overtime goals by Richard, including a 1-0 triple-overtime marathon that didn't end until 1:10 in the morning. The Wings knotted the series with a pair of wins at The Forum, but the Canadiens dethroned the champs with 5-2 and 3-2 victories. Howe and

Defenseman Bob Goldham was one of the hardest working men in snow business during his six seasons with the Wings. An integral member of all four Stanley Cup winners, Goldham had an uncanny ability to block shots, which made him one of the premier penalty killers in the league.

Two-way center Glen Skov was one of many players from the Wings' farm system that helped produce the nucleus of the Stanley Cup champions of the fifties. He later teamed with Marty Pavelich and Tony Leswick to form Detroit's top checking line. Skov spent half of his twelve-year career in Detroit, scoring a high of 17 goals in 1953-54, a figure he later reached playing in Chicago.

Arguably the greatest single-season team of all-time gathers around hockey's ultimate prize at Olympia Stadium on April 15, 1952. That evening the Wings defeated the Canadiens to complete their Stanley Cup quest in the minimum eight games, becoming the first team to sweep their opponents in both rounds of the playoffs.

The postwar version of Jolly Jack Adams was more Stalin than Santa, remembered Alex Delvecchio. "Whenever you'd make a mistake on the ice, you'd sit in front of your locker with your head down. You'd hope he wouldn't show up, but he always did. You'd be looking down at the carpet, and you'd see those pigeon feet in those black shoes, and you'd know it was coming. He'd start giving it to you good. He'd call you every name in the book. You sat there and took it. You didn't dare look up for fear he'd whack you on the head."

Richard each scored four goals in the series, leaving no conclusive evidence as to which player was better.

There was no question, however, that the team that ripped through the NHL the following season was the finest to represent the Detroit franchise since its inception. Far more than that, the '51-52 Red Wings—who finished 44-14-12—were arguably the greatest single-season team of all time. Once again Detroit hit triple digits in points while tying its own record for victories. Second-place Montreal was a distant 22 points behind. Howe won the Hart Trophy and his second straight scoring title with 86 points, including 47 goals, and Lindsay finished runner-up with 30 goals and 69 points. For the second straight year the linemates joined Kelly and Sawchuk on the First All-Star Team.

There were no statistics or hardware to measure the most important intangible: harmony. "We had great unity," recalled Glen Skov, the pivot on a checking line that included Marty Pavelich and newcomer Tony Leswick. "We did a lot of things together off the ice. On the ice, we defied anybody to beat us."

The Red Wings of the late forties and early fifties were like an extended family. As tired as that phrase has become, in this particular case there is no other way to describe their storied togetherness. To a degree, it was less a matter of choice than a reaction to the environment they suddenly found themselves in. Most of the players were single, pink-cheeked lads from small towns in Canada, suddenly plunked down in a noisy, crowded, confusing metropolis that, thanks to the booming auto industry, had grown into the fourth-largest city in the country. A church-going teetotalist, Jack Adams, was their surrogate father, while the prim, gray-haired matrons of the neighborhood boarding houses they stayed at during the season—Ma Shaw, Ma Tannahill—served as surrogate mothers. The wives of married players, most notably Gloria Abel, also fulfilled the role, hosting dinners and barbecues for team members.

Like any band of soldiers, students, or athletes pressed into a circumscribed universe, these Wings found an easy and practical comfort in doing things together and, along the way, discovered that they genuinely liked each other. They sneaked beer onto trains and whiled away hours playing pinochle or hearts for a penny a point. They reserved Monday nights for get-togethers at a local Italian restaurant, took in movies at the Fox Theatre, and bowled in leagues at the Lucky Strike, three blocks from Olympia. Many attended mass or started offseason businesses together. They double- and triple-dated, served as best man for each other's weddings, and buried their smiles when Adams—wholly convinced that sexual relations, even with a wife, robbed a player of his game legs—screamed at newlywed Glen Skov during one of his locker-room tirades that he was "spending too much time in the crease!"

It wasn't a perfect world, of course. There was always the fear that, in an era of stiff competition, capricious management, and 17-man rosters, one might suddenly find himself without an NHL job. And salaries were so low that even stars had to find summer employment. But all in all, Wings from that period reflect today, it was a wonderful life, getting paid to play a game one loved with a bunch of swell teammates. For all the uncertainty of employment and risk of injury, even those pseudo production workers—Howe, Lindsay, and Abel—knew that toiling for Jack Adams sure beat sweating on any of the city's real assembly lines.

The Wings' juggernaut made quick work of the 1952 postseason, sweeping the Maple Leafs and the Canadiens behind a bulletproof blueline and Sawchuk's sensational goaltending. Sawchuk, who had won his first of three consecutive Vezinas with a 1.94 goals-against average and a league-best 12 shutouts, surrendered but five goals in eight games. He racked up four shutouts—two each against Toronto and Montreal and all on home ice—as Detroit became the first team to skate through the playoffs undefeated. "He is their club," said Rocket Richard. "Another guy in the nets and we'd beat them."

At least Richard gave the victors *some* credit. Dick Irvin refused to acknowledge the Wings' superiority, despite having been beaten decisively in the title round by scores of 3-1, 2-1, 3-0, and 3-0. "Why should I pretend something I do not feel?" he said bitterly. "Let them celebrate their victory if they wish. I don't lose easily."

Today, members of that squad all use the same expression when describing their sense of invincibility. *We could have played all summer*, they say, *and kept on winning.*

"Those eight games, that was the ultimate," said Leo Reise Jr. "The team we had was great. The Canadiens were great. Toronto was great." The public reaction to a championship was nothing like it was to become, however. "Now they have a street parade, they meet the president. It's a show," said Reise. "We just got a pat on the back. The city of Detroit didn't give us recognition. It was a ho-hum deal."

The new Mrs. Howe gets a peck on the cheek from Red Kelly as her husband, Ted Lindsay, and Marty Pavelich look on (top). Howe's 1953 wedding was one of many involving team members during their Stanley Cup years, including Glen Skov's the following spring (bottom). Jack Adams frowned on his young players' nuptials, accusing Skov, for one, of "spending too much time in the crease." Recalled Alex Delvecchio: "Every time I had a bad game, he'd scream at me that my marriage was ruining my career. He'd say, 'Delvecchio, why don't you leave your wife alone? You're ruining your career.'"

**A**lex Delvecchio, while not the box-office draw that his linemates on the retooled Production Line were, was a graceful skater with deceptive speed and amazing endurance. In 24 seasons he missed just 43 games, in the process setting a team iron-man record of 548 consecutive games played. He also was a choirboy compared to his more fiery wingers, winning three Lady Byng trophies while averaging just 16 penalty minutes a season. "I don't think I had five fights in my life, and most of them were just grappling with the other guy," he recalled.

## THE DETROIT RED WINGS

In part that was because winning had become almost monotonous. The following season the original Production Line was broken up when Abel asked to be traded to Chicago. The woeful Blackhawks had been purchased by James Norris Jr. and Art Wirtz, who wanted him as coach. Second-year center Alex Delvecchio took Abel's place at center, Lindsay inherited Bootnose's captaincy, and the Wings didn't break stride. They received the Prince of Wales Trophy, given annually to the regular-season champion, for the fifth consecutive season. This broke the mark of four straight titles previously held by Boston and Montreal. And for the fifth straight year they led the NHL in scoring, on three different occasions scoring 10 goals or more goals against an opponent. It would be another dozen years before a Detroit team again reached double-digits in a game.

The only real excitement that winter was Howe's bid to break Rocket Richard's single-season mark of 50 goals. He officially wound up with 49, the result of a bad scoring decision during a late-season game with Boston. He deflected a shot from Red Kelly that bounced off a Bruin's skate and into the net. "Red knew that I was the last player to touch the puck," said Howe. Adams's argument for a scoring change fell on deaf ears. Howe, a notoriously unselfish player, shrugged his sloped shoulders. He knew that Kelly was chasing Flash Hollet's record of 20 goals by a defenseman; besides, he figured that he still had plenty of chances left. As fate would have it, his last chance at the record was in the season finale against Montreal. Tommy Ivan double- and triple-shifted him, but Dick Irvin had Bert Olmstead play practically inside Howe's sweater all evening. The big guy was blanked as the teams battled to a 1-1 draw. Afterwards Irvin taunted the disappointed Detroit crowd by grabbing Richard's arm and raising it into the air. "The winner and still champion," Irvin gloated to the press.

Despite missing out on the magical 50-goal mark, Howe's 95 points raised the bar on his own record and gave him an unprecedented third straight scoring title and his second Hart Trophy. Once again Lindsay finished runnerup, popping in 32 goals while piling up 71 points. Howe, Lindsay, Sawchuk, and Kelly (who wound up with 19 goals) were selected first-team All-Stars for the third year in a row. Delvecchio, a superb puck handler and playmaker, placed fifth in scoring with 59 points and was named center of the second team.

With all this firepower the Red Wings seemed a lock to successfully defend the Cup. They bombed Boston, 7-0, in the opener of the semifinals, but then the third-place Bruins bit Detroit in the pants. "Sugar Jim" Henry, a part of Adams's big nine-man trade with Chicago three years earlier, had been unable to find a spot in the Detroit system and wound up in Beantown. Henry was outstanding in the nets and Ed Sandford provided some clutch scoring as the surprising Bruins—who had won only two of fourteen regular-season meetings against Detroit, getting outscored 62-19—upset the Wings in six games. Howe, held to two goals, was despondent afterwards, claiming that his poor play had cost Detroit the series.

"What are you talking about?" argued Bob Goldham. "You're the guy who got us here."

## Silver Streak

Howe continued to take the defeat hard. Joining the rest of the team for a postgame drink, he shocked everybody by impulsively ordering a double bourbon. He was normally a beer drinker, but on this occasion he downed the bourbon. Then he ordered another one. He concluded the season by throwing up and swearing off the hard stuff.

The Red Wings grabbed a sixth consecutive league title in 1953-54, though the gap between them and perennial runner-up Montreal continued to grow more narrow. Detroit won 37, lost 19, and tied 14 for 88 points, seven ahead of the Canadiens. Red Kelly won his third Lady Byng trophy in four years and captured a new prize, the inaugural James Norris Trophy as the league's top blueliner. The award was created to honor the late owner of the Wings, who had died of a heart attack on December 4, 1952, while working at his desk. Kelly also joined Howe (who captured a fourth straight scoring title with 81 points) and Lindsay as first-team All-Stars.

Although they received scant recognition, except from their own teammates, the checking line of Skov, Pavelich, and Leswick played a huge role in the Wings' success. "Pavelich was one of the most underrated players that ever played," said Lindsay. "He and Skov and Leswick were always matched against the best lines in the league. They never scored that many goals, but by always playing against the best lines I always figured we were a half-goal ahead when the game started. They did such a great job defensively and never got the credit they should have."

One member of that unheralded trio, Leswick, was destined for glory that season. The sawed-off thirty-one-year-old left wing was a native of Humboldt,

The mouse that roared. Tony "Mighty Mouse" Leswick, once a 27-goal scorer for the Rangers, changed his game when he left Broadway for Detroit in 1951. But in the seventh game of the '54 finals, it was his scoring touch, not his zealous checking ability, that gave the Wings the Stanley Cup.

A 1953 trading card of Leonard "Red" Kelly, the legendary blueliner who could handle a puck as well with his feet as some could with their stick. Kelly broke into the NHL in 1947 and played 20 seasons, splitting his eight Stanley Cups evenly between Detroit and Toronto. He won the Lady Byng Trophy four times and in 1954 was the first recipient of the Norris Trophy, donated by the children of the late Detroit owner, James "Pops" Norris, to honor the league's top defenseman.

Hockey in your face. Bob Goldham and Toronto's Jim Morrison send the customers ducking for cover as they bang along the boards in 1953.

According to Jack Adams, Marty Pavelich "was one of the four key men around whom we built our hockey club." The defensive forward, a Detroit regular from 1947 to 1957, was at his best when matched against the league's top wingers, notably Montreal's Rocket Richard. An added benefit were the spaghetti dinners his mother cooked for team members when the Red Wings held training camp at The Soo.

Saskatchewan. He had learned the game from his older brother Jack, a forward on the Chicago team that beat the Wings in the 1934 finals. Jack drowned that summer, but another brother, Pete, later a member of the New York Americans, picked up the instruction. Tough Tony broke into the professional ranks with the Cleveland Barons in 1942, spent three years in the Canadian navy during the war, then was signed by the Rangers after his discharge. Although Detroit fans remember him as a spotty scorer, he was quite a marksman with New York. He was named a second-team All-Star behind Lindsay in 1950 and had a fine series against the Wings in that year's Cup finals.

Leswick stood five and a half feet tall and weighed 160 pounds, earning him the nickname "Mighty Mouse," after the popular cartoon character of the time. When he was picked up by Jack Adams in 1951, it was made clear that his future with the club rested primarily on his defensive abilities. The former 27-goal scorer for the Rangers concentrated on being a pest to the league's top forwards. He especially enraged Dick Irvin by hooking, grabbing, and harassing Rocket Richard whenever the Wings and Canadiens engaged in one of their grudge matches. If Leswick was a mugger and a hoodlum, as Irvin maintained, he also was one of the top money players in the league, as the Montreal coach would soon learn.

In the semifinals the Wings breezed past the Maple Leafs in five games. In the finals Montreal seemed ready to fall just as easily, dropping three of the first four games. Then Irvin, looking to shake up his team, benched Jacques Plante and installed Gerry McNeil between the pipes. The Canadiens stormed back to take game five, 1-0, on an overtime goal by Ken Mosdell, and then easily captured the sixth game, 4-1.

## Silver Streak

The seventh and decisive game was played April 16, 1954, in front of the usual packed house at Olympia. It turned out to be a classic. Kelly's second-period power-play goal tied the contest at 1-1, which remained the score after regulation time expired. The climactic rush to the championship began a little more than four minutes into overtime. Prystai passed deep out of his own zone to Skov, who sailed down the left side, across the Montreal blueline. He banged the puck off the boards behind the net and it bounced out to Leswick, who lifted a lazy shot towards the Montreal goal. Doug Harvey, one of the game's premier defenders and an accomplished semipro baseball player to boot, planned to knock the puck to the ice so that he could play it. Instead, to his horror and the crowd's delight, it unaccountably deflected off his glove and shot over the shoulder of McNeil.

Montreal was stunned. Ted Lindsay was ecstatic. "You little toad!" he said to Leswick moments after his Cup-winning goal. Irvin and his team, sore losers, stormed off the ice instead of congratulating the winners, as was customary. "If I had shaken hands," said Irvin, "I wouldn't have meant it. I refuse to be a hypocrite."

Before the puck was dropped on the next season, which would go down as one of the most tumultuous in history, Jimmy Skinner replaced Tommy Ivan behind the Detroit bench. Publicly, Ivan spoke of the opportunity to join the rebuilding Blackhawks as general manager. Privately, he was fed up with Adams's meddling and backseat coaching. Accompanying him in the move to Chicago was Metro Prystai, who later spoke glowingly of his contributions to author Roy MacSkimming. "Tommy was a terrific little coach—softspoken, just an ordinary guy. We'd have a bad period, and Adams'd come into the

April 16, 1954: In a scene that was becoming wonderfully familiar to Detroit fans, jubilant Red Wings took turns planting their lips on the Stanley Cup as it sat on a small wooden table on the Olympia ice. The lone female in the picture is Margerite Norris Riker, the twenty-seven-year-old daughter of the late owner. As president of the team in the three years following her father's death, she became the first woman to have her name inscribed on the Cup, as well as the youngest executive.

Howe shakes hands with an old friend, Harry Lumley, at the conclusion of the Detroit-Toronto semifinals in 1954. The Wings eliminated the Maple Leafs in five games.

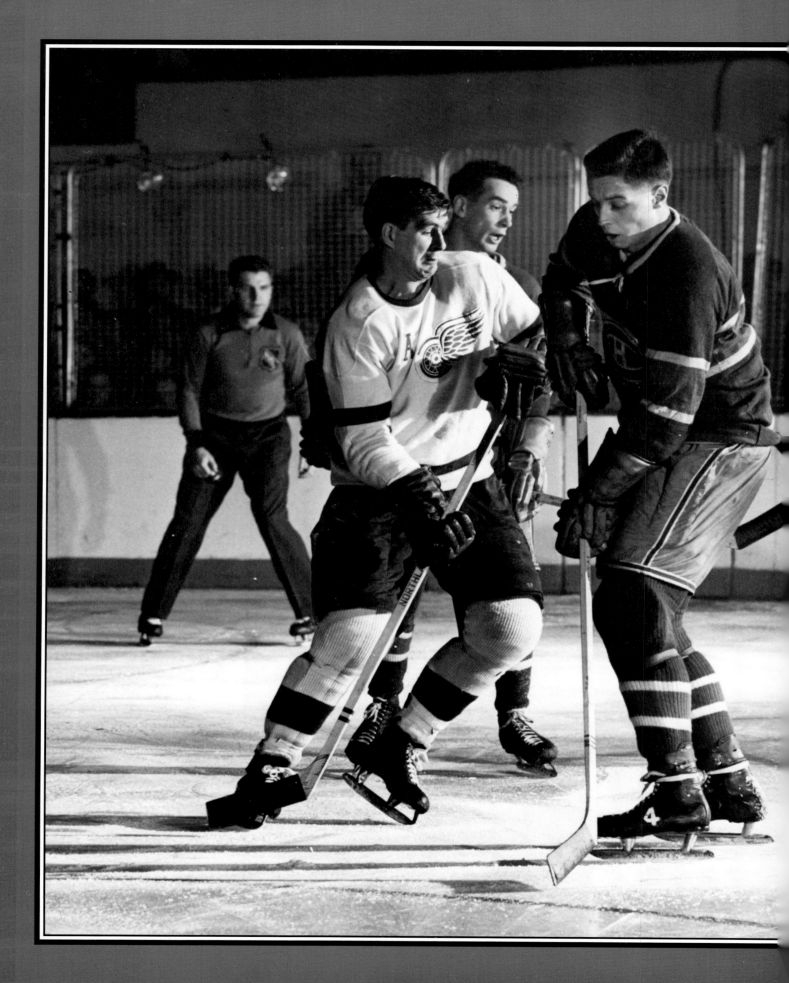

In 1953-54, Terry Sawchuk recorded his fourth of five straight seasons of allowing less than two goals per game. He was as steady as ever in the finals against Montreal, allowing just a dozen goals in seven games.

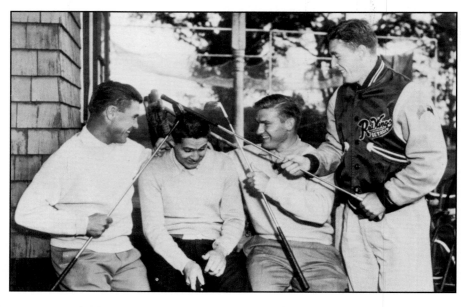

Earl "Dutch" Reibel gets his crewcut flattened by a trio of teammates during a golf outing. Reibel was voted the American Hockey League's top rookie in 1952 and the following season led the Western League in scoring. In his first NHL game, October 8, 1953, he set a record with four assists against the Blackhawks. The center's best seasons were 1954-55, when he scored 25 goals, and 1955-56, when he scored 17 goals and won the Lady Byng Trophy. Reibel ended his six-year NHL career with Chicago in 1959.

Never mind what cartoonists thought. The true artists of Jack Adams's dynasty were his players, as shown by this banged-up but happy band of warriors in 1954-55. From left: Howe, Marcel Bonin, Glen Skov, Johnny Wilson, Marty Pavelich. "We seemed to have such unity, probably because we all got along so well," said Skov. "We harmonized. There was so much confidence in one another that we felt we could beat any team."

dressing room and raise hell with us. Then after he'd left, Ivan'd say, 'Don't listen to that fat bugger, he doesn't know what he's talking about.' I don't know if they planned it that way, but he'd calm us down, and holy mackerel, we'd go out there and do anything for Tommy. He was that kind of guy."

Skinner, captain of the '45 Omaha team with which Howe had turned pro and later a coach of junior teams in Windsor Hamilton, was a NHL rookie in awe of his boss. He confessed that all he did was "open the door to let the players out onto the ice." Lindsay was more blunt: He was no more than "a yes-man for Adams," someone unable to give direction or make line changes. The concensus of the players today is that they won that year despite Skinner, not because of him.

Howe missed six games because of a shoulder injury, snapping his playing streak at 382 games and causing him to relinquish his traditional spot at the top of the league's scoring list. His 62 points didn't even lead the team. Earl

# Silver Streak

Jack Adams acted as the haberdasher after his number-one star collected three goals against Montreal in the fifth game of the 1955 finals. Detroit won, 5-1.

Howe established a new post-season mark with 20 points in the 1955 playoffs, including nine goals.

Dutch Reibel goes over the boards. Due to an injury that cost Howe six games during the 1954-55 campaign, Reibel squeaked by the perennial scoring leader with 66 points, good enough for fourth place in the scoring race.

"Dutch" Reibel, a shifty, crew-cutted center then in his second year with Detroit, had 25 goals and 66 points, good for fourth in the league behind a trio of Montreal snipers: Bernie "Boom Boom" Geoffrion, Rocket Richard, and Jean Beliveau. Despite Howe's off season, Skinner's inexperience, and Lindsay's suspension for punching a fan in Toronto, the Wings managed to stay close to the Canadiens in the standings. Home cooking helped. From the day after Christmas until the end of the regular season, the Wings did not lose a single game at Olympia, winning 13 and tying another five.

The Detroit-Montreal rivalry came down to a riotous home-and-home series. The Canadiens, two points ahead of Detroit at the time, went into the showdown without their top gun and inspirational leader. On March 13, Richard had attacked linesman Cliff Thompson in a game at Boston. The viciousness of his assault caused league president Clarence Campbell to suspend the fiery Frenchman for the remainder of the regular season and the

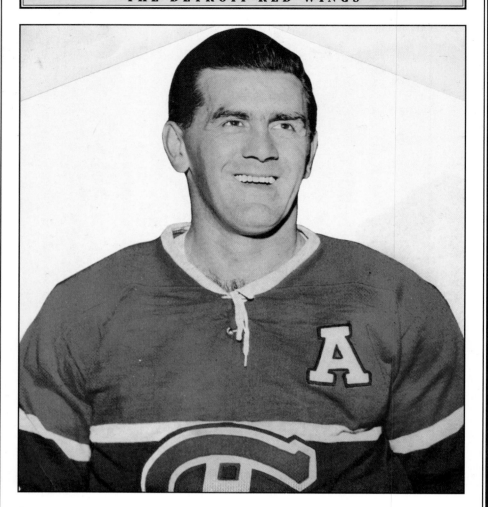

## THE DETROIT RED WINGS

**M**ontreal's Maurice "Rocket" Richard (right) was suspended for the last games of the 1955 season, including the playoffs. Angry Canadiens fans erupted on March 17, 1955, during a crucial late-season showdown against the Wings in the Montreal Forum.

In what became known as the "Richard Riot," a fan (above), choking from tear gas, is escorted out of the Forum by police.

forthcoming playoffs. Montreal fans were incensed. The suspension ended up costing Richard the scoring title, an honor that had always eluded him. More important, it put a serious crimp in Montreal's chances for regaining the Cup from the hated Wings.

On March 17, 1955, the Wings were enjoying a 4-1 lead during the first intermission when all hell broke loose at Montreal's Forum. A tear gas bomb exploded, causing a mass panic towards the exits that could have turned deadly. Campbell, who had stoically endured a torrent of garbage and slurs while watching the game and had been sucker-punched in the face by a fan, huddled with Montreal management.

Meanwhile, as the "Richard Riot" swirled around them, Detroit players hunkered down in the visitors' locker room. "We watered down some towels and pressed them into the crack of the door so none of the gas would come in," said Ross "Lefty" Wilson, the Wings' trainer and practice goalie. "Then we got a note came saying the game was forfeited. Now we had to get out of there."

**Gordie Howe in 1954**

**WINGS WIN ALL, 6-0**

*It's 7th Title in Row; Lindsay Gets 3*

**T**ed Lindsay, who always played well against Montreal, helped spark the Wings' drive to an unprecedented seventh straight title in 1954-55, notching a hat trick against his old enemies in the decisive final game of the regular season, then adding a four-goal game two weeks later in the Stanley Cup finals. He tied a record with 12 assists in the 1955 playoffs.

Outside, a mob roamed Ste. Catherine Street, looting stores, overturning cars, and battling police. Several bullets blew out an exterior window of the arena. The Wings took a roundabout way to the station, where they boarded a Detroit-bound train filled with several hooligans. They warned the Wings of further violence at Olympia Stadium.

With 70 Detroit policemen guarding the gates and patrol cars cruising Grand River, the only violence in the season finale was visited upon the Canadiens. A five-minute ovation greeted the Detroit players as they moved out onto the gleaming white surface of Olympia. With the title on the line, the Wings rolled to a 6-0 victory behind Lindsay's three scores. The Wings' ninth straight win to close out the season produced a final record of 42-17-11. The 95 points put them two ahead of the Canadiens.

In the semifinals, Detroit buried Toronto in four straight while Montreal eliminated Boston in five games. This set up the third Detroit-Montreal finals in four Aprils.

The opener, played at Olympia, saw Montreal hold a 2-1 lead midway through the third period, thanks to a pair of goals by Floyd Curry. But a short-handed tally by Pavelich put the Wings up, 3-2, and Lindsay added another with 18 seconds remaining to account for the final 4-2 score.

Two days later the Wings swamped the Canadiens, 7-1, behind Lindsay's four goals. Howe, Delvecchio, and Pronovost also scored. Some observers were foolishly predicting a sweep, but two straight victories by Montreal on its home ice quickly quieted them. In game three, Geoffrion scored twice to pace a 4-2 win. Following the fourth game, a 5-3 Montreal verdict, both teams boarded the train for a rematch the following day in Detroit. Behind Howe's hat trick, part of an eventual record postseason output of 20 points, the Wings pounded out a 5-1 victory. But the Richard-less Canadiens stayed alive with a 6-3, sixth-game verdict at the Forum. Once again, the Stanley Cup would be determined in a seventh game at Olympia.

On April 14, 1955, the Wings took the ice in front of a packed house of Detroit partisans. They were supremely confident, having not lost a home game in nearly four months. They certainly weren't going to fall down on the job in the seventh game of the finals.

And they didn't. Delvecchio scored twice, Howe once, and the Wings polished off Montreal, 3-1.

Afterward the players gathered at center ice for the presentation of the Stanley Cup—a ceremony that had become all-too-familiar to spoiled Detroit fans. After all, this was the fourth time in the last six years that the Wings had won the trophy in front of their fans.

There was a slight glitch. The microphone being lowered from the rafters got tangled several feet above Clarence Campbell's head. A couple of Wings hoisted Glen Skov onto their shoulders, the tall center untangled the cord, and then the president of the National Hockey League commenced to telling the crowd what it already knew—that, on this April evening, the Detroit Red Wings were the best hockey team in the world.

The planet continued to spin in 1955. The U.S. sent its first military advisors to Vietnam, while Congress appropriated $30 million for Dr. Jonas Salk's miracle polio vaccine. In Birmingham, Alabama, bone-tired Rosa Parks refused to give up her bus seat to a white man, launching the civil rights movement.

Locally, the Tigers' twenty-year-old right fielder, Al Kaline, became the youngest player to win a batting title, while Soupy Sales hosted the first Detroit-based television show to air nationally. Chevrolet introduced its legendary small-block V-8 engine. And the Red Wings' dynasty was broken up by an inexplicable series of trades with Boston and Chicago.

"I suppose I could understand some of us being sent to Chicago," said Skov, who after the season was shipped to the Windy City along with Tony Leswick, Johnny Wilson, and Benny Woit. "Tommy Ivan was the coach and the Norris family wanted to shore up the Blackhawks. But why four guys [Sawchuk, Marcel Bonin, Lorne Davis, and Vic Stasiuk] went to Boston, I just don't know. It was a total shock. Gordie was only twenty-seven and the rest of the team was younger than he was. There was no rhyme or reason to it."

Jack Adams's moves would help Montreal finally surpass Detroit as the NHL's dominant team. The following season the Canadiens snapped the Red Wings' string of seven straight regular-season crowns, then whipped them in five games in the finals to win the first of five consecutive Stanley Cups. Meanwhile, Detroit began a Cup-less drought that continues to this day.

"Montreal had great teams," admitted Skov. "But we had great teams, too. We weren't afraid of Montreal or Richard or anybody. If we had stayed together, we would've won a lot more Stanley Cups, I can tell you that."

**M**arguerite Norris Riker, Clarence Campbell, Bill Dineen, Ben Woit, and Gordie Howe watch rookie NHL coach Jimmy Skinner kiss the Stanley Cup, which the Wings have just captured with a 3-1 victory at Olympia on April 14, 1955. Later, captain Ted Lindsay spoke into the public address and radio microphones, telling the partisan crowd what it already knew: that Detroit remained the center of the hockey world.

On a typically bleak winter day in 1956, inmates work on the ice rink at Marquette Prison.

It was, insists Leonard "Oakie" Brumm, the damndest hockey game ever played. Here it was, the dead of winter and the middle of the NHL season, and the best hockey team in the world had chartered a plane to fly hundreds of miles to the rugged northern reaches of Michigan in order to slap rubber with a group of spaghetti-legged, middle-aged kidnappers, murderers, arsonists and thieves.

Howe. Lindsay. Kelly. Sawchuk. What were these future Hall of Famers doing squaring off on an outdoor pond against the likes of Bugsy Wisocki and an assortment of other four- and five-time losers?

According to Brumm, it was the result of a promise Wings general manager Jack Adams had made to the officials of Marquette Prison. "Build it," Jolly Jack

# Pen Pals

had said in a mood of off-handed largesse, or words to that effect, "and we will come."

"It" was a regulation-sized, walled hockey rink, something no prison in the country had ever had. But thanks to the efforts of Brumm, the prison's first athletic director and a top-drawer contractor to boot, the rink was built. And, miraculously, the Wings did come. To a tough, dreary, maximum-security prison justifiably known as the Alcatraz of the North.

The game was played on the afternoon of February 2, 1954. But the story really began many years earlier, back in 1927, when Adams arrived in the Motor City as the new coach of the Detroit Cougars. Prohibition made the twenties an uproarious decade, and nowhere was the noise louder than in Detroit, whose proximity to Canada made it the perfect conduit for illegal booze.

The city's most notorious bootleggers were a loosely organized band of young punks who grew up together on the near east side. Dubbed the Purple Gang by the press, they were known as flashy dressers, big spenders, and avid sportsmen. Nothing short of a swig of good hooch beat rubbing shoulders with the city's sporting elite. The Purples could be seen taking in baseball games at Navin Field, boxing matches at neighborhood gyms, and hockey games at the brand-new Olympia Stadium on Grand River. Somewhere along the line the ringleaders—Ray Bernstein, Irving Milberg and Harry Keywell—made the acquaintance of Adams, who had enough sense to just smile, shake hands, and politely turn down all invitations to join the boys for a night out on the town.

That, of course, was a wise decision. In 1931, several Purples were sent to Jackson State Prison for their part in the Collingwood Massacre, a bloody triple homicide inside a downtown apartment building. The gangsters' influence extended beyond prison walls, however, as witnessed by the baseball-loving Bernstein's ability to coax Tiger star Hank Greenberg to play an exhibition game at Jackson. The imprisoned Purples also continued their murderous ways, arranging (and, some say, participating in) the infamous slaying of state Senator Warren G. Hooper in 1945. For their suspected roles in the Hooper murder the Purples were shipped to Marquette Prison.

E mery's Boys, named after the warden, pose with their coach, Oakie Brumm, who stands at far right.

"You don't get into Marquette," said Brumm, "unless you've screwed up several times."

This was where inmates did the hardest time imaginable: sequestered in cramped cells with no toilets, and forced to endure the interminable, bone-numbing winters without long johns because the warden was afraid they'd give escapees an edge in the wilderness. And this was where Adams, touring the grounds as a guest of warden Emery Jacques one day in 1953, unexpectedly ran into a pair of old acquaintances: Bernstein and Keywell.

"Say Jack," the old Purples said, "how about bringing the Red Wings up for a scrimmage someday?"

"Sure, no problem," replied Jack, realizing the prison had no facility or team.

Not to be outdone, the warden piped in: "Anytime at all, Jack. Just let us know and we'll be ready."

Adams returned to Detroit and quickly forgot the matter. He didn't realize what his casual conversation had set in motion. Jacques firmly believed that organized recreation helped inmates blow off steam that might otherwise be channeled into riots like the one that had ripped apart Jackson Prison a year earlier. Unbeknownst to Adams, the warden was in the process of hiring Oakie Brumm as the prison's first athletic director. Brumm, a member of the University of Michigan's NCAA championship hockey team in 1948, had just come home to his native Marquette from the University of Alaska, where he had directed the hockey program and built the school's rink.

## Silver Streak

"Practically all I heard from inmates from the time I got hired by Jacques was, 'The Red Wings are coming! The Red Wings are coming!'" said Brumm. "And all I could think was, 'How am I supposed to get together some kind of team to play them?'"

Brumm, who today continues to move around the world as a construction project manager, can spend hours spinning tales of his four-year stint as the prison's athletic director, during which time he developed football, baseball, hockey, golf, and other recreational programs. He remembers how prison athletes, huffing and puffing their way through football and hockey practices, would nonetheless constantly smoke throughout the sessions. One goalie even installed an ashtray on top of his net. Inmates were known to throw a game for three cartons of cigarettes, conceal homemade weapons inside their uniforms (one convict was stabbed during a pileup), and honor the criminal's code to never snitch—even when opponents blithely robbed them of their equipment.

Since Marquette was designed for older prisoners (a convict had to be at least 28 to be assigned there), most of the inmates who tried out for Brumm's hockey team in late 1953 were in their thirties and forties. Few could skate very well. Those without barking ankles exhibited minimum hockey ability. And Brumm had to fight to get hockey sticks for the players. For years, the prison had disallowed sticks, fearing that inmates would use them to attack the guards or each other. Instead of ice hockey, inmates had played kick hockey, a kind of soccer on ice.

Brumm used his construction know-how and material donated by his father, a building contractor, to erect a walled rink in the corner of the prison yard. Jacques kept Adams appraised of Brumm's progress. When informed that the inmates had no pads, skates or goaltending equipment, Adams donated all of the equipment of the Omaha Knights, which had just recently ceased being a Wings farm club. As a joke, he had "Emery's Boys," in honor of the warden, sewn on the front of each jersey.

Brumm relentlessly drilled his squad of inmates over the winter of 1953-54. They scheduled games against teams from the free world and did surprisingly well against them. With a few such games under their belt, Emery's Boys finally felt confident enough to challenge the Wings.

At this point, Adams may very well have regretted ever having met the Purple Gang, or making such an off-the-cuff remark in front of a courtyard of prisoners. But true to his word, on the morning of February 2, 1954, the entire Wings squad arrived at Marquette County Airport (the future site of K.I. Sawyer Air Force Base) via a twin-prop DC-3 that cost the semipro Marquette Sentinels (the sponsor of the trip) $1,800 to charter. After checking into the Northland Hotel and enjoying a light lunch, the Red Wings were taken to the old brownstone prison. Some of the Detroit players, tough guys on the ice, were understandably apprehensive.

"The prison game generated all kinds of interest," Brumm said. "No one knew the caliber of the players or how the Wings and inmates would react to each other. Jack Adams got some criticism at the time. It was one thing to fight at Olympia against other real hockey players. But what would they do in a fight on the ice at

This was where inmates did the hardest time imaginable: sequestered in cramped cells with no toilets, and forced to endure the interminable, bone-numbing winters without long johns because the warden was afraid they'd give escapees an edge in the wilderness.

**T**he entire prison population of 600 convicts (minus those in solitary confinement) stood around the boards. The weather was perfect for hockey: about 21 degrees, overcast, and no wind. Not that Adams's troops needed any meteorological advantage.

Marquette Prison with someone who had already probably killed a couple of people? Not to mention being surrounded by hundreds of the toughest, most volatile 'fans' in the country."

The rousing reception the visitors got quickly put their fears to rest. After dressing in the carpenter's shack (the only building with a shower large enough to enable it to serve as a locker room) and getting patted down by guards, the Wings trooped onto the immaculately manicured ice, accompanied by shouts of encouragement and recognition from the assembled cons.

"Most of them were great hockey fans," recalled left winger Johnny Wilson. "They listened to all the games on the radio. They knew all the boys and were cheering us on, which was kind of nice."

Dutch Reibel, centering a line that included Lindsay and Howe, took the opening faceoff at 1:30 that afternoon. The entire prison population of 600 convicts (minus those in solitary confinement) stood around the boards. The weather was perfect for hockey: about 21 degrees, overcast, and no wind. Not that Adams's troops needed any meteorological advantage.

For the first several minutes, nary an inmate touched the puck. The Wings freely passed it back and forth several times on each rush, skating around the cons as if they were pylons. After about a minute of this dazzling stickwork, someone would finally pop the puck past the prisoners' goalie, Bugsy Wisocki, a habitual thief who had been released from solitary especially for this game.

"Howe would get the puck and circle the net three times before putting it in," said Wilson. "It was funny to watch."

After ten minutes, the Wings had a 10-0 lead. By the fifteen-minute mark it had grown to 15-0. It could easy have been 50-0. "The only time I touched the puck," lamented Brumm, who installed himself on defense, "was when I pulled it out of the back of the net."

Terry Sawchuk, bored by the inactivity at his end of the ice, sat atop his lonesome net. When he spied the puck finally coming his way, he raced up to it and took it halfway down the ice himself. After enduring several more minutes of idleness, he deliberately tripped one of Emery's Boys so he could be sent to the penalty box to sign a few autographs. Meanwhile, the inmates and guards were hooting and hollering and imploring the Wings to pour it on the overmatched cons. At one point Ted Lindsay handed the puck to the cons' best player, Ed Rilley. "Go, man, go," the Wings' captain told him.

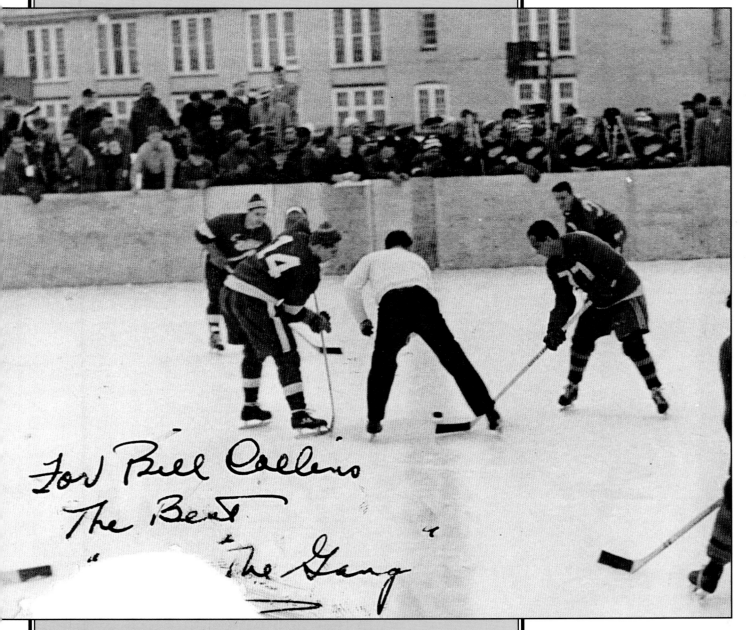

For Bill Collins
The Best
"The Gang"

Rilley, who had been embarrassed enough, thank you, looked Terrible Ted square in the face.

"Fuck you, Ted," responded Rilley. "I ain't going." Everyone within earshot of this exchange roared with laughter. Later, when some of the Wings donned the prisoners' green jerseys to even up the sides, Lindsay skated up to prison officials seated in the primitive press box and fired off the best line of the afternoon.

"We'll win this one, see," he said in his best James Cagney impersonation, "and be outta here in two years."

For Emery's Boys, it only seemed like two years. The first period ended with an 18-0 Wings lead, after which no one bothered to keep score. Everyone was too

**P**ros and cons. The opening faceoff between the Red Wings and inmates.

> "This is a great day," proclaimed Adams, hoisting the bucket high for all to see. "I'm proud to have such a fine 'farm' team up here in the north. The only trouble is, you guys sure have made it tough for me to recruit any of you."

engrossed watching the Wings' pinpoint passing, crisp shots, and graceful skating. It was a skills exhibition that had the inmates on the ice standing in their tracks, leaning on their sticks and whistling in admiration. Defensman Bob Goldham earned the cons' respect as perhaps the bravest man on the ice, as he repeatedly dropped in front of shots and blocked them with his special belly pad.

"They've won the Stanley Cup and a lot of other big prizes," Brumm said at the end of the exhibition, "but now the Red Wings will receive an award no other hockey team can ever claim." With that he handed Adams and coach Tommy Ivan a "honey bucket," a refuse pail prisoners used in their cells in lieu of toilets.

"This is a great day," proclaimed Adams, hoisting the bucket high for all to see. "I'm proud to have such a fine 'farm' team up here in the north. The only trouble is, you guys sure have made it tough for me to recruit any of you."

After showering, the Wings enjoyed dinner with the convict team and several guests from both sides of the prison walls. Each Wing was given a hand-tooled wallet with his name and winged-wheel logo on it. Gordie Howe, who earlier had magnanimously pronounced the ice surface the best he had ever skated on, gave a talk, as did the warden and Adams. Then at six o'clock it was off to the hotel, where the Wings rested an hour before playing another exhibition game at the indoor Marquette Palestra against the Sentinels.

The Wings toyed with the Sentinels, beating them soundly in front of a full house of 3,000 fans. Brumm, who had played earlier with Emery's Boys, took a regular shift with the Sentinels. This confused the Wings' Jim "Red Eye" Hays, who skated up to Brumm shortly after the puck was dropped at 8:30.

"He said, 'How in the hell did you get out to play down here tonight?'" laughed Brumm. "I guess throughout the entire afternoon he never realized I was working at the prison instead of doing time!"

The next morning, when it came time to board the plane for home, it was so cold the engines wouldn't start. Said Johnny Wilson: "We sat on the runway and froze. Meanwhile Jack was afraid half of his boys would get sick." The props finally turned and the first—and so far, the only—NHL team to play inside a maximum security prison headed back to Detroit, leaving a considerable share of equipment and goodwill behind. Ten weeks later, the Wings defeated Montreal to win their third Stanley Cup of the decade. The following year they won a fourth, cheered on by the residents of the largest penalty box any of the Wings would ever see.

The prison game's success made many wonder why more weren't scheduled. "We tried," Brumm admitted, "but not very hard. Somebody should've gone to Detroit, sat down with Jack Adams, and ironed out a plan. But he got busy, we got busy, and for some reason it never happened." Adams continued to donate equipment for the prison's hockey program, however, even after Brumm left the prison for his family's construction business in 1957.

Four decades later, the one-of-a-kind game remains fresh in the memories of all who participated or watched. Brumm, for one, recounts it with gusto in a book he has been working on for the last several years. He wryly calls it *We Only Played Home Games.*

"I'll tell you what it was," he said. "It was a hell of an entertaining game from this standpoint: When the best team in hockey played the worst, you saw all the skills, the passing and skating ability, that you missed in a tight-checking NHL game. In a game like ours, you realized just how good those Red Wing teams of the fifties really were."

After the game Jack Adams hoisted the Wings' symbol of dominance—a "honey bucket" given him by inmates.

# CHAPTER FIVE

**P**laying in the NHL during the days of the Original Six was not the most lucrative profession a man could choose. In New York, some players actually skipped practice to shovel snow during storms to make a few extra bucks. The paychecks weren't appreciably bigger for those who'd won a handful of Stanley Cups or scored a hatful of goals. Gordie Howe skated for all of $7,500 in 1953, the year he and his new wife—a pretty and

# Winters of Discontent

## 1955–1960

strong-willed blonde named Colleen Jaffe—set up house in a modest home on Stalwell Avenue in Detroit. "That was not a lot of money, especially for a player who was leading the league in scoring every year and was a first-team All-Star, but there was little that could have been done about it at that time," Colleen complained in their joint autobiography, *And Howe!* "It was a matter of too many players and too few teams."

Even winning the Cup was worth only about two or three thousand dollars a man, and that was before taxes and Jack Adams took a bite. "The first couple of times we won the Stanley Cup, we got about $3,000 a share," remembered Johnny Wilson, a member of all four of Detroit's Cup-winning teams in the fifties. "The

Team captain Ted Lindsay always maintained that he had the Red Wings' logo tattooed over his heart.

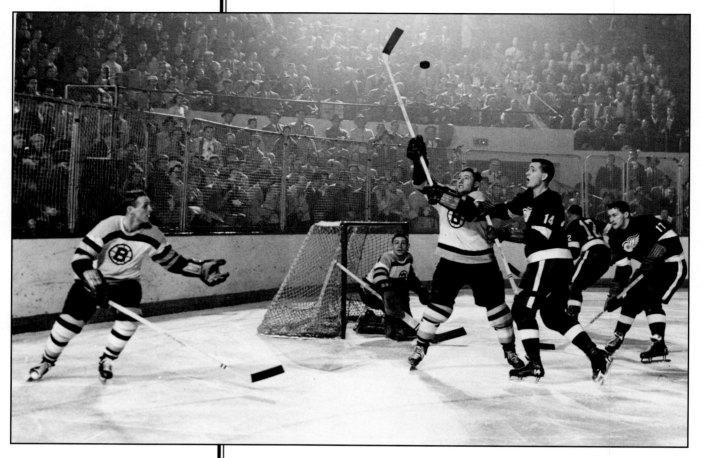

A familiar face is in goal for Boston as the Wings and Bruins duke it out during the 1955-56 season. Watching the flight of the puck with great interest are, from left, Boston defenders Doug Mohns, Terry Sawchuk, and Fern Flamon, and Wings Lorne Ferguson, Metro Prystai, and Bill Dineen.

next time we got $1,900. Ted Lindsay, being captain, went to Adams to find out why. Adams told him instead of 20 shares—17 players, two trainers, and the coach—we now had 30 shares: the head electrician, the plumber, the roofer, etc. . . ." Players knew better than to complain, Wilson added. "There was the 'shut up' clause in our contract: 'Shut up and play.' And that's what we did."

Howe shut up and played for an estimated $16,000 in 1955. Of course, a dollar was a bit more elastic then. A loaf of bread cost 17 cents, a gallon of gas averaged 29 cents, a half-gallon of milk went for 46 cents (delivered), and a three-bedroom house could be had for $12,500. However, stars in other major sports were making five and six times what the top draw in hockey was being paid. Adams had always assured Howe that he not only would be the highest-paid player on the squad but also the best-compensated in the league. This wasn't true (at least a couple of Canadiens were making more), but Howe trusted Adams and like all players dutifully kept the terms of his contract confidential. It cost him dearly. It wasn't until 1960, after fourteen super-productive years in the league, that hockey's greatest name could afford a second car. That came about not because of Adams's largesse but from Colleen striking an endorsement deal with a Canadian chain of hardware stores that doubled her husband's annual income.

## Winters of Discontent

Displays of independence were anathema to Adams, whose gruff paternalism was hardening with age into a kind of mule-headed absolutism. When Pops Norris died just before Christmas in 1952, ownership had passed to his daughter, Marguerite, and youngest son, Bruce. Neither felt wholly comfortable questioning Adams's ways; after all, he was a living legend and had just been appointed Detroit's representative on the league's powerful board of governors. After Tommy Ivan left the bench for Chicago two years later, Adams acted as puppetmaster to Jimmy Skinner, who was happy just to be where he was and thus not inclined to argue with the man who had put him there. Consequently, by 1955 the Wings were more than ever Adams's team, and he was pretty much free to exercise his cavalier and often capricious judgment without having it seriously challenged by owner or coach.

The moves Adams made in the wake of the Red Wings' victory in the 1955 finals rocked the hockey world. In a nine-player deal with Boston he swapped Terry Sawchuk, Vic Stasiuk, Marcel Bonin, and Lorne Davis for defenseman Warren Godfrey, goalie Gilles Boisvert, and forwards Ed Sandford, Norm Corcoran, and Real Chevrefils. In another multiplayer trade he sent Tony Leswick, Johnny Wilson, Glen Skov, and Benny Woit to Chicago for defenseman Bucky Hollingsworth and forwards Jerry Toppazzini and Dave Creighton. Of the eight players Detroit received, only two—Godfrey and Hollingsworth—were still around at the end of the season. Meanwhile, most of the men Adams traded continued their solid careers in other NHL cities. In fact, over the next couple of seasons Adams would bring back via trades some of the players he'd originally dispatched, including Sawchuk, Wilson, and Leswick.

"It was pathetic how Adams destroyed that team," said Lindsay, one of only nine members of the '55 Stanley Cup champions to return in red and white for the 1955-56 season. "Of course there was an uproar about it. But Adams generally was respected for what he had done for the Wings in other years—and then, he thought he was God anyway and could do no wrong."

Sawchuk's exit was at once the most shocking and yet the most plausible. In just six seasons he had won three Vezinas and backstopped three Cup winners; during this period his goals-against average had never risen above two a game. But he was becoming moody and, in Adams's estimation, puck-shy. Most signicantly, the team had a successor groomed. Glenn Hall, a twenty-three-year-old out of Humboldt, Saskatchewan, had been very impressive in a couple of brief NHL trials. If Adams was to trade the league's top goalie, everyone felt he should've gotten a front-line player in return, someone—preferably a defenseman—who could have kept the Detroit dynasty going. Montreal was known to be interested in trading either Tom Johnson or Doug Harvey for Sawchuk, but Adams didn't like the idea of strengthening his chief competitor.

It turned out that Montreal didn't need Sawchuk. With Jacques Plante between the pipes, a new coach, Toe Blake, behind the bench, and featuring a gallery of sharpshooters unseen in the history of the league, Montreal was poised to supercede Detroit's dominance in the second half of the Eisenhow-

Glenn Hall, dubbed "Mr. Goalie," started his eighteen-year Hall-of-Fame career in 1952 as Terry Sawchuk's backup. In his first full NHL season, 1955-56, he won the Calder Trophy, and the following season was selected to the first All-Star team. Between 1955 and 1962 Hall appeared in a record 554 consecutive games, including playoffs, although he frequently was so nervous before a game that he had to throw up. The prime of Hall's career was spent in Chicago and St. Louis, where he won or shared three Vezina trophies.

Alex Delvecchio (10) and Marty Pavelich storm the Chicago net as goalie Hank Bassen and a flock of Blackhawks work to keep the puck out. This action occurred during the 1955-56, the first season since 1947-48 that the Wings did not win the Prince of Wales Trophy for finishing in first place.

er decade. In 1955-56 the Canadiens' big center, Jean Beliveau, supplanted Howe as scoring champ, while Rocket Richard bumped him from his traditional spot on the first All-Star team. With talent like Boom-Boom Geoffrion, Claude Provost, and Henri Richard (the Rocket's younger brother) fueling hockey's top offense, and Harvey, Johnson, and rookie Jean Guy Talbot headlining the league's stingiest defense, the Canadiens snapped the Wings' streak of seven consecutive regular-season championships. The Montreal juggernaut then started a more impressive streak of its own, winning the first of five straight Stanley Cups. No one had ever won more than three in a row.

The Wings were mired in the middle of the standings for much of the 1955-56 season, before rallying to nose out New York for second place with 76 points. Montreal finished far out in front with an even 100 points, then easily dispatched the Rangers in the semifinals.

Detroit got rid of Toronto in five games in the other semifinal match, one that was leavened with black humor. Prior to game three, a crank repeatedly called the *Toronto Sun* and warned that he was going to shoot Lindsay and Howe if they dared play that night at Maple Leaf Gardens. This was in retaliation, he said, for the injury they supposedly had inflicted on the Leafs' Tod Sloan in the previous game. Security was beefed up, but the players tried to take the death threats in stride. Bob Goldham suggested that rookie Commy Burton test the would-be assassin's marksmanship by skating out for warm-ups in a jersey with Howe's number nine sewn on the back and Lindsay's number seven stitched on the front. Burton declined the offer.

"Once we got on the ice," recalled Lindsay, "some of the guys were saying, 'Don't skate too close to us because he's liable to be a bad shot.'" Contemptuous of the death threats and the hearty booing, Lindsay was his usual devilish

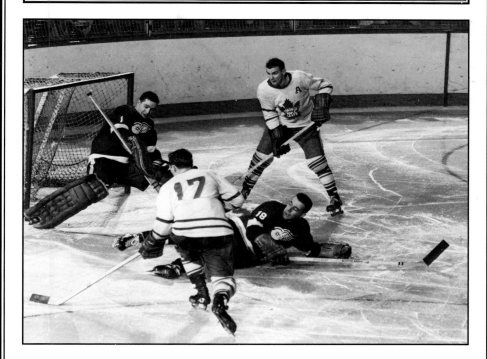

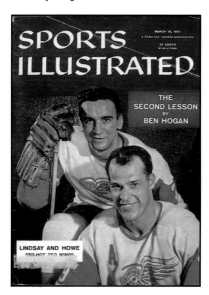

Glenn Hall and a sliding Bucky Hollingworth attempt to turn back Toronto's Dick Duff during the 1956 semifinals. Hall, who didn't wear a mask until late in his career, often paid the price for his barefaced heroics. During the 1957 playoffs he took a wicked shot to the face that delayed play for a half-hour as 23 inches were sewn into his mouth. Jack Adams, convinced that his goalie was puck-shy, traded him after the season to Chicago. Four years later, Hall gained a measure of revenge by backstopping the Hawks to victory over the Wings in the 1961 Stanley Cup finals.

By 1957 the Wings were back in their familiar position of leading the league, thanks to the scoring of two old reliables. In 1956-57 Howe and Lindsay finished first and second in league scoring, the third time in six seasons that they had accomplished that feat.

self, scoring the tying and winning goals in a 5-4 overtime victory. Afterwards, he circled the rink, aiming his stick like a machine gun as he sprayed imaginary bullets into the crowd. "Some of the people who were booing all of a sudden started applauding," he said. "I guess they thought, 'Jeez, here's a guy who's got a sense of humor. We didn't think Lindsay had one.'"

There wasn't much to smile over in the championship tilt, the third straight involving Detroit and Montreal. The Canadiens overcame a two-goal deficit in the opener, pouring four goals past Glenn Hall in the final period for a 6-4 victory, then followed up with a 5-1 walloping in the next game. Detroit managed to win the third contest, 3-1, but Montreal responded with 3-0 and 3-1 wins to finally eliminate the defending two-time Cup champions. The last game, played April 10, 1956 at Montreal, was notable in that it was the last time a team was allowed to score as many goals as possible while a member of the opposing team was off serving a minor penalty. In this instance, Jean Beliveau and Rocket Richard scored the game's first two goals in the second period while Marcel Pronovost was in the penalty box for tripping. Montreal's proficiency on the power play—it wasn't unheard of for the Canadiens to score even three goals on the same minor penalty—forced a significant rule change. Starting in 1956-57, a player serving a two-minute penalty was allowed to return to the ice if his team was scored on.

Glenn Hall had been less than spectacular in the '56 finals, but his regular-season goaltending—a 2.11 average and a league-high 12 shutouts—earned him the Calder Trophy as top rookie. The following season Hall joined Howe, Lindsay, and Red Kelly on the first All-Star team as the Red Wings rebounded to win their twelfth Prince of Wales trophy under Adams's stewardship. It was just like old times as Howe and Lindsay finished one-two in the scoring

Al Arbour was the Wings' bespectacled defenseman for three seasons in the fifties before spending another fourteen years with Chicago, Toronto, and St. Louis. Arbour would earn his greatest fame as coach and general manager of the New York Islanders, leading them to four consecutive Stanley Cups in the 1980s.

race with 89 and 85 points, respectively. Howe's 44 goals were far more than anybody else in the league and gained him his fifth Art Ross Trophy and third Hart Trophy, while Lindsay's 55 assists not only led all playmakers but tied his own team mark. Sophomore center Norm Ullman finished tenth in scoring with 16 goals and 52 points. For all the criticism directed Adams's way since his trading spree had gutted the squad, it was a fact that for the eighth time in nine years his team had finished the regular season on top of the standings. Detroit's 38-20-12 record in 1956-57 netted 88 points, six ahead of Montreal. Fans and reporters wondered if the previous season had been just an abberation.

It turned out that it hadn't. In the opening round of the '57 playoffs the Wings were embarrassed in five games by the fourth-place Bruins. Montreal, whose second-place finish owed more to injuries to several key players than to any resurgence by Detroit, regained its health in time to successfully defend its Cup.

Adams, looking for scapegoats, found two in Hall and Lindsay. After the '57 playoffs, he traded the two All-Stars to Chicago for veteran Johnny Wilson and three young players, William Preston, Forbes Kennedy, and Hank Bassen.

"When we lost to Boston in the playoffs he came into the dressing room and said it was all my fault," Hall said of Adams. "So, then he traded me to

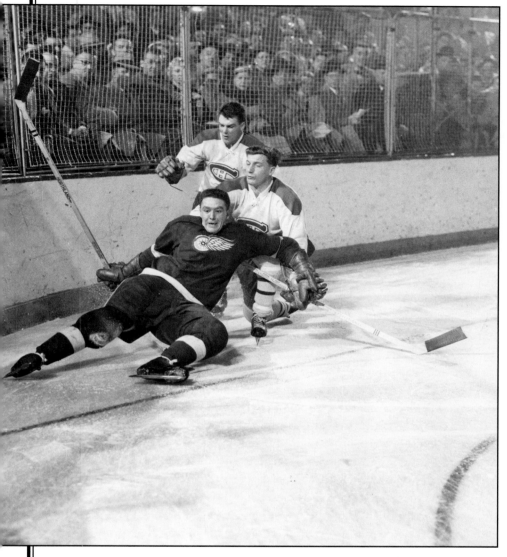

The Detroit-Montreal rivalry of the 1950s was the most hotly contested in professional sports and involved some of hockey's legendary figures. Between them the Wings and Canadiens won every Stanley Cup from 1950 to 1960 except one—1951, when Toronto temporarily broke their monopoly—and met in the finals four times.

"I never spoke to any of them," said Ted Lindsay, recalling the many train rides the two teams shared between Montreal and Detroit. "I hated them and they hated me. It was the way it was and the way it should be. It was wonderful."

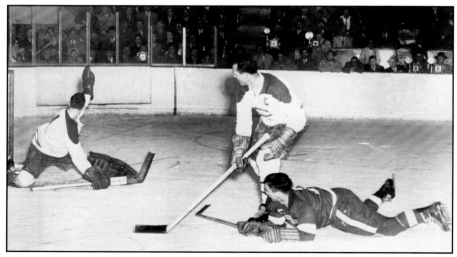

The Wings' winning chemistry included Johnny Wilson, a member of all four Stanley Cup champions in the fifties. The left wing had his best season for Detroit in 1952-53, when he scored 23 goals. Three seasons later he tallied 24 times for Chicago, to which he had just been traded. Wilson had a second tour of duty with the Wings from 1957 to 1959 before closing out a twelve-year NHL career in Toronto and New York. He later coached in Los Angeles and Detroit.

Chicago and when I did well with the Blackhawks what do you think Adams said? He said that he was doing them [the Blackhawks] a favor by trading me to them. That was Adams for you, always trying to make himself look good. Of course, I wasn't surprised at the way he was acting. After all, only a year earlier he had blamed Gordie Howe for our losses. So, by lumping me in a class with Gordie, I felt I was right in there with the best."

At the time, Hall's trade wasn't seen as a terribly controversial move, especially when Adams reacquired Sawchuk from Boston. But the trading of the thirty-one-year-old Lindsay—team captain, perennial All-Star, and the heart and soul of the Red Wings—caused an enormous outcry. The protestations were futile. Lindsay triggered Adams's wrath by daring to display his independence—first, by starting a successful offseason auto parts business with Marty Pavelich and then by spearheading the ill-fated attempt to organize the NHL Players Association. To Adams, his onetime favorite son suddenly was an ingrate and, worse, a clubhouse lawyer.

"My first ten years in the league, I could've kicked Jack in the ass and he would've hugged and kissed me," Lindsay said of their relationship. "When Marty and I went into business he became a different person. And the trade to Chicago—that was because of the players association. I'd just come off the best year I'd ever had as a Red Wing. See, Jack was losing control of his players, and like everybody else in management then, he couldn't stand the thought of that."

The association (players were uneasy calling it a union) had been formed in February 1957, with Lindsay serving as president. The NHLPA quickly filed a three-million-dollar lawsuit against the league and its member clubs in an attempt to win increased pension benefits and a larger share of television

The dynamic duo of Lindsay and Howe at Olympia in 1958. However, this time the two are opponents, not teammates. The first time they faced each other after Lindsay was traded to Chicago, Terrible Ted lowered the lumber on Howe's head right in front of the Detroit bench. Howe retaliated with a punch that knocked his old friend to the ice.

"What the hell are you doing?" exclaimed Howe. "You want to play this way?" "Friendship's not worth it," responded Lindsay. "Then keep your fucking stick away from my face," warned Howe. Lindsay played three seasons for the Blackhawks before retiring in 1960.

Jimmy Skinner began his long association with the Red Wings as the captain of the Omaha farm team during the war and continued it as head coach, scout, and general manager for the parent team. Skinner compiled a 123-79-46 record during his three and a half seasons behind the Wings' bench, which included two Prince of Wales trophies and a Stanley Cup in 1955.

revenue. By the following year, however, the association would be dissolved, its most militant members traded as punishment for their "betrayal." Subjected to harassment and thinly veiled threats from Adams, Detroit players would be the first to announce that they were withdrawing from the association. Potentially influential players like Howe and Red Kelly (the new Wings captain after Lindsay was banished) quickly caved in to the intimidation. Naive, scared, and programmed since youth to trust authority, they preferred to individually negotiate their differences rather than resort to a strike, the ultimate weapon of organized workers. "In those days," Kelly explained years later, "you didn't want to hurt the game or its reputation."

Instead, they chose to hurt themselves. In exchange for their agreement to drop legal action, players were tossed a few crumbs from the owners. Players received a slightly larger share of playoff money and saw their pension and

**B**ill Dineen, who played for Detroit from 1953 to 1957, scored 17 goals his rookie season, after which Jack Adams promised the young forward a raise to $6,500. "I thought I was getting a raise of $500," said Dineen. "What I didn't know at the time was that the NHL had raised its minimum salary from $6,000 to $6,500. So all Adams did was give me the minimum once again!" Later, as coach and general manager of World Hockey Association teams in Houston and New England, Dineen was reunited with an old teammate, Gordie Howe.

health benefits increased marginally. They received no part of the new television contract being negotiated, though the league agreed to raise the minimum salary from $6,500 to $7,000 a year. From that point owners and team executives kept a vigilant watch on potential troublemakers, squashing any subsequent attempts to re-establish union solidarity until lawyer and agent Alan Eagleson was successful in organizing dissidents in 1967.

Adams hated Lindsay to the end of his days. One Sunday he startled his players on their way up the church steps when somebody mentioned the turncoat's name. "You mention that son of a bitch!" he roared. "I want you to know, I get down on my knees every night and thank the Good Lord I got rid of that son of a bitch!"

By the spring of 1992, when a new generation of players started making noise about going out on strike over a new labor-management contract (they ultimately were locked out by the owners), Howe had emerged as one of the NHLPA's most vocal supporters and a potent symbol of past economic injustices. "Things today are pretty nice—salaries and everything else," he said. "But it's the future that is at stake. They have seen what the future has done to a lot of the older players."

Howe, sixty-four at the time, admitted that he and other players from the Original Six era hadn't given much thought to their post-hockey days.

"Leo Reise was playing in Detroit and he said, 'Gordie, the money we're going to get from the pension won't be worth the paper it's written on because of escalating costs.' But I thought, 'This is pretty nice. I'm getting $6,500 a year; I'm putting $900 into the pension. And it will protect me for the future, because when I get fifteen years or so in the league, when I turn forty-five, I'll get as much as I'm making now.' That sounded pretty good. As it turned out, I'm around $14,000 or $15,000 a year."

Not long afterwards, Howe and his poorly compensated contemporaries from the forties, fifties, and sixties were the beneficiaries of a successful class-action lawsuit against the league. As today's players routinely sign million-dollar contracts that guarantee them lifetime security before some are even able to grow a decent playoff beard, the warriors who built the game skate into old age with arthritic joints, a few extra dollars a month, and a lingering regret that, as young men, they hadn't battled management off the ice as spiritedly as they did each other on it.

S id Abel took over from Jimmy Skinner halfway through the 1957-58 season and coached the Wings a total of 12 seasons, during which time his teams won 340 games, only two more than they lost, and tied another 132. As a player, Abel was regarded as one of the greatest inspirational leaders in club history, but his motivational magic fell a little short when behind the bench. He remains the only coach to take a team to the Stanley Cup finals four times and never win.

T alented Johnny Bucyk arrived in Detroit in 1955 from Edmonton of the Western Hockey League but was soon gone, another victim of Jack Adams's irrational trading frenzy of the late fifties. "He wasn't good enough for Detroit," Lindsay later complained, "but he played twenty-one years for Boston and was one of the best players in the league." In 23 seasons, the Hall-of-Fame left winger scored 556 goals and 1,369 points and helped the Bruins win two Stanley Cups.

A fter Adams got rid of Lindsay, he tried to punish his close friend and business partner, Marty Pavelich, by assigning him to the minors. The twenty-nine-year-old left winger, still in the prime of his career but weary of Adams, got back at the King Wing the best way he could. He retired, then together with Lindsay built their fledgling company into a prosperous supplier to the Big Three automakers.

With fewer and fewer veterans from the club's recent championship past to call upon, Jimmy Skinner's shortcomings as coach became more exposed. His health declined. He had terrible migraine headaches and couldn't sleep at night. Halfway into the 1957-58 season, with the Wings sinking under a 13-18-7 record, he was replaced by Sid Abel. Abel, out of hockey at the time, returned to rally the club to a third-place finish, one point ahead of the Bru-

**M**arcel Pronovost's end-to-end dashes made him the Paul Coffey of the 1950s. Perhaps the best rushing defenseman of his era, Pronovost broke in with the Wings in the 1950 playoffs and stayed with the team through the end of 1965. After that he spent five more seasons with Toronto, where he won his fifth Stanley Cup.

**M**arcel Pronovost was nonchalant about the many injuries he suffered, including the broken nose that forced him to wear this crude face shield during the 1955-56 season. "To me," he once said, "accidents are as common as lacing up a pair of skates." However, the future Hall of Famer remained a cog from the once-great Wings Stanley Cup machine.

ins. For their trouble the Wings drew first-place Montreal, who blew past them in the first two games of the semifinals, 8-1 and 5-1, before completing the sweep with a pair of one-goal victories at Olympia.

Adams's petty vindictiveness continued to affect the team. Although it wasn't public knowledge at the time, Red Kelly played the last few games of the following season with a broken foot. In the final stages of the '58-59 campaign, Abel and Adams, anxious for the Wings to make the playoffs, had asked the ailing blueliner to remove his cast and suit up. Kelly normally used his skates a lot to move the puck, so the injury severely affected his play. Despite his quiet heroics the team continued to lose and plunged to the basement, marking the first time Detroit had missed the playoffs since 1938.

Midway through the following season, a Toronto reporter asked Kelly if he thought he was through. Kelly, tired of being blamed by the press for the Wings' late-season collapse—particularly since the stories were being leaked from the front office—admitted the truth. Newspapers jumped all over the revelation. "Was Red Kelly forced to play on a broken foot?" the *Detroit Free Press* demanded to know.

Just like that, another Detroit favorite bit the dust. On February 4, 1960, an infuriated Adams dealt Kelly and forward Billy McNeill to New York for Bill Gadsby and Eddie Shack. When Kelly refused to report, Adams was forced to kill the trade. Instead, he suspended Kelly, who in turn decided that, like Pavelich, he'd had quite enough of Adams, thank you. He retired and made plans to work fulltime for his offseason employer. Finally, with the league president's quiet intervention, Kelly went to Toronto for defenseman Marc Reaume. It was as lopsided a deal as has ever been struck in the NHL. While Reaume lasted two nonproductive seasons in Detroit, Kelly went on to play seven more seasons and win another four Stanley Cups with the Maple Leafs.

The banished redhead had a hand in the Maple Leafs' semifinal whipping of the fourth-place Wings that year, a season in which Howe won his fifth Hart Trophy and joined defenseman Marcel Pronovost on the first All-Star team. Kelly, moved from the blue line by the Leafs, centered a line with Frank Mahovlich on the left side. It was Mahovlich's goal three minutes into the third overtime that gave Toronto a 5-4 victory at Olympia and a two-game-to-one series edge. The Wings responded with a 2-1 sudden-death win of their own, but Toronto then took the next two games and the series.

The 1960 playoffs offered an opportunity to look back on a decade the Red Wings had owned, which in addition to all of the championships included 22 individual trophies and one-third of all postseason All-Star berths. How quickly things had changed. A mere five years after their last Stanley Cup victory, Howe, Pronovost, Delvecchio, and Sawchuk remained the only cogs of the once-great Red Wing machine.

However, this quartet of old reliables also was a solid nucleus around which the team would rebuild in the first half of the sixties. Detroit would unexpectedly reach the finals four times within a six-year period, as the front-office strategy shifted from one of patiently developing young players to that of acquiring veterans in an annual attempt to win the big prize now. The Wings would do so without their greatest link to the past.

On April 25, 1962, a press conference was held to announce that, after thirty-five seasons and seven Stanley Cups, Jack Adams was leaving the Detroit organization. The sixty-six-year-old general manager had been butting heads with his coach for some time. What Adams considered input was characterized as interference by Abel, whose complaints to Bruce Norris convinced the young owner that it was finally time for Jolly Jack, grown senile and corrosive with age, to step down. Adams, while acknowledging that he had been feeling the effects of his age, insisted that he could still do the job and that he had been fired. He was angry that Norris had ignored his personal choice as successor, Bud Poile, coach and manager of the Edmonton Oil Kings, and instead named Abel as the Wings' new general manager. "I guess they don't need my advice anymore," he said.

According to Norris, Adams had been retired at full pay. Whether needing the money or craving the action, over the next six years Adams kept busy in sports promotions around Detroit and also served as president of the Central Professional Hockey League. On May 2, 1968, he was working at the desk of his Detroit office when he suffered a fatal heart attack.

There was an outpouring of genuine sorrow at his passing. Obituaries skimmed his bad points and concentrated on his legacy as one of the game's true architects and as a man whose indomitable will to win was second to none. He was justifiably painted as a great booster of hockey and of the city of Detroit. Anecdotes concerning his religious faith and charitable acts revealed a side of Adams that was at odds with the one remembered from countless locker-room tirades, where he had roared at his men like some wild-eyed Old Testament prophet. At his funeral one of his former players conceded that maybe the old man hadn't been all bad. "I guess in the long run he was teaching me," he said.

Others in attendance remained skeptical. "Well," responded another ex-Wing, "he was a miserable son-of-a-bitch when he was alive and today's he's a *dead* miserable son-of-a-bitch."

Frank "Budd" Lynch, whose father died in the great flu epidemic after World War I, lost his right arm to a German artillery shell in World War II. He didn't let either misfortune hold him back, moving from a small radio station in Hamilton, Ontario, where he made $5.50 a week in 1936, to Detroit's powerful WWJ, where he started doing hockey telecasts in 1949.

The popular broadcaster retired from radio-TV work in 1975, then became the publicity director of the Wings for seven years. Since 1982 the "One-Armed Bandit"—a member of the Hockey Hall of Fame and winner of the Foster Hewitt Award for excellence in hockey broadcasting—has been the public address announcer at Joe Louis Arena.

# The Troubled Genius of Terry Sawchuk

**F**or storied performers like Terry Sawchuk, careers are not defined by numbers or seasons as much as by moments. One in particular stands out in the mind of Gary Bergman, who joined the Wings in 1964. "At the end of the season we were playing a big Saturday night game against Toronto at Maple Leaf Gardens," remembered Bergman. As the rookie defenseman sat nervously waiting for the game to begin, he overheard a pair of veterans discuss their chances.

"Ukey, how do you feel?" Gordie Howe asked his goalie.

"Big Guy, get me a couple tonight," responded Sawchuk. "I think that's all we're going to need."

The two men who personified the Red Wings for much of the fifties and sixties then proceeded to act out the script they had just written. Howe scored two goals, Sawchuk allowed one, and the Wings prevailed, 2-1.

"That just shows what The Uke could do when he set his mind to it," said Bergman. "I still get goose bumps when I think about it."

Thinking of Terry Sawchuk—known as "The Uke" or "Ukey" to his friends—produced a good share of goose bumps on March 6, 1994. That Sunday afternoon, in ceremonies preceding Detroit's game with Buffalo, the man many consider the finest goaltender in history had his jersey retired. A banner bearing his famous No. 1 was hoisted to the rafters of Joe Louis Arena, where it now flutters alongside those honoring four other Detroit greats: Howe (No. 9), Ted Lindsay (7), Alex Delvecchio (10), and Sid Abel (12).

The Hall-of-Fame netminder, who died a cloudy death in 1970, wasn't around for the ceremonies, which is just as well since The Uke never cared much for the limelight. But a passel of family members and former teammates were there. Talk revolved around such familiar highlights as his four shutouts in the '52 Stanley Cup playoffs, his three 1-0 victories in one week in 1954, and his stash of NHL regular-season records—21 seasons, 971 games, 103 shutouts—that no goalie will ever approach.

For some who knew him best, the talk centered around The Uke's complicated personality, a tapestry woven of talent and courage, as well as more than a few stray strands of moodiness and obstinance.

"It's almost a cliché to say that goaltenders are different," said Jack Berry, longtime hockey beat writer for United Press International and the *Detroit Free Press* and *News*. "But Sawchuk was. The Uke was tough. He went his own way. He was not really a happy guy most of the time. But you can chalk that up to the conditions under which he played. They really were iron men back then."

The Uke's iron constitution too often was betrayed by a cardboard body. As fabled as his career was, it would have been even greater had he not been beset by a nearly continuous string of ailments and injuries. "Dad was a medical freak," said his son, Jerry. "He had more operations than I can remember. Doctors could never figure out how he walked, much less played. He had a bad back from goaltending, so he walked hunched over all the time." A shriveled right arm, the result of a childhood injury that didn't mend properly, handicapped him to the end of his days. "He couldn't knot his tie. Mom had to knot all of his ties for him when he went on road trips."

The temperamental Sawchuk takes on some taunting Toronto Maple Leafs fans.

The Red Wings' goalie of the future is pictured in 1947. At the time eighteen-year-old Sawchuk was playing for Omaha of the U.S. Hockey League, where he would win Rookie-of-the-Year honors.

## THE DETROIT RED WINGS

Compounding the physical trauma was the psychological angst all goalies must battle. The war of nerves is bad today, but the pressure to perform was considerably worse in Sawchuk's time. Netminders were expected to play every minute of every game, come hell or high water. In the 1950s that meant 70 regular-season games plus as many as 14 more playoff contests, all squeezed into a six-month season.

"In those days clubs only carried one goalie," said longtime broadcaster Budd Lynch. "If he got cut, the team had ten minutes to get him sewn up and back on the ice. If he was hurt too bad to continue, usually the trainer would put on the pads and finish out the game."

"If you weren't up to it," said Jerry Sawchuk, "there were all sorts of guys in the minor leagues waiting for a shot. You always had to be looking over your shoulder for someone to replace you. Remember, there were only six goalies in the entire league when my dad played. It tells you something about the quality of the goalies then that the only way Lefty Wilson, who was a pretty good goalie in the American Hockey League, could make it to the NHL was by becoming the Wings' trainer."

Nonetheless, Sawchuk not only persevered, he excelled. He won or shared four Vezina Trophies (1952, 1953, 1955, 1965) and was a member of four Stanley Cup championship teams (1952, 1954, 1955, 1967). He was a first-team All-Star selection three consecutive seasons (1951-53) and a second-team pick four other times (1954, 1955, 1959, 1963). He remains the only goalie to be named Rookie of the Year in three different leagues.

"He could be a tough guy to get to know," admitted Lynch. "But he was number one back in the era when the Wings were kings."

Terrance Gordon Sawchuk was born in Winnipeg, Manitoba, on December 28, 1929. That he came into the world during the first winter of the Great Depression was indicative of his luck, which for the rest of his life would often prove to be bad.

His father had fled the impoverished Ukraine as a child and eked out a living as a tinsmith in a factory. Louis Sawchuk is remembered today as "a tough old goat" who once settled an argument with a former Canadian boxing champion by knocking him out with a single punch.

The Sawchuk home reflected the same kind of frontier hardiness. It was cramped and unimposing, its drafty rooms heavy with the clinging smells of cabbage rolls and woodsmoke. As much to generate heat as to conserve space, Terry shared a bed with his older brother, Mike.

By the time he was four years old, Terry was pushing a puck across his own little corner of western Canada. This was classic river hockey: newspapers stuffed into trousers, a frozen horse apple for a puck, the low-slung winter sun melting like a ball of butter into the horizon. Mike, a high school goalie, enjoyed giving his kid brother some pointers. "You have to have good balance and keep your eyes on the puck," he'd instruct. Terry would nod, trying to keep his balance in the mattresslike pads.

If Terry ever had an idol, it was his older brother. Mike is described by relatives as "the nicest kid; a big strong guy." Which made his death when Terry was ten a real tragedy. Today a heart murmur can be fixed as routinely as a flat tire; in 1939 Manitoba, the condition was fatal.

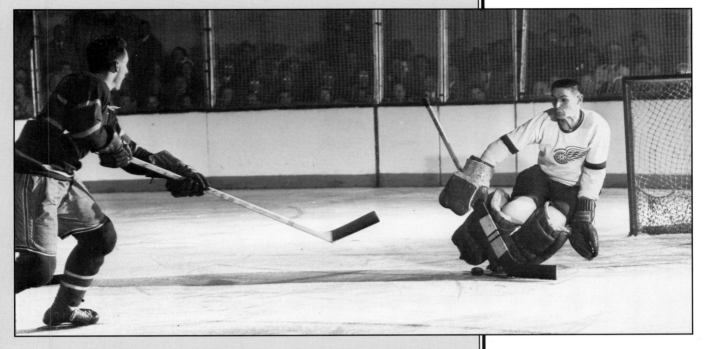

A second brother, Roger, died of pneumonia, also at a young age. Whether his brothers' early passing turned Terry introspective or merely confirmed an already fatalistic view of the world can only be guessed at. Surely Mike's death affected him. "He'd talk about Mike," one family member remembered. "He'd say how much he missed him."

Terry moved through the local amateur ranks—Pee Wees, Bantams, Midgets—wearing Mike's pads. When he wasn't playing hockey during the long Canadian winters he was hitting a baseball or kicking a football. The latter was responsible for a bizarre accident that crippled his right arm when he was twelve.

"Dad was on his way to church one Sunday when he ran across some boys playing rugby," said Jerry Sawchuk. "They were teasing him, so he decided to join in."

Terry emerged from a pileup with a throbbing pain in his right elbow. Too scared to tell his parents, he kept the pain to himself. Two years later, doctors discovered he had broken his arm. It had mended horribly, to the extent that it was two inches shorter than the left and had the range of motion of a rusty gate.

The goal for many kids born during the Depression was to reach fourteen. That was the magic number, the age when one could chuck the schoolbooks, acquire working papers, and start contributing to the family welfare. Terry dropped out of school and found work in a sheet-metal plant. His mother gave him an allowance out of what he brought home.

By now he had caught the eye of the Wings' organization. It placed him on a Junior team, the Winnipeg Flyers, then promoted him to its Junior "A" team in Galt, Ontario. This meant moving away from home. The Wings agreed to pay him $80 a month, which didn't go far even in 1946. Upon leaving, his mother pressed a $10 bill into her son's hand. "It was one of the few $10 bills she ever had," he later remembered.

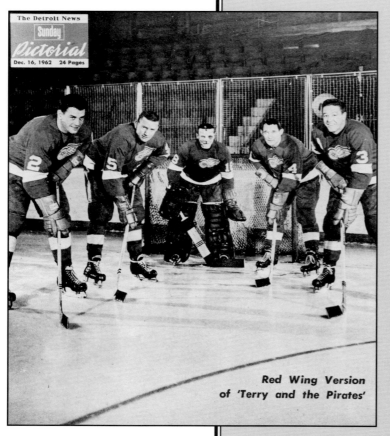

The Detroit News
Sunday
Pictorial
Dec. 16, 1962   24 Pages

**Red Wing Version
of 'Terry and the Pirates'**

The following year the promising goalie was sent to an even stronger Junior team, the Windsor Spitfires. There he could develop under the watchful eye of Wings general manager and coach Jack Adams. In November 1947, Adams sent his budding star to Omaha of the U.S. Hockey League.

Despite suffering a badly cut right eyeball during a game on his eighteenth birthday, the acrobatic youngster turned the league on its ear. He won Rookie of the Year accolades, an honor repeated the next season when he played for the Wings' top farm club in Indianapolis of the American Hockey League.

In early 1950, Sawchuk was enjoying a second productive AHL campaign when he was called up to Detroit to replace injured star goalie, Harry Lumley. His first NHL start was on January 8, 1950, against Boston. He managed to overcome a severe case of the jitters and played a steady game, but bad luck was with him. His defensemen kicked two pucks past him into the net and the Bruins won, 4-3. He played six more games as a fill-in, surrendering just two goals a game and posting his first NHL shutout. He was sent back to Indianapolis as the Wings, behind the recuperated Lumley, won their first Stanley Cup in nearly a decade.

**W**ho was that masked man? Careful readers of the *Detroit News* had to be asking themselves that question after seeing this cover of the paper's Sunday pictorial. The defensemen (from left, Howie Young, Doug Barkley, Bill Gadsby, and Marcel Pronovost) are who they appear to be, but the goalie is an imposter. Because Terry Sawchuk was unable to pose for one reason or another, the photographer had to substitute fellow blueliner Pete Goegan for the missing goalie. The subterfuge almost worked. Unfortunately, nobody thought to have the imposter change his jersey to one bearing Sawchuk's number.

In the wake of the Cup win, Adams had a decision to make. With a core group of young stars in place, the Wings had the makings of a dynasty. But who should mind the net for the next several years—the veteran Lumley or the kid in Indianapolis? In a terrific gamble, Adams sent Lumley to Chicago and promoted Terry.

Affable and eager to confirm Adams's faith in him, Sawchuk became the talk of the hockey world in the early 1950s. "In action, he was the most acrobatic goaltender of his time," observed Toronto sportswriter Trent Frayne. "He didn't move so much as he exploded into a desperate release of energy—down the glove, up the arm, over the stick, up the leg pad; he sometimes seemed a human pinwheel. He played the whole game in pent-up tension, shouting at his teammates, crouching, straightening, diving, scrambling, his pale face drawn and tense. . . ."

Adams initially frowned on Sawchuk's unique gorillalike crouch, which allowed him to follow the puck amid a forest of sticks and skates. But when other goalies started to abandon their traditional upright style and adopt similar stances, the Wings' boss quit complaining.

With the Production Line taking care of business on the far end of the rink and The Uke stopping nearly everything shot his way, the Wings racked up back-to-back 100-point seasons in Sawchuk's first two years, the first times any team had passed the century mark. Sawchuk missed winning the Vezina his freshman season of 1950-51 by a single goal, but with 11 shutouts and a 1.98 goals-against average he was the easy choice for the Calder Trophy as the NHL's top rookie.

The following season he earned his first Vezina, posting 12 shutouts and a sparkling 1.94 average. In fact, in each of his first five NHL seasons Terry's goals-against average stayed below two goals a game. He also turned in a shutout about once very six games. And his 44 wins in each of his first two campaigns remained a record until Bernie Parent, benefitting from an expanded schedule, recorded 47 victories for Philadelphia in 1973-74.

Although Detroit was upset in the 1951 semifinals, in 1952 the Wings did something no team had ever done before. They swept through the playoffs with eight consecutive wins over Toronto and Montreal. Four of them were shutouts by The Uke, who allowed but five goals overall for an unbelievable 0.62 average. He was all smiles as the Stanley Cup was presented to the Wings. "Life can be beautiful," he said.

It got even better. That summer he met Patricia Morey, a vivacious seventeen-year-old who was getting ready to start her senior year of high school. Pat was the adopted daughter of Ed Morey, the well-known proprietor of Morey's Golf Course in Union Lake. Like Terry, she understood hard times. Her mother had died in childbirth and her father had gone to sea. Pat and her siblings were scattered among various families. She was eleven years old and staying at the Guardian Angel Home in Detroit when the Moreys adopted her.

"My nephew Art played matchmaker," recalled Pat, now remarried and living in Florida. "He brought Terry out to golf. We talked for three hours that first day."

Although the twenty-two-year-old star had just completed one of the greatest goaltending feats in Stanley Cup history, Pat "knew nothing, absolutely nothing about hockey," she said. "I didn't know who Terry Sawchuk was and I didn't care. I was more for going out and having fun with my friends."

The two didn't date for some time following their initial meeting. What finally won Pat over was her suitor's persistence. "I'd come home from being out with my friends and Dad would say, 'That Terry Sawchuk called again,'" she recalled with a laugh.

On their first date they went to the Fox Theatre, where they put on 3-D glasses to see Vincent Price in *The House of Wax*. Not long afterward Terry proposed marriage. Since the Moreys were a very old-fashioned family, he first had to ask Ed Morey for permission to marry his daughter. Then he dropped to his knee to ask Patricia to marry him.

The wonder is not that Pat accepted—she said yes and they were married August 5, 1953—but that The Uke could get up from bended knee. Already he was suffering from an assortment of ailments. His back hurt, the beginning of a life-time of pain caused by his crouching style. In 1950 and 1951 he underwent operations to remove bone chips from his crippled elbow. In 1953 his appendix burst, and he later suffered severe chest injuries in a car accident.

He was a fairly big man: a shade under six feet tall and about 190 pounds, although his weight often fluctuated dramatically. In terms of dieting and training this was a decidedly less enlightened era. He smoked cigarettes, enjoyed his beer, and barely swatted at pucks during practice. "His philosophy was that he was paid to play games, not practice," explained his first-born child, Jerry.

He was a fairly big man: a shade under six feet tall and about 190 pounds, although his weight often fluctuated dramatically. In terms of dieting and training this was a decidedly less enlightened era. Sawchuk smoked cigarettes, enjoyed his beer, and barely swatted at pucks during practice.

With his velcro-strip haircut and hard-lined face, The Uke had the look of a Marine drill instructor and the temperament to go with it. As the years passed and the pressures of his job and providing for a growing family mounted, his early affability gave way to increased irritability.

Jerry Sawchuk, today a sales rep in the Detroit area, was born in 1954. He was followed by two brothers (Michael and Terry) and four sisters (Debbie, Carol, Kathy, and JoAnn). The family grew up on a ranch-style house built on Ed Morey's golf course.

During the offseason The Uke often worked for his father-in-law. Budd Lynch likes to tell of the time the two bullheaded men got into an argument.

"So Ukey took a job tending bar at his [Morey's] competitor," Lynch said. "Some of Uke's pals, like Marcel Pronovost, would show up at Morey's looking for him. Morey would just wave and tell 'em, 'He's working across the street.' He worked there all summer until training camp began."

Lynch laughed. "A little bit obstinate? I guess you could say so."

With his velcro-strip haircut and hard-lined face, The Uke had the look of a Marine drill instructor and the temperament to go with it. As the years passed and the pressures of his job and providing for a growing family mounted, his early affability gave way to increased irritability. He quarreled with fans, referees, writers, and anyone else who didn't see eye-to-eye with him. At times he shot off sparks like a downed power line. For a goalie he accumulated an unusually high number of penalty minutes, including 39 in 1957-58 alone.

Such intensity played havoc with his already over-wrought nerves. After one game, a sportswriter offered, "You never had a chance on the two shots that beat you, Terry."

"You're all wrong," he snapped back. "I have a chance on every shot taken on my goal."

A teammate tried to explain The Uke's mood swings. "Nothing less than perfection satisfies Terry. He takes personal blame for every puck that slips by him."

As Sawchuk's performance in the 1953-54 and 1954-55 seasons proved, not too many did slip by him. Including the regular season and playoffs, he notched 27 shutouts and backstopped the Wings to their last two Stanley Cups. By the spring of 1955 the hockey world was ready to canonize him.

But drop a halo a foot and you have a noose. Jack Adams, convinced that nerves were getting the best of his all-world goalie, shocked everybody by including him in a nine-player trade with Boston. He announced that the club would go with Glenn Hall, a talented goalie sitting in the wings. Sawchuk and his family were flabbergasted. He kept asking himself, "Am I washed up?"

The answer clearly was no. He had nine shutouts his first season with the lowly Bruins, but by his second year he hated the environment. He stayed in a boardinghouse while his family remained in Detroit. The isolation and capricious treatment from fans and writers caused him to become rude and uncooperative. He was booed, torn to pieces in the press, then expected to lead the Bruins to the promised land. The Uke brushed off autograph requests, bickered with the press, and said more than a few things that stoked the ongoing feud. "I get so wound up," he explained, "I don't even know what I'm saying."

By early 1957, Sawchuk had had enough of Beantown. He announced his retirement. Although he had just turned twenty-seven, he felt like an old man. "My nerves are shot," he said. "I can't eat or sleep. I'm getting out of the game."

Fans and sportswriters jeered his decision and questioned his fortitude, but a medical exam revealed that the worn-out goalie with the swollen neck glands was suffering from mononucleosis. After a hospital stay and convalescence back home, he felt like a new person. Jack Adams, disappointed with Glenn Hall's performance in the 1957 playoffs, wanted him back. He sent Hall to Chicago and then swapped promising forward Johnny Bucyk to Boston for the rights to The Uke.

Number 1 was back with the Wings, though it wasn't exactly like old times. The club was competitive, and he once again enjoyed playing one-on-ones for $100 a pop at practice, but the glory days of the early 1950s were impossible to recapture. Montreal, in the midst of winning five straight Cups, was the power in the league now, to be followed by Toronto in the early 1960s. Over the next seven seasons Sawchuk would help lead the Red Wings to the Cup finals three times. Each time they lost, although The Uke often played brilliantly, sometimes heroically.

Few knew the toll jitters were taking on him and his family, however. "The day of the game, Dad would lock himself in his bedroom, maybe make one or two appearances in the kitchen," said Jerry Sawchuk. "But he didn't want to be bothered. We knew not to approach him."

Behind closed doors, Sawchuk tried to rest and mentally prepare for the game at hand. As he got older he increasingly fretted and brooded, images of booming slap shots and deflected pucks flickering like a horror film behind his closed lids.

Imagine a mule kicking you in the face. Now you have some idea of the impact a frozen piece of rubber flying unpredictably through the air has when it crashes into a barefaced goalie at 90-100 miles per hour. The nervous tension caused some netminders to get physically ill or turn to the bottle for relief. Glenn Hall, for one, was famous for throwing up before each game. Others, invariably nicknamed "Ulcers" or "Shaky," downed Pepto-Bismol between periods and vowed to quit the game before they left one on a gurney.

By the early 1960s, artillerymen such as Boom-Boom Geoffrion and Bobby Hull had popularized the use of curved blades, which sent pucks whistling toward the net on nearly invisible trajectories. Deflections in front of the net, once an inadvertent and occasional hazard, now were an integral part of the offensive strategy. The trend toward rushing defensemen also left goalies vulnerable to more shots, increasing the chances for calamity. In his time Sawchuk took some 400 stitches in his face. That didn't include the occasional black eye, broken nose, cracked rib, cut hand, chipped tooth, or shattered cheekbone.

Sawchuk, seen here with a pair of blackened eyes, "was probably the worst practice goaltender who ever lived," said one of his defensemen, Doug Barkley. "He was a big-game goaltender, but he just hated the practices. If you shot one high at him in practice, he would just go stand over by the boards. He figured the game is when you play."

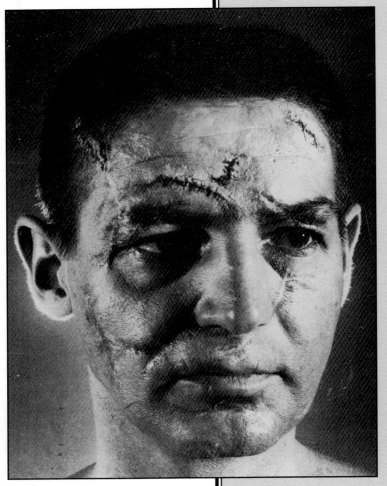

A national magazine once hired a make-up artist to reconstruct the many facial injuries Sawchuk had suffered during his career. This gargoyle-like look was the result.

"I remember a matinee game in Chicago, when Bobby Hull hit him in the face with a slap shot," said Budd Lynch. "It carved The Uke up pretty good. Afterward on the train, Adams told him, 'You're gonna wear a mask.' Uke said, 'I hate 'em.'"

Nonetheless, Sawchuk started the 1962-63 season sporting a mask fashioned by trainer Lefty Wilson. Like the one Montreal's Jacques Plante had introduced to the league three years earlier, it was made of molded fiberglass and fit close to the face. *Too* close, according to Jerry Sawchuk.

"The mask had these squares and circles for eye and nose openings," he recalled. "The only thing absorbing the shock was this thin layer of felt, which would disappear once it got sweaty. So when a shot hit my dad in the mask, it would actually cut a square or circle in his face."

Despite its primitive design and dubious protection, the mask boosted Sawchuk's confidence. With the Phantom of Olympia between the pipes, Detroit roared to its best start ever, going undefeated in its first 10 games. Sawchuk allowed but 13 goals during this streak.

Then on January 12, 1963, the snakebit goaltender suffered yet another serious injury. Toronto's Bob Pulford skated over his left hand. A two-hour operation repaired the lacerated fingers and muscles. "The doctor didn't remember how many stitches he took," Sawchuk said, "but I counted 79."

The Uke missed 17 games, but he returned to ring up a sterling 2.58 average for the year, his best since coming back to Detroit. He steered the Wings to the Cup finals, where they fell to Toronto in five games.

The following season, in the 1964 semifinals against Chicago, he left the hospital where he was being treated for a pinched nerve in his shoulder to rally the team to sixth- and seventh-game wins. For the second straight April, the Wings' silver dreams died in the finals against Toronto. The series went the distance, but the history books best remember the sixth game, when the Leafs' Bobby Baun—playing on a broken ankle—fired a shot in overtime that deflected off a Detroit defenseman and past the startled Uke. It was one of the most disheartening losses of Sawchuk's career.

The 1963-64 season was notable in another respect. It marked the last time an NHL goalie (Boston's Eddie Johnston) played every minute of every game. The two-goalie system, brought on by injuries, mental exhaustion, and a changing style of play, was now the norm. Sawchuk shared duties that season with Roger Crozier, a twenty-year-old rookie whose acrobatic style reminded some of the young Terry Sawchuk.

## Winters of Discontent

Looking to protect their prized prospect, the Wings exposed the old Terry Sawchuk to the draft, assuming that nobody would want him because of his age. They were wrong. Toronto claimed The Uke.

In Toronto, Sawchuk shared the job with another old warhorse, veteran Johnny Bower. Together they allowed the fewest goals in the league in 1964-65. But they refused to accept the Vezina Trophy unless both of their names were inscribed on it. More important, at least as far as Sawchuk was concerned, was that both goalies received the cash award that accompanied the prize.

His moodiness had long been an integral part of his persona. His best friend, defenseman Marcel Pronovost, played with him in Detroit and Toronto. "You had to understand him. I roomed with Ukey for years. When we got up in the morning I would say hello. If he answered, we'd talk the rest of the day. If he didn't answer, I just kept quiet."

He continued to go his own way, unaffected by how outsiders viewed him. He liked to drink, gamble, and chase women, and didn't give a damn who knew it. He had no patience for those who were not part of his troubled inner world.

"My father was Terry's age and grew up in Winnipeg," recounted Dan Diamond, a publishing consultant in Toronto. "Once in 1961, when I was seven years old, the Leafs and Wings were playing an exhibition in Winnipeg and he took me to the game.

"We went down to the locker room to catch a glimpse of the players. There probably were about thirty people milling around. All of a sudden the door bursts open and the first one out is Sawchuk. He pushes me in the chest and I hear the first words I ever heard an NHLer utter. 'Where's the broads?' he roars. And then he just blew past all of us."

Diamond's experience was not a solitary one. Reporter Jack Berry remembered covering the Wings after a playoff loss in Toronto. "These parents sent their son up to Terry after the game," said Berry. "Sawchuk wasn't interested. He told the kid, 'Fuck off, you little bastard.'"

"Some summers my dad sold cars," said Jerry Sawchuk. "Needless to say, he didn't have the temperament for it."

Sawchuk played three seasons with the Leafs. His final one, 1966-67, may have been his finest as a pro. Certainly it was his most satisfying. In addition to recording his 100th regular-season shutout, he was brilliant in the playoffs. Despite suffering from an injured shoulder, he relieved Bower in the fourth game of the semifinals against Chicago. He stopped all 37 shots sent his way, including

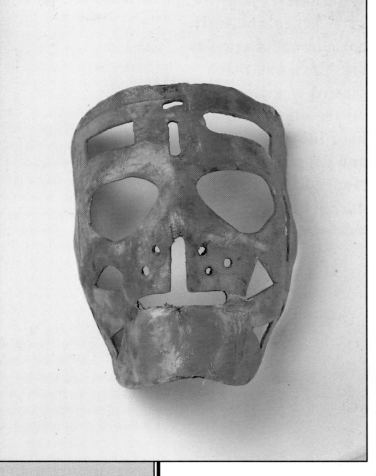

Lefty Wilson constructed Sawchuk's first mask in 1962, using three thins sheets of plexiglass. The Detroit trainer later sold versions of the mask to other goalies for $35 apiece.

Whatever happened, the entire episode was tragic and senseless, one that seemed of a piece with all the other grief and hard luck the moody and depressive goaltender had suffered during his life.

a slap shot from Bobby Hull that ripped like a bullet into his sore shoulder and floored him.

"Are you all right?" Toronto's trainer anxiously asked.

The thirty-seven-year-old Uke glared back at him. "I stopped the puck, didn't I?" he snapped.

The Leafs, who had been criticized as being too old and too slow, beat Chicago. Then they went on to topple the Canadiens for the Stanley Cup. In the Cup clincher, Sawchuk had 41 saves in a suffocating win that wasn't decided until the final minute.

Afterward, the Leafs' locker room was alive with jubilant players and club personnel slapping each other on the back and guzzling champagne. Meanwhile, observed one reporter, the two battered goalies "sat in a corner by themselves, dragging deeply on cigarettes and grappling silently with the frayed nerves and many physical ailments that are an inescapable part of life for aging men."

After the crowd had thinned out, Sawchuk finally lifted his aching body off the bench. On the way to the shower he paused to tell a reporter, "That's the way I'd like to go out. In style."

Although Sawchuk was past his prime and would have liked to retire, he felt trapped. He had a wife and seven children to care for and no other marketable skills. "I remember we were so scared one year when he had a back operation," said Pat Milford. "What would he do? What *could* he do? All he had was hockey."

The Leafs exposed their Cup-winning goalie to the expansion draft, as the Original Six doubled in size to 12 teams for the 1967-68 season. The Los Angeles Kings paid The Uke $40,000 to tend goal, which to the weary warrior was 40,000 good reasons to keep tugging on the pads. The Kings finished second, thanks in part to his 3.07 average in 36 games.

After the season he was traded to Detroit for Jimmy Peters Jr., a rangy center whose father had played with Sawchuk twenty long years earlier. Now in his third tour of duty with the Red Wings, he compiled a commendable 2.62 average in 13 games as a back-up to Roy Edwards and Roger Crozier.

The pressures of Sawchuk's chosen profession put a strain on his marriage. He and Pat were divorced in 1969, the year he was traded to the New York Rangers. This was a final, lost season, in more ways than one. Now forty years old, he played only sparingly in New York, though in eight games he did manage to post one more shutout. Counting playoffs, it was the 115th of his career—a staggering number that grows more imposing with each passing season.

He shared a rented house on Long Island with Ron Stewart, a teammate who, like Sawchuk, was divorced and considered a loner. On the evening of April 29, 1970, the two argued outdoors over who was going to clean the place before both left for the summer. It was a silly argument, one fueled by several hours of drinking inside a bar. A shoving match ensued, during which Sawchuk supposedly stumbled over an overturned barbecue grill and fell awkwardly onto Stewart's knee.

The Uke suffered internal injuries—some of which, his oldest son suggests, may have been undetected from previous accidents. His injured gall bladder was removed in an operation the following day. His condition turned critical, howev-

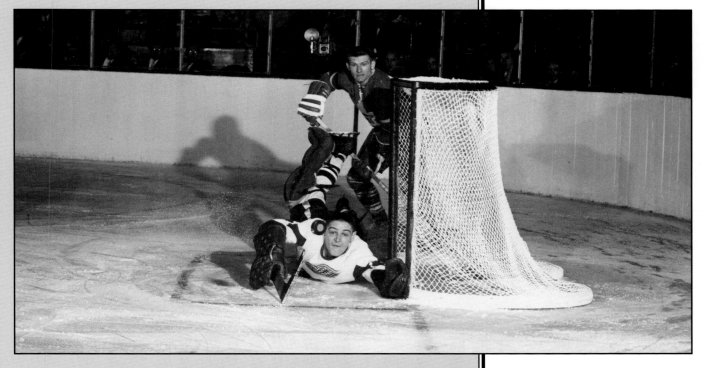

er, and he underwent a second operation to remove blood from his liver. On May 31, 1970, he died unexpectedly of a blood clot in a Manhattan hospital. There was considerable speculation that there was more to the story. But after a grand jury investigation, the local district attorney's office finally decided not to file any criminal charges.

"He fell on me," maintained the remorseful Stewart, who was absolved of any blame in the incident. "But through his career, Terry took much worse falls on the ice and he always bounced back. It doesn't make sense. It's all like a bad dream when I look back now."

Whatever happened, the entire episode was tragic and senseless, one that seemed of a piece with all the other grief and hard luck the moody and depressive goaltender had suffered during his life.

Sawchuk was buried at Mount Hope Cemetery in Pontiac. The Hockey Hall of Fame waived its usual five-year wait for candidates and inducted him the following year. His exhibit, filled with pads, masks, and other memorabilia of his hard and dangerous craft, remains one of the museum's most popular.

The Uke was not a sentimental man and he didn't care to be fussed over, so it's hard to say what he would have made of all the commotion surrounding the retiring of his jersey. It's harmless to imagine that maybe in some frozen, far-off stretch of the hereafter, he and his brother Mike took a break from a game of river hockey and smiled down on the proceedings.

What *is* certain is that when the red-and-white banner bearing The Uke's single digit was hoisted heavenward at The Joe, it finally made official what most hockey people have thought all along. That for all of his demons, Terry Sawchuk was, and always will be, number one.

Sawchuk played more games and more seasons, and had more shutouts, than any other goalie in history.

# CHAPTER SIX

By the early 1960s Gordie Howe was universally recognized as the finest player in NHL history. "Sincerely, I have never seen a greater hockey player," admitted Rocket Richard, who retired in 1960. "I mean a more complete player. Gordie Howe does everything and does it well." That opinion was echoed by stars like Jean Beliveau and Bobby Hull. "I wish I was half the player Gordie was," said Hull.

# The Heyday of Mr. Hockey

## 1960–1971

Although Howe would never play on another Stanley Cup winner after 1955, when he had just turned twenty-seven, the numbers he continued to compile over the next 15 seasons as a Red Wing would elevate him to a plane higher than legend. He broke, then embellished, dozens of records, including those for most goals, assists, and points in a career.

Nearly all of his production occurred during the days of Original Six competition, a golden era of goaltending and at a time when the hallmark of a scorer was a 20-goal season. Howe not only reached that level twenty-two consecutive years, he also finished in the league's top five scorers a stunning 20 straight seasons, a period in which he *averaged* 35 goals per campaign.

Still battling at age forty, Gordie Howe challenges Toronto rookie defenseman Pat Quinn in a 1968 game at Maple Leaf Gardens.

Gordie Howe's dry humor was in evidence during the Wings' traditional New Year's Eve game at Olympia in 1961. As Howe lined up to take a penalty shot against old fishing buddy Johnny Bower of Toronto, Leafs defenseman Carl Brewer hovered around the redline, doing his best to distract him. "Gordie!" he yelled. "Your shoelace is untied!" Seconds later, after he had slammed the puck past Bower, Howe skated past Brewer. "Guess I can tie my skates now," he said.

"When I first played for Chicago," said Metro Prystai, "everybody was always talking about Howe, Howe, Howe, and I'd wonder why. But when I went to Detroit and played with him and saw what he did game after game after game, then you wondered whether the guy was human. He killed penalties and was a threat out on the ice all the time and scored 40-45 goals, when there were only half a dozen guys who scored more than 25 a season."

Howe's year-in, year-out reliability, coupled to his durability, gave him an aura of invincibility. Unlike the man who would one day break his records, Wayne Gretzky, he didn't require a bodyguard. He was his own enforcer. He possessed the most educated elbows in the league and an elephantlike memory for remembering those who had wronged him. Sooner or later, he would extract retribution, and it was a good bet that neither the offending party nor the game officials would see what had happened.

Howe once recalled how he had handled a player who liked to use his stick a bit too spiritedly. "He used to spike me in the back of the legs with his stick. And I'd be bleeding. So I told him one night that if he touched me again he'd be very sorry, and he laughed at me. We went down the ice, and I flipped the puck over to Lindsay, who was going to the net all alone." With everybody's eyes on Lindsay, Howe suddenly turned around and punched his antagonist in the face. "Broke his cheekbone," he remembered. "A promise kept."

During his career Howe played with broken ribs, a fractured left wrist (the result of a vicious slash), and a broken collarbone that had been misdiagnosed as a bad sprain. He took 500 stitches in his face and had his nose broken 14 times. Once he stopped a Bobby Hull slapshot with his skate. "Cut my skate off, please!" he screamed at trainer Joe Alcott. "My toe's broken."

"It's a long way from your heart," said Alcott, referring to the hockey player's universal creed of playing through pain. The grimacing superstar wasn't in the mood to argue. "My fist is a foot from your damn nose if you don't start cutting," he warned. A short while later he limped back into the lineup.

Howe was playing with injured ribs the night of his most famous altercation, the one that cemented his reputation as some kind of superman. On February 1, 1959, he took apart Rangers defenseman Lou Fontinato in the climax of a feud that had been brewing for some time.

At 6-foot-1 and 195 pounds, Fontinato was a well-built enforcer with a reputation for mayhem. A few years earlier he had become the first NHLer to spend more than 200 minutes in the penalty box. During the 1958-59 season *Look* magazine helped build Fontinato's image as the toughest man in hockey with a six-page pictorial that showed him flexing his muscles and hammering opponents.

There had been years of mutual hostility between Howe and Fontinato. "Whenever I went on the ice against the Rangers, the coach sent Fontinato out," said Howe. "The idea was to work on me and distract me. Once, it cost me because I forgot a valuable bit of advice Ted Lindsay gave me. He said don't ever drop your stick until the other man does. So we get into one game and Louie says, 'You want to drop your stick?' and I said, 'Hell, yes!' and I threw it to the ice, and the guy hit me right over the head—on my forehead where there's no hair—about six stitches worth. He nailed me, and I stood there laughing over my stupidity, and Lindsay just shook his head.

"Another time I was leaning way over trying to hook the puck to Alex Delvecchio, and when Fontinato saw that, he came back with the hand holding his stick and split my lip and loosened a tooth. We sat in the penalty box and he says, 'What's the matter with your lip, Gordie?'—you know the whiny way he talks sometimes. I vowed it wouldn't happen to me again.

"Damned if I didn't find myself in the same position in our next game. When he went to hit me, I raised my stick and cross-checked him and damned near cut his ear off. Tit for tat. When he came back to the bench from the dressing room, he was wearing a bandage turban, real funny looking. The crowd threw beer and everything on me.

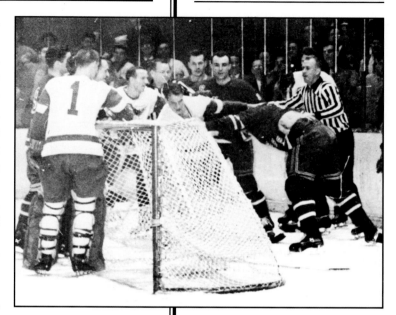

Any compilation of Gordie's greatest hits would have to include this 1959 demolition of Rangers strongman Lou Fontinato.

It was Hank Bassen's bad luck that he had to compete with iron men Terry Sawchuk and Roger Crozier during his six seasons with Detroit. Bassen, pictured with Howie Young and Alex Delvecchio, was obtained from Chicago in 1960. He split duties with Sawchuk his first season, posting a decent 2.89 average in 35 games. He only played 64 more games after that, however, before concluding his NHL career in 1967-68 with Pittsburgh.

Bruce Norris, owner of the Wings from 1955 to 1982, was a former collegiate player who occasionally liked to practice his Ivy League moves on his employees. Here Hank Bassen is getting ready to squeeze the pillows on his boss's shot during a post-practice session at Olympia in 1961.

"So that was the situation between us when we went into New York to play the Rangers again." That evening at Madison Square Garden, Fontinato took a break from reading his clippings to charge into a fracas involving Red Kelly and Eddie Shack behind the Rangers' net. Howe, who had intervened on Kelly's behalf, noticed the blur rushing towards him, recognized it as Fontinato, and ducked a punch aimed at his head. Then, as Howe later described it, "that honker of his was right there, and I drilled it. That first punch was what did it. It broke his nose a little bit."

Observers recalled Howe grabbing Fontinato's jersey with his left hand, then using his right hand to deliver a stream of vicious uppercuts—"whop, whop, whop, just like someone chopping wood," said one player in *Life* magazine, which devoted three pages to the incident. Millions of people across the country were treated to photos of the humbled Fontinato swathed with bandages. In as violent a half-minute as ever seen inside a prize ring, Howe had broken Fontinato's nose, dislocated his jaw, and destroyed his ego and reputation.

Howe's demolition of the NHL's top enforcer was all in a night's work for someone who clearly was in a league all by himself. "There are only four teams in the league," a rival player said at the time. "Montreal, Toronto, Chicago, and Howe."

The Red Wings made a surprise trip to the finals in 1961. Behind Gordie's 72 points and Norm Ullman's 70, the team survived a lackluster second half that saw it win only 10 times in 35 outings to finish fourth. After losing to a strong Toronto team, 3-2, in double overtime in the opener of the semifinals, Detroit seemed destined to be swept. But the Wings stunned the experts by taking the next four games by scores of 4-2, 2-0, 4-1, and 3-2. This put them in the championship round with the equally surprising Blackhawks, who had ended Montreal's five-year Stanley Cup reign.

This final was the first ever to feature third- and fourth-place finishers. Chicago, owned by Jim Norris Jr. and rebuilt into a contender by general manager Tommy Ivan, had another Detroit connection guarding the net. Glenn Hall, the man Jack Adams had blamed for the Wings' postseason loss four years earlier, was steady against his old teammates. Meanwhile, high-flying offensive talents like Bobby Hull, Stan Mikita, and Kenny Wharram kept the heat on the Wings' beleaguered goaltending duo of Terry Sawchuk and Hank Bassen, who had split chores during the season.

After rookie Bruce MacGregor's goal lifted Detroit to a 2-1 victory that squared the series at two games apiece, Chicago erupted for six goals in the fifth game and five more in the sixth to capture the Cup. It would turn out to be the only championship not won by either Detroit, Montreal, or Toronto during the entire six-team era.

## The Heyday of Mr. Hockey

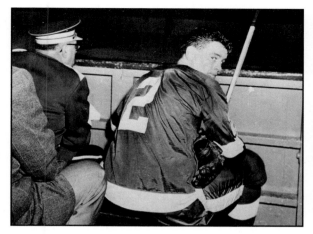

The Wings fell to fifth the next season, missing the postseason despite the addition of blueliner Bill Gadsby, acquired from the Rangers for minor leaguer Leslie Hunt. The fifteen-year veteran with the comfortably crumpled face was a character guy, someone who had beaten polio early in his NHL career and would later throw an old demon, alcoholism, to the mat. He confessed to being "happy to be back in a real hockey city. In New York you can walk down Fifth Avenue and nobody knows or cares who you are. In places like Chicago and Detroit, people have a feeling for their team."

Another character guy, one who was slowly emerging from Howe's Everest-like shadow, was Alex Delvecchio, a smooth and dependable operative and a fixture on the league's top-ten scoring list. Delvecchio, in the midst of an iron-man streak that would see him play a club-record 548 games in a row, took over the captaincy at the beginning of the 1962-63 season and would wear the large "C" on his sweater for the next dozen years.

Delvecchio's understated but consistently excellent career deserves a moment of reflection. During his 24 seasons in Detroit (an NHL tour of duty surpassed only by Howe), he would amass 456 goals and 1,281 points. Yet, because of the presence of his more famous and prolific linemate, he never once led the team in scoring or outright in goals scored (though he did tie Norm Ullman with 31 markers in 1965-66). Amazingly, despite his prowess as a playmaker, he only topped the team in assists on three occasions. He also was an All-Star selection only twice, each time picked for the second team. It would seem that he often got overlooked, even by his contemporaries. Nonetheless, the gentlemanly center was an overwhelming choice for the Hockey Hall of Fame when he became eligible.

Howie Young wasn't a character player, merely a character. The cocky, short-fused defenseman was a superb skater, though his erratic behavior while playing for Hershey in the American Hockey League turned many people off. At the time Detroit dealt for him he had already racked up 108 penalty minutes in just 29 games and had scored on his own goaltender. In his spare time Young was a cowboy, a bit actor (he worked with Frank Sinatra in *None But*

**B**ad boy Howie Young in two familiar poses: in a fight and inside the penalty box. In 1963 he went to Chicago in a deal that netted the Wings Roger Crozier, but three years later he returned for a second tour of duty.

**S**everal weary Wings rest between periods in a game played during the 1961-62 season, a year in which Detroit finished fifth and out of the money. From left: Norm Ullman, Bob Dillabough, Alex Delvecchio, Gordie Howe, and Warren Godfrey.

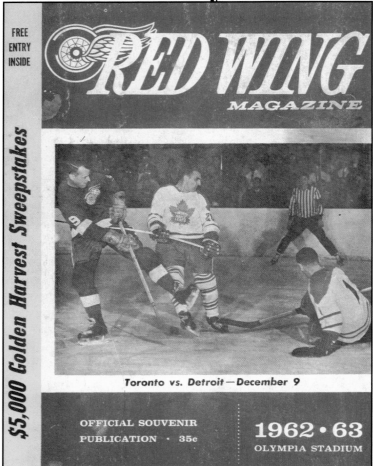

$5,000 Golden Harvest Sweepstakes

Toronto vs. Detroit—December 9

OFFICIAL SOUVENIR PUBLICATION · 35¢

1962 · 63
OLYMPIA STADIUM

**I**n 1962-63 Howe had 86 points to win his sixth, and last, Art Ross and Hart trophies. His 38 goals also gave him 540 for his career, just four shy of Rocket Richard's record. "I'd like to be half as good as Gordie," said Chicago superstar Bobby Hull.

*the Brave*), a movie stuntman, and a lush. He liked to hang out with cops and assorted low-lifes, a combination that guaranteed an unusually high number of appearances—social and otherwise—in precinct stations. On one occasion he left the saloon with a milkman. When his new friend failed to sober up in time to go to work, Young offered to take over his route. Losing the list of customers provided him, Young improvised by placing a bottle of milk on the doorstep of every house he drove past, taking care to ring the doorbell to announce the delivery. It wasn't long before the police showed up and placed him the municipal version of the penalty box.

Young's exploits could fill a book—and for a time they did, right under the category of penalty minutes in the NHL's media guide. During the 1962-63 season, his third with the Wings, the twenty-five-year-old wild-man accumulated a staggering 273 penalty minutes, shattering Lou Fontinato's seven-year-old mark of 202. The record fell in a game against the Canadiens on February 17, 1963, when a high-sticking incident led to Young being assessed a major, minor, misconduct, and game misconduct—a total of 27 minutes. The league suspended him for three games, but he returned in plenty of time to join in on the fun as the Wings made another unexpected run at the Stanley Cup.

That year Young's roommate on the road, Howe, took his sixth and last scoring championship with 86 points. He also earned his sixth and final Hart Trophy as league MVP. Parker MacDonald, a left winger acquired three years earlier from New York, had the best season of his fourteen-year NHL career,

Terry Sawchuk began wearing a mask with the start of the 1962-63 campaign. The face protection restored his confidence and resulted in a 2.48 average, his best in six years. Unfortunately, there still was no way to protect against a shot in the back from Toronto's Eddie Shack (left). In the 1963 Cup finals, Shack and company beat the Wings in five games.

Howe, who led all playoff scorers with 16 points, shares a toast with Toronto coach Punch Imlach on April 18, 1963, shortly after the Leafs had defeated Detroit, 3-1, to wrap up the Stanley Cup.

finding the net 33 times and adding 28 assists. Norm Ullman, developing into one of the game's finest snipers, had 26 goals. Delvecchio had 24. Bolstering the resurgent offense was Doug Barkley, a tall and tough defenseman picked up from the Chicago organization. A banger on the blueline, Barkley also was adept at carrying and firing the puck. He scored 27 points, just one less than Gadsby among Detroit's defensemen. The following year he would top all NHL backliners with 11 goals.

Detroit finished fourth, but only five points behind first-place Toronto, in the tightest race in NHL history. The Blackhawks, big favorites to oust the Wings in the first round of playoff action, put five pucks past Sawchuk in each of the first two games. But Detroit stormed back to sweep the next four games, bombing Glenn Hall for a total of 19 goals. This qualified the Red Wings for the finals against Toronto.

The tone of the series was set in the first minute and eight seconds of game one, when Toronto's Dick Duff scored twice on Sawchuk. The Leafs won the opener, 4-2, then followed up with another 4-2 victory. The Wings claimed their only win on Alex Faulkner's second-period goal in game three, but the tight-checking Leafs returned from the 3-2 loss to hammer out 4-2 and 3-1 decisions in the next two games to win the championship.

The loss to Toronto in the '63 finals wasn't nearly as painful as the one in the next year's would be. Once again the Wings finished fourth, and again they upset the high-scoring Blackhawks—this time battling back to win games six and seven—to earn a rematch in the finals against the Maple Leafs. While the league's top goal scorer, Bobby Hull, was limited to only two goals, Ullman had 13 points against Chicago, including a pair of hat tricks. They were the first by a Detroit postseason performer since Howe lit the lamp three times against Montreal in the 1955 finals.

Although Ullman captured headlines with his effort against the Hawks, Howe remained the year's top story, even as the Wings prepared to meet the

**N**umber 545! The crowd explodes at Olympia on November 10, 1963, as Howe finally breaks Richard's record. The man of the hour waited out the stoppage of play with Terry Sawchuk, then playfully plucked the hair of Billy McNeill, whose assist would turn out to be the last of his six-year NHL career. Almost lost in all of the commotion was that the 3-0 blanking of Montreal was the 94th shutout of Sawchuk's career, tying George Hainsworth's record.

two-time defending Cup champion Leafs. He had started his 18th NHL season with 540 lifetime goals, needing just five more to break Rocket Richard's league record of 544. He tied the mark on October 27, 1963, at Olympia, tallying on the power play against the Canadiens' Gump Worsley. Then came two long weeks of trying to pot the record-breaker. The team fell into a slump as Howe's teammates concentrated harder on setting him up than on the little things that go into winning a game. As Howe and the Wings struggled, the air leaked out of the balloons that had been stored at Olympia in anticipation of the historic event.

Finally, on November 10, 1963, he did it. Appropriately, the historic goal came against Richard's old team. Late in the second period, with Montreal on the power play, Howe, Gadsby, and Billy McNeill suddenly broke out of their own zone. McNeill flew up the right side, cut over to the middle as he crossed the Canadiens' blueline, then slid the puck to Howe, who let go a wrist shot from the top of the right face-off circle. Charlie Hodge, in net for the injured Worsley, dove to his left a fraction of a second too late. At 15:06, the puck zipped past into the short side of the net, touching off a prolonged celebration at the old red barn.

Among the gifts Howe received in recognition of his 545th goal was an oil painting presented on behalf of the Canadiens by Jean Beliveau. Montreal's captain, a good friend off the ice, confessed that he was glad to see Howe finally score. "I've been carrying this around for days," he said.

All in the family. The line of Mark, Gordie, and Marty Howe in January 1964.

"There was a standing ovation for about 20 or 25 minutes," recalled his son Mark, who was then eight years old. "I've seen my dad get many ovations but nothing close to that. I remember sitting in the crowd. People were cheering so loud that when you yelled, you couldn't hear it in your own ears. It was incredible."

With the pressure off, the Wings slowly got back on track. After scoring a paltry 74 goals in their first 33 games, they averaged four goals a game the rest of the way. They peaked at the right time, blasting the powerful second-place Blackhawks 7-2 and 4-2 to cap a comeback in the semifinals.

Some of the octane was missing against Toronto, but not the thrills. In the opener in Toronto, penalty killer Bob Pulford swiped an errant pass and broke in alone on Sawchuk, scoring the game-winning goal with just two seconds left on the clock. The Wings could have been demoralized beyond repair by the 3-2 loss. Instead, they countered with a 4-3 victory, Larry Jeffrey scoring the winner at 7:52 of the first extra session.

The series moved to Olympia, where the Wings blew a three-goal lead before Delvecchio's tap-in with 17 seconds remaining produced another thrilling 4-3 win. Toronto knotted what was turning into a classic series with a 4-2 win in game four, but Detroit regained the advantage with a 2-1 verdict at Maple Leaf Gardens. This put the Wings just one victory away from their first Stanley Cup in nine years.

The game played April 23, 1964 at Olympia has become an integral part of hockey lore. The score was tied at three each late in the third stanza when

135

The arrow points to Bobby Baun, the hobbled Toronto defenseman who has just launched a routine shot towards the Detroit net from near the blue-line. Somehow, the puck found its way through a tangle of defenders and past Terry Sawchuk to hand Toronto a dramatic 3-2 overtime win in the sixth game of the 1964 Cup finals. "Baun hit my stick," Bill Gadsby said later. "If I hadn't put my stick up it would have hit me in the face. It might have been better."

On March 29, 1964, Bob Champoux became a footnote to Wings history, coming out of the stands at Chicago Stadium to replace an injured Terry Sawchuk in the second game of the semifinals against the powerful Blackhawks. It was the first NHL game for the twenty-one-year-old goalie, who had just completed his first pro season with Cincinnati in the Central Hockey League.

Champoux allowed four goals, but his teammates scored five to win and knot the series at a game apiece. Sawchuk came back to play the rest of the series, which the Wings won in seven games. Champoux drifted back into obscurity, finally re-emerging nine years later to play briefly for the California Golden Seals.

Leafs defenseman Bob Baun took a slapshot off his skate and was taken by stretcher to the locker room. Despite the pain, Baun insisted on having the trainer tightly wrap what was later diagnosed as a broken ankle. At 1:43 of the first overtime period, the hobbled defenseman shoveled the puck from just inside the blueline towards the Wings' goal. The harmless looking shot turned deadly, however, bouncing off Bill Gadsby and finding its way past Doug Barkley and Sawchuk into the net for a dramatic 4-3 Toronto victory. Detroit fans, primed for a celebration to equal the one that had accompanied Howe's milestone goal six months earlier, instead filed out of Olympia in stunned silence. The Wings resembled the few stray balloons still left in the rafters: deflated. Two days later they lost the decisive seventh game at Maple Leaf Gardens, the Leafs opening up a quick 1-0 lead and then scoring three times in the third period to salt the game away.

Sid Abel had taken his team to the finals three times in four years, largely because of his dependence on veterans. In the fall of 1964 he outdid himself, convincing an old favorite to shake off four years of accumulated rust and come out of retirement. Ted Lindsay, then thirty-nine years old and away from the NHL wars since the spring of 1960, impressed Abel with his conditioning during an exhibition game that reunited the original members of the Production Line. Why not give the NHL another try? suggested Abel.

"I thought he was kidding," recalled Lindsay, who took Abel up on his offer. "The only favor I asked was to let me skate the eight o'clock shift every morning in training camp because I still had to go to work to make a living. That way I could go to lunch with customers and make sales calls in the afternoon."

## The Heyday of Mr. Hockey

On opening night against Toronto, Lindsay—now sporting number 15 on his sweater—skated out to a deafening standing ovation from Detroit fans, then showed that he hadn't lost any of his desire to screw opponents' heads into the ice. He punched out the Leafs' Tim Horton and received a ten-minute misconduct, part of a season total of 173 penalty minutes. That season he played on a line with Bruce MacGregor and Pit Martin, bagging 14 goals and 14 assists in his swan song as a Red Wing.

That same year Roger Crozier, seventeen years Lindsay's junior, took over netminding duties after Sawchuk was claimed by the Leafs in the intra-league draft. The little goalie, all of 5-foot-8 and 140 pounds, had been impressive in the 15 games he had played the previous season. The wiry goalie excited onlookers with his acrobatic saves and gallant style, sliding out farther than any other goaltender to meet an onrushing skater, braving slap shots with his bare face and quicksilver reflexes. In 1964-65, Crozier joined Sawchuk and Glenn Hall as Detroit goalies who have been named the NHL's top rookie. Crozier earned the Calder Trophy on the basis of his six shutouts and a 2.42 goals-against average, both league bests. He also became the last goalie to appear in all 70 games, as every other team had switched to a two-goalie rotation. Crozier lost the Vezina Trophy on the last night of the season to the Toronto tandem of Sawchuk and Johnny Bower. A superstitious sort, Crozier blamed it on somebody swiping his lucky black fedora inside a Toronto

I n the fall of 1964, four years after retiring from the Blackhawks, thirty-nine-year-old Ted Lindsay suited up again for the Red Wings. His comeback year included 14 goals, 173 penalty minutes, numerous scuffles, and a new jersey number, 15. "It's certainly not the money," he said of his motivation. "I'm well off. I just had this desire to wind up my career with the Red Wings."

A fter playing every game of the schedule for seven consecutive seasons, Alex Delvecchio saw his streak end during the 1964-65 season. Undeterred by a broken jaw, he missed just two games while finishing with 25 goals and 67 points, good for fifth place on the scoring list.

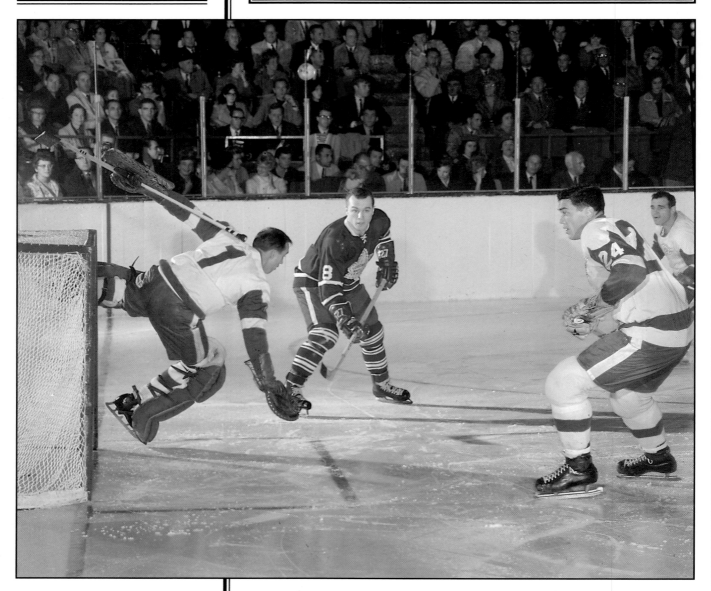

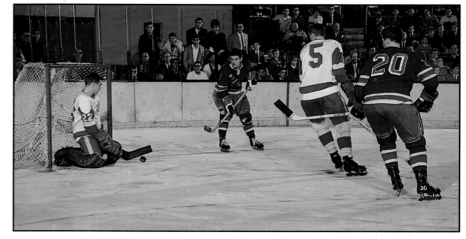

**R**oger Crozier wore number 22 in 1963-64 (right), his first season with Detroit. The following year the nimble netminder was number one in every way, the Wings having unexpectedly lost their thirty-four-year-old regular goalie, Terry Sawchuk, to Toronto in the draft. Crozier didn't disappoint, winning the Calder Trophy while leading all goalies with a 2.42 average and six shutouts.

restaurant. To make matters worse, the lack of a hat caused the prematurely balding goalie to catch a head cold.

Lindsay and Crozier were only part of the story as Detroit zoomed past Montreal and Chicago with 25 wins in its last 39 games. On March 9, 1965, the streaking Wings finally overhauled Chicago for the top spot with a 3-2 win over the Canadiens at Olympia, as Delvecchio scored the winner with just five seconds left to play. Sixteen days later, they clinched their first Prince of Wales Trophy in eight years with a 7-4 drubbing of the Rangers. The Wings, with a final record of 40-23-7, four points better than the Canadiens, had three of the league's top scorers. Norm Ullman, with 15 goals in his last 13 games, overtook perennial goal-scor-

ing champ Bobby Hull and finished with a league-high 42. His 41 assists gave him 83 points, four behind Chicago's Stan Mikita. Howe finished third with 76 points and Delvecchio placed fifth with 67. Ullman and Crozier were named to the first All-Star team, while Gadsby and Howe were selected for the second squad.

The red-hot Wings opened Stanley Cup play with a pair of wins over Chicago at Olympia, 4-3 and 6-3. Back in the Windy City, the Hawks responded with 5-2 and 2-1 victories to draw even. In game five, Ullman erased a 2-1 Chicago lead by scoring twice within five seconds, an achievement still listed in the NHL official guide as the fastest two goals in Stanley Cup history.

"Both were fairly long shots," Ullman said of his goals, scored at 17:30 and 17:35 of the second period. "I used the defenseman as a screen. On the first one, I cut across, shot it. Lo and behold, I got it. The second one was off the faceoff. [Chicago's Eric] Nesterenko picked it up. I intercepted it. The defenseman came at me. I used him as a screen. It went in." Ullman completed his third playoff hat trick against the Hawks in two Aprils by snapping an insurance goal past Glenn Hall with two minutes left in the third period. The 4-2 win put Detroit just one victory shy of reaching the finals. But Chicago pasted the Wings 4-0 on its home ice, then returned to Olympia to end the series with a 4-2 victory.

The old man of the team, Lindsay, had enjoyed a good series against Chicago, scoring three times. His plans for returning for another season at age forty were sabotaged, however, by Toronto's front office, which wouldn't pass on him in the waiver draft. "I wasn't going to play in Toronto," said Lindsay, "so I just quit, this time for good."

Abel and his Toronto counterpart, Punch Imlach, pulled off one of the biggest trades in years. Abel shipped Marcel Pronovost, Larry Jeffrey, center Ed Joyal, and two other players to the Leafs for veteran right wing Andy Bathgate, center Billy Harris, and an unproven left winger named Gary Jarrett.

**C**elebrating the Wings' surprising first-place finish in the spring of 1965 are (from left) Ed Joyal, Norm Ullman, Paul Henderson, Alex Delvecchio, and Roger Crozier. It was the first time since 1957-58 that the club had finished higher than fourth.

Doug Barkley keeps stride with Toronto's Red Kelly, an early proponent of head protection. Barkley, destined to have his career ended by an errant blade, would have benefitted from an eyeshield, still years away from being introduced to the NHL.

Bryan "Bugsy" Watson

During the course of the 1965-66 season Abel picked up several more veterans, including forwards Ab McDonald and Dean Prentice and defensemen Bob McCord and Leo Boivin.

After battling Chicago and Toronto for the second and third spots in the standings, the Wings settled into fourth. A tragic incident probably kept the team from finishing higher than it did. On January 29, 1966, Doug Barkley's career was ended when Chicago's Doug Mohns attempted to lift his stick as he got off a shot. The blade of Mohns' stick struck Barkley in the right eye, severely tearing the retina. The Wings' superb blueliner underwent several futile operations to save his vision and never played again.

For the fourth year in a row Detroit drew Chicago as its opening-round opponent in the playoffs. Bobby Hull was the talk of the sports world, having shattered the magical 50-goal mark that season. But soon the name Bryan "Bugsy" Watson was on everybody's lips. The pesty defenseman, drafted from Chicago, was assigned by Abel to shadow Hull's every move, creating more than a few pyrotechnics during the six-game series.

"Watson, who's Watson?" snapped Chicago coach Billy Reay. "They're trying to make a national hero out of a guy who hangs all over the greatest scorer in hockey. What kind of logic is that? Who pulls them into the stadium—Bobby or this guy Watson? What makes it so great about doing nothing but hanging on a guy all night?" Although Reay was loathe to acknowledge it, Watson did do more than just frustrate Hull. Bugsy, who'd managed all of two goals in 70 regular-season games, equalled his total against Chicago.

The Blackhawks won the curtain-raiser, 2-1. The second game, played April 10 at Chicago Stadium, was the first nationally televised game ever in the United States. The Wings embarrassed the home team, 7-0, behind four power-play goals. Chicago eked out another 2-1 win in game three, but then

## The Heyday of Mr. Hockey

Semifinal action in 1966: Bruce MacGregor's shot glances off the arm of Glenn Hall as Pierre Pilote looks helplessly on. The Hawks won the game, 2-1, but lost the series.

Norm Ullman was one of the finest clutch players in club history. In the 1964 playoffs he had two hat tricks against Chicago, then added a third against the Hawks the following postseason. In 1966 he led all Stanley Cup performers in scoring with 15 points, the last Red Wing to do so.

the Wings rolled past the Hawks to win three straight and the series. Chicago's "Golden Jet," who'd found the net 54 times during the season, was limited to just two goals, both when Watson was on the bench.

"I don't think he ever got over it," Watson recently said of Hull's performance. "A few years ago I had an accident with a chain saw. I almost lost my hand. I heard that Hull said, 'How's the chain saw doing?'"

Watson's antics had gotten the Wings into the finals. They faced the first-place Canadiens, who'd finished 16 points ahead of Detroit and swept Toronto in their semifinal match. Montreal was a big favorite. The Wings, however, seemed a team of destiny. They beat the Habs in the opener, 3-2, on Paul Henderson's goal, then exploded for four third-period goals to win the second game, 5-2. It was the first time in its long and glorious history that Montreal had dropped the first two games of a playoff series at home.

The underdogs took the Detroit-bound train filled with confidence. The next two games were scheduled for Olympia. More important, Crozier—who'd once again led the loop in appearances and shutouts—was in top form. Better yet, fate seemed to be conspiring against the Canadiens. To change their luck, coach Toe Blake moved the team from the downtown Sheraton-Cadillac to a Dearborn hotel. Trouble was, a national convention for barbershop quartets was being held at the same time. "As a result," Jean Beliveau wrote in his autobiography, "harmony-heavy renditions of 'Sweet Adeline' and 'By the Light of the Silvery Moon' could be heard at all hours of the day and night. I remember Toe, running up and down the halls in his pajamas, trying to get the conventioneers to shut up."

Perhaps the lack of sleep took some of the edge off the Canadiens. They won game three, 4-2, then grabbed game four, 2-1, on Ralph Backstrom's goal with seven minutes left in regulation. Hank Bassen allowed both Montreal

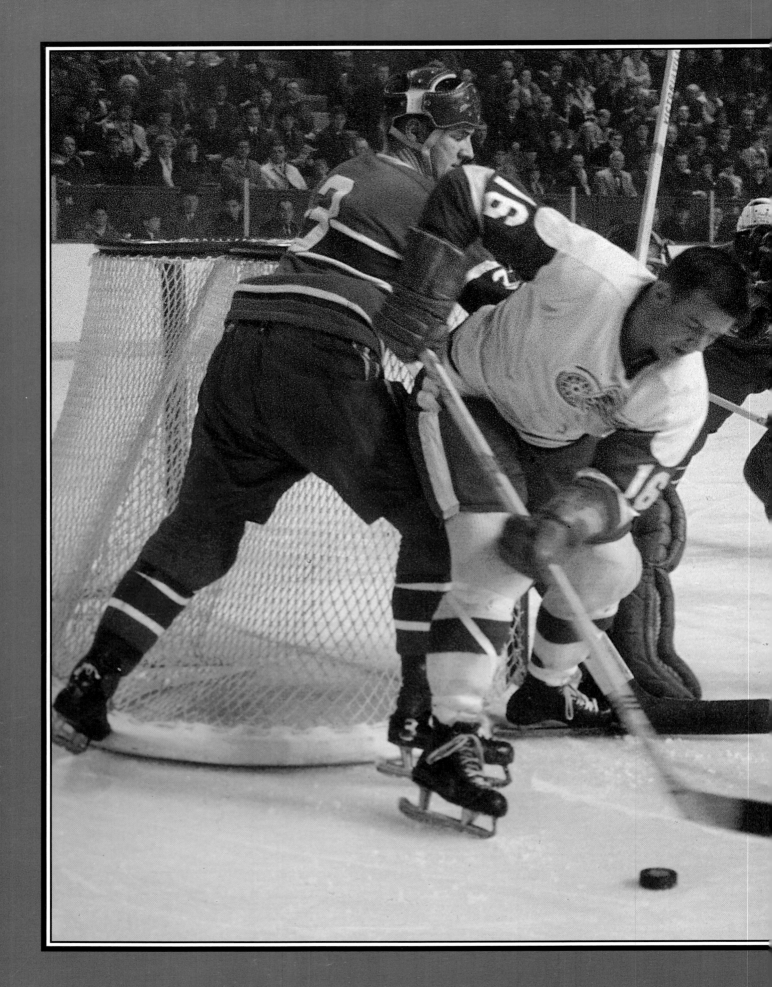

**T**he 1966 finals between Detroit and Montreal was a memorable scrap, the first to involve the two traditional rivals in a decade. The Canadiens, after losing the first two games at home, came back to sweep the next four games, the last on a controversial overtime goal.

R oger Crozier was injured in this collision with Montreal's Bob Rousseau in the fourth game of the 1966 Cup finals. The Canadiens won the Stanley Cup, but Crozier's acrobatics earned him the Conn Smythe Trophy as playoff MVP. It was the first time a player from the losing side had won the trophy.

goals, as Crozier had been forced out of action early in the first period after a goal-mouth collision with Bobby Rousseau.

Playing with a wrenched left knee, Crozier turned in a subpar performance in game five, won by the Canadiens, 5-1. Sid Abel defended his goalie, explaining that "we didn't give the little guy any protection. With his heavily taped knee, he just couldn't move out there." The series switched to Motown, where on the evening of May 5, 1966, the Red Wings hosted the last Stanley Cup final game ever played at Olympia.

It was one of the most controversial ever seen at Grand River and McGraw. Crozier surrendered first-period goals to Jean Beliveau and Leon Rochefort, but Ullman's shorthanded tally in the second frame whittled Montreal's advantage to 2-1. Then halfway through the third period, Floyd Smith scored to make it 2-2.

It remained that way through the first couple minutes of overtime, when Henri Richard steamed towards the Detroit net. Gary Bergman was in hot pursuit as Canadiens left winger Dave Balon passed the puck from the corner towards the crease. Richard, who by now had been upended by Bergman's check and was sliding towards Crozier like an out-of-control toboggan, arrived at the same time as the puck. The rubber biscuit hit Richard as both slid past Crozier and into the net for the Cup-winning goal. The Wings were livid. They maintained that Richard had shoved the puck in with his glove, arm, or elbow. "That shouldn't have been a goal," Bill Gadsby continues to argue to this day. "I forget who the referee was, but he just didn't call it. Oh, I was sick. . . ." Toe Blake, not taking any chances on referee Frank Udvari waving the disputed goal off, yelled at his players, "On the ice! Everybody on the ice!" The celebratory Canadiens took turns smooching the Stanley Cup as Detroit players and fans moaned about the injustice done them. Nobody suspected then that it would be another four decades until the Red Wings played for the championship again.

T he Wings missed the playoffs the next three seasons. Their recently concluded six-year run, which included four appearances in the finals, had been impressive, considering how the team had been disassembled by Jack Adams. But the squad had been rebuilt at the expense of player development, never one of Sid Abel's strong points. By the middle sixties other clubs had passed Detroit in the area of signing and developing young players.

The 1966-67 season saw the Wings flop into fifth place. Opponents scored 241 times, a number exceeded only by last-place Boston. Barkley and Gadsby

## The Heyday of Mr. Hockey

There wasn't much for Detroit to cheer about in 1966-67, because the Wings finished a poor fifth in the last year of the Original Six era. Detroit fans did get to witness Dean Prentice score his 250th career goal, however. The historic marker came on January 6, 1967, against Chicago's Denis DeJordy. The left wing scored 60 of an eventual 391 NHL goals during his three and a half seasons in Detroit.

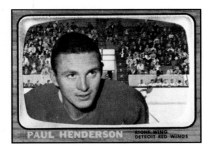

Paul Henderson contributed 22 goals to the Wings' attack in 1965-66 and 21 the following season. The right wing spent the lion's share of his eighteen-year professional career in Toronto, playing for that city's entries in both the NHL and World Hockey Association. His most famous goal was one that isn't listed in *The Hockey Register*. In 1972, he scored late in the final game to decide the bitterly contested landmark series between Russia and a group of NHL all-stars.

were sorely missed on the blueline. In desperation the club signed ancient Doug Harvey, who was attempting an NHL comeback, *a la* Ted Lindsay. The forty-two-year-old former Norris Trophy winner, 20 pounds overweight, huffed and puffed through two games before being sent back to the minors. Howe, on the other hand, kept rolling along. At thirty-nine, he popped in 25 goals and had 40 assists to finish with the fourth-best point total in the league. Ullman's 70 points placed him third.

The era of the Original Six came to an end in the fall of 1967, as the NHL started play with expansion teams in six cities: St. Louis, Los Angeles, Pittsburgh, Minnesota, Philadelphia, and Oakland. Detroit, its once-rich farm system already in disrepair, was further depleted by the draft on June 6, 1967 that helped stock the new teams. The Wings lost 20 players: goalies Don Caley and Joe Daley, and skaters Andy Bathgate, Norm Beaudin, Leo Boivin, Ray Cullen, Dwight Carruthers, Val Fonteyne, Pete Goegan, Terry Gray, Billy Har-

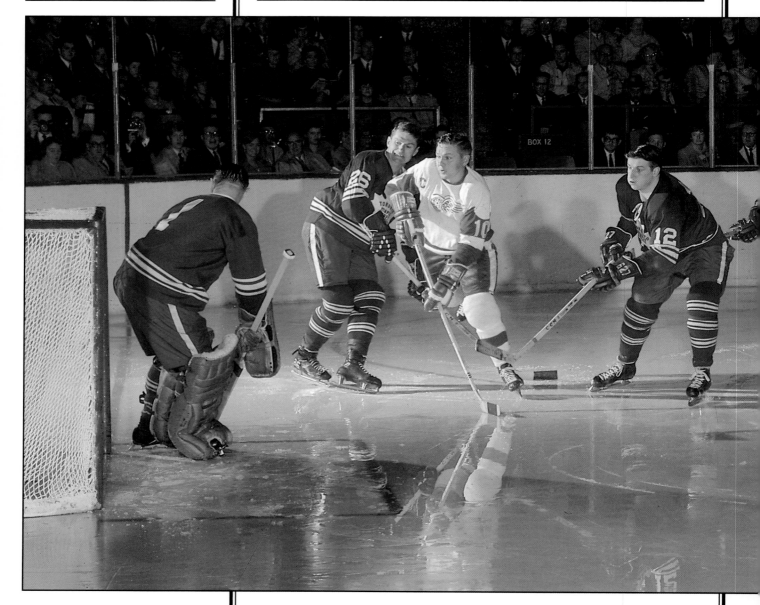

In 1967-68, his 18th season as a Wing, Alex Delvecchio finally led the team in assists. His 48 dish-offs were just one less than league-leader Phil Esposito of the Boston Bruins and helped him place eighth on the scoring list with 70 points.

ris, Brent Hughes, Real Lemieux, Parker MacDonald, Ab McDonald, Don McKenney, Andre Pronovost, Ted Taylor, Bob Wall, and Bugsy Watson. Minnesota selected the most Wings, six, while Oakland and Philadelphia chose the least, one each.

For the first time since 1937-38, the league was split into two conferences. The established clubs were put in the Eastern Division while the expansion teams were placed in the Western Division. The schedule was expanded to 74 games. This worked out to 50 games within the division and 24 outside of it. This meant the number of battles with such longtime rivals as the Canadiens and Maple Leafs had shrunk from 14 to 10 each season. Traditionalists moaned, but it wouldn't be too many more years before Original Six teams like Boston and Montreal visited Detroit just once each winter.

Detroit's first match with an expansion team was October 22, 1967, against the St. Louis Blues. The Wings won, 1-0, on Paul Henderson's third-period goal. Playing expansion teams did nothing to improve Detroit's fortunes; it finished last in the East, its 66 points surpassed by every team in the league except Oakland. Although the offense (a team-record 245 goals) was second only to Boston, the defense (a team-record 257 goals allowed) was easily the worst in the NHL. After the season Abel was relieved of his coaching duties by Bruce Norris, who gained some public relations points by bringing back an old favorite to take his place.

Bill Gadsby had retired after the 1966 Cup finals, packing it in after twenty futile years of trying to win a Stanley Cup. During this time he and his wife had carefully planned for retirement. The plans, which included a stake in a golf course in Edmonton, went *poof!* when Gadsby's partner died and the property was sold to settle the estate. A coaching position with the Edmonton Oil Kings evaporated when he and his boss had a disagreement. Then, unexpectedly, Norris offered him the Detroit head coaching job. After years of shuffling back and forth between western Canada and various NHL cities, of packing and unpacking suitcases and pulling their four daughters in and out of schools, the Gadsbys had a difficult decision to make: Stay put in Edmonton or make another move back to Detroit? After much agonizing, Gadsby decided to take Norris's offer. He was so confident of his future that he didn't even bother to get a written contract.

**B**ill Gadsby came to Detroit in 1961 and helped solidify the Wings' defense. He retired after the 1966 Stanley Cup finals, then returned to coach the Wings to a 33-31-12 record in 1968-69.

**N**earing his fortieth birthday, Gordie Howe was still dominating and intimidating.

Gadsby guided the Wings to a 33-31-12 record in 1968-69, which was an improvement over the previous two seasons but still placed the club fifth in the strong Eastern Division and out of the playoffs. A trade with Toronto during the previous season had turned out nicely, with the Maple Leafs sending Pete Stemkowski, Frank Mahovlich, and Garry Unger to Detroit in return for Floyd Smith, Norm Ullman, and Paul Henderson. In his first full season in Detroit, left winger Mahovlich—a proven scorer long known as "The Big M"—combined with Howe and Delvecchio to create a devastating triple-threat.

"I grew up in a little town in northern Ontario named Schumacher," recounted Mahovlich. "The founder of the town, Mr. Schumacher, always gave Christmas presents to all the kids who lived there and one year, I think when I was eight or nine, I got a Red Wings sweater. From that day on, until I joined the Toronto organization when I was fifteen in 1953, I was a Red Wings fan."

In 1968-69 this newest version of the Production Line was the most prolific the league had yet seen, chalking up 118 goals and a then-record 264 points between them. "Why were we so successful? We all thought the same," Mahovlich said. "We were on the same wave length. You can't explain it. You can't explain a lot of things that happen in hockey. I just know that I was fortunate to play with many great players during my career, and Alex and Gordie were two of the best."

Mahovlich tied Howe's club record of 49 goals and set a new team mark with four hat tricks, while Delvecchio's dead-on passes earned him 58 assists to go with his 25 tallies. At age forty, Howe scored more points than ever before. On March 30, 1969, he accounted for a goal in a 9-5 loss at Chicago to become the first Wing to record 100 points in a season. He finished with 44 goals and 59 assists for 103 points. Playing against expansion teams helped

down circuit managed to outscore the Wings' grey-beard. That year Boston's Phil Esposito (126 points) and Bobby Hull (107) joined Howe as the first NHL players to break the century mark in scoring.

Gadsby earned his $25,000 salary by enduring the meddling of Norris, who had grown increasingly erratic because of his drinking. One night in Pittsburgh the owner accosted his coach after the first period and demanded he quit using Dean Prentice. Gadsby was dumbfounded. At the time the veteran forward was on a scoring binge. "I don't want to see him on the ice again tonight," Norris commanded, offering no explanation.

"What's going on?" Gadsby asked Abel after Norris had left.

"I dunno," said Abel, "but you'd better do what he says."

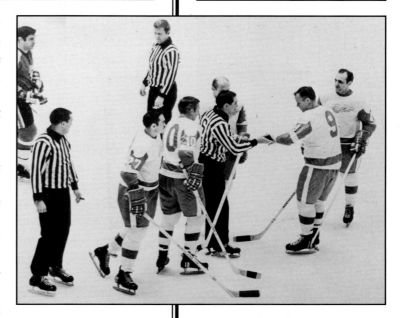

Nonetheless, Gadsby inserted Prentice into the game in the second period to kill a penalty. "Didn't you get my message?" Norris told Gadsby in the locker room between periods. "I don't want to see Prentice on the ice." Gadsby, irritated at Norris's interference, benched Prentice for the rest of the game. When Prentice asked about it on the bus, Gadsby told him it was because he wasn't hustling. "I felt terrible for a long time, lying to him," Gadsby said later. "It was degrading to have to do it, yet if I told the truth it would have gotten around that I wasn't in charge of the team, and in a sense that would have been even more degrading."

Home games at Olympia became nearly unbearable. Norris, slowly getting stewed inside his private suite, often phoned the bench in the middle of the action. "What's the matter with Bergman?" he'd demand. Or, "Why isn't Bathgate shooting more?" This impressed his cronies and satisfied his need to be a bully. Once, in exasperation, Gadsby ripped the phone right off the wall. "I couldn't be yakking with him during a game," he explained. "I had other things to think about."

The following October it was Gadsby who was abruptly disconnected. The Wings beat Toronto on opening night and followed that up with a victory in Chicago. As the unbeaten team was getting ready for a home game against Minnesota, Gadsby was called into Norris's office, where the owner sat with a martini on his desk. "Bill," he said, "I'm relieving you of your responsibilities as coach of the club."

**M**ahovlich arrived in time to celebrate Howe's 700th career goal, a milestone reached December 4, 1968 in Pittsburgh. In 1968-69 the "Big M" scored 49 times to tie Howe's team record, then added 38 more in 1969-70. He played another half-season before being dealt to Montreal.

**F**rank Mahovlich, a gifted left wing on his way to the Hall of Fame, maintained his high-scoring ways after being traded to the Wings from the Toronto Maple Leafs during the 1967-68 campaign.

**Bill Gadsby**

**Ned Harkness**

The reason why was never spelled out, although the old blueliner came to believe that Abel—afraid that his own job might be jeopardized by Gadsby's popularity and success—had helped turn Norris against him. Pickets appeared outside Olympia protesting the firing, but it was to no avail. The behind-the-scenes intrigue resulted in Abel taking over the coaching duties. Meanwhile, Gadsby discovered that he was legally obligated to swallow his bile. In a letter, Norris agreed to pay him through the end of the season. However, beneath his signature was a handwritten addendum: "If you make any derogatory remarks about the Detroit Red Wing hockey organization, your pay will cease as of that date." In order to earn his pay, Gadsby did some scouting. "Sid kept saying to me that we'd have to have lunch, talk about the firing," he recalled. "I said, 'Just give me a call.' He never called."

Gadsby stuck around town. Over the next several years he lost his life savings in a failed auto parts business, battled alcoholism, and had his battered hip replaced. Displaying the same grit that had made him a Hall-of-Fame defenseman (he was inducted in 1970, a year after Abel and Norris), he bounced back from all of these ordeals to become a successful sales rep and hockey-school instructor.

Under Abel the team participated in a wild, wooly, and farcical finish to the 1969-70 season. With two games to go, five points separated the top five teams in the Eastern Division, all of whom were competing for four playoff berths. As Detroit prepared for a final home-and-home series with the Rangers, a computer figured that there were 125 different combinations possible. The Rangers took the Olympia ice on Saturday, April 4, 1970, with the crowded Eastern Division standings looking like this:

|  | Won | Lost | Tied | Pts |
|---|---|---|---|---|
| Chicago | 43 | 22 | 9 | 95 |
| Boston | 38 | 17 | 9 | 95 |
| Detroit | 39 | 20 | 15 | 93 |
| Montreal | 38 | 20 | 16 | 92 |
| New York | 37 | 21 | 16 | 90 |
| Toronto | 29 | 32 | 13 | 71 |

The Wings clinched a playoff spot with a 6-2 victory, but Chicago and Boston also won to remain two points in front. If Detroit won on Sunday and Chicago and Boston each lost their final game, there would be a three-way tie for first. However, Chicago would be awarded the top spot based on the first tiebreaker: most victories. The Wings could still finish second, but only if they won on Sunday and Toronto upset Boston. Figuring that the Bruins were not about to lose at home against the last-place Leafs, Abel resigned himself to a third-place finish. He allowed the team to guzzle champagne on the plane ride to New York and planned on resting several of his veterans.

This was good news for the Rangers, who were still in the hunt. If they could beat Detroit and the Canadiens lost in Chicago, New York and Montreal would finish tied for the fourth and final playoff spot with identical records. The tiebreaker would be total goals scored for the season, a problem for New York since Montreal had a five-goal edge going into the last game. The Rangers' dilemma was that they not only had to beat the Wings, they had to score as many goals as possible if they were to pass the Canadiens in that department.

The packed house at Madison Square Garden, as well as a national television audience, were treated to a rousing, all-out display of offensive hockey. Rangers coach Emile Francis sent a forechecking forward into each corner and positioned his defensemen a few feet in front of the Wings' net. With some of the Wings suffering from hangovers and the rest merely going through the

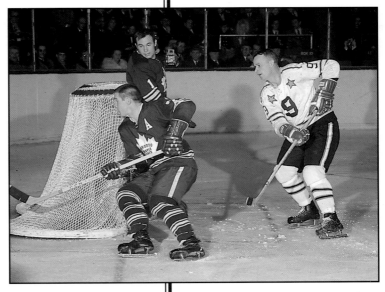

**G**ordie Howe was voted to the first All-Star team in 1968, 1969, and 1970.

motions, the Rangers spent practically the entire afternoon in the Wings' zone. Roger Crozier was bombarded with 65 shots as the Rangers built a 9-3 lead late in the third period. That still wasn't enough offense for Francis, who with 3:38 to play pulled his goalie for a sixth attacker in hopes of potting more goals. Instead, Detroit slipped a couple of pucks into the empty net, resulting in the final 9-5 score. It had been a ludicrous display, but it did the trick for New York. That evening, Montreal lost to Chicago and scored only twice in the process; thus the Rangers wound up squeezing into the playoffs by a final margin of two goals. The Wings finished third with 95 points, the most by a Detroit squad since 1954-55.

Abel caught considerable flack for the team's lack of effort in the finale. "Mathematically, I didn't think we could make second place because the odds were that Boston would beat Toronto," he explained. "Why should I tell my guys to go out and beat their heads against a wall?" Abel's rested Wings were beaten in four straight games by the Blackhawks in the opening round of the playoffs, each time by the score of 4-2. Not long afterwards, Norris booted Abel back upstairs to make room for a collegiate coaching sensation named Ned Harkness.

The forty-seven-year-old Harkness had an extremely impressive resume. In 21 seasons as head hockey coach at Rensselaer Polytechnic Institute and Cornell University he had built an outstanding 339-123-9 record. In his last season at Cornell, Harkness's squad—featuring future Montreal great Ken Dryden in goal—went unbeaten in 29 games and won the NCAA title, the third of Harkness' career. The 1970 Cornell squad remains the only major hockey team to go through an entire season undefeated. Harkness also had been a successful lacrosse coach, winning a national championship in that sport as well.

There was a sense of excitement surrounding Harkness's revolutionary hiring. After all, no rookie NHL coach had ever come directly from the col-

**G**ary Bergman (left) and Garry Unger prepare to move out of their own end in a game during the 1970-71 season.

lege ranks. But it was for that very reason that there also was a good deal of apprehension. How would professionals react to a man who had coached nothing but amateurs his entire life?

The grizzled older Wings did not respond well at all to Harkness's rah-rah collegiate style, a fact reflected in the club's poor start to the 1970-71 season. Harkness dismissed rumors that, after just four wins in the first 16 outings, his neck was already on the chopping block. "If I get fired, it'll be my pride that will suffer. I can always get another job." An interesting aspect of the new coach's personality was that, for all his Ivy League credentials, he swore like a Teamster caught in traffic. Once, as Harkness tore into the team between periods, Howe occupied himself by counting the number of times the coach used the word "fuck" or one of its many variations. He lost count after 80.

On January 2, 1971, the Wings were annihilated in Toronto by the score of 13-0. It remains the worst beating in the team's history as well as one of the most lopsided NHL defeats ever. Players presented management with a petition. Abel asked Norris, who'd been warned by Howe that the team could not win with Harkness at the helm, if he had the authority as general manager to fire the coach. When Norris said no, Abel quit, severing a thirty-three-year relationship with the club as player and executive (though he would return to the organization as a scout and a broadcaster). The power struggle resulted in Harkness taking over Abel's job. Doug Barkley, who had been serving as general manager and coach of the Wings' Fort Worth affiliate in the Central Hockey League, was brought in to coach. He inherited Harkness's dismal 12-22-4 record.

It was not a smooth transition, admitted Barkley. "The move up to the NHL at that time was the biggest mistake I ever made," he said later. "I didn't have that much experience and I was taking over a team with most of the same personnel who once were my teammates. Besides, now I was younger than a lot of the players I was coaching. They knew I lacked coaching experience and I knew it, too. Except, I wasn't willing to admit it at the time."

Harkness, similarly mule-headed about acknowledging his own deficiencies, occupied himself with dismantling the team that Abel had put together. He dispatched Frank Mahovlich to Montreal and Bruce MacGregor and Pete Stemkowski to New York. The most controversial swap occurred in February, when he traded Garry Unger and Wayne Connolly to St. Louis for Tim Ecclestone and Red Berenson. Fans in both cities were outraged. Unger was a young, flashy center who had scored 42 goals the previous season, just one less than league leader Phil Esposito. True, at the time of the trade he had but nine goals, but he was still considered by nearly everybody in town as a budding superstar and thus an untouchable. Harkness defended the transaction. "We hated to give up Unger," he said, "but in Berenson I feel we have acquired a superstar who can lead this team. . . . We owe it to our fans to improve this club, and moving Unger was one of the ways I felt I could do it." The fact that the thirty-one-year-old Berenson had once been a standout at the University of Michigan (in 1962 he had become the first player to go directly from an American college to the NHL) may have entered into the former collegiate coach's decision. That Unger was one more reminder of the previous regime undoubtedly contributed, too.

Due to Harkness's wheeling and dealing, new faces kept appearing in the Wings' dressing room. There was little cohesiveness on or off the ice. For the first time in its history the team placed seventh. To add to the embarrassment, it finished behind an expansion club, Vancouver, which had been added to the division that year. It also recorded its lowest point total since Jack Adams had worked behind the bench. This despite the fact that it played 18 more games than the 1946-47 edition, the last Detroit squad to manage as few as 55 points.

That was the year a young and galloping Gordie Howe had broken in with the Wings. Now, a full quarter-century later, he had closed out his silver-anniversary campaign with an assortment of injuries that had cost him much pain and one-fifth of the schedule. An arthritic left wrist had forced him to play practically one-handed many nights. He'd also had a severe case of "tennis elbow," missed 10 games with torn rib cartilage, and had the flu so bad that management sent him to Florida for 10 days to shake it.

Not that hockey's Methuselah was exactly skating over his beard. On the night of Saturday, April 4, 1971, a few days after celebrating his forty-third birthday, he scored a second-period goal against Chicago's Tony Esposito in a 4-1 loss at Olympia. It was his 23rd of the season—a solid number that most players half his age would be satisfied with. For that reason, and the fact that he had another season left on a $100,000-a-year contract, most speculation over his future revolved around his chances for bagging career goal number 800. With 786, he was only 14 goals short of extending his record to a magical, unattainable mark, one that he had often expressed a desire to reach. Surely he would be back.

The following night the Wings ended a dismal year with a 6-0 loss to the Rangers. As Howe sat on the team bus, waiting to be driven to the airport for the flight back to Detroit, he puffed on a cigar and talked with reporters. "Am I coming back?" he asked rhetorically. "Right now I don't honestly know. I'll be at training camp . . . and that's probably when I'll make up my mind."

The Olympia employee in charge of holding the pucks near the time clock knew better. After scoring against Chicago, Howe had quickly fished the puck out of the net and exchanged it for a new one. Nobody had noticed, but he was fulfilling a promise he had made long ago to his wife to give her the puck with which he had scored his last NHL goal. With that gesture, the heyday of Mr. Hockey in Detroit was over.

The travels of journeyman Ab McDonald embodied the growth of pro hockey in the late sixties. The tall left wing was acquired from Boston in 1965, lost to Pittsburgh in the expansion draft two years later, then reacquired in 1971.

After scoring five points in his second tour of duty in Detroit, the 36-year-old vagabond found new life in the World Hockey Association. Before quitting in 1974, he had seen the once-provincial world of the Original Six explode to 28 professional teams in two leagues.

# CHAPTER SEVEN

**T**he seventies were a dispiriting decade in Detroit. Leisure suits . . . lava lamps . . . gas lines . . . the Pacer . . . plant closings . . . stagflation . . . avocado-colored appliances. The city's four professional sports franchises, all bottom feeders in the standings and all talking of pulling up stakes for the suburbs, did little to improve the mood.

Today, Detroit's hockey fans recall the period with a visible shudder. The 1970s and early eighties were the time of the dead Wings, when years of darkness with Harkness gave way to a long, deep freeze with the likes of Larry Lozinski, Barry Salo-

# Dead Wings

## 1971–1986

vaara, and Fern LeBlanc doing their best to imitate Howe, Kelly, and Sawchuk. These players, along with a dizzying succession of coaches and general managers, passed through town so quickly it was rumored that the entrances to the Wings' front office and locker room had been fitted with turnstiles.

Between 1970 and 1986, a period of 16 seasons, the Wings dressed some of the worst squads ever to represent the franchise and made the playoffs only three times. Sixteen different men coached the team, some more than once, and six worked as general managers. Nineteen players served as captain of this rudderless ship, including center Red Berenson, who came to town in early 1971.

Marcel Dionne in the spring of 1975, wrapping up a season in which he set new Red Wings records with 74 assists and 121 points.

The Wings' dynamic center of the early seventies, Marcel Dionne, picks up a head of steam.

Red Berenson scored his first NHL goal against Detroit on the final day of the 1961-62 season while playing for Montreal. Berenson later became captain of the expansion St. Louis Blues, where he played for Scotty Bowman and once scored six goals in a 1968 game against Philadelphia.

Berenson brought his work ethic and scoring touch to Detroit, popping 28 into the net in 1971-72. All told he had 111 goals as a Wing before being traded back to St. Louis in 1974.

"It was a difficult time in Detroit," Berenson recalled with considerable understatement. "The team was in turmoil. There were more players living in the hotel than in their own places. The organization was very unstable at the top and whenever that is the case, it's going to show on the ice."

Apathy reached new lows. Some fans jeered their chronic losers by wearing bags over their heads. Others registered their disgust by throwing ink bottles, chickens, and live hamsters onto the ice. One night a huge banner was dropped from Olympia's rafters, calling a certain Wings player "chicken." On another occasion a more plaintive sign was unveiled at Joe Louis Arena. "Please Try," it pleaded.

The long litany of mediocrity began with a seventh-place finish in 1970-71. The Wings moved up a couple of notches in 1971-72, but did so without coach Doug Barkley, who resigned on Halloween, evidently frightened by the team's direction. "I feel this team still has a chance to make the playoffs," he explained. "I couldn't turn it around, and if I waited any longer it might be too late." Barkley was replaced by Johnny Wilson, a link to the glorious 1950s.

Wilson, who'd coached at Princeton and in Los Angeles, was thought to have a way with young players. He had three dandies under his command in Detroit. Fifth-year left wing Nick Libett was on his way to his most productive of 14 NHL seasons: 31 goals and 53 points. Two other fleet forwards, Mickey Redmond and Marcel Dionne, also gave fans at Olympia a regular reason to climb out of their seats. Dionne, a small, speedy center with a solid shot, played on a line with Libett and racked up 77 points, setting a new NHL standard for rookies.

Redmond, a high school dropout from Kirkland, Ontario, had been fortunate enough to break in with two Stanley Cup winners in Montreal. The strong right winger, part of the deal that sent Frank Mahovlich to the Canadiens, blossomed as an everyday player in Detroit. He scored 42 times in 1971-72, then posted an even stronger performance his sophomore year. When Redmond beat Ron Low in Toronto on March 27, 1973, he simultaneously broke Gordie Howe's team record of 49 goals and became the first 50-goal scorer in team history. He added two more to finish with 52 and a berth on the first All-Star team. "Mickey could easily score 75 goals a year," maintained Wilson, "if only he could develop a little finesse. He thinks he can blast that puck through anything. . . . Once he learns the knack of being a little tricky, he'll break all the records."

The Wings showed considerable improvement in Wilson's second year, finishing 37-29-12 for 86 points. Although this would have put them in second place in the Western Division, it was only good enough for another fifth-place finish in the much stronger East. At the end of the season Wilson was fired. He was replaced by Ted Garvin (a minor league coach and friend of Ned Harkness) who was removed after his charges won just two of the first 11 games of the 1973-74 campaign. This was to make room for an old favorite, Alex Delvecchio, who had just announced his retirement after 24 seasons.

However, the Wings couldn't even pull off a coaching change without a bit of slapstick. Garvin was canned just hours before a game with Philadelphia. Because Delvecchio had not yet officially tendered his resignation to the league office, he still was technically on the roster. A playing coach was against NHL rules, so the freshly fired Garvin was prevailed upon to work the bench that night. With about three minutes left to play, Garvin abruptly left Olympia. Delvecchio, who hadn't played or coached that night, wound up officially getting credit for the 4-1 loss.

Delvecchio, given a three-year contract, was no saviour. He was about break-even as a coach (27-31-9) as the team fell to sixth, despite Redmond's 51-goal performance. But Delvecchio's solid standing with Norris caused Ned Harkness to finally consider other career options. On February 6, 1974, the embattled general manager resigned, having done, in most observers' eyes, nearly irreparable damage to the franchise during his four years at Olympia. Few were willing to credit him with drafting Marcel Dionne or trading for Mickey Redmond, both of whom would soon be gone anyway.

In 1974-75, Dionne scored 47 goals and shattered Gordie Howe's club records for assists (74) and points (121). Danny Grant, acquired from Min-

Andy Brown, a Red Wing from 1971 to 1973, was the last goalie to play without a face mask. Such daring came naturally to Brown, who raced cars during the offseason.

**L**eft winger Nick Libett was known principally as a defensive player during his eleven years with Detroit, used mainly on a checking line and as a penalty-killer. His most memorable season was 1971-72, when he scored 31 goals and had a brawl with Chicago's Keith Magnuson "that seemed to go on forever," he said. Twenty-five years later, most people have forgotten the goals but still ask him about the fight.

nesota for center Henry Boucha, played on the left side and popped in 50 goals, an increasingly common figure that still was exceeded by only two others in the league. They took up some of the slack caused by Redmond's absence. Redmond, in the second season of a five-year, one-million-dollar contract (another increasingly common number) ruptured a disc and underwent back surgery. He was limited to just 15 goals in 29 games.

Newspapers reported that Delvecchio, now general manager as well as coach, had a communication problem with his young players. This undoubtedly had that legendary disciplinarian, Jack Adams, guffawing in the clouds. *Throw a little fruit at 'em and threaten them with a one-way ride to Indianapolis!* he might have roared at Delvecchio. But this was a different era, as long hair, head bands, player agents, and the smell of marijuana drifting through the dank corridors of Olympia Stadium made all too clear. Players no longer exhibited automatic and unquestioning obedience to management. There were many more teams and many more options. This included jumping to the new league on the block, the World Hockey Association, which was distributing dollars in the same cavalier fashion that a hungover Howie Young had once delivered milk bottles.

In 1975 Delvecchio traded the dynamic but disgruntled Dionne to Los Angeles for left winger Dan Maloney, aging defenseman Terry Harper, and a second-round draft choice. Dionne, who'd aped Delvecchio by winning the Lady Byng Award in his final year as a Wing, was less than gentlemanly upon leaving, blasting Detroit's management as not having a clue as to how to put together a winning, harmonious team. If playing well is the best revenge, Dionne got the upper hand in the transaction. He went on to become one of the most prolific scorers in NHL history, retiring in 1989 with 731 goals, 1,040 assists, and 1,771 points, numbers that at the time were second only to Gordie Howe.

Delvecchio then got into a pissing contest with Mickey Redmond. The star right winger had not endeared himself to management by employing Alan Eagleson (roundly despised by owners) as his agent and then using the threat of jumping to the WHA to leverage the first million-dollar deal in the club's history. After missing most of the '74-75 season, his sore back caused him to sit out the last 43 games in 1975-76. This equalled the number of games Delvecchio had missed in 24 seasons. The old iron man clearly thought Redmond was a slacker. In early 1976 he suspended him and announced that he had been placed on waivers, available to any team that wanted to pay the $30,000 fee. "He doesn't want to play in Detroit," he explained. "Otherwise he'd be here. We've gone long enough without him. He's no good to us. I'm tired of hearing players' excuses for mediocre work. I don't want to have such disruptive influences on my team."

Later it was revealed that Redmond had suffered neurological damage to his right leg. He could play, though not at 100 percent, or he could retire. He and his agent negotiated a buyout from his Wings contract. At twenty-eight, Redmond's once-promising NHL career was over, though he was to return several years later as a Wings broadcaster.

## Dead Wings

Without Dionne and Redmond the Wings lurched through another couple of woeful seasons. Doug Barkley had been brought back to coach at the start of the 1975-76 season, freeing Delvecchio to concentrate on the increasingly complex duties of general manager. There were problems, Barkley confessed. "Detroit had drafted a lot of young players who didn't like hard work and the physical fitness aspect of training. They were prima donnas with long-term contracts who knew that even if they didn't produce they wouldn't be sent down to the minors. It was important for us to work on conditioning because our club didn't have enough talent and I figured we could compensate by working hard."

Once again, the frustrations of the job got to the temperamental ex-defenseman. One night in New York, after watching his team get smoked by the Rangers, Barkley got into a shoving match with Walter McPeek, a hockey writer for the *Newark Star-Ledger*. McPeek filed a criminal complaint with the New York City police, claiming that he'd been struck. "He sued and they had a warrant out for my arrest in New York," said Barkley, "but before we ever returned

**M**ickey Redmond, Detroit's first 50-goal scorer, breaks out of the pack in a game against the Los Angeles Kings.

The 1977-78 Red Wings rose from the ashes and brought record crowds to Olympia Stadium.

Front row (from left): Jim Rutherford, Dennis Hextall (captain), coach Bobby Kromm, owner Bruce Norris, general manager Ted Lindsay, Nick Libett, Ron Low.

Middle row (from left): Greg Joly, Al Cameron, Bill Lochead, Vaclav Nedomansky, Terry Harper, Thommie Bergman, Rick Bowness, Larry Wright, Reed Larson.

Top row (from left): assistant trainer Dan Olesevich, Dennis Polonich, Andre St. Laurent, Errol Thompson, Dale McCourt, Paul Woods, Dennis Hull, Jean Hamel, Perry Miller, trainer Lefty Wilson.

there for another game I had been fired as coach." Barkley later apologized and the charges were dropped. Meanwhile the Wings unapologetically completed the season with two more coaches, Delvecchio and Billy Dea, and another out-of-the-money finish. This time they placed fourth in the new five-team Norris Division. The previous season the league had been realigned into two conferences comprised of four divisions, two of which—the Norris and the Adams—bore the names of Detroit hockey icons. The Wings would be the only original member of the Norris Division to remain in it for the entire 19 seasons of its existence, until expansion forced a name change and realignment in 1993.

Dea, a reluctant interim coach, gratefully went back to scouting after the team brought in Larry Wilson midway through the 1976-77 season. The former Wings forward and minor-league coach fared no better than his older brother, Johnny. He won just three of 36 games, part of a final 16-55-9 mark that buried Detroit in the basement. The losses were a new low for the franchise, as were the 41 points. No Detroit team had compiled fewer points since the 1937-38 squad, which had played 32 fewer games! In an era of high scoring, the Wings managed an anemic 183 goals, easily the worst output of any of the 18 teams in the league. Meanwhile, the defense missed being the loop's most porous by a single goal.

This abysmal performance made what happened the following year just that much more memorable. In 1977-78 the dead Wings rose from the ashes, doubled their number of wins, and made the playoffs for the first time in eight seasons.

"Aggressive hockey is back in town!" That was the promise made on billboards and promotional literature during the summer of 1977 by the Wings' new general manager. Considering the source—scarfaced Ted Lindsay—nobody dared doubt that it would be true.

Lindsay was hired to replace Delvecchio in March 1977 during the midst of a 19-game winless streak that lasted five agonizing weeks. After the season,

## Dead Wings

Larry Wilson was reassigned to the Wings' Kansas City farm club, while veteran coach Bobby Kromm was brought in to restore some competitiveness and pride to the parent team. Kromm had excellent credentials, having won three Central Hockey League crowns with the Dallas Blackhawks and the 1976 Avco Cup, the World Hockey Association's version of the Stanley Cup, with Winnipeg. At the time he was hired, Kromm had just taken the Jets to the seventh game of the 1977 Avco Cup finals before losing.

Kromm and Lindsay went about revamping the Wings' image from unorganized patsies to stand-up guys unafraid of a good rumble. "Myself, Nick Libett, and Dan Maloney were the tough guys here in Detroit," said Dennis Hextall, a gritty center whose resumé included two years of boxing at the University of North Dakota. "We wanted people to know we weren't afraid to play." There also was a feisty fellow named Dennis Polonich cuffing the opposition around; the flat-nosed right winger led the club in penalty minutes three years running.

The new regime opened with two losses and two ties, but then the club played .500 hockey the rest of the way to finish 32-34-14. This was good for 78 points and the second rung in the Norris Division. The 37-point improvement was the biggest by any NHL team in the last two decades. Lindsay had promised that his players would give an all-out effort and that "the fans would be hanging from the Olympia rafters." He was right on both accounts. His players hustled, and appreciative fans set a new single-game attendance mark on six separate occasions during the course of the season, including all three games in the postseason.

"It was an interesting season," said Libett, a 23-goal scorer who was the only member of the team to have played in the Wings' last playoff series, back in 1970. "Management wanted a youth movement, but some of us veterans proved them wrong. We had Paul Woods, Perry Miller, Andre St. Laurant, and had just drafted Dale McCourt. As the year progressed, we really came together as a team."

St. Laurant, an aggressive center acquired from the New York Islanders two games into the season, had his best year, racking up 31 goals and 39 assists. Woods, obtained from Montreal for $50,000 in the intra-league draft, had 19 goals playing on the Wings' "Kid Line." The line was pivoted by another rookie, twenty-year-old Dale McCourt, who led all Detroit scorers with 33 goals and 72 points. Playing on the right side was Bill Lochead, the club's top pick in the 1974 draft, who enjoyed his only 20-goal season.

The most exciting newcomer was Reed Larson, a smooth-skating defenseman out of the University of Minnesota. Larson's booming slapshot, often compared to Bobby Hull's in terms of velocity, made him the trigger on the power play and helped account for his 60 points, which tied an NHL record for rookie defensemen. Jimmy Rutherford, in his sixth Detroit season, shared goaltending duties with Ron Low, whom Lindsay had picked up from Washington for veteran center Walt McKechnie and two draft picks.

This blend of youth and experience put the Wings into a best-of-three preliminary against the Atlanta Flames in the opener of the 1978 playoffs.

Dale McCourt, Detroit's first pick in the 1977 draft, was a remarkably consistent scorer, collecting 33, 28, 30, and 30 goals in his first four seasons.

In the summer of 1979 the center was the object of a legal tug-of-war when an arbitrator awarded him to Los Angeles as compensation for Detroit's signing of free-agent goalie Rogie Vachon.

General manager Ted Lindsay instructed McCourt not to report to the Kings, who eventually settled the acrimonious matter by agreeing to take Andre St. Laurent and the Wings' first-round picks in the 1980 and 1981 entry drafts.

During the 1981-82 season, McCourt was packaged with Mike Foligno and Brent Peterson in a trade with Buffalo that brought Danny Gare, Derek Smith, and Jim Schoenfeld to Detroit.

**T**hanks to a wicked slapshot, Reed Larson shattered all scoring records for Detroit defensemen during his ten years with the club. "No matter what anyone says," said Washington goalie Ron Low, "Bobby Hull never shot the puck as hard as Reed does."

"We went into Atlanta with a lot of enthusiasm," said Hextall. "We were determined not to lose." They didn't, scoring one shorthanded and three power-play goals in the first period, enroute to a 5-3 victory. In the rematch two nights later, Bill Lochead practically brought the roof down on a rollicking Olympia crowd. With a minute and a half left in a 2-2 game, he busted down the left wing, shook off a defenseman, deked the goalie, then shot the puck from a nearly impossible angle into the Atlanta net to complete the series sweep. Euphoric fans clogged the corridor outside the Wings' dressing room, shouting Lochead's name and chanting "We're number one!"

"I don't think crowds yelled that when I played with Montreal," remarked thirty-eight-year-old Terry Harper, who had broken in with the Canadiens fifteen years earlier. "At least I don't remember hearing it. That seems so long ago now. This is much more exciting."

Next up were Harper's old employer. Scotty Bowman's Canadiens, one of the strongest teams in history, had won the previous two Stanley Cups in easy fashion and finished a mind-bending 51 points ahead of the Wings in the Norris Division. The only disagreement most experts had was in naming the number of games it would take for the Canadiens to eliminate the Wings in the best-of-seven series. Most figured the minimum, four.

The Wings fell to Montreal in the opener at The Forum but then shocked the complacent and spoiled Canadiens fans by winning the rematch, 4-2, two days later. After that the games moved to Detroit, where raucous record crowds were awaiting their heroes' return.

After 40 minutes of action in game three, 16,672 fans were rocking and rolling and talking upset as the organist banged out an ear-splitting rendition of "It's Only Make Believe." Nick Libett had scored twice, giving Detroit a 2-1 lead. The haughty Canadiens were obviously frustrated, with even the elegant Guy Lafleur losing his composure and slashing at his pesky antagonists. Fans, intoxicated by the Wings' earnest play and countless 12-ounce cups of beer, had flung more than 40 octopi onto the ice and bombarded the opponents' bench with garbage, forcing Scotty Bowman to don a helmet for protection. But the Canadiens came out skating in the third period like the champions they were. In short order Jacques Lemaire, Pierre Larouche, and Yvan Cournoyer all scored, spoiling the crowd's reverie and giving Montreal a 4-2 comeback win.

## Dead Wings

Shaken from their lethargy, the Canadiens moved in for the kill. In a Sunday matinee played April 23, 1978, Doug Risebrough and Bob Gainey scored shorthanded goals 24 seconds apart in the first period to start an 8-0 rout. "Seventeen thousand people saw a great hockey team tonight," said a dejected Dennis Hextall, "and it wasn't wearing red and white."

To be precise, 16,673 people were on hand, at the time the most people ever to watch a game at Olympia. In the last five minutes several thousand of them stood and gave their resolute but overmatched blue-collar heroes an ovation. With the series moving back to Montreal, and the Canadiens needing only one more win to close out the series, they correctly guessed that neither they nor their team would be returning to Olympia that spring.

**Vaclav Nedomansky**

Olympia Stadium's last hurrah took place in the fall of 1979. That year the NHL grew to 21 teams as it made peace with the World Hockey Association by agreeing to take in its four strongest clubs: Winnipeg, Quebec, Edmonton, and Hartford. Not only would Detroit fans now be able to watch rising stars like teenaged sensation Wayne Gretzky, they also would get one last glimpse of Father Time himself, fifty-one-year-old Gordie Howe, skating with his sons, Mark and Marty, in the uniform of the Hartford Whalers.

They'd already had a good look at Vaclav Nedomansky, a refugee from Communist Czechoslovakia and then the WHA. Nedomansky's arrival at the end of the 1977-78 season foreshadowed what would in a few years become a Red Wings specialty: signing talented—if slightly confused—European and Russian skaters to NHL contracts. "It was difficult understanding the mind of the players here," admitted the 6-foot-2, 206-pound center. "Why do they shoot from far away? Why don't they pass more? Why do guys fight? It's different from the things I was used to."

Big Ned adjusted well enough to lead the club with 38 goals and 73 points in his first full season, 1978-79. The Wings, however, greatly disappointed fans that year. A record number of them—16,678—showed up on November 1, 1978 for the Canadiens' first visit since the previous spring's playoffs. After building expectations with their storybook run against Atlanta and Montreal, the Wings fizzled. They lost to Montreal, 4-1, that night. It turned out to be just one more loss in a season that saw them revert to form and crash into the Norris Division cellar.

A trademark pose: Dale McCourt cocks his stick before blasting the puck on the power play.

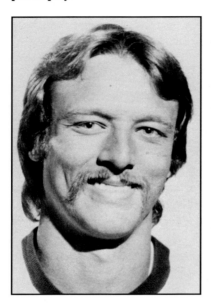

Defenseman Dave Hanson appeared in only 11 games as a Red Wing, but before leaving town the minor cult hero of the movie *Slapshot* was credited by some with coining the phrase, "Aggressive hockey is back in town." Ted Lindsay used the slogan to great marketing success when he took over the general manager's position.

Bobby Kromm, destined to get the axe before the end of yet another last-place finish in 1979-80, was still behind the bench on December 15, 1979, when the Wings wrapped up fifty-two years of up-and-down memories at the corner of Grand River and McGraw with a Saturday night game against the Quebec Nordiques.

"I think we'll feel some sadness in moving," said Paul Woods of the impending move to a brand new waterfront arena. Most players, however,

An aerial view of Olympia shows the addition built in the back in 1965 to accommodate more seats and a new elevator.

shared Reed Larson's sentiments. "I'm glad about the move," he said. "Nothing against the rink, but the new place looks beautiful on the water. It'll be good for the crowd and players. This is getting a little dingy down here."

The neighborhood around Olympia had grown shabby and dangerous, a consequence of the bloody riot in July 1967 that had left 43 Detroiters dead and thousands more jamming "House for Sale" signs into their lawns. The flight to the suburbs had accelerated during the seventies, leaving behind a slowly crumbling urban landscape. The four-story Olympia, with its leaking roof, broken railings, littered aisleways, and spray-painted graffiti, was representative of this sad neglect. Two murders in the neighborhood, including one of a suburbanite right across the street from Olympia, fueled Bruce Norris's anxiety to find a new igloo for his team. Meanwhile, hockey fans continued to drive in from outside the city to a big, lighted parking lot ringed by barbed wire.

After William Clay Ford moved his football team from downtown Tiger Stadium to a new domed stadium in Pontiac in 1974, Norris had entered into

**D**ecember 27, 1979: the opening faceoff of the last game played at Olympia.

serious negotiations with developers to build a hockey arena, Olympia II, nearby. At the same time, Detroit's new mayor, Coleman Young, had secured five million dollars in federal public works money and announced that he was getting ready to build an indoor stadium adjacent to Cobo Hall. Young lacked a tenant for his proposed facility, but to forestall the Wings' anticipated move to Oakland County he filed a lawsuit, claiming that such a move would remove jobs from an economically depressed area.

Despite Norris's public disinterest in a downtown arena, some influential businessmen anxious to aid the city's comeback finally convinced Lincoln Cavalieri, Wings vice president and manager of Olympia, to talk seriously with the mayor. In August 1977, the two sides fashioned a unique deal that moved the team downtown. The Wings created the Olympia Stadium Corporation to lease and book events for the new arena and Cobo Hall.

The lease from the city gave Norris the exclusive right to all profits from the two municipally owned facilities for the next thirty years, with an option for another thirty. His rent and tax payments would total $702,000 a year. The city's only other income would be from parking receipts and a 50-to-75-cent surcharge on every ticket sold. Thanks to additional federal loans, the fifty-three-million-dollar facility was built and ready for its first hockey game by the end of 1979. To the disappointment of some, the new facility wasn't christened Olympia II, but Joe Louis Arena. Detroit's first black mayor liked to joke that he named it after that great hockey player from Detroit's ghetto, heavyweight champion Joe Louis.

Ten days before Christmas 1979, a rowdy crowd of 15,609 attended the last of 1,790 NHL games at Olympia. As the Wings rallied from a four-goal deficit against Quebec to earn a 4-4 tie on Greg Joly's late goal, fans took pictures, unfurled banners, sounded boat horns, showered the ice with eggs, toilet paper, and fish, and booed the mention of Joe Louis Arena on the public address system. They then hung around after the game to hear the organist play "Auld Lang Syne" before heading for home, their heads heavy with memories. With that a unique chapter in hockey history came to a close. A couple of days earlier, told that the old red barn was probably slated for demolition, Gordie Howe had asked a reporter, "Save a brick for me."

The Wings opened play at Joe Louis Arena on December 27, 1979 with a 3-2 loss to St. Louis. The Blues' Brian Sutter scored the first goal in the new building, beating Rogie Vachon with a backhander at 11:05 of the first period. Lanky center Dennis Sobchuk, a WHA castoff playing his only season in Detroit, secured his spot in Red Wings trivia by banging in the equalizer at 1:43 of the second period. Sobchuk's fourth and final goal as a member of the Wings was the franchise's first at what local sportscaster Al Ackerman dubbed "The Joe."

After Dan Balduc made it 2-1 for Detroit late in the second period, the Blues came back with a pair of third-period scores to dampen the spirits of the all-time record Detroit crowd of 19,742. Bobby Kromm and Ted Lindsay both expressed disappointment with the outcome. "I thought it was the night we would start a new era," said Kromm. "It's sad for the loyal fans," said Lindsay. "They were ready to raise the roof off the new building."

They were already using the stairwells and sinks as urinals. Builders had miscalculated the number of rest rooms needed, an error compounded by larger crowds and 24-ounce beer cups, double the size of those that had been sold at Olympia. The new sports palace inspired other complaints, including seats that were too far from the action and not properly tiered to allow a person to see over the heads of spectators in front. "I liked the atmosphere at Olympia better," said one longtime season-ticket holder. "This is too large. We don't hear the puck, we don't hear the sticks, nothing. But you can see okay as long as people don't walk up and down the aisles."

A few weeks later, on February 7, 1980, the NHL All-Star Game was held in Detroit. That evening 21,002 people, the largest crowd ever to attend a hockey game anywhere, jammed The Joe, eager to bust their lungs cheering for a returning hero.

Gordie Howe had left Detroit several years earlier with a bitter taste in his mouth. In 1969 he had become Detroit's first $100,000-a-year player, but only

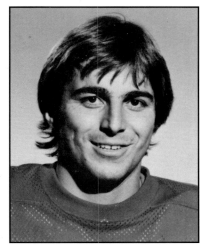

The final game at Olympia featured several fights and a Red Wings comeback. Down 4-0 to Quebec, the Wings gained a 4-4 tie on Greg Joly's late goal, the last ever scored at the old red barn.

G illes Gilbert, masked and unmasked. The lanky netminder, who'd spent 11 seasons with Minnesota and Boston, finished his career with a three-year tour in Detroit. He is perhaps best remembered for giving up two goals on penalty shots in a 1982 game with Vancouver at Joe Louis Arena.

after catching Bruce Norris in an egregious lie. Norris had always assured Howe that he would be the highest paid Wing. The trusting superstar had taken him at his word, only to discover in a conversation with teammate Bobby Baun that the newly acquired defenseman was making nearly double Howe's 45,000-dollar salary. Another teammate, Carl Brewer, also was paid more. Norris had no choice but to boost Howe's contract into the six-figure category, where it had rightfully belonged for some time.

Howe's relationship with Norris turned even more sour when he retired in 1971. Promised important responsibilities as a Wings vice president, he instead spent most of his time on the rubber-chicken circuit. He was given the "mushroom treatment," he said, kept in the dark until every once in a while somebody opened the door to his tiny Olympia office to shovel some more manure on him. In June 1973, he quit the club and came out of retirement to play alongside his sons with the Houston Aeros of the World Hockey Association. At the same time that the Wings and other NHL teams were trying to keep their players from switching to the WHA, Howe's signing embarrassed the Wings and gave the struggling circuit a big shot of credibility and a huge dose of publicity. Defying natural law, he then scored 100 points, was named the league's most valuable player, and led the Aeros to their first of two straight Avco Cups.

Howe's WHA days burnished his image as a tough, ageless phenomenon. During a brawl with the Indianapolis Racers, Roger Cote had Marty Howe on the ice. "He was running his jersey across his throat," remembered Mark Howe. "I was trying to get to him, but I was being held back."

That's when Pops got involved. "My dad went over to the guy and said, 'Get up.' The guy looked at him kind of funny and went right back to it. My dad said it again, 'Get up.' He still didn't.

"So my dad took his two fingers—and they're thick—and rammed them up the guy's nose and lifted him off. The guy flew off. It was the ugliest thing I've seen."

After retiring from the Wings with 786 goals, 1,023 assists, and 1,809 points, and more than 20 other NHL records, Howe added 174 goals and 508 points in six WHA seasons. The last two were spent in Hartford, which gave him a ten-year, five-million-dollar personal services contract after the Howes' attempts to return to the Wings in 1977 were rebuffed by general manager Ted Lindsay. Howe might have hung up his skates for good when the WHA died in 1979, but the news that Hartford had been absorbed by the NHL meant that the Howes could finally realize a lifelong dream of playing an NHL game together in Detroit. During the 1979-80 season, Hartford—now a member of the Norris Division—played three times in the city. In the first contest, Howe and his sons lined up for the opening faceoff as the crowd serenaded him with chants of "Gor-die! Gor-die!" Afterwards he said, "I've been waiting for it for thirty-two years."

Howe's relationship with the public has always been magical. He remains a rarity among top athletes, a genuinely humble, likable fellow who always gave his all and never lost his common touch. There are countless stories dealing with his unaffectedness and generosity of spirit: how he signed autographs for three hours after a tough loss, treated an entire neighborhood of children to ice cream, promised a sick kid a goal, or helped push a motorist out of the snow on the way to practice. He could never willingly turn down an autograph request, he explained. He had worked too hard for the privilege.

All of this and more were on the minds of the thousands of fans who squeezed into Joe Louis Arena for the 32nd annual All-Star Game. Cheers were abundant as the members of the teams representing the Prince of Wales and Clarence Campbell conferences were introduced. Then Howe, a grandfather just a few weeks shy of his fifty-second birthday, the scorer of 15 goals in his 32nd major-league season, skated out. The handclaps and scattered chants of "Gor-die! Gor-die!" quickly built into a frenzied ovation, the loudest and most pro-

longed ever heard in the building. The cheers continued to flow down from the angled stands and wash over the balding, slope-shouldered guest of honor, who stood awkwardly at center ice before skating over to the bench, where Lefty Wilson was assisting the Prince of Wales squad. "Lefty, help me," he pleaded. The trainer responded in the rough humor of the locker room. "Fuck you, Gordie," he said.

The thunderous ovation on a Tuesday night in the dead of winter lasted nearly three full minutes. It demonstrated what Detroiters felt about the man. Gordie Howe was still the greatest, even if the team he had once so ably represented no longer was.

The change of venue didn't help the Wings, who proved they could lose as easily on the waterfront as they had in the inner city. The losses kept the revolving door spinning. Bobby Kromm was fired a month after the 1980 All-Star Game and Ted Lindsay officially named coach. Lindsay's surrogate behind the bench, Marcel Pronovost, who'd steered Buffalo to a 105-point season a couple of years earlier, presided over the team's final nine games, seven of them losses.

By the following October Lindsay, on the outs with Norris, had been replaced as general manager by Jimmy Skinner and was doing his best to right the Wings' ship as coach. He lasted 20 games, during which the team won only three times, before leaving in favor of Wayne Maxner. Skinner and Maxner would both last only two years in their respective positions. When Billy Dea took over Maxner's duties with 11 games left in the 1981-82 campaign, it marked the 16th head coaching change in 13 seasons—a stretch of instability

The Wings' fortunes didn't automatically improve upon moving into Joe Louis Arena. Here Jim Rutherford forlornly stares at the puck resting in his net in one of the first games played at The Joe.

that would have been remarkable even for a floundering expansion team. That it was happening to one of professional sports' oldest and proudest franchises was considered almost criminal.

The Red Wings' crumbling fortunes reflected those of their owner. By 1982, Bruce Norris was selling off pieces of the once formidable Norris Grain Company, a business empire that at its height included not only the Red Wings and the Chicago Blackhawks, but also sausage companies, wheat mills, and ranches stretching from South Dakota to South Africa. When he'd been divorced in 1961, the dissolute playboy had listed his personal wealth as twenty million dollars, though that included millions of dollars borrowed against his own company in the form of interest-free loans.

Since then Norris had squandered the family fortune and was now busy fending off creditors. He was being sued by Lindsay, Mickey Redmond, and Nick Libett for a total of $805,000 owed in deferred salaries and other payments. In addition, the developers of the proposed Oakland County arena were on their way to winning a 3.4-million-dollar judgment against him for reneging on his promise to move the Wings to Pontiac.

In June of 1982, Norris ended his family's fifty-year association with the Red Wings. He sold the team to Mike Ilitch, an ex-Marine and former Detroit Tigers farmhand who had created the Little Caesars pizza chain from the single store he had opened in Garden City, Michigan, in 1959. The Detroit native had long been a major supporter of amateur sports programs, especially hockey, but he

**M**ike and Marian Ilitch bought the team from Bruce Norris in 1982.

had been frustrated in his attempts to buy his first love, the Tigers. The team ultimately was sold for fifty-three million dollars to his chief competitor, Tom Monaghan, creator of Domino's Pizza and another ex-Marine and wannabe Tigers shortstop.

Although Monaghan was lucky enough to have his team win a World Series title his first year as owner, while Ilitch continues to wait in vain for his first Stanley Cup, in the long run the new boss of the Red Wings got the much better deal, financially speaking. At Norris's bankruptcy hearings in 1985, it was revealed that Ilitch had bought the Wings with little more than a handshake. Norris had received seven million dollars in promissory notes plus the pledge of a one-million-dollar cash down payment, to be made from the receipts for tickets sold over the coming season. A few months later, Ilitch bought the lucrative leases to Joe Louis Arena and Cobo Arena for fifteen million dollars, including nine million dollars in promissory notes. Freed from the indifferent ownership of Norris, the value of the team would quickly escalate. Within a decade of being bought by Ilitch, the Red Wings were rated the most valuable NHL franchise. According to the estimate of one leading financial magazine, today the team is worth in the neighborhood of 175 million dollars.

In 1982-83, Ilitch's first season as owner, the Red Wings finished last for the fifth straight time. However, there were immediate signs that the franchise was finally being stabilized, creating optimism for the future. Jimmy Devellano, a super scout credited with building the expansion New York Islanders into a four-time Stanley Cup champion, replaced Jimmy Skinner as general manager and formulated long-range plans. "We had no farm system and only two or three players who were any good," he recalled. "I knew we were going to have to rebuild completely and we set out to do that through the draft. It was a slow and painstaking process, but by 1987 or so we had a pretty good team."

Nick Polano, a rising star in the Buffalo organization, was hired as coach and quickly tabbed a former Sabre, Danny Gare, as on-ice leader. Gare, a scrappy right wing obtained the previous season from Buffalo, would end the team's musical-chairs approach to the captaincy by wearing the "C" on his sweater for the next four years.

"We were in no way Stanley Cup contenders, but it was a great atmosphere," recalled Dwight Foster, a gimpy-kneed center picked up from New Jersey for the grand total of one dollar. "You knew Mike Ilitch was in the process of building the kind of team that is on the ice today. It was great to be part of that building process at the very beginning."

Foster played on a unit that included Gare and Bob Manno. The trio of grinders was an early favorite at The Joe, where appreciative fans dubbed them the "Troll Line." That's because they were ugly but effective, explained Foster. "Danny was here a season before me," he said, "but he had come from Buffalo, where he had been relegated to a situational role. No doubt he was losing a step or two, but he was capable of more than that. Manno was a defenseman who converted to forward, and the three of us just kind of clicked together."

**D**anny Gare was past his prime when acquired from Buffalo, but his gritty, grinding style made him the perfect choice for captain between 1981 and 1986.

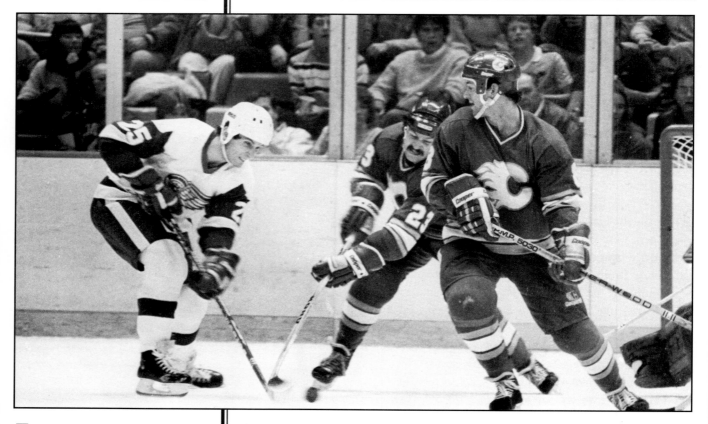

John Ogrodnick led the Wings in goals six straight seasons in the eighties, including 1984-85 when he bagged 55 and was named to the first All-Star team.

The greatest offensive force of the early Ilitch era was John Ogrodnick, a dour, hatchet-faced left winger from Ottawa, Ontario. "Johnny O," the team's fourth-round pick in the '79 draft, scored 35 goals in 1980-81, his first full NHL season. It was the first of six straight seasons of leading the Wings in goals, including the 1984-85 campaign. That year he broke Mickey Redmond's club record with 55, earning him a spot on the first All-Star team. He finished seventh on the league's scoring list, the first time in a decade that a Wing had cracked the top ten.

In the fall of 1983, an offensive wunderkind from the Peterborough Petes made his first appearance at The Joe. Eighteen-year-old Steve Yzerman, Jim Devellano's number-one pick in the '83 draft, was heralded as the start of Detroit's hockey renaissance. Yzerman lived up to expectations by establishing new team records for scoring by a rookie, notching 39 goals and 87 points, best on the club. Also contributing to the club's rejuvenation that year was the signing of Brad Park as a free agent. The thirty-five-year-old defenseman was a certain Hall-of-Famer who'd enjoyed 20-plus-goal seasons in New York and Boston. He was dangerous as the point man on the power play. When he assisted on Ivan Boldirev's goal with 13 seconds left in the season, he broke Reed Larson's club record for assists by a defenseman, with 53. Behind Ogrodnick, Yzerman, and Park, Detroit moved up to third place, just two points behind St. Louis. Although the Blues eliminated the Wings three games to one in the 1984 Norris Division semifinals, the future looked bright indeed.

Other history was made during the '83-84 season. That year the league introduced a five-minute, sudden-death overtime period as a way of injecting excitement into the high number of tied games. On October 5, 1983, Detroit and Winnipeg played the first regular-season overtime game since 1942, settling for a 6-6 tie. Also that season, Brian Johnson, a tough twenty-three-year-old right winger from Montreal, became the eighth black to play in the NHL and the first for Detroit.

Johnson didn't consider himself a pioneer, though attitudes towards black players clearly hadn't changed much since Boston forward Willie O'Ree cracked the all-alabaster NHL during the 1957-58 season. When Johnson skated in exhibitions at Joe Louis Arena, one belligerent fan wanted to know, "Why aren't you playing basketball?" Some opponents called him "nigger." Even a Red Wings teammate couldn't resist asking, "Guess who's coming to dinner?" when the locker-room discussion turned to food.

The Wings liked his roughhouse style. Johnson was the prototypal enforcer, garnering six goals and 250 penalty minutes in 67 American Hockey League games. The 6-foot-1, 185-pound policeman maintained that the slurs and needling didn't bother him. "As long as they call me names, it means I'm doing something right. It's 1983. Racial problems are going to be around in the year 2000. I try to better myself. If a person uses racial slurs, he's a small person. He has no class. I try to overcome that. If it's a player, I don't get mad, I get even. Even if it takes me all year." Unfortunately for Johnson, he didn't stick around nearly that long. The rookie went pointless in three games before being sent back to the minors for good.

Polano coached the club to another third-place finish in 1984-85. Once again the Wings fell in the opening round of the playoffs, this time getting swept by the Blackhawks in three straight. Despite Ilitch's impatience—Polano was promoted to assistant G.M. after the season—anticipation contin-

**S**teve Yzerman, the first player drafted in the Ilitch era, paid immediate dividends. Number 19 had 39 goals and 48 assists in his rookie season of 1983-84, and fans immediately began professing their love—much to the chagrin of Troll Line veteran Dwight Foster.

**Brian Johnson**

175

By the middle eighties bench-clearing brawls like this one between Detroit and Toronto had become distressingly familiar, prompting the NHL to enact rules severely penalizing players who left the bench to join an on-ice fracas.

Chris Cichocki, one of several high-priced free agents brought to town in 1985 by Mike Ilitch, broke in with a bang. On October 10, 1985, he scored two goals against Minnesota in his first NHL game. However, injuries limited the right wing to just nine more goals over the rest of his career, split between Detroit and Pittsburgh.

ued to run high, as imports like Ron Duguay continued to deliver. Duguay, obtained in a six-player deal with the Rangers prior to the '83-84 season, scored a cumulative 71 goals his first two years in Detroit. The big center was a sight, his long blond locks flowing in the slipstream as he hurtled down the ice. It was great theatre, especially as all but a handful of players now wore helmets.

Looking to take a short cut to respectability, Ilitch went on an unprecedented spending spree prior to the start of the 1985-86 season. His pizza dough got him NHL free agents Mike McEwen, Warren Young, and Harold Snepts; collegiate free agents Adam Oates, Ray Staszak, Dale Krentz, Tim Friday, and Chris Cichocki; and Czech defector Petr Klima (who wore number 85 on his jersey to honor the year of his defection). He signed Harry Neale, whose experience bridged both the NHL and university ranks, to coach, then sat back in his private suite at The Joe and awaited what he hoped would be an unforgettable season.

It was unforgettable—the worst in franchise history. The free agents flopped, core players like Yzerman, Gare, Ogrodnick, and goalie Greg Stefan either were injured or had off-years, and the defense resembled Swiss cheese. By Christmas the Wings had given up 10 goals in a game four times, had the worst record of any team in the league, and were about to broom Neale. Park took over on December 30, but the club continued to slip, slide, and stumble to a horrific final mark of 17-57-6.

"What is so stunning is not the number of goals the Red Wings have given up," marveled Joe Falls in the *Detroit News*, "or even the number of shots on the net. Computers have not been built yet to record this amount. It is the velocity of these shots. It is almost scary the way the opposition loads up on the Detroit goaltenders. While the Red Wings are using pop guns, the opponents are using cannons. It doesn't seem very fair." In addition to allowing the most power-play goals in league history, 111, Detroit's defense was scored

## Dead Wings

**V**eteran blueliner Brad Park was appointed coach when Harry Neale was fired midway through the 1985-86 schedule, but his defensive savvy could do little to stop the flood of goals. The Wings surrendered more than five a game while losing 57 times, their worst season ever.

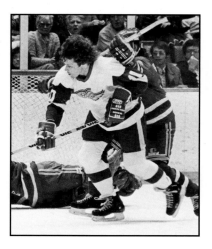

**H**is flowing locks made Ron Duguay a fan favorite at The Joe. He was traded towards the end of the 1985-86 season, having averaged 30 goals and 72 points during his three-year stay.

upon 415 times. To this day only one NHL team, the 1974-75 Washington Capitals, in their first year of existence, has given up more goals.

"There's nothing I want to remember about this season," said the-soon-to-be-fired Park, echoing a universal sentiment. Before another season began, Red Wings fans were jarred out of their amnesiac state by the announcement that a new coach had been hired. Ilitch and Devellano had been conducting secret negotiations with one of the game's finest young coaches, and now an emotionally charged malapropian from Montreal was ready to deliver Detroit from the dark ages.

# The World Hockey Association

**F**ormer Wing Larry Johnston was captain of the ill-fated Michigan Stags.

**A**sk anyone under the age of twenty-five about the World Hockey Association and you're liable to get a blank look. *The WHA?* some might respond feebly. *What's that—the call letters for a radio station in Kalkaska?* If the WHA is the WHO? to young fans, those with longer memories know it as an upstart league strong on ambition and innovation but light on cash and principle. Overall play may not have approached the talent level of the NHL, but individually the WHA boasted some of sport's greatest names during its seven seasons of existence, ranging from established stars like Gordie Howe to promising youngsters like Wayne Gretzky.

Viewed at from different angles, the WHA was either a force for needed change in the game or a circus run by carpetbaggers. Winnipeg's shocking signing of Chicago Blackhawks superstar Bobby Hull to a $2.75-million contract in 1972 had the effect of boosting artificially low salaries across the board. But with the big bucks came player agents (practically unheard of in the NHL before then) and franchise-hopping on an unprecedented scale. Between 1972 and 1979 the WHA fielded 32 teams in 24 different cities. Only four would eventually survive.

Curiously, although Detroit has always been recognized as a hockey hotbed, the city had a WHA franchise for just a few months. In the summer of 1974 Chuck Nolton and Pete Shagena, a couple of local entrepreneurs with interests in the chemical business, bought the moribund Los Angeles Sharks. They moved the franchise to Detroit and renamed it the Michigan Stags.

The Stags, coached by ex-Wings player and coach Johnny Wilson, held its training camp at the University of Michigan's Yost Arena. The team got little respect. A circus kept them out out of their home, Cobo Arena, until the seventh game of the season. The play-by-play announcer for their inaugural game, a veteran broadcaster, was so underwhelmed by the assignment that he didn't even bother to study the roster before going on the air. "Number 14 passes to number 8," he told his audience. "He takes it into the corner and passes to number 16. . . ."

The Michigan Stags quickly proved to be a disaster, financially and competitively. Attendance fell far short of what was needed for the club to break even. "I'd say they'd draw a couple of thousand a game," said Jack Berry, then the hockey writer for the *Detroit News*. "You never had to worry about finding a parking space, I remember that."

"You want a couple of minutes to talk about the Stags?" asked Larry Johnston, the former Wings defenseman who was captain of the team. "That's about all it'll take."

Johnston, who today operates a sports memorabilia shop in Redford, Michigan, had played three seasons with the Red Wings before signing with the Stags.

"I got a little more money," he said. "I thought they'd stay around for awhile. Instead it was a disaster."

According to Johnston, the new owners hadn't realized how much money it took to operate a professional hockey team. They were strapped for cash almost from the get-go. "Hotels wouldn't let us check in on credit, so we had to sit around in the lobby until somebody came up with the money to pay for the rooms in cash," he recalled. "We'd get off an airplane and the bus driver wouldn't take off until he was paid in advance. All of our sticks were neutrals; they'd gotten them wholesale from someplace. It was all pretty sad."

In addition to Johnston (who returned to play three more NHL seasons), the Stags did feature some other fine individual players. Heading the herd was Marc Tardif, an accomplished scorer who had jumped from the Montreal Canadiens to Los Angeles the previous season. The twenty-five-year-old left winger started the 1974-75 campaign with the Stags and finished it with Quebec, bagging 50 goals between the two teams. Tardif went on to capture a couple of scoring titles in a Nordiques uniform, including a WHA-record 154 points in 1977-78. His point totals predictably went down when he returned to the NHL, but he was still good for 25-30 goals a season playing in the senior circuit. All told, Tardif popped 510 pucks into NHL and WHA nets during his fourteen-year, two-league career.

Another notable Stag alum was a husky forward from Royal Oak named Bill Evo. The former Peterboro Pete had been selected by the Red Wings in the third round of the 1974 draft, but he opted to sign with the Stags. After five WHA seasons, including tours with Cleveland and Edmonton, he quit hockey to pursue a law career. In 1995 Evo was named the Red Wings' president, partially because of the experience he had picked up in the WHA. Part of that experience was being informed in the middle of a road trip that the owners had defaulted. This occured in the early part of 1975, when creditors caught up to the Stags in Cleveland.

"That last game they weren't even the Stags," said Berry. "That night when the players trooped into Richfield Arena, they had their jerseys taken away from them." The Stags' red, green, and brown uniforms were replaced with generic, logo-less outfits. Afterwards, the players were free to strike their own deal. Many wound up in Baltimore, where the franchise was resuscitated as the Blades.

The Michigan-Baltimore club, which scored fewer goals (205) and surrendered more (341) than any other in the league, finished with a 21-53-4 record for 46 points. Only the expansion Indianapolis Racers had a more woeful record. The Racers, at least, quickly turned things around and won a division title the next season. The Baltimore franchise folded.

The Stags' owners need not have felt bad. More franchise shifts and failures followed. In four years the WHA shrank from an ambitious three-division, 14-team league to a barely breathing circuit of six clubs, four of which (Winnipeg, New England, Quebec, and Edmonton) were absorbed into the NHL for the 1979-80 season.

Asked to summarize the brief history of the World Hockey Association, Jack Berry responded: "The players weren't as skilled as those in the NHL, but they were entertaining. It was certainly minor-league hockey. But you know what? Today, with expansion, all of those guys would be playing in the NHL."

> "We'd get off an airplane and the bus driver wouldn't take off until he was paid in advance. All of our sticks were neutrals; they'd gotten them wholesale from someplace. It was all pretty sad."

# CHAPTER EIGHT

The renaissance of Mike Ilitch's Red Wings began one June day in 1986, when Jacques Demers—who had just missed steering the St. Louis Blues into the Stanley Cup finals—was introduced as the twenty-second head coach in the club's history. The forty-two-year-old Demers was the seventeenth different person to work behind Detroit's bench in the last seventeen years, but the only one of them to turn into a genuine folk hero.

# A New Show at The Joe

## 1986–Present

"I cannot remember the last time a coach caused so much commotion in a major city," *Free Press* columnist Mitch Albom would marvel at the end of Demers's first season in Detroit, a year in which the pudgy, emotional, and eternally optimistic miracle worker made wine out of water, transforming the Wings from NHL doormats to final-four contenders.

Demers's stay in town would be short—just four years—but during that period he would be named Coach of the Year in back-to-back seasons, win two Norris Division crowns (and lose another on the last shot of the season), take his team into the conference finals twice, and even open a popular Southfield restaurant bearing his name.

**Wayward winger Bob Probert made headlines with his numerous battles on and off the ice.**

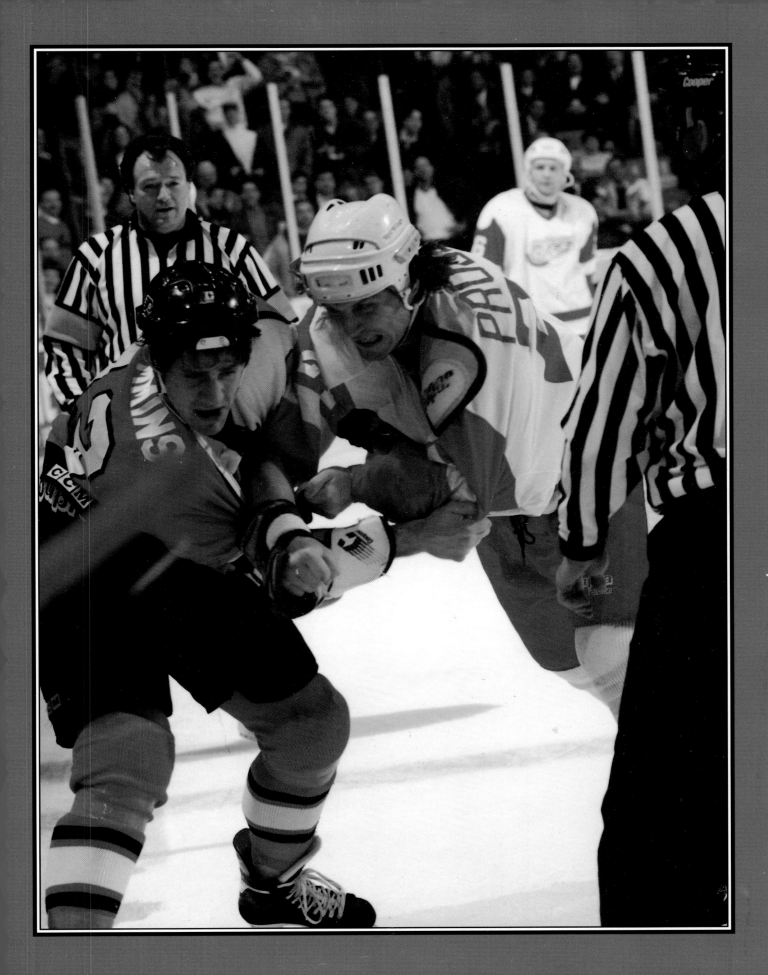

**B**rent Ashton pokes in one of his team-high 40 goals during the 1986-87 season. The left wing slipped to 26 the next season, after which he was traded to Winnipeg for Paul MacLean.

The son of a Montreal butcher, Demers was working on a loading dock when he got his first coaching job. He rose through the minor hockey ranks and into the World Hockey Association, where he was Quebec's coach when the Nordiques were admitted into the NHL in 1979. Let go the following year, he was all set to take a job as a computer operator when St. Louis hired him in 1983. By the spring of 1986 he had guided the Blues to within a goal of playing Montreal for the Stanley Cup, St. Louis falling 2-1 to Calgary in the seventh game of the Campbell Conference finals. Not long afterwards he left the Gateway City for Detroit.

Demers's signing caused considerable commotion. While Motown percolated with anticipation over the coming season, St. Louis accused the Wings of violating the league's tampering rules, which forbids a team from negotiating with another team's coach without that club's permission. Intrigue was nothing new to Detroit's front office, where Jimmy Devellano had just survived a power struggle with Brad Park and was involved in clandestine operations to get Russian stars to defect. The Wings and Blues ultimately reached a settlement: The teams would play a series of exhibitions, with all the proceeds from the games going to St. Louis.

One of Demers's first moves was to appoint Steve Yzerman captain. Judging by the number of fans wearing jerseys sporting his number 19 at The Joe, the handsome, baby-faced center was clearly the darling of the crowd, particularly among females.

Yzerman, only twenty-one, was starting his fourth NHL season. Although a decade later he would pass Alex Delvecchio to become the second most pro-

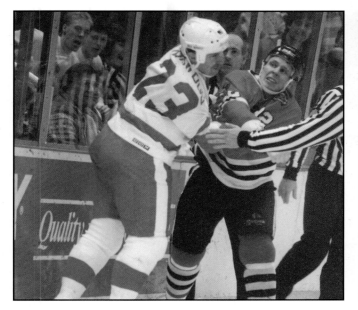

lific scorer in team history and sign a 17.5-million-dollar contract that would make him a Red Wing for life, in the fall of 1986 his impact on the franchise's fortunes was still more apparent than real. A fractured collarbone had forced him to miss the final 29 games of the previous season, limiting him to a mere 14 goals. He also seemed miscast as captain, though he was clearly the most gifted player on the team when healthy. His quiet and reclusive nature worked against him being a "yapper," as he liked to call his more boisterous brethren. He didn't care for the responsibilities that went with being captain. Not only was he unwilling to reproach slackers, he preferred to belong to his own little clique inside the clubhouse. Despite his understated ways, a cauldron of ambition burned inside him. "Steve wants to win more than anybody," said Gerard Gallant, his best friend during their nine years together on the Wings.

Demers's debut was less than smashing. Quebec rolled over the Wings, 6-1, causing Demers to announce to his players: "This won't do. We can't have this." The rebuilding was an ongoing process, with several players jettisoned during the season. The most significant trades involved swapping center Kelly Kisio, a steady 20-goal scorer during his three full seasons in Detroit, for veteran Rangers goalie Glen Hanlon, and sending John Ogrodnick to Quebec for left winger Brent Ashton. Ashton scored 40 goals to lead the club, ending Johnny O's six-year domination of that category, while Hanlon split netminding chores with Greg Stefan. While a quartet of 30-goal scorers—Ashton, Yzerman (31 goals, 59 assists), Gallant (38 goals), and Petr Klima (30 goals)—fueled the offense, the clutch-and-grab antics of veteran blueliners Harold Snepts, Mike O'Connell, Dave Lewis, Gilbert Delorme, and Lee Norwood—all acquired via trades or free agency—helped solidify the once-porous defense.

A pair of young head-banging forwards also contributed to the remarkable improvement in the Wings' goals-against figures, which in just one year shrunk from an average of 5.2 to 3.4 a game. Joe Kocur and Bob Probert, col-

The defensive duo of Lee Norwood (left) and Gilbert Delorme (right) came to be known as "Hack" and "Whack" for their chippy style of play. Both had played for Demers in St. Louis.

**Jacques Demers**

Joe Kocur, one half of the Wings' "Bruise Brothers" of the 1980s, in a heated discussion with Vancouver's Craig Coxe in 1987.

The last two Wings to disdain helmets were veteran defensemen Mike O'Connell (top) and Harold Snepts (bottom). Snepts, acquired from Minnesota in 1985, played three seasons before departing. O'Connell, who'd scored as many as 18 goals in a season with Boston, came over from the Bruins during the 1985-86 campaign. He hung up his skates in the spring of 1990.

lectively known as the "Bruise Brothers," may have been, pound for pound, the most destructive duo of enforcers ever to play in the NHL. Kocur, a 6-foot, 205-pound right wing from Calgary, had led the loop with a team record 377 penalty minutes the previous season, his first full NHL campaign. His thunderbolt right hand, tough enough to crack helmets, would eventually become so mangled that it would require a series of operations to repair. This would include grafting a chunk of his buttocks to replace tissue gouged out around his knuckles. But at age twenty-two, his lethal fist was still in peak shape. He explained that he always aimed a punch at the center of his opponent's head. "That way you're always going to hit something."

Probert, his twenty-one-year-old tag-team partner, weighed in at 6-foot-3 and 225 pounds. He'd grown up in Windsor, which accounted in part for his huge popularity at The Joe. Unlike Kocur, the battling left winger had soft hands around the puck, netting 13 goals in '86-87. However, like Kocur, Probert was unapologetic about his pugilistic chores. Early in the season, he got into a fight with Toronto's hard-nosed defenseman, Bob McGill. Probert ended the altercation with a well-timed head butt, for which he received a match penalty. "My arms were tired," he explained.

As the Wings continued to clutch, grab, hustle, scrap, and head-butt their way through the tightest divisional race in memory (only nine points would separate the five teams at the end), their coach became a minor celebrity. With his mustache, glasses, fedora, and accent, Demers was a Inspector Clouseau lookalike whose most appealing characteristic was the linguistic bloopers he committed as he moved back and forth from English to his native French. He described himself to a reporter from *Sports Illustrated*: "Everyone said when he gets to Detroit he'll take a landslide, but I think I've done a commandable job. . . ." Fans took to Demers's sincerity and ebullience with wide-open arms; he was a welcome change from years of blandness behind the bench.

## A New Show at The Joe

The Joe was crammed to the rafters all winter. The string of sellouts always included a peculiar looking retired schoolteacher named Joe "The Brow" Diroff, who gained his nickname from the astonishing thicket of hair that swept across the top of his eyes. His trademark homemade signs, such as SEAT OF WINGSDOM and SPIRIT—DON'T LEAVE HOME WITHOUT IT, became fixtures at Joe Louis Arena, as did his madcap, cornball cheers. A favorite was his strawberry shortcake cheer:

Strawberry shortcake
Gooseberry pie
V-I-C-T-O-R-Y!

When not detained by other engagements (he also attended all home games for the Tigers, Lions, Pistons, and several college teams), The Brow regularly visited the airport, setting up his lawn chair in an empty terminal in the wee hours of the morning to welcome the team back from a road trip. Later, he would even visit Probert in jail to give the troubled player a heart-felt cheer. "I am not a man who makes judgments," Diroff explained. "I won't cast any first stones. Everyone needs someone to care. And cheer."

"The Brow is a good man," remarked Demers. "He cares about the right things. And our players like him. He's a little eccentric, I think. But he's harmless. There are some superfans out there that I consider dangerous. The Brow—he's just a good guy."

Even The Brow's cheerleading couldn't prevent a minor collapse, as the Red Wings blew a comfortable lead in the standings in the last two weeks of the season, dropping six of eight games, five by a single goal. St. Louis, trailing Detroit by a point, checked into Joe Louis Arena for the finale, needing a victory to snatch first place. The hard-charging Blues grabbed the Norris Division crown when Rob Ramage scored with just 71 seconds remaining in overtime. Detroit finished in second place with a 34-36-10 record, good for 78 points and an appointment to meet third-place Chicago in the opening round of the playoffs.

After stubbing their toe in the regular season, the Wings figured to have some trouble against one of their most bitter foes. Instead, to the immense delight of The Brow and other members of the faithful, they swept the Hawks, setting up a Norris Division final with fourth-seeded Toronto.

The Leafs, who had upset St. Louis, dominated the Wings in the first two games, winning by scores of 4-2 and 7-2. Stefan was benched in favor of Hanlon, who played the rest of the series. A 4-2 victory at Maple Leaf Gardens restored some confidence into the Wings' locker room, but then a 3-2 overtime loss pushed Detroit to the brink of elimination. Demers continued to speak optimistically of moving onto the third round, despite Toronto's commanding three-games-to-one edge. Back home at The Joe, Hanlon threw a 3-0 shutout. "No excuses," Demers said when the teams reassembled in Toronto for game six. "We have played 90 games this season. If you want to play 91, you better win this."

Shawn Burr was a rugged, talkative forward who was the Wings' number-one pick in the 1984 draft. In 11 seasons with Detroit he delivered 148 goals and countless bone-crushing body-checks, including an occasional errant one that knocked out a teammate.

**G**len Hanlon replaced Greg Stefan during the 1987 play-offs and led the Wings to a stirring comeback, beating the Maple Leafs three straight times, twice by shutout.

They did, 4-2. Two nights later Adam Oates, Yzerman, and Darren Veitch all scored in a 3-0 victory to complete the Wings' marvelous comeback against their traditional arch-rival. The crowd noise threatened to blow the doors off Joe Louis Arena. Detroit fans, who only a year earlier had suffered through the most embarrassing season in franchise history, now celebrated their former doormats' extraordinary inclusion into the NHL's final four. "I am so proud of these players," a moist-eyed Demers said after the game. "They had plenty of chances to quit. People would have said, 'Hey, you swept Chicago. That was good enough.' But they wouldn't accept that."

Demers was so pumped up that, at the final buzzer, he slid across the ice in his street shoes and suddenly leaped into the air, a fist thrust towards the heavens. It was a nice bit of symbolism for a religious man who regularly visited a Quebec shrine named for St. Anne de Beaupre. Unfortunately, the powerful Edmonton Oilers awaited in the Campbell Conference finals, and nothing less than the intervention of this popular saint could prevent Demers and his band of overachieving, blue-collar players from crashing back to earth.

Wayne Gretzky's Oilers, enroute to claiming their third Stanley Cup in four seasons, shook off the pesky Wings in five games, though not before the overmatched Detroiters shocked them in the series' opener at Edmonton. The Wings' grabbing and holding tactics frustrated Gretzky, who had added a seventh straight Art Ross Trophy and an eighth consecutive Hart Trophy to his already groaning mantel. "We used to call Wayne 'Weener,'" recalled Greg Stefan, who had grown up best friends with The Great One in Brantford, Ontario. "He was dominant even then. He'd score seven or eight goals a game." Edmonton, for all of its offensive pyrotechnics, was far from being a one-dimensional team. Its defense shut down the Wings over the next four games, allowing a total of only eight goals.

The Wings never quit. The final game was still a one-goal affair until the closing seconds, when, with Stefan pulled for an extra skater, Kent Nilsson's clearing pass banged off the boards and headed for the empty Detroit net. As his teammates looked on helplessly, Gilbert Delorme futilely chased after the sliding puck. He arrived too late, the goal finally bringing the Wings' storybook season to an end. Delorme wearily slumped over the net, his head cradled in gloves blackened by sweat. It was the perfect image, the embodiment of a gallant, scrapping team that had gone farther than anybody ever thought possible before succumbing.

A few hours later, flying back to Detroit, Demers's exhausted band took up a collection for Joe Diroff. The Wings' most loyal fan, who had paid his own way to Edmonton for game five, had been invited to fly home with the players. Now, six miles up in the sky somewhere over Canada, The Brow led his heroes in one final cheer for an amazing season:

Strawberry shortcake
Gooseberry pie
V-I-C-T-O-R-Y!

## A New Show at The Joe

Detroit's second season under Demers was a virtual repeat of the first, only this time the battling Wings finished on top of the Norris Division with a 41-28-11 record. The 93 points were the best by a Detroit squad in eighteen years. Once again the team fought its way to the third round of the playoffs before losing to eventual Stanley Cup champion Edmonton in five games, and once again Demers took home the Jack Adams Trophy as the coach of the year. Key contributors to the Wings' first divisional crown since 1964-65 included Probert, who popped in 29 goals while serving a league-high 398 penalty minutes; Gallant, who racked up 34 goals and 242 penalty minutes; Klima, whose nocturnal activities didn't prevent him from scoring 37 times; and Glen Hanlon, who posted a 3.23 goals-against average and four shutouts, best in the league. Yzerman emerged as a bonafide superstar, accumulating 102 points—his first of six straight 100-plus seasons. He also displayed the kind of quiet grit that went a long way towards establishing him as a real team leader. On March 1, 1988, just moments after scoring his 50th goal of the season against Buffalo, a broken skate caused him to crash into the Sabres' goalpost. He had torn the posterior cruciate ligament in his right knee, an injury that seemed certain to end his season, if not his career.

Yzerman spurned a risky operation that involved grafting the ligament from a cadaver into his knee and then screwing it to his leg bones. "Now, if they wanted to give me Bobby Orr's ligament, or Gordie Howe's, then maybe I would have done it," he joked later. Instead he threw himself into a rigorous program of weight-lifting and other physical therapy designed to strengthen the muscles surrounding the torn ligament. As the team noisily skated to the top of the standings and through the first two rounds of the playoffs, Yzerman silently and uncomplainingly underwent two to three hours of arduous rehabilitation each day. Filling in for the captain were third-year center Adam Oates, a playmaker with superb instincts; grinding Mel Bridgman, acquired the previous season from New Jersey; and John Chabot, a valuable free agent who contributed 13 goals and 44 assists.

In the playoffs Oates, Chabot, Klima, and Probert all shined. Chabot set a team record with 15 postseason assists, Klima notched the franchise's first two postseason hat tricks in twenty-three years, and Probert broke one of Gordie Howe's records with 21 playoff points. The Wings made their way past the Maple Leafs in six games and the Blues in five. The rematch with Edmonton in the Campbell Conference finals didn't seem to scare the Detroiters, half of whom spray-painted their hair red and white for the occasion.

The Wings played Edmonton tough, splitting the first two games. After being out of the lineup for two and a half months, Yzerman returned to play the rest of the series, picking up a goal and three assists. Despite the emotional lift his presence provided, the Oilers proved too talented. They wore down the Wings, sweeping the next three games, including a heartbreaking 4-3 overtime win at Detroit in game four and an 8-4 rout in the clincher.

The result of the final game, as well as the eventual fate of Demers, were determined the night before the game when seven players were caught breaking

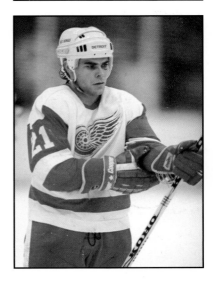

Adam Oates came into his own after Steve Yzerman was hurt in March 1988. The young center had a superb postseason and returned in 1988-89 to score 78 points, 62 of them on assists. To the horror of Detroit fans, Oates was then traded, whereupon he blossomed into a number-one center and a consistent 100-point scorer for St. Louis and then Boston.

The Red Wings made the final four in 1987 and '88, falling to the eventual Stanley Cup champion, Edmonton, each year in five games. In this shot from the '88 series, Mark Messier bores in on Glen Hanlon as Rick Zombo does his best to deter him.

Right wing Petr Klima was the Czechoslovakian version of Bob Probert, without the fists. He had immense ability, averaging 31 goals his four full seasons with the Wings, but he squandered a good deal of it through his fervent pursuit of the American dream: fast cars, young women, and drinking.

Klima had two hat tricks and scored on a penalty shot during the 1988 playoffs, but he also was responsible for the Goose Loonies incident and the dissension that divided the clubhouse.

Ironically, he was traded to Edmonton towards the end of the 1989-90 season and helped the Oilers to another Stanley Cup.

curfew. Klima, out with a broken thumb, talked fellow alcoholic Probert into joining him for some drinks at an Edmonton nightclub called Goose Loonies. Probert and Darren Veitch were nabbed by an assistant coach and returned to the Wings' hotel drunk; Klima, Chabot, Joe Kocur, third-string goalie Darren Eliot, and rookie defenseman Steve Chiasson also were busted. Feeling that he owed it to the rest of the team to put the best squad he could on the ice for game five, Demers decided not to bench Probert. "It definitely had an effect on our whole team," he admitted after watching his spiritless team get crushed. "We came out flat in the first period. There was a loss of respect going on."

Demers's concern for Probert and Klima was genuine; his own father had died an alcoholic. But his subsequent attempt at discipline was torpedoed by Mike Ilitch, who quietly, and without Demers's knowledge, repaid the $5,000 each of the offending players was fined. Other players, increasingly upset by what they perceived to be a double standard at work, staged a quiet palace revolt. Over the next couple of seasons the clubhouse was balkanized. Harmony and trust, such crucial ingredients for overachievers like this band of Wings, evaporated.

Yzerman had a huge season in 1988-89: 65 goals, 90 assists, and 155 points. All were team records. Only Gretzky and Pittsburgh's Mario Lemieux, two superstars in whose shadows it would always be Yzerman's misfortune to have to skate, outpointed him. For his efforts he won the Lester B. Pearson Award, a most valuable player award voted on by NHL players. One player unable to cast a ballot was Probert, whose substance abuse problems had spiraled out of control.

Probert's erratic behavior had first made headlines in the summer of 1985, when Redford police had charged him with driving under the influence and with fleeing and eluding. A long series of traffic violations and brushes with the law followed. After years of trying to deal with their troubled star through counseling and clinics, the Wings had attempted to trade him during the season. There were no takers. In the early morning hours of March 2, 1989, he was arrested on the American side of the Detroit-Windsor Tunnel by a customs agent, who had found 14 grams of cocaine stuffed down his shorts. He was charged with smuggling drugs, a felony punishable by up to twenty years in prison. The team suspended him and hurriedly cleaned out his locker. "I guess this ends our Bob Probert problem," Yzerman said, "in the wrong way." The distracted, divisive Wings won a second straight Norris Division crown with an uninspired 34-34-12 record. When they were upset, four games to two, in the first round of the playoffs by fourth-place Chicago, Demers blamed the whole lost season on Probert and Klima, another wayward talent who had been suspended for an alcohol-related offense.

The 1989-90 season began with Probert on his way to serving a plea-bargained sentence of three months at a federal facility in Minnesota, followed by an additional three months at a halfway house. It ended with the Wings, desperately trying to make the playoffs, reinstating Probert for a crucial game against Minnesota. On March 22, 1990, Probert received a tumultuous ovation at The Joe and scored the team's only goal in a 5-1 loss to the North Stars. Although the U.S. Immigration Service had ordered him deported, an appeal allowed him to play for the Wings as long as he didn't travel to Canada. This meant no road trips to Toronto and no visits to his mother in Windsor.

In less than four years, Demers's act had grown stale. The preseason trade of Adam Oates and Paul MacLean to St. Louis for forwards Bernie Federko and Tony McKegney, both of whom were past their prime, had stirred up fans, the media, and especially the players. One Wing reproached Demers for "trading for your buddy Bernie Federko." The team had gotten rid of one cancer when Klima was sent to Edmonton during the season, but the deal for Detroit-born center Jimmy Carson had also cost the Wings two good, young players in forwards Adam Graves and Joe Murphy. Another trade sent tough left winger Kris King, a character guy, to the New York Rangers for Chris McRae, who was a bust. The clubhouse was rife with cliques. Several key players, including Yzerman, told Mike Ilitch that the coach could no longer motivate the team—an opinion seconded by an assistant coach angling for the head position.

**P**aul MacLean, a consistent 30-to-40 goal scorer during his seven years with Winnipeg, put 36 into the net in 1988-89, his only season as a Red Wing. The right winger was part of the package that sent Adam Oates to St. Louis for Bernie Federko, a trade that left most Detroit fans and players shaking their heads.

# THE DETROIT RED WINGS

Detroit finished the '89-90 season dead last in the Norris Division. On July 13, 1990—Friday the 13th—Demers was fired with three years remaining on his contract. Brian Murray was named coach and general manager that same day. Less than two weeks later, Probert was ticketed for speeding on his Harley Davidson. Two weeks after that he was ticketed again, this time for going 102 miles-per-hour in his black Corvette. Demers may have left Detroit, but his greatest headache remained behind.

Under Murray the rebuilding of the Red Wings began anew. Jimmy Devellano, claiming burnout, was named senior vice president and surrendered his general manager duties to the new coach. Thus the forty-seven-year-old Murray became the sixth man in team history to assume both roles at the same time.

Murray was a proven winner, if one didn't look too closely at his playoff record. A graduate of McGill University in Montreal, where he served four years as hockey coach and athletic director, he proved his ability in the junior ranks by taking the Regina Pats to a league title in 1980 after it had finished last the previous year. He then moved up to Hershey of the American Hockey League, guiding the Washington Capitals' farm team to its best record in forty years. Midway through the following season he was named head coach of the Capitals. In his seven full seasons with the Caps, Murray averaged 43 victories and 95 points, figures second only to Edmonton's Glen Sather during that period. However, Murray had a haunted playoff history: None of his teams had ever gotten beyond the second round.

Murray swung several deals, sending Lee Norwood to New Jersey for right wing Paul Ysebaert and picking up center Kevin Miller in a five-player trade that sent Joe Kocur to the Rangers. Defenseman Brad McCrimmon came over from Calgary in exchange for a second-round draft pick. Murray also was the beneficiary of the Wings' European scouting system, which was in place years before the rest of the league. The 1989 draft included Swedish defenseman Niklas Lidstrom and Soviet stars Sergei Fedorov and Vladimir Konstantinov. Fedorov, a member of the Central Red Army team, defected in the summer of 1990 while playing for the Soviets in the Goodwill Games at Seattle and became an immediate sensation in Detroit. In Murray's first season the twenty-year-old center would wind up with 31 goals and 48 assists, finishing second in team scoring and in voting for the Calder Trophy. Lidstrom and Konstantinov would join the Wings' blueline corps the following season.

Murray restored some respectability to the Wings his first year. The team compiled a 34-38-8 record, good for third place in the Norris Division. Yzerman had his fourth straight 50-goal season, banging in 51 pucks and adding 57 assists for 108 points. Probert, subject to random drug tests as part of his probation, stayed chemical-free but otherwise continued his outlaw ways, picking up 315 penalty minutes and several more moving violations during the course of the season. The Wings went up against St. Louis in the first round of Stanley Cup action. The Blues, with 105 points, were 29 points bet-

**G**reg Stefan is gently helped off the ice on November 27, 1989, after blowing out his right knee in a goal-mouth collision during a 6-2 loss to Edmonton. The accident closed the books on the goalie's nine-year career, spent entirely in Detroit.

**D**emers hugs his players as they come off the ice after winning an important game late in the 1989-90 season. By now, however, the emotional coach's act had grown old. In three more months he would be fired, though he would later resurface to win the 1993 Stanley Cup as coach of the Montreal Canadiens.

## A New Show at The Joe

Jimmy Carson had grown up in the Detroit area but was passed over in favor of Joe Murphy in the 1986 draft. He was only nineteen years old when he scored 55 goals for Los Angeles, but that became the high-water mark of his career.

As part of the blockbuster deal that brought Wayne Gretzky to L.A., Carson didn't come close to making Oiler fans forget The Great One. In his second year in Edmonton he quit the team after some players, upset over his refusal to play a more physical game, reportedly hung him on some hooks in the dressing room.

The Wings got him for Petr Klima, but despite the best efforts of coaches and players to have him get more involved, Carson continued to practice his own brand of non-violence.

After scoring 100 goals and 202 points in 240 games for his hometown team, Carson was sent to Los Angeles in early 1993 in a six-player trade that made Paul Coffey a Red Wing.

**Bryan Murray**

The Alka-Seltzer Plus Award isn't quite the Hart or Art Ross Trophy, but it still honors a significant achievement. In 1992, Paul Ysebaert led the NHL with a plus-minus rating of +44. That, along with his 35 goals, took some of the sting out of a season that ended with the Norris Division champs getting swept by the Blackhawks in the second round of the playoffs.

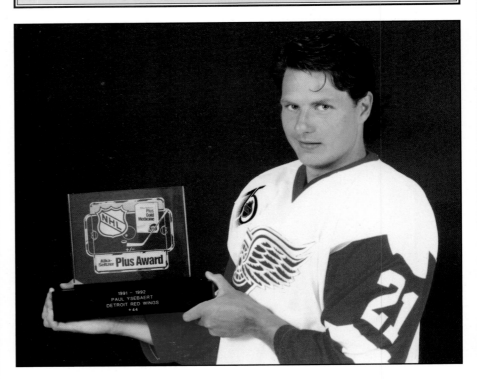

Tim Cheveldae's best of six seasons in Detroit was 1991-92, when he led all NHL goaltenders in games (72) and victories (38). That spring he became the first Detroit goalie to post two straight playoff shutouts since Terry Sawchuk forty years earlier.

Good-natured but sensitive, Cheveldae took a positive-thinking seminar the following summer after fans blamed him for the team's postseason collapse against Toronto. The booing became so bad Bryan Murray was soon forced into a trade he really didn't want to make, sending Cheveldae to Winnipeg for Bob Essensa in early 1994.

ter than Detroit during the season, but it was the Wings who won three of the first four games. However, a riotous game five in Detroit, in which the teams combined for a record 298 penalty minutes, ended as a 6-1 Blues victory and set St. Louis back on course. The Blues swept games six and seven to complete a back-from-the-grave comeback that started Detroit fans mumbling about Murray's well-known playoff woes.

By the following spring Murray had assembled the ingredients of a first-place team and a legitimate Stanley Cup contender. Tim Cheveldae, an unassuming and likable netminder from Sid Abel's hometown of Melville, Saskatoon, had earned the starting job the previous season. In 1991-92, he led NHL goalies with 72 games and 38 victories as the Wings captured the Norris Division crown with 98 points. Yzerman had another solid year with 45 goals and 103 points, Fedorov added 32 goals and 86 points, and ex-Ranger Ray Sheppard, signed by Murray as a free agent, knocked in 36 pucks, one more than Paul Ysebaert. Probert, having grown a bit mellower and more selective about fighting, scored 20 goals and cut his penalty total by a minute a game. The young and improving blueline corps included Lidstrom, Konstaninov, Steve Chiasson, and Yves Racine.

Shades of Ebbie Goodfellow. As part of the NHL's 75th anniversary celebration in 1991-92, Original Six teams wore replica jerseys dating back to their first years in the league. Rick Miller is sporting the same kind of sweater worn by the Detroit Cougars in 1927. Mercifully for the players' sake, these were not made of heavy wool.

# SPLAT!
# An Eight-Legged Salute to Excellence

When Scotty Bowman won his 1,000th NHL game (including playoffs) in early 1994 at Tampa Bay, transplanted Red Wings fans in the Sunshine State celebrated in time-honored fashion. They threw an octopus out onto the ice. And then another. And then a third.

Each time, a grimacing official or arena employee timorously skated over, scooped up the mass of tangled tentacles with a shovel or stick, and deposited the disgusting mess over the glass.

It's a scene that has been replayed more times in more arenas around the hockey world than anyone can guess. One even appeared during the Olympic Winter Games. Although its original meaning is lost on most octopus-tossers, each eight-legged splat is a tribute to Pete Cusimano, the super fan who literally launched the sport's most bizzare tradition more than forty years ago.

"The mistake most people make today is that they throw out a raw octopus," explains Cusimano, who has spent most of his seven decades in the seafood and restaurant business in the Detroit area and thus knows his fish. "We boiled ours. That firmed it up, so the tentacles rolled up."

Pete was born and raised on Detroit's east side, near Mack and Mount Elliott. The oldest of nine children, including six boys, he took his turn working in the family fish store. Like all Detroit hockey fans in the 1950s, Pete and his brothers lived and died with the fortunes of Howe, Lindsay, Abel, and Company. In the spring of 1952, the Cusimano boys were rooting for the Wings to complete an unprecedented eight-game sweep of Toronto and Montreal in the playoffs.

"My brother Jerry and I were working in the store Thursday afternoon, putting together the display for Friday," he recalls. "And Jerry picks up this octopus and says, 'Hey Pete, an octopus has eight legs. Let's throw it on the ice on Sunday as a good luck omen. You know, eight legs, eight wins.' We laughed about it and said, 'Okay, let's do it.'"

According to Pete, a properly cooked octopus has a certain glow to it—"a nice red-wine color"—and will bounce when it hits the ice. Which is exactly

Jerry and Pete's brother, Fritz, poses in front of the family's eastside fish market in about 1950. Evidently there were no octopi on hand that day.

what happened on Sunday, April 15, 1952, when Pete—sitting in the lower bowl of Olympia Stadium—flung the octopus in celebration of the Wings' first goal of the game, a first-period tally by Metro Prystai. It hit near the faceoff circle and skidded all the way to the blueline.

The linesman skated over to take a look. He moved to pick it up—then suddenly drew back his hand. Marcel Pronovost gallantly whacked the creature from the deep with his stick. Meanwhile, the public address announcer scolded the crowd: "Octopi shall not occupy the ice. Please refrain from throwing same."

"When it's boiled, octopus wiggles like Jell-O," says Pete. "Pronovost thought it was alive, but it was dead and cooked."

The same would have been said of the Cusimano brothers, had they been caught. In those days you simply didn't throw things onto an NHL rink. But except for some conspiratorial friends and ushers, for years no one knew the identity of the mysterious octopus launcher.

"We considered it just a one-time deal," Pete says. The Wings won the game, 3-0, and became the first team to win the Cup in eight straight. But the next year, with the Wings preparing for the playoffs, the three Detroit dailies—the *News*, *Free Press* and *Times*—all started asking, "Will the octopus make its annual appearance?"

So Pete and Jerry, who appreciated the value of tradition, pitched another out onto the ice at the start of the '53 playoffs. Unfortunately, the Wings were upset in the semifinals by fourth-place Boston. But the charm held the next two Aprils, as Detroit captured two more Cups. As Pete points out, three out of four ain't bad.

Tragically, Jerry died in an auto accident in 1954. But Pete kept the tradition alive. By the end of the decade imitators had arrived on the scene, smuggling their slimy bombs inside paper sacks, coat pockets and purses. Unlike Pete, who always threw but one, imitators pitch them indiscriminately and in volume. Many heave them, somewhat optimistically, from the far reaches of Joe Louis Arena. Unless one has a bionic arm, these are doomed to fall onto the heads of unsuspecting patrons many rows short of the ice surface.

Some, lacking the Cusimano daring, have a change of heart. To this day, the Wings' postgame cleanup crew finds abandoned bags of rotting octopi stuffed under seats. These are tossed into the Detroit River, where they're gobbled up by fish and turtles.

Pete Cusimano has grown to become the paterfamilias of octopi since his historic first toss. He's been written up in various publications, been given an all-expenses-paid trip to Toronto to repeat his feat on Canadian ice, even been made the subject of a Trivial Pursuit card. People seek him out, asking his advice on the proper pitching technique.

"Don't try throwing it like a baseball," he always tells them. "You'll throw your shoulder out doing that. You have to side-arm an octopus, like a grenade."

Pete enjoys his cult status, but admits he's the fortunate son of serendipity. Who could have predicted that an innocent prank would grow into an international tradition? He sometimes thinks the whole thing has gotten out of hand, all these airborne octopi. They're a mess, they arrive with little rhyme or reason, and they're potentially dangerous. Still, all things considered, it could have been worse.

His dad could have owned a dairy farm.

Jerry (left) and Pete Cusimano, all dressed up for their sister's wedding in 1951, launched hockey's strangest tradition the following spring. The day after the first octopus hit the Olympia ice, the *Detroit News* observed: "Over the years, galoshes, girdles, beefsteaks and buttons, and all brands of normal fish have appeared upon the ice, but never an octopus."

**P**aul Coffey, an integral member of three Stanley Cup winners in Edmonton and another in Pittsburgh, was traded to Detroit on January 29, 1993. In 1994-95 the highest scoring blueliner in hockey history became the first defenseman ever to lead the Wings in points. "It's scary," said teammate Ray Sheppard. "I don't think I've played with anybody who sees the ice so well."

Detroit's opponent in the first round was fourth-place Minnesota, which barged out to a three-games-to-one series lead before the Wings knew what hit them. But Cheveldae blanked the North Stars in game five, 3-0, and then game six, 1-0. The winning goal came at 16:13 of overtime when Fedorov's shot hit the back crossbar of the Minnesota net and caromed out. The instant-replay judge reviewed the video and declared the goal good—the first time instant replay had determined the outcome of a playoff game. A couple of nights later, Fedorov scored the first of five Detroit goals as the rejuvenated Wings swamped Minnesota, 5-2, to cap off their comeback. Cheveldae's scoreless streak was finally broken at 3:50 of the third period, ending 188 minutes, 36 seconds of shutout hockey.

The Norris Division wars continued with a second-round match with Chicago. It was thought that Detroit had the superior team. The Wings had dominated the Hawks during the season, dropping only one of eight meetings. But it was the Hawks who really came to play, shocking the Wings with a four-game sweep. Three of the games were decided by a goal, which made a couple of the soft shots Cheveldae allowed to get past him that much more noticeable. Meanwhile, his counterpart, Eddie Belfour, was practically impenetrable, holding the Wings' high-powered offense to just six goals. "If there was one legitimate time I thought we could win the Stanley Cup," said a disheartened Gerard Gallant, "it was this time."

But the Wings improved themselves considerably the next year, Murray picking up Dino Ciccarelli from Washington and Paul Coffey from Los Angeles. Both were well on their way to the Hall of Fame and gave a kick to an already high-powered offense. With Yzerman cranking out 137 points, including 58 goals, and the in-your-face style of Ciccarelli paying off to the tune of 41 goals and 56 assists, Detroit set team records with 47 wins, 103 points, and 369 goals. Chicago, however, was three points better, resulting in an opening-round matchup between second-place Detroit and third-place Toronto, which had piled up 99 points.

Working in the Wings' favor was a ruling by the U.S. Immigration Service allowing Probert to travel to Canada. The team had gone 14-26-9 in the 49 road games he had been forced to sit out in the previous four years. But in 1992-93, the Wings won three of the first four games he played across the border, illustrating his importance as a brawler and scorer in hostile arenas.

## A New Show at The Joe

Bob Probert's attempt to put his personal house in order oddly led to whispers that no longer living on the edge had adversely affected his game. The league's heavyweight champ lost a few fights, putting dents in his image of invincibility. But he silenced critics with his convincing thrashing of Tie Domi in their eagerly anticipated rematch at Madison Square Garden on December 2, 1992. On his way to the penalty box, Domi still had enough strength left to gesture towards the Wings' bench, which was alive with laughter and mock applause.

Early in the season Probert had his most famous fight, a rematch with Tie Domi. The Rangers' resident cementhead had split Probert's eye open in a fight at Madison Square Garden in February 1992, then skated off the ice buckling an imaginary heavyweight belt around his waist. The mocking gesture underscored what many around the league were privately thinking: Probie's mild ways away from the arena had affected his wild ways in uniform. But Probert's reputation was restored on December 2, 1992, when he and Domi met in their heavily hyped rematch at the Garden. The gloves flew off seconds after the opening faceoff, after which Probert pounded the pretender to his crown with a flurry of jackhammer punches. Video of the fight was shown on the replay board at Joe Louis Arena during the Wings' next home game, drawing roars from the crowd. One fan heaved a weightlifting belt onto the ice. On it was written "Probert."

Gerard Gallant sets up shop in front of Toronto's Felix Potvin in the opening game of the 1993 Norris Division semifinals. Gallant was nicknamed "Spuddy" because he hailed from potato-producing Prince Edward Island. The bristly left winger had four straight seasons of at least 34 goals and 200-plus penalty minutes, earning a berth on the second All-Star team in 1989. The '93 playoff against Toronto was his last action as a Red Wing; he signed with Tampa Bay after Detroit failed to offer him a contract.

But Probert was a nonfactor in the '93 playoffs, which started with a pair of blowout wins at The Joe, 6-3 and 6-2. Toronto bounced back with two home-ice victories, 4-2 and 3-2. Dave Andreychuk scored the winner in the fourth game with a wrap-around goal against Cheveldae. In the fifth game, Detroit blew a 4-1 lead and lost, 5-4, in overtime. The tying goal bounced off Cheveldae and the winner went through his legs, causing abuse to pour down from the stands at Joe Louis Arena. Ciccarelli's hat trick paced a 7-3 rout in game six at Toronto, setting up the climax at The Joe. It ended in disaster, as the Wings failed to protect a 3-2 lead in the third period. Doug Gilmour's tip-in knotted the score with less than three minutes left in regulation, and then Nikolai Borschevsky's deflection two and a half minutes into overtime sent the Wings home for the summer.

Two scapegoats emerged from this debacle. Cheveldae was so emotionally devastated by his subpar playoff performance, the death of his mother a few weeks later, and the widespread blame for the team's early exit, that Murray sent him to a four-day positive-thinking seminar. And Murray, himself the butt of criticism for yet another postseason failure, reluctantly relinquished his coaching duties to a man he didn't care to hire, Scotty Bowman.

## A New Show at The Joe

It's May 1, 1993, and Steve Yzerman, coming off a 137-point year, has just seen the season turn to sawdust on Nikolai Borschevsky's overtime goal in the seventh game of the Detroit-Toronto playoff. John Cullen is the Leafs player offering his condolences.

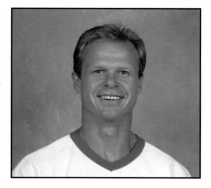

Mark Howe, the thirty-seven-year-old son of Gordie Howe, signed a free-agent contract with the Wings on July 8, 1992 and went on to play three seasons with his father's old club.

Mark, born the month after the Wings' last Stanley Cup in 1955, had already crafted a Hall-of-Fame-caliber career as a high-scoring defenseman—first with Houston and New England of the WHA, then during a ten-year stint with the Philadelphia Flyers, where he was selected to the first All-Star team three times.

A chronic bad back seriously cut into his playing time in Detroit and finally forced him to retire in 1995. By then he had amassed 407 goals and 1,246 points in 22 WHA and NHL seasons. Unlike his dad, however, he never played on a Stanley Cup winner.

William Scott Bowman was thought to have a computer for a brain and a block of ice for a heart. He was a stickler for detail. In Pittsburgh, his most recent stop before coming to Detroit on June 15, 1993, his players dubbed him "Rainman" after the character, an idiot savant, in the movie by the same name. Detroit players, some of whom had an immediate dislike of their new coach, quickly picked it up.

The fifty-nine-year-old Bowman had been raised in a blue-collar neighborhood outside Montreal. When he was a seventeen-year-old left winger for the Montreal Junior Canadiens, he was clubbed in the head during a playoff game. He suffered a fractured skull, ending his career. He worked at a paint factory and coached junior teams, eventually breaking into the NHL as an assistant coach in St. Louis in 1967. He took over the head job in mid-season, guiding the expansion Blues to the first of three straight appearances in the Stanley Cup finals. In 1971 he became the coach in Montreal, where he led the veteran squad to five Stanley Cup championships in eight years. He left Montreal in 1979 and settled in Buffalo, where he won no titles but cemented his image as a cold, aloof tactician. Moving on to Pittsburgh, he earned two more Stanley Cup rings—the first as general manager, the second as an emergency

**D**allas Drake goes to the net against Chicago in 1994. He was later traded to the Winnipeg Jets in a deal that brought goalie Bob Essensa to the Wings.

fill-in for the cheery and popular Bob Johnson, who was dying of brain cancer.

Ilitch paid the winningest coach in NHL history a lot of money to do one thing: take a talent-laden team that was a chronic underachiever and turn it into a Stanley Cup champion. "This Detroit team is going to learn quickly that we're going to do whatever it takes—maybe building up some confidence, maybe some other type of motivation," Bowman said.

Bowman's arrival coincided with the restructuring of the league along geographical lines. The former Campbell and Wales conferences were renamed the Western and Eastern conferences. The four divisions also took on less colorful names, the former Norris Division becoming the Central. Its members included all of the traditional Norris rivals, as well as a newcomer, Winnipeg. Gary Bettmann, a marketing whiz who had helped turn the National Basketball Association into a big success, was starting his second year as hockey's first commissioner. Canada's national game was increasingly referred to as a "product," with the changes designed to make the game "more meaningful for the new fan," explained Bryan Murray. "It takes a little away from the tradition, there's no question about that. But I think with the marketing strategy, it's probably a good move."

It was interesting that Bowman, a coach from the old school, would find himself a cover boy for the splashy, uptempo NHL of the nineties. He and Murray had major differences of opinion on personnel. Bowman didn't like Yzerman's one-dimensional play, and he wasn't happy with the goaltending or many of the defensemen. Bowman wanted to win now, but his suggested moves were stymied by Murray, who believed his mandate as general manager was to build a solid team that would compete for the Cup for years to come.

The Wings, preseason picks of many to win it all, instead started the first weeks of the Bowman era nearly losing them all. They dropped seven of their first 10 games, as Bowman took a good look at what he had to work with. He didn't care for several players, particularly Probert, who had resumed drinking over the summer, and Cheveldae, who he finally quit playing in home games because of the abuse he took. As Detroit battled Toronto and Dallas (formerly Minnesota) for the Central Division crown, goaltending became the sore spot. Murray, unwilling to pull the trigger on a major trade that would bring an experienced big-time goalie to town, settled on getting Bob Essensa from Winnipeg in exchange for Cheveldae and second-year forward Dallas Drake. The Wings wound up winning the division with 100 points, two better than Toronto, but it wasn't because of anything Essensa did. In fact, Chris Osgood, a twenty-one-

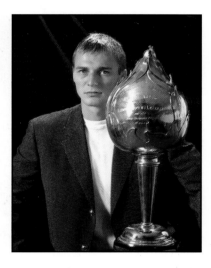

Keith Primeau was Detroit's top pick in the 1990 draft but experienced problems growing into his 6-foot-4, 220-pound frame. In 1993-94 he lit the lamp 31 times, his finest effort before leaving the team prior to the start of the 1996-97 season.

In 1993-94, Sergei Fedorov filled in for the disabled Steve Yzerman and had the season of his life, scoring 56 goals, 120 points, and becoming the first European skater to win the Hart Trophy. That year the dazzling two-way center also was presented with his first of two Selke Awards as the league's top defensive forward. On December 26, 1996, Fedorov electrified The Joe by scoring five goals in a 5-4 overtime win over Washington.

year-old netminder up from the Wings' Adirondack farm club, played more than any of the five goalies employed during the season.

The offense carried the day, producing a league-best 356 goals. When Yzerman went down with a neck injury in November, Sergei Fedorov jumped into the breech as the number-one center. Principally a defensive specialist who'd always had to be encouraged to shoot more, Fedorov became the first European to win the Hart Trophy. He scored 56 goals and added 64 assists to finish just 10 points behind scoring champion Wayne Gretzky. He also earned the Selke Award as the league's top defensive forward. Ray Sheppard had 52 goals, Paul Coffey scored 77 points to set a team mark for defensemen, and Keith Primeau, a towering if ungainly center, showed signs of living up to his

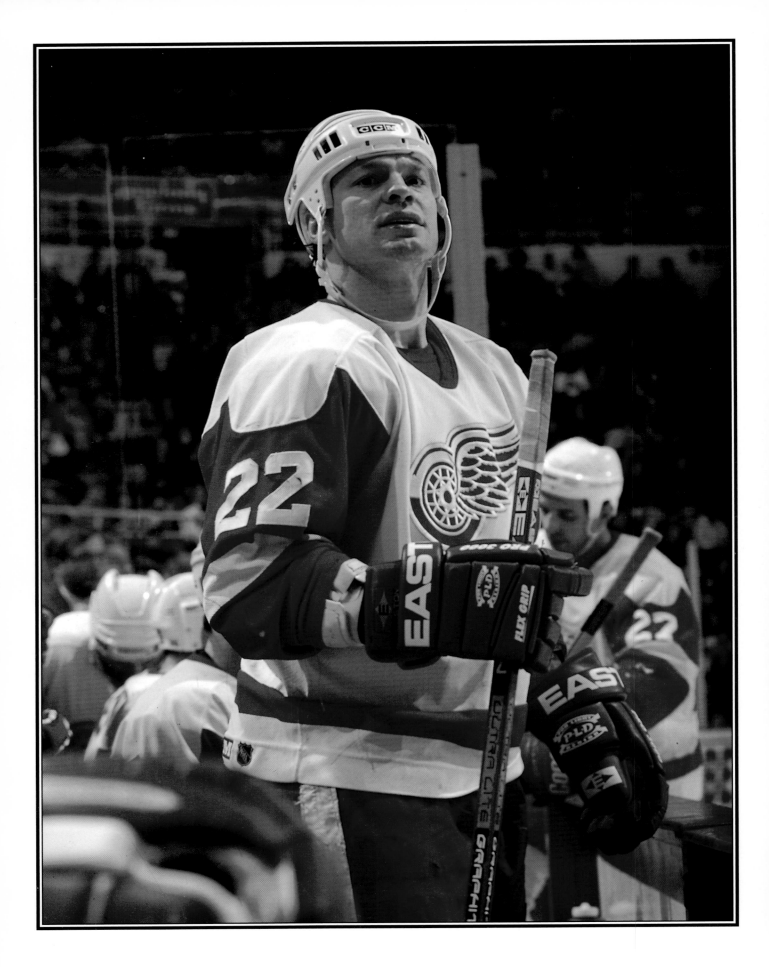

potential with 31 goals. Slava Kozlov, a small but gutsy Russian winger who had survived a car crash that killed a teammate, had recuperated to the point that he scored 34 goals. And Yzerman, despite missing 26 games, contributed 82 points. It all added up to a substantial force squaring off against a vastly inferior foe as postseason play started.

The San Jose Sharks, a third-year expansion team that had won all of 11 games the previous season, was the eighth seed in the Western Conference play-offs and drew top-seeded Detroit. The Sharks shocked Detroit with a 5-4 win in the opener at The Joe, but the Wings woke up for games two and three. They won 4-0 and 3-2, but then the Sharks bit twice, squeaking out a 4-3 verdict in San Jose after trailing by two goals, then taking a 6-4 decision in Detroit. The Sharks' three-games-to-two series edge had players baffled. Ciccarelli complained that the Sharks were so nice to him in front of their net, it was hard to work up a hatred for them. It was like being nibbled to death by goldfish.

**P**ound for pound, right wing Dino Ciccarelli was one of the toughest competitors ever to wear the winged wheel. His style also made him a huge fan favorite during his four seasons at The Joe (1992-96). Ciccarelli, who grew up in Sarnia, Ontario, averaged a point per game and was a force on the power play and in the playoffs, all of which made his trade to Tampa Bay for a third-round draft pick all the more difficult for fans to accept.

**S**an Jose goalie Arturs Irbe continually frustrated the Wings in the opening round of the 1994 playoffs. The lowly Sharks, only in their third year of existence, pulled off one of the greatest shockers in playoff history, beating Detroit in seven games.

**D**arren McCarty saw his dream come true in 1993, crashing the Wings' lineup as a twenty-one-year-old rookie right wing and being part of a team that entered the playoffs as a favorite to win the Stanley Cup. But the bubble burst in the first round against the San Jose Sharks.

**Probie in a more mellow moment.**

The Wings crushed San Jose, 7-1, in game six and then flew home to apply the clincher. Osgood had replaced the ineffective Essensa earlier in the series, but it was one major mistake by the rookie goalie that determined the outcome. After Kris Draper and Kozlov had scored to wipe out a 2-0 Sharks lead, Osgood and his counterpart in teal and white, Arturs Irbe, took turns preserving the tie with timely saves. Then, with 6:35 left, Osgood wandered far from the crease to clear a pass from his own end. San Jose's Jamie Baker picked it off along the boards and snapped it into the wide-open net before Osgood could recover. Joe Louis Arena was shocked into silence. As the clock wound down, the booing began. For the second straight year, the Wings had lost a game seven on home ice. For the fourth time in five years, they had been eliminated in the first round. One bellicose fan summed up the feelings of the nearly 20,000 on hand when he stood up at the buzzer and roared into the eerie quiet, "Same old shit!"

Pictures of a disconsolate Osgood crying in the locker room made it into the newspapers. The kid was forgiven. Murray was not. A few days later he and assistant general manager Doug MacLean were broomed. Bowman was given the additional title of director of player personnel. Now he would be free to make over the team in the way he wanted.

That summer the Wings finally said goodbye to Bob Probert, who had been arrested after smashing his motorcycle into a car while drunk. He was given his unconditional release, making him free to sign with any club that wanted to gamble on him. (He soon signed with Chicago.) They then said hello to Calgary goaltender Mike Vernon, obtained for Steve Chiasson. Vernon had backstopped the Flames to the 1986 Stanley Cup and was thought to be the man who could do the same in Detroit. Bowman also acquired veteran defensemen Bob Rouse and Mike Ramsey.

Their debut was delayed by the prolonged labor dispute between owners and the NHL Players Association. The two sides had been working on a new

contract for sixteen months but were still far apart as the opening of the 1994-95 season approached. There were four main points of contention: a rookie salary cap, free agency, salary arbitration, and revenue splits to aid small-market clubs. The players were bargaining in good faith, promising not to strike during the regular season or playoffs. But owners wished to play hardball.

On October 1, 1994, the night the Wings were to open the season against the St. Louis Blues, Joe Louis Arena stood silent. The day before, owners announced that the season would be "delayed" two weeks. Players called the postponement a lockout. That evening frustrated fans obtained their fix at The Palace of Auburn Hills, where 20,182 of them showed up to watch the Detroit Vipers make their International Hockey League debut with a 7-3 victory over the Cleveland Lumberjacks. The crowd easily eclipsed the IHL single-game attendance record.

While the new guys in town were competitive and put on a fun show (players skated out of a giant smoke-breathing snake's mouth), they still weren't the real deal. The Red Wings stayed home, working out informally to stay in shape. Their solidarity was admirable. Stars like Yzerman, who was out $17,460 a day in salary, stood shoulder-to-shoulder with lesser-paid brethren like Chris Osgood, who was losing $1,085 a day, as the lockout continued through the early autumn. "We're not going to break," insisted Shawn Burr. "When hockey players get down to crunch time, that's when we stick together. That's how we've been raised since we were three years old. I'll live on nothing before I turn on my friends."

Reacting to charges that the team wasn't tough enough, the Wings picked up enforcer Stu "The Grim Reaper" Grimson just before the 1995 playoffs. Grimson was bloodied in his first game in Detroit, taking on San Jose tough guy Jim Kyte to the obvious delight of Joe Louis Arena fans.

207

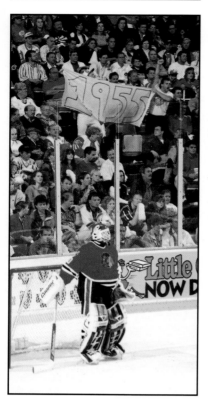

Expectations were high for the Wings when they won the President's Trophy for compiling the best record in the strike-shortened 1995 season. Fans unfurled this banner behind Chicago goalie Eddie Belfour during the Western Conference finals as a reminder of how long it had been since the team's last Stanley Cup.

The league's labor problems mystified Detroit's Russian players. "This would never happen in Russia," said Vlady Konstantinov. "They tell you to go play in Siberia, you go play in Siberia."

Mike Ilitch had mixed emotions. As the owner of the NHL's most valuable franchise, he was the kind of overly generous boss who had placed new VCRs in players' lockers at Christmas, given Yzerman a $50,000 bonus for scoring his 50th goal, and bought a private jet for the team so that the players wouldn't have to spend as many evenings away from their families.

But he also knew that the economics of professional sports had changed. A few weeks earlier, a similar disagreement had resulted in the cancellation of the balance of the major-league baseball season. Ilitch, who now also owned the Detroit Tigers, understood that annual increases in ticket prices could not keep up with ever-escalating salaries. (Of course, he conveniently forgot that a few years earlier he had helped unleash the beast now devouring hockey through his own extravagant signings of free agents.) "Our payroll has gone up six million dollars this year," he said. "We're exceeding where we should be for our team to be profitable. It's common-sense arithmetic. If the payroll goes up six million dollars, where's the money going to come from? The poor fans keep getting taxed. . . . If a player is entitled to make seven million dollars, isn't the owner entitled to make a million or two? What I'd like to ask players is, 'What can we work out, because we're bleeding.' Let's do something for the game, for the fans, or we're going to price ourselves out of business. We've got to make it economically viable."

Finally, just as it appeared that the NHL would become the second major sport that year to lose a season because of labor strife, owners and players reached a compromise agreement. Ilitch was one of a handful of hardliners who thought that the owners should stand firm on the issue of a team salary cap, but he was outvoted by fellow magnates. The final deal provided for free agency beginning at age thirty-two and a salary cap on entry-level players only.

An abbreviated, 48-game schedule was put together. The Wings opened January 20, 1995, with a 4-1 over Chicago at The Joe. They quickly climbed to the top of the overall standings and never looked back.

The key was a whole-team dedication to defense built around a system that assistant coach Barry Smith had brought back from a trip to Europe. Called the left-wing lock, it was a safety system that limited the number of odd-man rushes by having either the center or left winger hang around the blueline. The local dailies marveled over how Bowman had "sold" the system to the troops. Yzerman set the record straight. "Scotty wasn't selling us," the captain said. "He was *telling* us."

Despite sliding a bit in the final two weeks, the Wings finished with a 33-11-4 record and 70 points. It was the best showing in the league, giving the Wings the President's Trophy and home-ice advantage throughout the playoffs. The team had bought into Bowman's defensive-minded system while barely skipping a beat offensively. They finished third in scoring and narrowly lost out to Chicago in allowing the fewest goals. Vernon had proven as good as advertised, allowing 2.52 goals a game in 30 appearances, but Osgood had been equally impressive, with a 2.26 average in 19 games. Paul Coffey won the third Norris Trophy of his career, his 58 points placing him seventh in league scoring. He became the first blueliner ever to lead a Detroit club in points. Ray Sheppard had 30 goals, which translated into a 50-plus season had a full schedule been played. *The Hockey News* and other publications made the Wings favorites to take the Stanley Cup. As if that wasn't pressure enough, Bowman had a giant photograph of the '55 Wings, the last Detroit squad to win the Cup, placed in the clubhouse. As the playoffs began, players drew a crude drawing of the Cup along with a countdown listing how many victories they needed to win the elusive prize themselves.

The Wings easily eliminated Dallas in the opening round in five games, the Stars' lone victory coming after they had dropped the first three. This allowed Detroit to wrap up the series on home ice with a convincing 3-1 victory. Joe Louis Arena fans, between heaving record numbers of octopi over the glass—a messy tradition that local fish merchants Jerry and Pete Cusimano had started in 1952—breathed a collective sigh of relief. It was the first time since 1992 that one of the league's perennial powerhouses had moved into the second round. Somebody updated the board inside the clubhouse: 12 victories to go.

San Jose was next. To a man, the Wings insisted that there was no revenge factor involved; after all, 10 of them hadn't even been members of the team that had been embarrassed by the Sharks the previous spring. Detroit gutted the Sharks in four straight, outscoring them 24-6 and outshooting them by a nearly three-to-one margin. "I think they're the best team in hockey," Sharks forward Chris Tancill said. "When you combine that amount of talent with that much hard work, you've got a great team."

Eight to go. Chicago came to Joe Louis Arena for the opener of the Western Conference finals boasting the stingiest defense in the league. The octopus watch continued, five being tossed during the national anthem and another 19 after Ciccarelli countered Chris Chelios' goal with a power play tally towards the end of the first period. Later Tony Amonte beat Vernon with a backhander, giving the Blackhawks a 2-1 lead after two periods. But constant pressure by the Wings resulted in the win. Eight minutes into the third stanza, Doug Brown snapped a rebound past Belfour high on the glove side. "That's the type of blue-collar goal you need to beat a guy like Eddie," said another unheralded Wing, Kris Draper. "You just keep going to the net, keep shooting and hope you can jimmy one. "Ten minutes later it was Draper's turn to be a lunchbucket hero. Draper, a grinding center who had been acquired from Winnipeg two years ear-

**I**n the pandemonium surrounding the Wings' advancement into the 1995 Stanley Cup finals, scores of octopi were thrown.

**T**he victorious Red Wings are pictured with the spoils of victory for winnning the 1995 Western Conference title: the Clarence Campbell Bowl.

lier for the grand total of one dollar ("It was a Canadian buck," he acknowledged), was johnny-on-the-spot when Lidstrom's slapper bounced off Belfour's pads. Draper, in the crease to the left of Belfour, flicked the rebound upstairs for the game-winner, which incidentally was the Wings' 1,000th playoff goal in their history.

The third meeting was a repeat of the first two contests. Goals by Primeau, Coffey, and Stu Grimson, of all people, built a 3-2 lead after two periods. The game was a chippy affair. In the third, Coffey's clearing pass was intercepted, allowing Jeff Shantz to bang home the tying goal. The Hawks, desperate for any kind of an edge, had announced that anybody caught throwing a foreign object onto the ice would be escorted out of the arena. One of Chicago's biggest fish houses issued a press release declaring that no octopi would be sold to people from Michigan. Positive I.D. would be required on any sale. Devoid of octopi (although a rubber chicken did make it onto the ice), the Wings fought the Hawks hammer and tong through one overtime period and into a second. Finally, Vladimir Konstantinov—who, like Grimson, had never scored a playoff goal—swept up a loose puck in the neutral zone, crossed center ice, then let loose a wobbly shot a couple of strides inside the blue line. To the horror of Chicago fans, Belfour overplayed it and the puck floated between his blocker and shoulder and into the net. After a bruising 81 minutes and 25 seconds, the gritty Wings had earned their third straight one-goal victory.

Coming off eight consecutive wins, the Wings were due for a stinker. Vernon let in four of Chicago's first ten shots as the Hawks rolled to a 5-2 win. It was the only time in the series that either team had led by more than a goal. It also served warning to the noticeably lackluster Wings that Chicago was not going to just roll over and die for them.

The fifth game was at The Joe. As he had in game four, Savard popped one past Vernon for the game's first tally. Yzerman countered in the second period, when the Wings outshot their opponents by a 20-2 margin. Detroit had the Hawks back on their heels most of the evening, but Belfour was brilliant as the teams battled into overtime tied at a single goal apiece. The minutes continued to run off the clock. Then, not long after Joe Murphy clanked a shot off the post early in the second OT, Slava Kozlov turned Chris Chelios around with a drive towards the net. Belfour, who had been peppered by pucks all evening, may have been fatigued. He closed his legs a fraction of a second

**C**aptain Steve Yzerman hoists the Clarence Campbell Bowl aloft on June 11, 1995, minutes after Slava Kozlov electrified the crowd with an overtime goal that put the Wings in the Stanley Cup finals for first time since 1966.

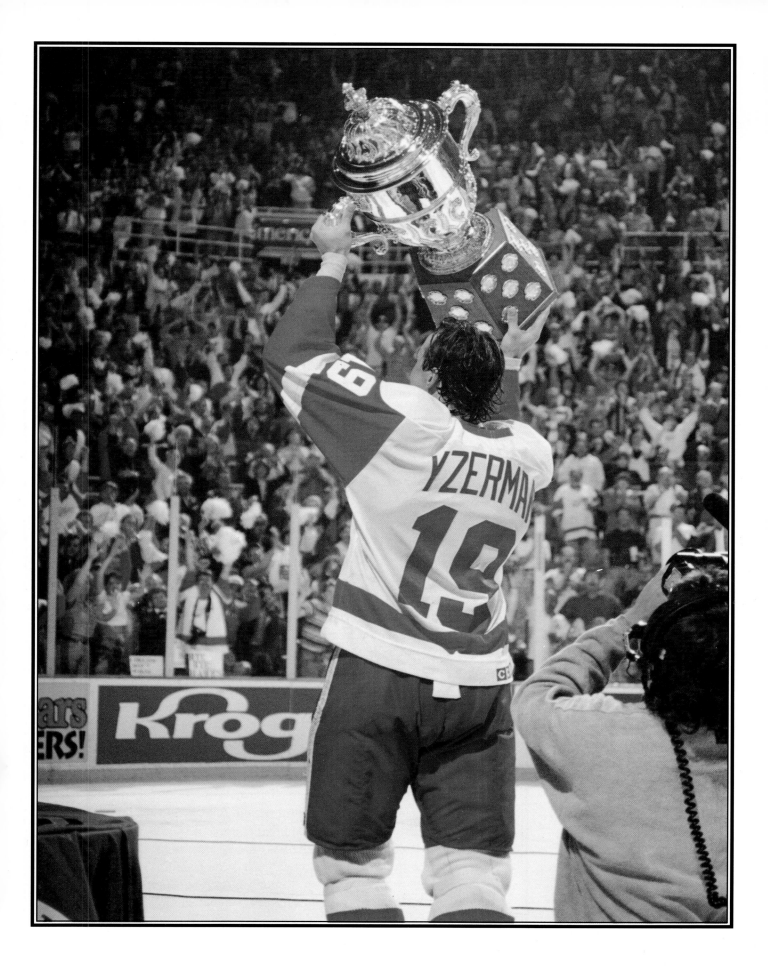

**R**ay Sheppard in a pre-game skate prior to the opener of the 1995 Stanley Cup finals. The right winger, who'd had 52 goals the previous season, had 30 in 43 games during the strike season—nearly a 60-goal pace.

too late as Kozlov's slapper zipped between his pads for a 2-1 victory. Just like that, it was hello, Stanley Cup finals.

Yzerman held the Clarence Campbell Bowl—symbol of Western Conference supremecy—aloft to pandemonium and skated to the runway. As thrilling as this was—no Wings team had made it to the finals since 1966, the year before Yzerman was born—wiser heads like Coffey knew there was no sense getting too excited. "Let's get out of here," he told Yzerman, who seemed uncertain about what to do next. In the clubhouse, somebody updated the legend that accompanied the drawing of the Stanley Cup. Four more wins to go. To the absolute shock of the hockey world, the heavily favored Wings never got any closer to their dream.

The New Jersey Devils, a squad whose trapping, opportunistic style of play had enabled it to climb over more stylish teams into the finals, were heavy underdogs. The year before, they had been eliminated in the seventh game of the conference finals by the New York Rangers, who'd gone on to win their first Stanley Cup since 1940. Now the Devils, who'd finished with the ninth best record in the league, had to contend with a flashy Detroit team that nearly all observers predicted would end their own Cup drought of forty years.

The battle between flash and trash started on June 17. By the time the last notes of the national anthem had floated to the rafters of The Joe, 14 octopi had splattered onto the ice, including a 25-pound monster that Devils goalie Martin Brodeur eyed warily as it was hauled away.

It was as close to the net as any Detroiter got for most of the rest of the night. Ciccarelli did counter Stephane Richer's power-play goal midway through the second period to tie the game at one apiece, but overall New Jersey smothered the Wings' sharpshooters. They were limited to a mere 17 shots, their lowest total of the season. Frustrated and impatient, they couldn't skate through New Jersey's center-ice web. Meanwhile, the Devils played their usual waiting game, finally pouncing on a turnover to score the goal that gave them the game. Early in the third period, John MacLean stole the puck from Niklas Lidstrom and took a shot that bounced off Coffey's stick. Claude Lemieux, a belligerent right winger who the Wings would quickly learn to loathe, whacked the deflection between Mike Vernon's pillows.

"We were real rusty, for whatever reason," said Coffey. "But it's a positive sign when 20 guys in this dressing room stink the joint out and we only lose 2-1."

However, the tone of the series had been established. The heavyweight Devils banged, battered, and bruised the Wings' lightweights in their next meeting, hammering out a 4-2 victory. "Hit grandpa! Kill grandpa!" the Devils yelled to each on the bench as they took turns zeroing in on Coffey. The homeboys also played hard but appeared simply overmatched and frustrated. The visitors also exposed Vernon, an excellent standup netminder with a quick glove. His standup style, although taking away goals from the corner of the net, made him susceptible to between-the-legs shots. The Devils found the five hole several times during the series.

Motown was in a panic. Only two teams had ever come back from losing the first two games at home to win the Cup: Toronto in 1942 and Montreal in 1966, both times at the expense of the Wings. But instead of coming out smokin', as promised, in game three, the Wings had their ears pinned back, 5-2. The game was more lopsided than the score indicated. "I was embarrassed and humiliated," Bowman fumed afterwards. "I've coached a lot of teams in the finals. We never were humiliated. It's totally unacceptable, an embarrassment to the National Hockey League. The Devils won every aspect of the game." Yzerman didn't disagree with his coach's harsh assessment. "We were on TV throughout the U.S. and Canada. It was an embarrassment. It's not that we didn't try. It's just the way we played. We were totally dominated in the Stanley Cup finals. We're supposed to be one of the top clubs in the league, and we looked like we didn't belong out on the ice."

In less than a week's time, the giddy, expectant atmosphere surrounding hockey's winningest team had turned funereal. Octopus sales plummeted. Superior Fish in Royal Oak, which typically sold about 200 pounds a week to restaurants, had brought in 6,000 pounds for the playoffs. After the third-game loss, the market slashed the going price from $4 to $1.99 a pound.

**T**he Wings, heavy favorites to defeat New Jersey for the Cup, were instead humbled as the Devils outmuscled them in four straight games. "Up to tonight, I've enjoyed the thrill of it all," a glum Steve Yzerman said after the final game. "Losing spoils it all."

**S**cotty Bowman flanked by his assistant coaches, Barry Smith (left) and Dave Lewis.

Two nights later the Devils put the pitchfork into the Wings with another 5-2 victory. After the buzzer the downcast Detroiters were only spectators, not participants, as the Devils whooped it up in front of the home folks. Keith Primeau stood by his net and watched the entire party. "I wanted it to hurt as long as possible," he explained. "That way I never forget it."

**A**fter winning two of three road games to launch the 1995-96 campaign, the Wings opened their home season on October 13, an unlucky Friday for the Edmonton Oilers. The visitors were thrashed, 9-0. Banners representing their divisional and conference championships and best overall record were unfurled. But the ceremony felt hollow. "We had a great opening night in our building," said Kris Draper. "We hung four banners. We did a lot of nice things last year, but New Jersey did the ultimate. We'd trade all four of our banners for that one of theirs."

"Well, I certainly think about it a lot," Yzerman said of the finals sweep. "Whenever I think back into last season, that's the first thing that pops into my mind, the finals." Said Darren McCarty: "We spent our individual time dealing with what happened, dealing with the letdown of the final series. But nothing you can do about it now. Just improve for the future."

To that end Ray Sheppard was traded to San Jose on October 24 for Igor Larionov. In his prime the slender and bookish-looking, thirty-five-year-old center had been the Wayne Gretzky of Russia, the quarterback of the team that won Olympic gold medals in 1984 and 1988, as well as a slew of world championships. In Detroit he was reunited with Slava Fetisov, the defenseman Bowman got from New Jersey before the '95 playoffs. The thirty-seven-year-old Fetisov, born in Moscow during the height of the cold war, had been regarded as the greatest hockey player in his country's history. A major in the Red Army, he had captained the national team to two Olympic gold medals and eight world titles and the Central Red Army team to 13 straight league championships. Youngsters like Fedorov and Kozlov had grown up worshipping this pair's exploits. To have them suddenly in their midst, casting a critical but paternal eye, was akin to having Gordie Howe and Ted Lindsay suddenly suit up as Steve Yzerman's wingmates.

With Konstantinov added to the mix, Bowman had assembled the first all-Russian unit outside of the former Soviet Union. This hammer-and-sickle version of The Fab Five ("Velikolyepnaya Pyatyorka" in Russian) proved

deadly. "Their playing style obviously meshes," said Barry Smith. "Their drop passes, skating, puck control—it all works a lot better together. They're not a line that just stays in their lanes." At the time of the Larionov trade the Wings were 4-3-2. Afterwards they lost only 10 of their next 73 games, a testament in part to the unit's effectiveness.

The '95-96 season was a record-breaking one, with several team and league records set and various personal milestones reached. In mid-December, Coffey became the first blueliner to register 1,000 career assists on his drop pass to Larionov in a 3-1 win over Chicago. Five weeks later, Yzerman scored against Colorado to join only 20 other NHL players in the exclusive 500-goal club. One was Ciccarelli, who during the season tallied his 545th goal to pass Rocket Richard.

The juggernaut clinched a playoff spot in late February, with a quarter of the schedule still to play. Curiously, there was little joy. Winning had become routine, expected, almost monotonous. Instead of fully appreciating just what they were accomplishing, the players had adopted a wait-and-see attitude. Records are nice, they reasoned, but it's what happens when the octopi start to fly that really counts. "If you don't win the Stanley Cup," said defenseman Mike Ramsey, "you can trash the regular season. And that's sad because you should put some stock in what this team has done this year." Ciccarelli

Sergei Fedorov kills a few idle moments with elder statesmen Slava Fetisov and Igor Larionov, both former stars with the Soviet national team who had found new homes in the NHL.

The '95-96 season was a historic one, beyond Detroit's record-setting 62 wins. On December 13 against Chicago, Paul Coffey (above) picked up his 1,000th career assist, an unprecedented milestone for defensemen. And on January 17 against Colorado, Steve Yzerman (right) celebrated his 500th career goal.

chimed in: "All of the players know that anything short of winning it all will be a disappointment, no question. But people forget how tough it is to even get to the finals, let alone win it. And it'll be tougher this year." The proof was that New Jersey failed to even make the playoffs, thus becoming the first defending Cup champion in a quarter-century to spend the postseason at home.

The goaltending was superb. Osgood compiled a 39-6-5 record with a sparkling 2.17 goals-against average and five shutouts. Vernon had a 2.26 average and three shutouts in 32 games. Rookie Kevin Hodson got in the act, too, blanking Chicago in his first NHL start. It was the first time in club history that three different goalies had hurled shutouts. Of course, they were aided by a system that emphasized team defense. Both Yzerman and Fedorov were finalists for the Selke Award. Fedorov won, but that a previously one-dimensional player like Yzerman had altered his game so dramatically so to be considered one of the league's top defensive forwards was tribute to player, coach, and system. On 57 occasions the Wings allowed two or fewer goals in a game, enroute to a final tally of only 181, easily the fewest goals surrendered in the league. The offense remained potent and well-balanced, finishing third in goals. Fedorov accounted for 39 of them, followed by Yzerman and Kozlov, with 36 apiece. Primeau had 27. Larionov and Ciccarelli chipped in with 22 each, while Lidstrom and Konstantinov both reached career highs in goals and points. Even Osgood put his paddle to use. On March 6, 1996, near the end of a game at Hartford, he joined Philadelphia's Ron Hextall as the only NHL netminder ever to score a goal in regular season play.

A late-season game against Colorado was illustrative of the team's dominance. The talented Avalanche squad came into Joe Louis Arena trailing only the Wings in points, but left shaking their heads in wonderment. The Wings administered the Avalanche's worst beating of the season, snowing them 7-0 behind three shorthanded goals and three power-play markers. Colorado managed a measly 15 shots on net as the Wings clinched their third straight Central Division title and second consecutive President's Trophy under Scotty Bowman.

Having once again clinched home-ice throughout the postseason, the only challenge for the Wings as they waited for the playoffs to begin was the all-time single-season record for victories. Bowman's Canadiens had won 60 games in 1976-77. The Wings tied the record on April 10 with a 5-2 win over Winnipeg, then broke it two nights later with a come-from-behind 5-3 victory against the Blackhawks that also matched Philadelphia's NHL mark for most home victories in a season (36 in 1975-76). They extended it to 62 on the final Sunday of the regular season, whipping the Stars at Dallas, 5-1. During the record-break-

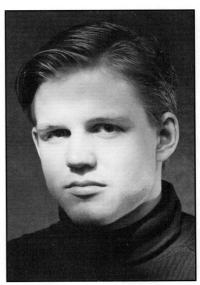

**B**y the spring of 1996 baby-faced Chris Osgood had emerged as the Wings' number-one goaltender.

217

Dubbed "Vlad the Impaler" for his aggressive stickwork, Vladimir Konstantinov was one-fifth of an all-Russian unit that Scotty Bowman unveiled during the 1995-96 season.

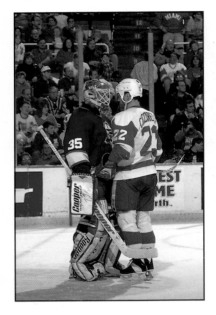

S cenes from a historic season: (clockwise from top left) Dino Ciccarelli faces down a Winnipeg goalie; Kris Draper exults after scoring a goal; Mike Vernon kicks out a Montreal shot.

ing game fans filled The Joe with chants of "Sixty-one! Sixty-one!" The public relations people wanted a photograph to commemorate the milestone victory, but the players said no. "We'll take a picture at the end of the season," said Yzerman. "Hopefully, we'll have the Stanley Cup in front of us. That's the only picture we need."

The picture of domination grew fuzzy in the playoffs. The Wings' opening-round opponent was eighth-seeded Winnipeg, the only team to have beaten them twice during the season. The Jets were on their way to Phoenix after the season, where they would become the Coyotes—one more franchise shift by a small-market Canadian team to the United States. In the first two games in Detroit, Osgood backstopped the Wings to rather easy 4-1 and 4-0 victories.

The storyline changed when the venue shifted to Winnipeg. Jets fans, upset over their team's move after 17 seasons in Manitoba, packed the Winnipeg Arena nearly 16,000 strong to express their support for the team and their distaste for anything American. With most of them dressed from head to toe in white, they booed the U.S. national anthem and kept up a nonstop wall of sound—the ear-splitting "White Noise" that was a tradition in Winnipeg. The Jets, their adrenalin pumped to new levels, played with abandon along the boards and knocked the Wings back on their heels, 4-1.

In game four, however, the Wings returned to the defensive scheme that had stifled opponents all year. Konstantinov opened the scoring just 82 seconds into the game. After Craig Janney tied it early in the second period, the

Wings deflated the crowd with power-play markers by Larionov, Kozlov, and Ciccarelli to build a 4-1 lead after 40 minutes. The cushion grew to 6-1 on Greg Johnson's and Yzerman's goals, at which point fans realized they were probably watching the Jets' final game in Winnipeg. In the waning minutes a growing shower of garbage rained down on the ice, including glass bottles, coins, batteries, mustard containers, pop cans, and even a can of blue paint. Vernon, starting his second straight game, got bopped by a roll of toilet paper and retreated into the safety of his net. At the horn there was none of the traditional celebrating. The Wings hustled into the dressing room, determined not to come back for a game six.

However, Nikolai Khabibulin saw that they did. The Jets' little netminder did everything but stand on his ear in the fifth game, stopping 51 of 52 shots as Winnipeg handed the Wings only their fourth home loss of the season, 3-1. The Wings were more irritated at themselves for their indiscriminate shooting than frustrated by Khabibulin's acrobatics.

They were more disciplined, more patient, in their return to raucous Winnipeg Arena. They scored on their first shot of the afternoon, Kozlov snapping one over the top of Khabibulin's catching glove less than four minutes into the game. By the end of the period Kozlov had added a second goal and

**A** panoramic view of The Joe in 1996. The Wings' 36 home victories in 1995-96 tied the NHL regular-season record set by the Philadelphia Flyers in 1976-77.

**Steve Yzerman**

Yzerman had also scored, creating a 3-0 lead that effectively ended the game and the series. Norm Mackiver blistered one from the slot past Vernon with 12 minutes left to play, re-energizing the becalmed Winnipeg crowd, but Primeau scored an empty-netter to account for the final 4-1 verdict.

"A little adversity is good," Yzerman said afterwards. "It's good to lose a tough game, then rebound. Everyone was mad we had to play again, but we did what we had to do. We're delighted to win, but our goal is to win the Stanley Cup, not the first round."

The next step was getting past St. Louis, which had finished 51 points behind Detroit in the regular season. The Blues, with an average age of thirty, had the oldest lineup in the NHL. However, the veteran roster boasted a collective 33 Stanley Cup rings, and that experience would prove invaluable as they took the Wings to the very limit. These greybeards were captained by Wayne Gretzky, obtained by coach Mike Keenan earlier in the season from Los Angeles. If the thirty-five-year-old center was no longer the greatest player in hockey, he remained the game's most marketable name and was still a formidable presence.

During the regular season the smothering Wings defense had registered the league's highest penalty-killing percentage in twenty-two years. It went on to hold the Jets to zero goals in 28 power-play opportunities in the first round of the playoffs. But in the series opener, St. Louis put two pucks past Osgood while enjoying the man advantage. The first, by Shane Corson, was payback for Ciccarelli's own power-play goal; the second, by Dennis Hull, knotted the game at two goals apiece. However, with two minutes left to play, Fedorov jumped into a two-on-one break and, taking a pass from Kozlov, buried the puck for a 3-2 Wings win.

Game two was over shortly after it began. Detroit scored four goals within an eight-minute span in the first period, then coasted to an easy 8-3 victory as the Blues were repeatedly whistled for foolish penalties. Yzerman scored twice and set up three teammates, tying Norm Ullman's team record of five points in a playoff game.

Any thoughts that the Blues would roll over and die were dispelled when the series shifted to St. Louis. In game three the Blues, playing with greater discipline and distributing bodychecks all over the ice, scored on their first three shots on Mike Vernon, building a 3-1 lead, then overcame a Yzerman hat trick to win in overtime, 5-4. Two nights later Jon Casey turned aside 29 shots and Gretzky whistled a low slap shot between Osgood's pads to produce a 1-0 victory. Just like that, the hard-banging Blues had tied the series.

## A New Show at The Joe

Returning to home ice for game five did the Wings no good. St. Louis won the Sunday matinee, 3-2, to put Detroit on the brink of elimination. After three straight one-goal losses the Wings seemed as frustrated as their opponents had been just one week earlier. It wasn't a question of talent, most observers agreed, but one of character. "We will be back," Yzerman grimly predicted in the locker room. "It's not going to end. . . . We'll be back for game seven."

Bowman shook up the routine. He moved the team into a different hotel, canceled the game-day skate, installed Stu Grimson behind the bench as a cheerleader, then watched his troops play loose and confidently in a 4-2 victory. Maybe the charm was the baby alligator's head assistant trainer Ken Boyer got from a helpful witch and placed in a box near the bench. In any event, Larionov's goal midway through the opening frame was a huge psychological lift. It was the first time the Wings had played with a lead since the third period of the third game.

The Wings returned to Detroit to find the city haunted by ghosts of seventh games past. Fans and media types couldn't help but recall that two recent upsets had occurred in final games at The Joe: in 1993 against Toronto and in 1994 against San Jose. If the populace was panicking, the players were not. A good thing, too, as the Wings and Blues proceeded to play one of the most intense, nerve-wracking contests in recent memory.

Teammates pile onto Steve Yzerman after the captain's overtime goal beat St. Louis, 1-0, in the seventh game of the Norris Division finals.

The game remained scoreless through three periods. Osgood, who had permanently replaced Vernon as Bowman's playoff goalie, and Casey kept out everything thrown their way. Coming off the ice at the end of regulation time, Yzerman walked past a reporter whose look seemed to say, *Here we go again. Another Wings collapse*. "Wipe that smirk off your face," the captain commanded. The referees had, in time-honored fashion, swallowed their whistles by now, leaving it up to the players to trip, whack, and wrestle each other until a decision was reached. They skated through one overtime period, then trudged back onto the ice for another. Finally, at 1:15 of double overtime, Yzerman skated across the St. Louis blueline and whistled a 58-footer past Jon Casey for a heart-stopping 1-0 victory. A giant anthill of red-and-white bodies immediately grew behind the net, as players rushed off the bench to mob the captain. "It happened so fast, I don't think anybody expected it," said Bowman. "We were having trouble getting a shot at the net. It was a game nobody should lose, *really*."

**K**ris Draper takes a faceoff in the first game of the 1996 Western Conference finals against the Colorado Avalanche.

Yzerman's heroics temporarily deflected attention from a growing concern: the lack of production from the team's big guns. Fedorov and Primeau had produced a single goal apiece, and Primeau's had been an empty-netter. And Coffey's back was acting up again, the result of getting continually hammered every other night for a month. Still, Detroit went into the Western Conference finals against Colorado as the favorite.

The Wings could be excused for licking their chops at the sight of Patrick Roy in goal. After all, in the five games in which Roy had faced the Wings during the season he had been terrible: five losses with a 5.41 goals-against average. The irony was that Detroit was responsible for the former Montreal netminder being in Colorado. Roy had won the Conn Smythe Trophy as the most valuable player of the 1986 and 1993 playoffs, each time leading the Canadiens to the Stanley Cup. On December 2, 1995, however, the Wings bombed him for nine goals during an 11-1 wipeout at The Forum. After being yanked he exchanged a murderous glare with his coach, then informed the team president, seated behind the bench, that he had played his last game in Montreal. Four days later he was on a plane bound for Denver. Another key pickup was ex-Devil Claude Lemieux, who'd played with Roy on the '86 Cup winner. Together they would foil Detroit's drive to win its first Cup in 41 seasons.

Once again the Wings appeared neither tough enough, hungry enough, nor lucky enough to get over the hump. The Rockies beat them in the opener, 3-2, on Mike Keane's 35-foot wrist shot at 17:31 of overtime. Osgood could only look up at the ceiling in disgust after the puck found a hole through his arm. It was the same expression Coffey had worn earlier, when he'd reflexively batted a

clearing pass into his own net in the second period to tie the game, 1-1. The miscue accounted for one-third of Coffey's unofficial hat trick, as he'd also put two pucks into the Colorado net.

Compounding the loss was a mysterious injury to Yzerman that kept him out of the last half of the game. A groin pull, Wings officials announced. Some suspected it was his knee giving him problems again. In any event, he was unable to dress for the second game. With their leading playoff scorer on the sidelines, the Wings were shut out, 3-0.

The situation had become distressingly familiar to the previous season's debacle against the Devils, when New Jersey left Detroit with two wins stashed in its back pocket. "They're looking the same way they did last year in that they're getting a little frustrated," said Lemieux. "When we had them down last year with New Jersey, our goal was to shut the door on them when we got home. And that's our goal this year."

The Denver press had a field day at the Wings' expense. Woody Paige's column in the *Denver Post* was typical. After the Avalanche bolted to a 2-0 series

A rare sight: Slava Kozlov has plenty of ice surface to work with against the Avalanche, who ended Detroit's dream season with a six-game series win.

225

**P**aul Coffey and the rest of the Wings had their hands full dealing with Claude Lemieux, hero of New Jersey's sweep the previous spring and author of the most controversial hits in the '96 conference finals.

lead, Paige wrote: "Last night they should have been hurling calamari. The Avalanche reduced the Detroit Red Wings to fried squid. Pass the cocktail sauce. . . . If the Avalanche can win two games in Denver, the Red Wings will become The Greatest Gagging, Heaving, Choking Team In The National Hockey League. . . . The Red Wings will get about half their normal oxygen at a mile-high attitude. But they're already having problems breathing because it's difficult when you have your own gloves around your throat. . . ."

The Wings' bandwagon needed new leafsprings after they shredded Roy in a 6-4 victory highlighted by Fedorov's four assists and Yzerman's pregame lecture to his underachieving teammates. "Our top players have to take on a stronger leadership role," he said. "They have to start asserting themselves. This is the time in their careers when it's becoming their hockey team."

Detroit had never had any kind of rivalry with Colorado, but with so much at stake it was inevitable that the two teams would reach new levels of intensity. Although the Wings had just blitzed Colorado, Bowman was still seething an hour later about Lemieux's sucker punch of Slava Kozlov.

"You fucking asshole!" Bowman screamed at Lemieux as the team boarded its bus in the parking lot outside McNichols Arena. "I hope the league suspends you!" The outburst from the sixty-two-year-old Bowman startled Lemieux, who was with his wife and two-month-old child at the time.

After reviewing a tape of the incident, the league did suspend Lemieux for one game. Avalanche coach Marc Crawford, citing Bowman's propensity for playing mind games, lashed back with a cheap shot of his own. "It's all a sideshow," he told the press. "He's a great thinker, but he thinks so much, he even gets the plate in his head causing interference on our headsets." Crawford's reference to Bowman's career-ending injury produced a few nervous chuckles. Bowman's response: "He's really getting down there."

In game four the Lemieux-less Avalanche got down to a 4-2 victory that gave them a 3-1 series edge. The mountain the Wings needed to climb now seemed more insurmountable than those in Colorado. They made it partway up the slope with a 5-2 victory at The Joe. Kozlov swatted a waist-high pass from Doug Brown past Roy at 11:35 of the first period and Detroit was never headed. The ailing Coffey, out the last two games with back spasms, set up a couple goals, as the Wings trooped off the ice still needing two more wins to advance to the finals. A sign behind their bench said it all: "We still believe."

At the end of game six two nights later the only things to believe were that Colorado was the better team, and that Claude Lemieux was, hands-down, the dirtiest player in hockey. The Avalanche, who would go on to sweep the surprising third-year Florida Panthers (managed by Bryan Murray) for the Stanley Cup, proved the former by rolling to a 4-1 victory to sew up the series. And Lemieux proved the latter by hitting Kris Draper with a cheap shot that had the jaw of the Wings' smiling center sewn up for weeks.

Lemieux's hit came 14 minutes into the game, after he had already blindsided Yzerman and Larionov as they approached the bench on line changes. This time Draper had just chipped the puck past Joe Sakic, when Lemieux barreled into him from behind. Draper, absolutely defenseless, was driven like a tent peg into the boards and had to be helped, dazed and bleeding, into the clubhouse. Lemieux got a match penalty and ultimately received a suspension, but he protested that it was a clean hit.

"I think anyone who knows anything about hockey realizes that it wasn't a clean hit," Draper later said. "I had a fractured eye socket. I broke my nose, fractured a cheekbone, and broke my jaw. My teeth also needed to be worked on. All together I had more than 50 stitches." Draper underwent three hours of surgery and had his jaw wired shut for 16 days, a period in which his teammates once again groped to explain what had gone wrong.

What had happened? The team that had lost only 13 times in six months had lost nine of 19 playoff games, including several at home, where they had been nearly invincible. For the second straight spring, the winningest team in the NHL had entered the postseason tournament as the odds-on favorite to

The 1996 playoffs brought out the usual share of octopi, including this monster being hauled off the ice by zamboni driver Al Sobotka.

**B**rendan Shanahan, the kind of proven power forward the Wings had long coveted, arrived in Detroit just minutes before the 1996-97 season opened.

**B**ulked-up Martin Lapointe, the Wings' penalty leader in 1996–97, had a breakout season at right wing.

bring home the Cup, only to confound and disappoint. "There are some things missing," said defenseman Marc Bergevin, "but this team could still win the Stanley Cup. It's not like it's a onetime shot and we're done. This team is not far from winning the Cup. But some things have to be done. I don't know what it is. Let the brains figure it out."

In the absence of a Stanley Cup to celebrate, local fans and media had "the hit" to chew on all summer—which was more than Draper, restricted to a liquid diet, could do. About the time Draper finally sipped his last milkshake, Keith Primeau decided that he'd had the last straw, too. Primeau, criticized for his poor postseason, was tired of being a third-string center, parttime winger, and—in his view—fulltime scapegoat. Before camp opened he demanded to be traded.

The gang that had compiled the league's best record the last two seasons was slowly breaking up. During the offseason Mike Ramsey had retired, Marc Bergevin had signed a free-agent contract with St. Louis, and Dino Ciccarelli— a favorite of everyone in Detroit except Bowman—had been sent to Tampa Bay for a conditional draft choice. Now Primeau's holdout set in motion not only his own departure, but also that of two popular veterans. After a week of bizarre on-again, off-again negotiations involving Bowman, Primeau, his agent, the Hartford Whalers, and other clubs interested in a three-way deal, the Wings traded Primeau, a number-one draft pick, and a reluctant Paul Coffey for left winger Brendan Shanahan and defenseman Brian Glynn. Because Primeau needed to be added to the active roster in order to be traded, a player had to be dropped and exposed to the waiver draft. That player, Stu Grimson, wound up going to Hartford, too.

The trade occurred October 9. Mike Ilitch dispatched his private jet to fetch Shanahan. Twice a 50-goal scorer while with St. Louis and the kind of hard-nosed power forward the Wings had long coveted, Shanahan arrived just in time to be introduced at center ice before the home opener with Edmonton. He got a huge ovation from a sellout crowd that clearly viewed him as the missing piece to the Stanley Cup puzzle. The temperamental twenty-seven-year-old made an immediate impression, getting into a fight in his second shift as a Wing and soon rocketing to the top of the team's goal-scoring list. Utilizing his size (6-foot-3, 215 pounds) and a blistering shot, he would wind up with 47 for the season, including a league-best 20 on the power play, just one shy of the team record. He also established himself as a force in the clubhouse, taking some of the burden off Yzerman's shoulders.

The revamped Detroit lineup got off to a less than dazzling start to the '96–97 season, as the newest Wings, including rookie defensemen Jamie Pushor, Aaron Ward, and Anders Eriksson, needed time to mesh. "Right now we're trying to find our identity guys, like Dino, Stu, Preems, and Coff," said Darren McCarty, one of thirteen Detroit players aged twenty-five or younger. "It's not the same as last year around here, and there's a real different feeling in the dressing room. We're young. We're trying to find ourselves."

Two-thirds through the schedule the club found itself mired solidly in second place behind Dallas in the Central Division, and third overall in the conference standings behind the Stars and Colorado.

Bowman expertly blended more size and maturity into the lineup. He traded Greg Johnson to Pittsburgh for Tomas Sandstrom, a versatile winger whose savvy, scoring touch, and snarly disposition was nearly on a par with Shanahan's. He then picked up Murphy from Toronto on March 18, the trading deadline. The big veteran defenseman of seventeen NHL seasons had won two Stanley Cups with the Penguins and was a sure-fire Hall of Famer. Nobody on the Wings could claim as much playoff experience as Sandstrom or Murphy.

Bubbling beneath the surface all season long was the subplot involving Draper and his antagonist, Claude Lemieux. Neither the press nor the fans wanted to let the controversy go; meanwhile, players on both sides admitted that they just didn't like each other. It was bad enough that Lemieux never apologized or personally inquired about his victim's health. Exacerbating the bad feelings between the teams was his comment that his hit had actually made Draper "famous."

The schedule maker had Detroit and Colorado butting heads four times. Injury kept Lemieux out of the first two tilts, both won by Colorado. Lemieux was healthy for the third game, played in Denver and again won by the Avs. Ten days later, Colorado, on its way to supplanting Detroit as the President's Trophy winner, arrived at Joe Louis Arena for the rivals' last go-around before the playoffs began. This was Lemieux's first appearance in Detroit since "the hit" ten months earlier, and the Motor City was up in arms. "The emotions are still there," admitted Draper. "The juices are going to be flowing." Lemieux, meanwhile, tried to downplay the significance. "I'm not going to comment about Detroit," he told reporters. "Show's over."

How wrong he was. The show was just starting. In what was instantly branded as one of the classic games in franchise history—and what would emerge in retrospect as the defining moment of the Red Wings' season—the reigning Stanley Cup champions skated onto The Joe's ice on the evening of March 26, 1997, typically smug and remorseless. They left it bloodied and dazed and with a seed of doubt driven into their psyche.

A hockey game turned into Fight Night at The Joe. By the end there were 39 penalties called and at least nine bouts, with Detroit combatants—including lightweights Igor Larionov and Mike Vernon—winning nearly every match on the card. The main event was the one-sided thrashing Darren McCarty gave Lemieux, a cathartic beating that brought out the blood lust in fans, players, and more than a few reporters.

The ten-minute battle royal started late in the opening period when the professorial-looking Larionov grabbed Peter Forsberg around the neck in a scrum along the boards. Players began to pair off. McCarty—Draper's good friend and roommate—whirled away from a linesman and, seeing Lemieux standing there unattended, blindsided him with a punch to the face. Lemieux dropped to his knees and tried to cover up. McCarty threw several more punches before grabbing him by the scruff of his neck and dragging him towards the Wings' bench,

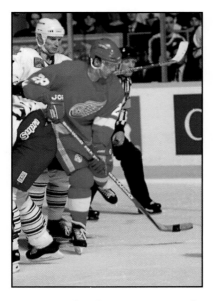

**T**omas Sandstrom was one of several newcomers that added more muscle to the Detroit lineup.

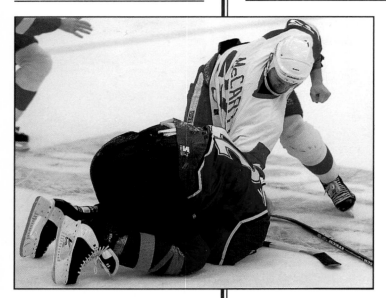

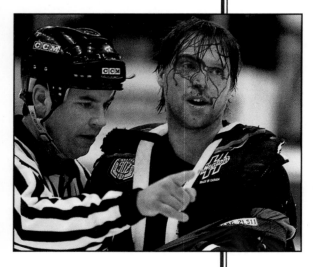

where he kneed him and continued to fire punches at the back of his head. Meanwhile, Patrick Roy moved out of the Colorado net to help Lemieux. Shanahan, looking to intercept Roy, knocked his man down with a flying leap that looked like something out of the World Wrestling Federation. After Shanahan got in a few swings, he was jumped by the Avs' Adam Foote, which allowed Roy to take on Mike Vernon, who had waddled at high speed from his crease. They met at center ice, where the two overstuffed goaltenders flailed away at each other for what seemed minutes until their arms felt like cement. The much smaller Vernon got the decision, as the Detroit bench and a full house stood on their feet and cheered him on.

Joe Louis Arena was absolute bedlam. Forsberg had been bloodied and Vernon had opened a cut over Roy's right eye. Lemieux needed fifteen stitches to close the cut in the back of his head. Emotions remained high the rest of the night, at one point Aaron Ward battling a bare-chested Brent Severyn. The pumped-up Wings continued to take the play to the Avs. With Colorado ahead, 5–3, midway through the third period, Martin Lapointe and Shanahan scored a half-minute apart to tie the game. Then, in the first few seconds of overtime, Shanahan shoveled the puck to McCarty, who smacked it past Roy for the 6–5 victory. The Joe shook to its foundations.

"What I did wasn't just for me," McCarty said. "It came from everyone on the team." And make no mistake about it, this collection of players—a number of whom hadn't been around the previous spring—was now a *team*. "This was a game that brought the Red Wings together," insisted Vernon.

Ultimately, sky-high emotions have no place to go but down. The squad played .500 hockey the last three weeks of the season, as Bowman continued to fine-tune his lineup for the playoffs. Vernon, who up until the Colorado game had played just once in two weeks, began to see more playing time. He had been more or less resigned to leaving Detroit once his contract expired at the end of the season, making room for the talented, younger, and much less expensive Kevin Hodson to become Chris Osgood's backup. However, when the playoffs began it was the feisty, well-rested Vernon—the veteran of three Stanley Cup finals—who was between the pipes. He would stay there night after night, his clutch gatekeeping justifying Bowman's decision, for the first time as a Detroit coach, to ride one goalie through the postseason.

In the opening round the Wings drew sixth-seeded St. Louis. The Blues were ailing, but still boasted Grant Fuhr, the man who had backstopped Edmonton to five Stanley Cups. Playing as well as he had in his prime, the veteran netminder kept the Wings off the board for more than five periods. He tossed a 2–0 shutout in the curtain raiser, then

**F**ight Night at The Joe. The festering feud between the Wings and Avalanche exploded into an all-out war on the night of March 26, 1997. Delighted Detroit fans were treated to the sight of Darren McCarty thumping a turtling Claude Lemieux while Avs goalie Patrick Roy was bloodied by his counterpart in the nets, Mike Vernon.

blanked the Wings through the first couple periods of game two. At this point Fuhr, who'd surrendered but one goal all week in three games at The Joe (counting the regular-season finale), seemed bulletproof. The Blues were leading, 1–0, four minutes into the third period, when Draper, on the ice killing a penalty, swept down the right wing and sent an ordinary shot towards the net. Unaccountably, the puck whistled between Fuhr's legs, knotting the score and lifting the pall of dread hanging over The Joe. "If they wouldn't have scored here," Fuhr said later, "it would have given us a big lift and would have taken them right out of it." Instead, three minutes later, Larry Murphy batted in a rebound for the 2–1 win.

Power-play goals produced a 3–2 Detroit victory two nights later at the Kiel Center, where fans entertained themselves by chanting "U.S.A! U.S.A.!" whenever Bowman sent the Russian Five over the boards. One, convinced that the Wings' top scorer was guilty by association, displayed a sign that declared, "Shanahan is a Russian." Forty-eight hours later, the Blues whipped Detroit 4–0. The four-goal loss matched the Wings' worst margin of defeat of the season.

Although Vernon had been pulled in game four, nobody blamed him for the team's faltering effort against an inferior foe. He had matched Fuhr save for save and had clearly been the difference the two times the Wings had managed to squeak by the Blues. Inspired by a postgame speech by Yzerman, his teammates ratcheted their game up a notch. This was no "win one for the Gipper" talk. "No secret philosophies," shrugged Shanahan. "Just put the puck on net and go after it." The result were 5–2 and 3–1 victories that advanced the Wings into the second round against Anaheim.

Detroit had been winless in 1996–97 against the vastly improved Mighty Ducks. The Wings had scored a grand total of three goals in their three losses and a tie against the unflappable Guy Hebert and his backup, Mikhail Shtalenkov. The Ducks, making their first appearance in the postseason, had another dynamic duo in Paul Kariya and Teemu Selanne—shifty forwards capable of finding the net in any arena.

A goal by Kariya gave Anaheim a 1–0 lead in the series opener after forty minutes. Anaheim's trapping defense and Hebert's excellent netminding continued to frustrate the Wings until Fedorov beat Hebert midway through the third period. Fedorov's tally ended a dry spell of 145 minutes and 15 seconds against the Mighty Ducks stretching back to the regular season. The game wound up in overtime. Previous editions of the Wings might have panicked, but this group remained composed. Fifty-nine seconds into the extra period, Martin Lapointe took a pass from Shanahan and one-timed it past Hebert for a 2–1 victory. "There's nothing like overtime," Lapointe said afterwards, "especially when you score the goal. You always want to be the hero." Two days later the teams skated through another nail-biter at The Joe. This time it was Slava Kozlov whose name made headlines, scoring at 1:31 of the third extra period to gain his hard-working teammates a 3–2 decision.

The series moved to the West Coast. Kozlov doubled his production in the third game, as he and fellow countrymen Fedorov and Igor Larionov combined

**N**iklas Lidstrom, who had tied Marcel Dionne's freshman assist mark with 49 in 1991–92 and finished runner-up to Pavel Bure for the Calder Trophy, had another quietly brilliant season in '96–97. The durable Swedish import—third among NHL blueliners with 57 points—quarterbacked the power play and played a nearly flawless defense. "He's probably the most important player on our team," said Steve Yzerman. "He plays in all situations and is expected to do a lot of things. He's a quiet guy, he doesn't get much attention, but he's an amazing player."

A group hug is in order after the Wings score one of their five goals in a 5–3 comeback win over Anaheim in the third game of the Western Conference semifinals.

for four goals in a 5–3 comeback victory. The three-hour time difference meant that fans back in the Motor City had to stay up past one o'clock in the morning to catch the entire game on television. The next meeting really tested the staying power of Detroit's hockey-mad insomniacs. The Red Wings eked out a 3–2 win on Shanahan's goal at 17:03 of the second extra session. His goal—Detroit's seventy-third shot of the night—came at 3:27 A.M. Eastern Standard Time, five hours after the marathon began. "I hope people stayed up to watch it," Shanahan said.

Was he kidding? Red Wings fever, like the team itself, had gathered momentum with six straight wins, half of them of the adrenaline-pumping overtime variety. Souvenir vendors were making a killing, the most popular item being a Red Wings flag that flapped proudly from the windows of tens of thousands of cars and trucks. Meanwhile, Colorado ousted Edmonton in their playoff series, setting up a rematch of last spring's Western Conference final between the Wings and the Avalanche. For hockey fans in Detroit, life rarely got any better than this.

As the teams prepared, Marc Crawford's comments in the immediate after-match of the March 26 donnybrook were dusted off. "I think that team has no heart," the Colorado coach had declared that night. "Detroit had the opportunity to do that in our building, but they didn't. . . . Everyone is gutless on that team, and I'd love to see them in the playoffs."

Colorado entered the series flashing the league's most potent offense and deadliest power play, as well as the best money goalie around. But the Wings outplayed, outhit, and outhustled the Avalanche in all but one of their six games. Thanks to their bulkier look, they were more aggressive—and more disciplined. "We have more players that can not only dish out the hits, but take them," explained Shanahan. "Guys that won't get rattled into retaliating and not get worn down. We've worn other teams down."

Colorado grabbed the first game, played May 15 at McNichols Arena, by a 2–1 score, despite being outshot by the same margin. It wasn't a good omen for Detroit, which hadn't won a best-of-seven series that opened on the road since 1966. Nobody in the Detroit locker room was offering excuses. The Wings simply came back and in workmanlike fashion turned the tables on Colorado, coming back from a two-goal deficit to win, 4–2. In the third period Fedorov scored the tying goal, Yzerman the winner, and McCarty the insurance tally. Back in Detroit, Vernon's spectacular goalkeeping and Kozlov's two goals were the story of a 2–1 victory that had a frustrated Patrick Roy openly challenging the Wings to step up for the crucial fourth game. "I really want to see how much Detroit is ready to play," he taunted. "That's what I want to see."

The Wings quickly shoved Roy's bravado down his throat. Larionov scored twice in the first period, Kirk Maltby added two goals, and before they knew exactly what had hit them, the complacent and arrogant Avs had had their world rocked, 6–0. Crawford, who had warned that Detroit hadn't "seen our best yet," pulled Roy before the game turned ugly in the third period. "You get a little emotional when they question your heart," said Joe Kocur, back with the team with which he had made his reputation in the 1980s. The popular enforcer, cut adrift by Vancouver, had played his way back into shape with a variety of pick-up and minor-league teams before signing with Detroit at midseason. "I always dreamed of playing against you and running into the corners with you," an opponent in a thirty-and-over, no-check league had told Kocur. "It just wasn't in this league that I pictured it." Kocur sported a new baseball cap during the playoffs. The lettering on it said it all: "Let the Ass Kicking Begin."

The ass-kicking got out of hand as the clock wound down on the Avs' embarrassing loss. Crawford, looking to deliver a message for game five, sent his players out with orders to hack and whack at the Wings' stars. The predictable result was a series of battles, with the Avs once again coming out on the short end of most of them. Officials handed out 204 minutes in penalties to the teams in the third period alone, including several game misconducts. The most entertaining exchanges involved Crawford, Bowman, and what few players were left, a wordfest that held up play for ten minutes. The words between the two benches got so heated that Avs assistant coach Mike Foligno, a former Wing, ripped off his headset and prepared to join Crawford in climbing over the glass to get at their antagonists.

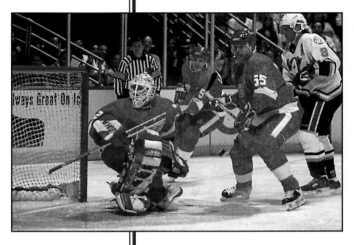

**N**iklas Lidstrom (5) and Larry Murphy (55) come to Mike Vernon's aid in the fourth game of the Detroit-Anaheim series. The Wings swept the Mighty Ducks to advance into the conference finals against Colorado.

Even Denver sportswriters were humbled by the spectacle of their organization falling to pieces in front of a national audience. "Denver vs. Detroit on Thursday night turned out to be an ice cube against a blowtorch," wrote Woody Paige. "The Avalanche was octopied, liquified, then liquidated. Only a small puddle remains. . . . The 'Lanchers were humiliated in the first two periods at Joe Louis Arena, then embarrassed themselves in the final period with a shameful goonfest and an infantile tirade by coach Marc Crawford." "Detroit is not—repeat, not—heartless and gutless," observed Bob Kravitz, referring to Colorado player Mike Keane's comments after the infamous March 26 game. "Thursday night, the only heartless, gutless team was the Colorado Avalanche."

To the Avs' credit, they regrouped on their home ice and blew out the Wings by the identical 6–0 score. Even Crawford, who was fined $10,000 for his eye-bulging rampage, salvaged some self-respect by publicly apologizing. However, the Red Wings closed out the series with a commanding sixth-game performance in Detroit, 3–1. "They did to us what we did to them last year," summarized Joe Sakic in the Avs' locker room. "They forechecked well, did well in their end and controlled the neutral zone. . . . They outhustled us everywhere."

But, stressed Bob Kravitz in the *Rocky Mountain News*, the memorable brawl of two months earlier had also played a major role: "It becomes clearer with each passing night [that the] evening of March 26 changed the psychological dynamics of hockey's most heated rivalry. . . ." Enemies to the bitter end, Drap-

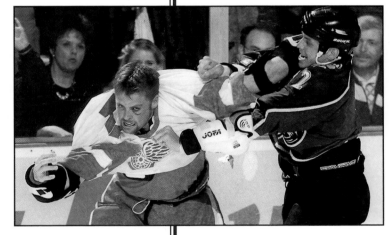

**A**aron Ward dukes it out with the Avs' Sylvain Lefebvre during the '97 playoffs. The fight was a draw, but the Wings knocked out the Avalanche in six games for the right to meet Philadelphia for the Stanley Cup.

er refused the traditional postgame handshake with Lemieux, who in turn ignored McCarty's outstretched hand.

**D**etroit had no history of animosity with its opponent in the Stanley Cup finals, Philadelphia. In fact, the Wings had little history of any kind with the Flyers, having played them only twice in the regular season (earning a tie and a win in a home-and-home series in January) and never in the postseason.

Philadelphia was a formidable foe, led by a rugged, intimidating front line nicknamed the "Legion of Doom." Its captain and franchise player was Eric Lindros, the 6-foot-4, 236-pound center who skated, hit, passed, and scored like Superman with a mean streak. His brawny wingers, John LeClair and Mikael Renberg, tipped the scales at 220 pounds. "They're obviously very talented and have a lot of ability," analyzed Larry Murphy, "but what's unique about them is their physical presence. They just seem to steamroll over everybody." Over the last year Detroit's lineup had gotten a much-needed boost in size. But the Flyers *averaged* six feet, two inches and 209 pounds a man, making them two inches and a dozen pounds bigger than the average Red Wing. The Eastern Conference champs, who had bulldozed each of their three playoff opponents in five games, more than blocked out the sun. They were healthy, confident, and deep in talent. They even had Paul Coffey, who had successfully requested Hartford to trade him to a contender. However, according to Draper, Detroit had a leg up on motivation as Philadelphia prepared to host the Wings in the opener on May 31. "We have so many guys here who went through the New Jersey sweep, the ultimate disappointment of our careers," he said. "You learn by losing. It takes failure to mature, and that's what we did."

These Detroiters also were a calmer bunch than the one that had preceded it to the finals. Yzerman spoke of the difference. "You kind of know what to expect a little more, you feel more comfortable in the situation. The fact that you're playing in the finals again, and the excitement and attention that comes along with it, I don't find as big a deal. . . . A bigger deal would be winning it."

After enduring years of coaching changes and trade rumors, Yzerman had signed a four-year, $17-million deal at the beginning of the season. Despite the security and the fact that the Wings figured to be a contender for the foreseeable future, he understood that he might never get another kick at the can. How many players get this close even once in their career, much less twice? He was the ultimate team man, still a leader who preferred to lead by example, not words. "When your captain lays down and blocks shots, when he sacrifices his body, it's a great example to the rest of the players," said Shanahan. When he did feel the need to speak up, Yzerman picked his spots. One was after the Wings had been shut out in the fourth game against the Blues. He could feel the season slipping away. "Steve didn't stand there and scream and yell," recalled McCarty. "He said, 'If we want to do something in the playoffs, we have to pick it up to a man.' We've just gone out after that and played hard."

It was a pair of unheralded grinders who unexpectedly scored the first

---

# The 1996–97 Red Wings

| | Won | Lost | Tied | Pts |
|---|---|---|---|---|
| '96–'97 | 38 | 26 | 18 | 94 |

| GF | GA | Finish |
|---|---|---|
| 253 | 197 | 2nd Central Division |

Defeated St. Louis 4–2 in Western Conference quarterfinals

Defeated Anaheim 4–0 in Western Conference semifinals

Defeated Colorado 4–2 in Western Conference finals

Defeated Philadelphia 4–0 in Stanley Cup finals

## Season Leaders

**Points**—Brendan Shanahan, 88

**Goals**—Brendan Shanahan, 47

**Assists**—Steve Yzerman, 63

**Penalties**—Martin Lapointe, 167 PIM

**Goaltending**—Chris Osgood, 47 Games, 2.30 GAA, 6Sh0

## A New Show at The Joe

Detroit goals of the title round. Less than seven minutes into the game, penalty killer Maltby broke in with Draper on a rare two-on-none and beat a sprawling Ron Hextall with the Wings' first shorthanded goal the playoffs. Philadelphia, still on the power play, tied it a minute later on Rod Brind'Amour's tally. But then with four minutes left, Joe Kocur intercepted a sloppy pass deep in the Philadelphia zone, deked Hextall to the ice, and nonchalantly backhanded the puck into the roof of the net for a lead the Wings never relinquished. "My reaction was more of a shock than elation," said Kocur.

His reaction mirrored that of the rest of the crowd at the CoreStates Center. The score was 3–2, Detroit, early in the third period when Yzerman applied the clincher. He let loose a 56-foot slap shot that Hextall somehow let past, sapping whatever momentum his team had built up. The 4–2 victory was Detroit's first in a Stanley Cup final game since 1966.

There was a different goalie in game two, but the result was the same. Shanahan and Yzerman scored on Garth Snow by the 9:22 mark of the first period. A pair of power-play goals by Brind'Amour just 69 seconds apart late in the period got the Philadelphia fans back behind their team again. But when it came to giving up bad goals, Snow proved no better than the man he replaced, allowing a long second-period blast from Maltby to slip by for what proved to be the game-winner. Shanahan sealed the 4–2 win with a third-period goal.

The oppressive weight of playoff history—something the Wings had experienced two years earlier against New Jersey—now pinned Philadelphia to the mat. Only two teams had ever rebounded from losing the first two games of the finals at home to win the Stanley Cup. As the Flyers continued to blame themselves for not playing up to their potential—an excuse the Avalanche had used while being cuffed around in the conference finals—the Wings went about their business in game three. Highlighted by the efforts of Shanahan and Fedorov (who would lead the team with 20 playoff points despite playing with cracked ribs), they skated to an easy 6–1 win at The Joe. This put them on the precipice of the franchise's biggest game since the seventh game of the 1955 finals. Many of the members of that team were on hand Saturday night, June 7, as the entire town rocked in anticipation of a sweet sweep. Brooms were duct-taped to the fronts and backs of cars; even the Washington Boulevard trolley sported brooms front and aft. The greatest symbol of municipal pride was the giant Spirit of Detroit statue downtown, which had been clothed in a huge Red Wings jersey. "It's sort of cool to watch," said McCarty. "But we don't get caught up in that. We just go out and play. We're a hardworking team, that's what we do."

It was McCarty who would end up scoring the Wings' final, and most dazzling, goal of the postseason. It would also turn out to be the Cup winner. The Red Wings, anxious to finish the job, played tentatively at first. But with a half-minute left in the first period, Niklas Lidstrom one-timed a slap shot from the blue line past Hextall, who'd returned to the nets after Garth Snow's meltdown in game two.

The "Grind Line" of Darren McCarty, Kris Draper, Kirk Maltby, and Joe Kocur gave opponents fits throughout the '97 playoffs, with Maltby and Kocur scoring Detroit's first two goals of the Stanley Cup finals.

Conn Smythe Trophy winner Mike Vernon helped shut down Eric Lindros and the Flyers in four games in the '97 Stanley Cup finals.

## THE DETROIT RED WINGS

The Wings nursed the narrow lead until McCarty showed moves of the kind usually only displayed by guys like Yzerman and Fedorov. Midway through the second period he took a pass from Tomas Sandstrom at center ice and was met by Janne Niinimaa. McCarty faked to his left, then cut to his right, a deke that caused the Flyers' defenseman to fall to the ice. As Hextall moved to his right, McCarty pulled the puck back, then flicked a wrist shot to Hextall's left. According to the clock, the game was a little more than halfway over at this point. But everybody in the building knew that it was *really* over.

The noise in the stands expanded to an unprecedented level at the last couple of minutes ticked away. Twenty thousand people were on their feet. Even Eric Lindros's goal with 15 seconds remaining barely produced a hiccup in the pandemonium. Finally, at 10:50 P.M., the horn blasted, fireworks exploded, confetti rained down from the rafters, and gloves, sticks, and helmets were jubilantly tossed into the air. Yzerman didn't know how to describe the last moments of the 2–1 victory that finally lifted more than four decades of frustration. He was glad the game was over, he later admitted, but at the same time he was wishing that it would never end.

With victory came the spoils. Vernon, who had won 16 of 20 playoff games with a sparkling 1.75 average, was named the winner of the Conn Smyth Trophy. But it was the captain's name that the crowd started chanting when the Stanley Cup, borne by two white-gloved assistants from the league, was brought out onto the ice. Then Yzerman, sporting a smile as wide as a goalie crease, did what he had dreamed of doing since he was a kid: lofting the silver-barreled trophy over his head and doing a slow victory waltz around the ice. He skated over to the bench where he presented hockey's top prize to the emotionally wrung-out Mike and Marian Ilitch. Then it was the team's two elder statesmen, Fetisov and Larionov, who did a victory lap. The rest of the players, the trainers, and even the zamboni driver took their turns. Scotty Bowman, who'd just become the first man to coach three different teams to an NHL title, laced on skates and took an unprecedented whirl.

The Wings had exposed the big, bad Flyers as being too slow, too disorganized, too lacking in poise, confidence, and esprit de corps. It was as convincing a clobbering as Detroit had suffered at the hands of New Jersey two years earlier. Actually, more so. Philadelphia had played with the lead for all of two minutes during the entire series. "They beat us four straight and I didn't think that could happen to our hockey club," Lindros said afterwards. "I'm still in shock."

Meanwhile, Detroit was in ecstasy. It had been 42 frustrating years between Stanley Cups, but now fans were savoring the eighth championship in team history—still more, despite the long drought, than any NHL franchise except Montreal and Toronto. In the after glow of victory, there would arise questions of personnel. Would Vernon, Fedorov, Larionov, Kocur, Fetisov, and Bowman remain in town? Trades, free agency, and retirement are unavoidable aspects of the game. What was certain was that Detroit's hockey faithful, as has been their custom for nearly three-quarters of a century, would continue to live and die with the fortunes of whoever wears the winged wheel.

# Season-by-Season Record

| Season | W | L | T | Pts | GF | GA | Finish |
|--------|---|---|---|-----|-----|-----|--------|
| 1926-27 | 12 | 28 | 4 | 28 | 76 | 105 | 5th American Division |
| 1927-28 | 19 | 19 | 6 | 44 | 88 | 79 | 4th American Division |
| 1928-29 | 19 | 16 | 9 | 47 | 72 | 63 | 3rd American Division |

*Lost to Toronto 0-2 in quarterfinals*

| Season | W | L | T | Pts | GF | GA | Finish |
|--------|---|---|---|-----|-----|-----|--------|
| 1929-30 | 14 | 24 | 6 | 34 | 117 | 133 | 4th American Division |
| 1930-31 | 16 | 21 | 7 | 39 | 102 | 105 | 4th American Division |
| 1931-32 | 18 | 20 | 10 | 46 | 95 | 108 | 3rd American Division |

*Lost to Montreal Maroons 0-1 (1 tie) in quarterfinals*

| 1932-33 | 25 | 15 | 8 | 58 | 111 | 93 | 2nd American Division |
|--------|---|---|---|-----|-----|-----|--------|

*Defeated Montreal Maroons 2-0 in quarterfinals*
*Lost to New York Rangers 0-2 in semifinals*

| 1933-34 | 24 | 14 | 10 | 58 | 113 | 98 | 1st American Division |
|--------|---|---|---|-----|-----|-----|--------|

*Defeated Toronto 3-2 in semifinals*
*Lost to Chicago 1-3 in Stanley Cup finals*

| 1934-35 | 19 | 22 | 7 | 45 | 127 | 114 | 4th American Division |
| 1935-36 | 24 | 16 | 8 | 56 | 124 | 103 | 1st American Division |

*Defeated Montreal Maroons 3-0 in semifinals*
*Defeated Toronto 3-1 in Stanley Cup finals*

| 1936-37 | 25 | 14 | 9 | 59 | 128 | 102 | 1st American Division |
|--------|---|---|---|-----|-----|-----|--------|

*Defeated Montreal Canadiens 3-2 in semifinals*
*Defeated New York Rangers 3-2 in Stanley Cup finals*

| 1937-38 | 12 | 25 | 11 | 35 | 99 | 133 | 4th American Division |
| 1938-39 | 18 | 24 | 6 | 42 | 107 | 128 | 5th National Hockey League |

*Defeated Montreal Canadiens 2-1 in quarterfinals*
*Lost to Toronto 1-2 in semifinals*

| 1939-40 | 16 | 26 | 6 | 38 | 90 | 126 | 5th National Hockey League |
|--------|---|---|---|-----|-----|-----|--------|

*Defeated New York Americans 2-1 in quarterfinals*
*Lost to Toronto 0-2 in semifinals*

| 1940-41 | 21 | 16 | 11 | 53 | 112 | 102 | 3rd National Hockey League |
|--------|---|---|---|-----|-----|-----|--------|

*Defeated New York Rangers 2-1 in quarterfinals*
*Defeated Chicago 2-0 in semifinals*
*Lost to Boston 0-4 in Stanley Cup finals*

| 1941-42 | 19 | 25 | 4 | 42 | 140 | 147 | 5th National Hockey League |
|--------|---|---|---|-----|-----|-----|--------|

*Defeated Montreal Canadiens 2-1 in quarterfinals*
*Defeated Chicago 2-0 in semifinals*
*Lost to Toronto 3-4 in Stanley Cup finals*

| 1942-43 | 25 | 14 | 11 | 61 | 169 | 124 | 1st National Hockey League |
|--------|---|---|---|-----|-----|-----|--------|

*Defeated Toronto 4-2 in semifinals*
*Defeated Boston 4-0 in Stanley Cup finals*

| 1943-44 | 26 | 18 | 6 | 58 | 214 | 177 | 2nd National Hockey League |
|--------|---|---|---|-----|-----|-----|--------|

*Lost to Chicago 1-4 in semifinals*

| 1944-45 | 31 | 14 | 5 | 67 | 218 | 161 | 2nd National Hockey League |
|--------|---|---|---|-----|-----|-----|--------|

*Defeated Boston 4-3 in semifinals*
*Lost to Toronto 3-4 in Stanley Cup finals*

| 1945-46 | 20 | 20 | 10 | 50 | 146 | 159 | 4th National Hockey League |
|--------|---|---|---|-----|-----|-----|--------|

*Lost to Boston 1-4 in semifinals*

| Season | W | L | T | Pts | GF | GA | Finish |
|--------|---|---|---|-----|-----|-----|--------|
| 1946-47 | 22 | 27 | 11 | 55 | 190 | 193 | 4th National Hockey League |

*Lost to Toronto 1-4 in semifinals*

| 1947-48 | 30 | 18 | 12 | 72 | 187 | 148 | 2nd National Hockey League |
|--------|---|---|---|-----|-----|-----|--------|

*Defeated New York Rangers 4-2 in semifinals*
*Lost to Toronto 0-4 in Stanley Cup finals*

| 1948-49 | 34 | 19 | 7 | 75 | 195 | 145 | 1st National Hockey League |
|--------|---|---|---|-----|-----|-----|--------|

*Defeated Montreal Canadiens 4-3 in semifinals*
*Lost to Toronto 0-4 in Stanley Cup finals*

| 1949-50 | 37 | 19 | 14 | 88 | 229 | 164 | 1st National Hockey League |
|--------|---|---|---|-----|-----|-----|--------|

*Defeated Toronto 4-3 in semifinals*
*Defeated New York Rangers 4-3 in Stanley Cup finals*

| 1950-51 | 44 | 13 | 13 | 101 | 236 | 139 | 1st National Hockey League |
|--------|---|---|---|-----|-----|-----|--------|

*Lost to Montreal Canadiens 2-4 in semifinals*

| 1951-52 | 44 | 14 | 12 | 100 | 215 | 133 | 1st National Hockey League |
|--------|---|---|---|-----|-----|-----|--------|

*Defeated Toronto 4-0 in semifinals*
*Defeated Montreal Canadiens 4-0 in Stanley Cup finals*

| 1952-53 | 36 | 16 | 18 | 90 | 222 | 133 | 1st National Hockey League |
|--------|---|---|---|-----|-----|-----|--------|

*Lost to Boston 2-4 in semifinals*

| 1953-54 | 37 | 19 | 14 | 88 | 191 | 132 | 1st National Hockey League |
|--------|---|---|---|-----|-----|-----|--------|

*Defeated Toronto 4-1 in semifinals*
*Defeated Montreal Canadiens 4-3 in Stanley Cup finals*

| 1954-55 | 42 | 17 | 11 | 95 | 204 | 134 | 1st National Hockey League |
|--------|---|---|---|-----|-----|-----|--------|

*Defeated Toronto 4-0 in semifinals*
*Defeated Montreal Canadiens 4-3 in Stanley Cup finals*

| 1955-56 | 30 | 24 | 16 | 76 | 183 | 148 | 2nd National Hockey League |
|--------|---|---|---|-----|-----|-----|--------|

*Defeated Toronto 4-1 in semifinals*
*Lost to Montreal Canadiens 1-4 in Stanley Cup finals*

| 1956-57 | 38 | 20 | 12 | 88 | 198 | 157 | 1st National Hockey League |
|--------|---|---|---|-----|-----|-----|--------|

*Lost to Boston 1-4 in semifinals*

| 1957-58 | 29 | 29 | 12 | 70 | 176 | 207 | 3rd National Hockey League |
|--------|---|---|---|-----|-----|-----|--------|

*Lost to Montreal Canadiens 0-4 in semifinals*

| 1958-59 | 25 | 37 | 8 | 58 | 167 | 218 | 6th National Hockey League |
| 1959-60 | 26 | 29 | 15 | 67 | 186 | 197 | 4th National Hockey League |

*Lost to Toronto 2-4 in semifinals*

| 1960-61 | 25 | 29 | 16 | 66 | 195 | 215 | 4th National Hockey League |
|--------|---|---|---|-----|-----|-----|--------|

*Defeated Toronto 4-1 in semifinals*
*Lost to Chicago 2-4 in Stanley Cup finals*

| 1961-62 | 23 | 33 | 14 | 60 | 184 | 219 | 5th National Hockey League |
| 1962-63 | 32 | 25 | 13 | 77 | 200 | 194 | 4th National Hockey League |

*Defeated Chicago 4-2 in semifinals*
*Lost to Toronto 1-4 in Stanley Cup finals*

| 1963-64 | 30 | 29 | 11 | 71 | 191 | 204 | 4th National Hockey League |
|--------|---|---|---|-----|-----|-----|--------|

*Defeated Chicago 4-3 in semifinals*
*Lost to Toronto 3-4 in Stanley Cup finals*

| 1964-65 | 40 | 23 | 7 | 87 | 224 | 175 | 1st National Hockey League |
|--------|---|---|---|-----|-----|-----|--------|

*Lost to Chicago 3-4 in semifinals*

**Season  W  L  T  Pts GF GA  Finish**

**1965-66**  31 27 12  74 221 194  4th  **National Hockey League**
*Defeated Chicago 4-2 in semifinals*
*Lost to Montreal Canadiens 2-4 in Stanley Cup finals*
**1966-67**  27 39  4  58 212 241  5th  **National Hockey League**
**1967-68**  27 35 12  66 245 257  6th  **Eastern Division**
**1968-69**  33 31 12  78 239 221  5th  **Eastern Division**
**1969-70**  40 21 15  95 246 199  3rd  **Eastern Division**
*Lost to Chicago 0-4 in Eastern Division semifinals*
**1970-71**  22 45 11  55 209 308  7th  **Eastern Division**
**1971-72**  33 35 10  76 261 262  5th  **Eastern Division**
**1972-73**  37 29 12  86 265 243  5th  **Eastern Division**
**1973-74**  29 39 10  68 255 319  6th  **Eastern Division**
**1974-75**  23 45 12  58 259 335  4th  **Norris Division**
**1975-76**  26 44 10  62 226 300  4th  **Norris Division**
**1976-77**  16 55  9  41 183 309  5th  **Norris Division**
**1977-78**  32 34 14  78 252 266  2nd  **Norris Division**
*Defeated Atlanta 2-0 in preliminary round*
*Lost to Montreal Canadiens 1-4 in Norris Division quarterfinals*
**1978-79**  23 41 16  62 252 295  5th  **Norris Division**
**1979-80**  26 43 11  63 268 306  5th  **Norris Division**
**1980-81**  19 43 18  56 252 339  5th  **Norris Division**
**1981-82**  21 47 12  54 270 351  6th  **Norris Division**
**1982-83**  21 44 15  57 263 344  5th  **Norris Division**
**1983-84**  31 42  7  69 298 323  3rd  **Norris Division**
*Lost to St. Louis 1-3 in Norris Division semifinals*
**1984-85**  27 41 12  66 313 357  3rd  **Norris Division**
*Lost to Chicago 0-3 in Norris Division semifinals*
**1985-86**  17 57  6  40 266 415  5th  **Norris Division**
**1986-87**  34 36 10  78 260 274  2nd  **Norris Division**
*Defeated Chicago 4-0 in Norris Division semifinals*
*Defeated Toronto 4-3 in Norris Division finals*
*Lost to Edmonton 1-4 in Campbell Conference finals*
**1987-88**  41 28 11  93 322 269  1st  **Norris Division**
*Defeated Toronto 4-2 in Norris Division semifinals*
*Defeated St. Louis 4-1 in Norris Division finals*
*Lost to Edmonton 1-4 in Campbell Conference finals*
**1988-89**  34 34 12  80 313 316  1st  **Norris Division**
*Lost to Chicago 2-4 in Norris Division semifinals*
**1989-90**  28 38 14  70 288 323  5th  **Norris Division**
**1990-91**  34 38  8  76 273 298  3rd  **Norris Division**
*Lost to St. Louis 3-4 in Norris Division semifinals*
**1991-92**  43 25 12  98 320 256  1st  **Norris Division**
*Defeated Minnesota 4-3 in Norris Division semifinals*
*Lost to Chicago 0-4 in Norris Division finals*
**1992-93**  47 28  9 103 369 280  2nd  **Norris Division**
*Lost to Toronto 3-4 in Norris Division semifinals*
**1993-94**  46 30  8 100 356 275  1st  **Central Division**
*Lost to San Jose 3-4 in Western Conference quarterfinals*
**1995**    33 11  4  70 180 117  1st  **Central Division**
*Defeated Dallas 4-1 in Western Conference quarterfinals*

**Season  W  L  T  Pts GF GA  Finish**

*Defeated San Jose 4-0 in Western Conference semifinals*
*Defeated Chicago 4-1 in Western Conference finals*
*Lost to New Jersey 0-4 in Stanley Cup finals*
**1995-96**  62 13  7 131 325 181  1st  **Central Division**
*Defeated Winnipeg 4-2 in Western Conference quarterfinals*
*Defeated St. Louis 4-3 in Western Conference semifinals*
*Lost to Colorado 2-4 in Western Conference finals*

## Detroit's Top 25 All-Time Scorers

| Rank | Player | Seasons | Gms. | Goals | Assists | Points |
|---|---|---|---|---|---|---|
| 1. | Gordie Howe | 25 | 1,687 | 786 | 1,023 | 1,809 |
| 2. | Alex Delvecchio | 24 | 1,549 | 456 | 825 | 1,281 |
| 3. | Steve Yzerman | 13 | 942 | 517 | 738 | 1,255 |
| 4. | Norm Ullman | 13 | 875 | 324 | 434 | 758 |
| 5. | Ted Lindsay | 14 | 862 | 335 | 393 | 728 |
| 6. | Reed Larson | 10 | 708 | 188 | 382 | 570 |
| 7. | John Ogrodnick | 9 | 558 | 265 | 281 | 546 |
| 8. | Sergei Fedorov | 6 | 433 | 212 | 317 | 529 |
| 9. | Gerard Gallant | 9 | 563 | 207 | 260 | 467 |
| 10. | Nick Libett | 12 | 861 | 217 | 250 | 467 |
| 11. | Sid Abel | 10 | 571 | 184 | 279 | 463 |
| 12. | Red Kelly | 13 | 846 | 154 | 297 | 451 |
| 13. | Syd Howe | 11 | 793 | 202 | 231 | 433 |
| 14. | Marcel Dionne | 4 | 309 | 139 | 227 | 366 |
| 15. | Shawn Burr | 11 | 659 | 148 | 214 | 362 |
| 16. | Dale McCourt | 5 | 341 | 134 | 203 | 337 |
| 17. | Bruce MacGregor | 11 | 673 | 151 | 184 | 335 |
| 18. | Ebbie Goodfellow | 14 | 575 | 134 | 190 | 324 |
| 19. | Mickey Redmond | 6 | 317 | 177 | 132 | 309 |
| 20. | Herbie Lewis | 11 | 481 | 148 | 161 | 309 |
| 21. | Gary Bergman | 11 | 706 | 60 | 243 | 303 |
| 22. | Marcel Pronovost | 15 | 983 | 80 | 217 | 297 |
| 23. | Carl Liscombe | 9 | 378 | 137 | 140 | 277 |
| 24. | Mud Bruneteau | 11 | 399 | 139 | 138 | 277 |
| 25. | Larry Aurie | 12 | 490 | 147 | 129 | 276 |

## Detroit's Top 10 All-Time Goaltenders

### (Ranked by Wins)

| Rank | Goalie | Seasons | Gms. | W | L | T | Avg. | ShO |
|---|---|---|---|---|---|---|---|---|
| 1. | Terry Sawchuk | 14 | 734 | 352 | 244 | 130 | 2.46 | 85 |
| 2. | Harry Lumley | 7 | 324 | 163 | 107 | 54 | 2.73 | 26 |
| 3. | Roger Crozier | 7 | 310 | 130 | 119 | 43 | 2.94 | 20 |
| 4. | Tim Cheveldae | 6 | 264 | 128 | 93 | 30 | 3.39 | 9 |
| 5. | Greg Stefan | 9 | 299 | 115 | 127 | 30 | 3.92 | 5 |
| 6. | Jim Rutherford | 10 | 314 | 97 | 165 | 43 | 3.68 | 10 |
| 7. | Roy Edwards | 6 | 221 | 95 | 74 | 34 | 2.94 | 14 |
| 8. | Norm Smith | 7 | 178 | 76 | 68 | 34 | 2.34 | 17 |
| 9. | Chris Osgood | 3 | 110 | 76 | 19 | 10 | 2.43 | 8 |
| 10. | Glenn Hall | 4 | 148 | 74 | 45 | 29 | 2.14 | 17 |

# Season Leaders

## Points

| Season | Player | G | A | Pts |
|---|---|---|---|---|
| 1926-27 | John Sheppard | 13 | 8 | 21 |
| 1927-28 | George Hay | 22 | 13 | 35 |
| 1928-29 | Carson Cooper | 18 | 9 | 27 |
| 1929-30 | Carson Cooper | 18 | 18 | 36 |
| 1930-31 | Ebbie Goodfellow | 25 | 23 | 48 |
| 1931-32 | Ebbie Goodfellow | 14 | 16 | 30 |
| 1932-33 | Herbie Lewis | 20 | 14 | 34 |
| 1933-34 | Larry Aurie | 16 | 19 | 35 |
| 1934-35 | Syd Howe | 22 | 25 | 47 |
| 1935-36 | Marty Barry | 21 | 19 | 40 |
| 1936-37 | Marty Barry | 17 | 27 | 44 |
| 1937-38 | Herbie Lewis | 13 | 18 | 31 |
| 1938-39 | Marty Barry | 13 | 28 | 41 |
| 1939-40 | Syd Howe | 14 | 23 | 37 |
| 1940-41 | Syd Howe | 20 | 24 | 44 |
| 1941-42 | Don Grosso | 23 | 30 | 53 |
| 1942-43 | Syd Howe | 20 | 35 | 55 |
| 1943-44 | Carl Liscombe | 36 | 37 | 73 |
| 1944-45 | Joe Carveth | 26 | 28 | 54 |
| 1945-46 | Joe Carveth | 17 | 18 | 35 |
| 1946-47 | Billy Taylor | 17 | **46** | 63 |
| 1947-48 | Ted Lindsay | **33** | 19 | 52 |
| 1948-49 | Sid Abel | **28** | 26 | 54 |
|  | Ted Lindsay | 26 | 28 | 54 |
| 1949-50 | Ted Lindsay | 23 | 55 | **78** |
| 1950-51 | Gordie Howe | **43** | 43 | 86 |
| 1951-52 | Gordie Howe | **47** | **39** | 86 |
| 1952-53 | Gordie Howe | **49** | 46 | 95 |
| 1953-54 | Gordie Howe | 33 | **48** | 81 |
| 1954-55 | Dutch Reibel | 25 | 41 | 66 |
| 1955-56 | Gordie Howe | 38 | 41 | 79 |
| 1956-57 | Gordie Howe | **44** | 45 | **89** |
| 1957-58 | Gordie Howe | 33 | 44 | 77 |
| 1958-59 | Gordie Howe | 32 | 46 | 78 |
| 1959-60 | Gordie Howe | 28 | 45 | 73 |
| 1960-61 | Gordie Howe | 23 | 49 | 72 |
| 1961-62 | Gordie Howe | 33 | 44 | 77 |
| 1962-63 | Gordie Howe | **38** | 48 | 86 |
| 1963-64 | Gordie Howe | 26 | 47 | 73 |
| 1964-65 | Norm Ullman | **42** | 41 | 83 |
| 1965-66 | Gordie Howe | 29 | 46 | 75 |
| 1966-67 | Norm Ullman | 26 | 44 | 70 |
| 1967-68 | Gordie Howe | 39 | 43 | 82 |

| Season | Player | G | A | Pts |
|---|---|---|---|---|
| 1968-69 | Gordie Howe | 44 | 59 | 103 |
| 1969-70 | Gordie Howe | 31 | 40 | 71 |
| 1970-71 | Tom Webster | 30 | 37 | 67 |
| 1971-72 | Marcel Dionne | 28 | 49 | 77 |
| 1972-73 | Mickey Redmond | 52 | 41 | 93 |
| 1973-74 | Marcel Dionne | 24 | 54 | 78 |
| 1974-75 | Marcel Dionne | 47 | 74 | 121 |
| 1975-76 | Walt McKechnie | 26 | 56 | 82 |
| 1976-77 | Walt McKechnie | 25 | 34 | 59 |
| 1977-78 | Dale McCourt | 33 | 39 | 72 |
| 1978-79 | Vaclav Nedomansky | 38 | 35 | 73 |
| 1979-80 | Dale McCourt | 30 | 51 | 81 |
| 1980-81 | Dale McCourt | 30 | 56 | 86 |
| 1981-82 | Mark Osborne | 26 | 41 | 67 |

| Season | Player | G | A | Pts |
|---|---|---|---|---|
| 1982-83 | John Ogrodnick | 41 | 44 | 85 |
| 1983-84 | Steve Yzerman | 39 | 48 | 87 |
| 1984-85 | John Ogrodnick | 55 | 50 | 105 |
| 1985-86 | Doug Shedden | 34 | 37 | 71 |
| 1986-87 | Steve Yzerman | 31 | 59 | 90 |
| 1987-88 | Steve Yzerman | 50 | 52 | 102 |
| 1988-89 | Steve Yzerman | 65 | 90 | 155 |
| 1989-90 | Steve Yzerman | 62 | 65 | 127 |
| 1990-91 | Steve Yzerman | 51 | 57 | 108 |
| 1991-92 | Steve Yzerman | 45 | 58 | 103 |
| 1992-93 | Steve Yzerman | 58 | 79 | 137 |
| 1993-94 | Sergei Fedorov | 56 | 64 | 120 |
| 1995 | Paul Coffey | 14 | 44 | 58 |
| 1995-96 | Sergei Fedorov | 39 | 68 | 107 |

**Dutch Reibel led the club in points in 1954-55.**

# Goals

| Season | Player | Goals |
|---|---|---|
| 1926-27 | John Sheppard | 13 |
| 1927-28 | George Hay | 22 |
| 1928-29 | Carson Cooper | 18 |
| 1929-30 | Herbie Lewis | 20 |
| 1930-31 | Ebbie Goodfellow | 25 |
| 1931-32 | Ebbie Goodfellow | 14 |
| 1932-33 | Herbie Lewis | 20 |
| 1933-34 | John Sorrell | 21 |
| 1934-35 | Syd Howe | 22 |
| 1935-36 | Marty Barry | 21 |
| 1936-37 | Larry Aurie | **23** |
| 1937-38 | Carl Liscombe | 14 |
| 1938-39 | Syd Howe | 16 |
| 1939-40 | Syd Howe | 14 |
| 1940-41 | Syd Howe | 20 |
| 1941-42 | Don Grosso | 23 |
| 1942-43 | Mud Bruneteau | 23 |
| 1943-44 | Carl Liscombe | 36 |
| 1944-45 | Joe Carveth | 26 |
| 1945-46 | Adam Brown | 20 |
| 1946-47 | Roy Conacher | 30 |
| 1947-48 | Ted Lindsay | **33** |
| 1948-49 | Sid Abel | **28** |
| 1949-50 | Gordie Howe | 35 |
| 1950-51 | Gordie Howe | **43** |
| 1951-52 | Gordie Howe | **47** |
| 1952-53 | Gordie Howe | **49** |
| 1953-54 | Gordie Howe | 33 |
| 1954-55 | Gordie Howe | 29 |
| 1955-56 | Gordie Howe | 38 |
| 1956-57 | Gordie Howe | **44** |
| 1957-58 | Gordie Howe | 33 |
| 1958-59 | Gordie Howe | 32 |
| 1959-60 | Gordie Howe | 28 |
| 1960-61 | Norm Ullman | 28 |
| 1961-62 | Gordie Howe | 33 |
| 1962-63 | Gordie Howe | **38** |
| 1963-64 | Gordie Howe | 26 |
| 1964-65 | Norm Ullman | **42** |
| 1965-66 | Norm Ullman | 31 |
|  | Alex Delvecchio | 31 |
| 1966-67 | Bruce MacGregor | 28 |
| 1967-68 | Gordie Howe | 39 |
| 1968-69 | Frank Mahovlich | 49 |
| 1969-70 | Gary Unger | 42 |
| 1970-71 | Tom Webster | 30 |
| 1971-72 | Mickey Redmond | 42 |

| Season | Player | Goals |
|---|---|---|
| 1972-73 | Mickey Redmond | 52 |
| 1973-74 | Mickey Redmond | 51 |
| 1974-75 | Danny Grant | 50 |
| 1975-76 | Michel Bergeron | 32 |
| 1976-77 | Walt McKechnie | 25 |
| 1977-78 | Dale McCourt | 33 |
| 1978-79 | Vaclav Nedomansky | 38 |
| 1979-80 | Mike Foligno | 36 |
| 1980-81 | John Ogrodnick | 35 |
| 1981-82 | John Ogrodnick | 28 |
| 1982-83 | John Ogrodnick | 41 |
| 1983-84 | John Ogrodnick | 42 |
| 1984-85 | John Ogrodnick | 55 |
| 1985-86 | John Ogrodnick | 38 |
| 1986-87 | Brent Ashton | 40 |
| 1987-88 | Steve Yzerman | 50 |
| 1988-89 | Steve Yzerman | 65 |
| 1989-90 | Steve Yzerman | 62 |
| 1990-91 | Steve Yzerman | 51 |
| 1991-92 | Steve Yzerman | 45 |
| 1992-93 | Steve Yzerman | 58 |
| 1993-94 | Sergei Fedorov | 56 |
| 1995 | Ray Sheppard | 30 |
| 1995-96 | Sergei Fedorov | 39 |

# Assists

| Season | Player | Assists |
|---|---|---|
| 1926-27 | John Sheppard | 8 |
| 1927-28 | George Hay | 13 |
| 1928-29 | Carson Cooper | 9 |
| 1929-30 | Carson Cooper | 18 |
| 1930-31 | Ebbie Goodfellow | 23 |
| 1931-32 | Ebbie Goodfellow | 16 |
| 1932-33 | Herbie Lewis | 14 |
| 1933-34 | Larry Aurie | 19 |
| 1934-35 | Larry Aurie | 29 |
| 1935-36 | Herbie Lewis | 23 |
| 1936-37 | Marty Barry | 27 |
| 1937-38 | Marty Barry | 20 |
| 1938-39 | Marty Barry | 28 |
| 1939-40 | Syd Howe | 23 |
| 1940-41 | Syd Howe | 24 |
| 1941-42 | Sid Abel | 31 |
| 1942-43 | Syd Howe | 35 |
| 1943-44 | Carl Liscombe | 37 |
| 1944-45 | Syd Howe | 36 |
| 1945-46 | Joe Carveth | 18 |
|  | Murray Armstrong | 18 |

| Season | Player | Assists |
|---|---|---|
| 1946-47 | Billy Taylor | **46** |
| 1947-48 | Sid Abel | 30 |
| 1948-49 | Ted Lindsay | 28 |
| 1949-50 | Ted Lindsay | 55 |
| 1950-51 | Gordie Howe | **43** |
| 1951-52 | Gordie Howe | **39** |
| 1952-53 | Gordie Howe | **46** |
| 1953-54 | Gordie Howe | **48** |
| 1954-55 | Dutch Reibel | 41 |
| 1955-56 | Gordie Howe | 41 |
| 1956-57 | Ted Lindsay | 55 |
| 1957-58 | Gordie Howe | 44 |
| 1958-59 | Gordie Howe | 46 |
| 1959-60 | Gordie Howe | 45 |
| 1960-61 | Gordie Howe | 49 |
| 1961-62 | Gordie Howe | 44 |
| 1962-63 | Gordie Howe | 48 |
| 1963-64 | Gordie Howe | 47 |
| 1964-65 | Gordie Howe | 47 |
| 1965-66 | Gordie Howe | 46 |
| 1966-67 | Norm Ullman | 44 |
| 1967-68 | Alex Delvecchio | 48 |
| 1968-69 | Gordie Howe | 59 |
| 1969-70 | Alex Delvecchio | 47 |
| 1970-71 | Tom Webster | 37 |
| 1971-72 | Marcel Dionne | 49 |
| 1972-73 | Alex Delvecchio | 53 |
| 1973-74 | Marcel Dionne | 54 |
| 1974-75 | Marcel Dionne | 74 |
| 1975-76 | Walt McKechnie | 56 |
| 1976-77 | Walt McKechnie | 34 |
| 1977-78 | Reed Larson | 41 |
| 1978-79 | Reed Larson | 49 |
| 1979-80 | Dale McCourt | 51 |
| 1980-81 | Dale McCourt | 56 |
| 1981-82 | Mark Osborne | 41 |
| 1982-83 | Reed Larson | 52 |
| 1983-84 | Brad Park | 53 |
| 1984-85 | Steve Yzerman | 59 |
| 1985-86 | Kelly Kisio | 48 |
| 1986-87 | Steve Yzerman | 59 |
| 1987-88 | Steve Yzerman | 52 |
| 1988-89 | Steve Yzerman | 90 |
| 1989-90 | Steve Yzerman | 65 |
| 1990-91 | Steve Yzerman | 57 |
| 1991-92 | Steve Yzerman | 58 |
| 1992-93 | Steve Yzerman | 79 |
| 1993-94 | Sergei Fedorov | 64 |
| 1995 | Paul Coffey | 44 |
| 1995-96 | Sergei Fedorov | 68 |

# Penalties

| Season | Player | PIM |
|---|---|---|
| 1926-27 | John Sheppard | 60 |
| 1927-28 | Percy Traub | 78 |
| 1928-29 | Bob Connors | 68 |
| 1929-30 | Harvey Rockburn | 97 |
| 1930-31 | Harvey Rockburn | **118** |
| 1931-32 | Reg Noble | 72 |
| 1932-33 | Stu Evans | 74 |
| 1933-34 | Hap Emms | 51 |
| 1934-35 | Ebbie Goodfellow | 44 |
| 1935-36 | Ebbie Goodfellow | 69 |
| 1936-37 | Ebbie Goodfellow | 43 |
| 1937-38 | Marty Barry | 34 |
| 1938-39 | Charlie Conacher | 39 |
| 1939-40 | Jimmy Orlando | 54 |
| 1940-41 | Jimmy Orlando | **99** |
| 1941-42 | Jimmy Orlando | **111** |
| 1942-43 | Jimmy Orlando | **99** |
| 1943-44 | Hal Jackson | 76 |
| 1944-45 | Hal Jackson | 45 |
| 1945-46 | Jack Stewart | **73** |
| 1946-47 | Jack Stewart | 83 |
| 1947-48 | Ted Lindsay | 95 |
| 1948-49 | Ted Lindsay | 97 |
| 1949-50 | Ted Lindsay | 141 |
| 1950-51 | Ted Lindsay | 110 |
| 1951-52 | Ted Lindsay | 123 |
| 1952-53 | Ted Lindsay | 111 |
| 1953-54 | Ted Lindsay | 112 |
| 1954-55 | Tony Leswick | 137 |
| 1955-56 | Ted Lindsay | 161 |
| 1956-57 | Ted Lindsay | 103 |
|  | Warren Godfrey | 103 |
| 1957-58 | Forbes Kennedy | 135 |
| 1958-59 | Pete Goegan | 111 |
| 1959-60 | Jim Morrison | 62 |
| 1960-61 | Howie Young | 108 |
| 1961-62 | Bill Gadsby | 88 |
| 1962-63 | Howie Young | **273** |
| 1963-64 | Doug Barkley | 115 |
| 1964-65 | Ted Lindsay | 173 |
| 1965-66 | Bryan Watson | 133 |
| 1966-67 | Gary Bergman | 129 |
| 1967-68 | Kent Douglas | 126 |
| 1968-69 | Bobby Baun | 121 |
| 1969-70 | Gary Bergman | 122 |
| 1970-71 | Gary Bergman | 149 |
| 1971-72 | Gary Bergman | 138 |

| Season | Player | PIM |
|---|---|---|
| 1972-73 | Larry Johnston | 169 |
| 1973-74 | Larry Johnston | 139 |
| 1974-75 | Bryan Watson | 238 |
| 1975-76 | Bryan Watson | 322 |
| 1976-77 | Dennis Polonich | 274 |
| 1977-78 | Dennis Polonich | 254 |
| 1978-79 | Dennis Polonich | 208 |
| 1979-80 | Willie Huber | 164 |
| 1980-81 | Jim Korn | 246 |
| 1981-82 | Reed Larson | 112 |
| 1982-83 | Danny Gare | 107 |
| 1983-84 | Joe Paterson | 148 |
| 1984-85 | Danny Gare | 163 |
| 1985-86 | Joe Kocur | **377** |
| 1986-87 | Joe Kocur | 276 |
| 1987-88 | Bob Probert | **398** |
| 1988-89 | Gerard Gallant | 230 |
| 1989-90 | Joe Kocur | 268 |
| 1990-91 | Bob Probert | 315 |
| 1991-92 | Bob Probert | 276 |
| 1992-93 | Bob Probert | 292 |
| 1993-94 | Bob Probert | 275 |
| 1995 | Stu Grimson | 147 |
| 1995-96 | Keith Primeau | 168 |

# Goaltending

| Season | Goalie | GP | GAA | ShO |
|---|---|---|---|---|
| 1926-27 | Hap Holmes | 43 | 2.33 | 6 |
| 1927-28 | Hap Holmes | **44** | 1.80 | 11 |
| 1928-29 | Dolly Dolson | 44 | 1.43 | 10 |
| 1929-30 | Bill Beveridge | 39 | 2.79 | 2 |
| 1930-31 | Dolly Dolson | **44** | 2.39 | 6 |
| 1931-32 | Alex Connell | **48** | 2.25 | 6 |
| 1932-33 | John Ross Roach | 48 | 1.94 | 10 |
| 1933-34 | Wilf Cude | 29 | 1.62 | 4 |
| 1934-35 | Norm Smith | 25 | 2.08 | 2 |
| 1935-36 | Norm Smith | 48 | 2.15 | 6 |
| 1936-37 | Norm Smith | **48** | **2.13** | **6** |
| 1937-38 | Norm Smith | 47 | 2.77 | 3 |
| 1938-39 | Cecil Thompson | 39 | 2.69 | 4 |
| 1939-40 | Cecil Thompson | 46 | 2.61 | 3 |
| 1940-41 | Johnny Mowers | 48 | 2.13 | 4 |
| 1941-42 | Johnny Mowers | 47 | 3.06 | 5 |
| 1942-43 | Johnny Mowers | **50** | **2.47** | **6** |
| 1943-44 | Connie Dion | 26 | 3.08 | 1 |
| 1944-45 | Harry Lumley | 37 | 3.22 | 1 |
| 1945-46 | Harry Lumley | 50 | 3.18 | 2 |
| 1946-47 | Harry Lumley | 52 | 3.06 | 3 |
| 1947-48 | Harry Lumley | **60** | 2.46 | 7 |

| Season | Goalie | GP | GAA | ShO |
|---|---|---|---|---|
| 1948-49 | Harry Lumley | **60** | 2.42 | 6 |
| 1949-50 | Harry Lumley | 63 | 2.35 | 7 |
| 1950-51 | Terry Sawchuk | **70** | 1.99 | **11** |
| 1951-52 | Terry Sawchuk | **70** | **1.90** | 12 |
| 1952-53 | Terry Sawchuk | 63 | 1.90 | 9 |
| 1953-54 | Terry Sawchuk | 67 | 1.94 | 12 |
| 1954-55 | Terry Sawchuk | 68 | 1.96 | **12** |
| 1955-56 | Glenn Hall | **70** | 2.11 | 12 |
| 1956-57 | Glenn Hall | **70** | 2.24 | 4 |
| 1957-58 | Terry Sawchuk | **70** | 2.96 | 3 |
| 1958-59 | Terry Sawchuk | 67 | 3.12 | 5 |
| 1959-60 | Terry Sawchuk | 58 | 2.69 | 5 |
| 1960-61 | Terry Sawchuk | 37 | 3.05 | 2 |
| 1961-62 | Terry Sawchuk | 43 | 3.33 | 5 |
| 1962-63 | Terry Sawchuk | 48 | 2.48 | 3 |
| 1963-64 | Terry Sawchuk | 53 | 2.60 | 5 |
| 1964-65 | Roger Crozier | **70** | **2.42** | 6 |
| 1965-66 | Roger Crozier | **64** | 2.78 | 7 |
| 1966-67 | Roger Crozier | 58 | 3.35 | 4 |
| 1967-68 | Roy Edwards | 41 | 3.50 | 0 |
| 1968-69 | Roy Edwards | 40 | 2.54 | 4 |
| 1969-70 | Roy Edwards | 47 | 2.59 | 2 |
| 1970-71 | Roy Edwards | 38 | 3.39 | 0 |
| 1971-72 | Al Smith | 43 | 3.24 | 4 |
| 1972-73 | Roy Edwards | 52 | 2.63 | **6** |
| 1973-74 | Jim Rutherford | 51 | 3.53 | 0 |
| 1974-75 | Jim Rutherford | 59 | 3.74 | 2 |
| 1975-76 | Jim Rutherford | 44 | 3.59 | 4 |
| 1976-77 | Jim Rutherford | 48 | 3.94 | 0 |
| 1977-78 | Jim Rutherford | 43 | 3.26 | 1 |
| 1978-79 | Rogie Vachon | 50 | 3.90 | 0 |
| 1979-80 | Rogie Vachon | 59 | 3.61 | 4 |
| 1980-81 | Gilles Gilbert | 48 | 4.01 | 0 |
| 1981-82 | Bob Sauve | 41 | 4.19 | 0 |
| 1982-83 | Corrado Micalef | 34 | 3.62 | 2 |
| 1983-84 | Greg Stefan | 50 | 3.51 | 2 |
| 1984-85 | Greg Stefan | 46 | 4.33 | 0 |
| 1985-86 | Greg Stefan | 37 | 4.50 | 1 |
| 1986-87 | Glen Hanlon | 36 | 3.18 | 1 |
| 1987-88 | Glen Hanlon | 47 | 3.23 | **4** |
| 1988-89 | Glen Hanlon | 39 | 3.56 | 1 |
| 1989-90 | Glen Hanlon | 45 | 4.03 | 1 |
| 1990-91 | Tim Cheveldae | 65 | 3.55 | 2 |
| 1991-92 | Tim Cheveldae | 72 | 3.20 | 2 |
| 1992-93 | Tim Cheveldae | 67 | 3.25 | 4 |
| 1993-94 | Chris Osgood | 41 | 2.86 | 2 |
| 1995 | Mike Vernon | 30 | 2.52 | 1 |
| 1995-96 | Chris Osgood | 50 | 2.17 | 5 |

**Bold indicates led NHL**

# Individual Records

## Service

**Most Seasons**
25 Gordie Howe, 1946-47 to 1970-71

**Most Seasons by Center**
24 Alex Delvecchio, 1950-51 to 1973-74

**Most Seasons by Right Wing**
25 Gordie Howe, 1946-47 to 1970-71

**Most Seasons by Left Wing**
14 Ted Lindsay, 1944-45 to 1956-57, 1964-65

**Most Seasons by Defenseman**
15 Marcel Pronovost, 1949-50 to 1964-65

**Most Seasons by Goalie**
14 Terry Sawchuk, 1949-50 to 1954-55, 1957-58 to 1963-64, 1968-69

**Most Games, Career**
1,687 Gordie Howe, 1946-47 to 1970-71

**Most Games by Center, Career**
1,549 Alex Delvecchio, 1950-51 to 1973-74

**Most Games by Right Wing, Career**
1,687 Gordie Howe, 1946-47 to 1970-71

**Most Games by Left Wing, Career**
862 Ted Lindsay, 1944-45 to 1956-57, 1964-65

**Most Games by Defenseman, Career**
983 Marcel Pronovost, 1949-50 to 1964-65

**Most Games by Goalie, Career**
734 Terry Sawchuk, 1949-50 to 1954-55, 1957-58 to 1963-64, 1968-69

**Most Games, Season**
84 Nicklas Lidstrom, 1992-93
Steve Yzerman, 1992-93
Nicklas Lidstrom, 1993-94

**Most Consecutive Games Played**
548 Alex Delvecchio, Dec. 13, 1956-Nov. 11, 1964

## Points

**Most Points, Career**
1,809 Gordie Howe, 1946-47 to 1970-71

**Most Points by Center, Career**
1,281 Alex Delvecchio, 1950-51 to 1973-74

**Most Points by Right Wing, Career**
1,809 Gordie Howe, 1946-47 to 1970-71

**Most Points by Left Wing, Career**
728 Ted Lindsay, 1944-45 to 1956-57, 1964-65

**Most Points by Defenseman, Career**
570 Reed Larson, 1976-77 to 1985-86

**Most Points by Goalie, Career**
15 Tim Cheveldae, 1988-89 to 1993-94

**Most Points, Season**
155 Steve Yzerman, 1988-89

**Most Points by Center, Season**
155 Steve Yzerman, 1988-89

**Most Points by Right Wing, Season**
103 Gordie Howe, 1968-69

**Most Points by Left Wing, Season**
105 John Ogrodnick, 1984-85

**Most Points by Defenseman, Season**
77 Paul Coffey, 1993-94

**Most Points by Goalie, Season**
5 Tim Cheveldae, 1990-91

**Most Points, Rookie Season**
87 Steve Yzerman, 1983-84

**Most Points by Defenseman, Rookie Season**
60 Reed Larson, 1977-78
Nicklas Lidstrom, 1991-92

**Most Points, Game**
7 Carl Liscombe vs. New York Rangers, Nov. 5, 1942
Don Grosso vs. New York Rangers, Feb. 3, 1944
Billy Taylor vs. Chicago, March 16, 1947

**Most Points by Defenseman, Game**
5 Reed Larson vs. Vancouver, Feb. 27, 1985

**Most Points, First NHL Game**
4 Dutch Reibel vs. New York Rangers, Oct. 8, 1953

**Most Points, Period**
4 Several times. *Last:*
Sergei Fedorov vs. Philadelphia, Jan. 21, 1992

**Most Consecutive Games Scoring Point**
28 Steve Yzerman, Nov. 1, 1988-Jan. 4, 1989

## Goals

**Most Goals, Career**
786 Gordie Howe, 1946-47 to 1970-71

**Most Goals by Center, Career**
517 Steve Yzerman, 1983-84 to 1995-96

**Most Goals by Right Wing, Career**
786 Gordie Howe, 1946-47 to 1970-71

**Most Goals by Left Wing, Career**
335 Ted Lindsay, 1944-45 to 1956-57, 1964-65

**Most Goals by Defenseman, Career**
188 Reed Larson, 1976-77 to 1985-86

**Most Goals by Goalie, Career**
1 Chris Osgood, 1993-94 to 1995-96

**Most Goals, Season**
65 Steve Yzerman, 1988-89

**Most Goals by Center, Season**
65 Steve Yzerman, 1988-89

**Most Goals by Right Wing, Season**
52 Mickey Redmond, 1972-73
Ray Sheppard, 1993-94

**Most Goals by Left Wing, Season**
55 John Ogrodnick, 1984-85

**Most Goals by Defenseman, Season**
27 Reed Larson, 1980-81

**Most Goals by Goalie, Season**
1 Chris Osgood, 1995-96

**Most Goals, Rookie Season**
39 Steve Yzerman, 1983-84

**Most Goals by Defenseman, Rookie Season**
19 Reed Larson, 1977-78

**Most Goals, Game**
6 Syd Howe vs. New York Rangers, Feb. 3, 1944

**Most Goals by Defenseman, Game**
3 Several times. *Last:*
Reed Larson vs. Vancouver, Feb. 27, 1985

**Most Goals, First NHL Game**
2 Chris Cichocki vs. Minnesota, Oct. 10, 1985

**Most Goals, Period**
3 Several times. *Last:*
Brendan Shanahan vs. San Jose, Feb. 12, 1997

**Most Consecutive Games Scoring Goal**
9 Steve Yzerman, Nov. 18-Dec. 5, 1988
Steve Yzerman, Jan. 29-Feb. 12, 1992

## Fastest Goals

**Fastest Goal From Start of Game**
0:06 Henry Boucha vs. Montreal Canadiens, Jan. 28, 1973

**Fastest Goal From Start of Period**
0:06 Henry Boucha vs. Montreal Canadiens, Jan. 28, 1973

**Fastest Two Goals**
0:08 apart Don Grosso vs. Chicago, March 19, 1942

**Fastest Three Goals**
1:52 apart Carl Liscombe vs. Chicago, March 13, 1938

## Power-Play Goals

**Most Power-Play Goals, Career**
211 Gordie Howe, 1946-47 to 1970-71

**Most Power-Play Goals by Defenseman, Career**
68 Reed Larson, 1976-77 to 1985-86

**Most Power-Play Goals, Season**
21 Mickey Redmond, 1973-74
Dino Ciccarelli, 1992-93

**Most Power-Play Goals by Defenseman, Season**
11 Reed Larson, 1985-86

**Most Power-Play Goals, Rookie Season**
13 Steve Yzerman, 1983-84

**Most Power-Play Goals, Game**
3 Ted Lindsay vs. Montreal Canadiens, March 20, 1955
Jimmy Carson vs. Toronto, Dec. 27, 1989

**Most Power-Play Goals, Period**
3 Jimmy Carson vs. Toronto, Dec. 27, 1989

## Shorthanded Goals

**Most Shorthanded Goals, Career**
43 Steve Yzerman, 1983-84 to 1995-96

**Most Shorthanded Goals, Season**
10 Marcel Dionne, 1974-75

**Most Shorthanded Goals, Game**
2 Lorne Ferguson vs. NY Rangers, Feb. 2, 1957
Shawn Burr vs. Minnesota, Jan. 9, 1990
Steve Yzerman vs. Minnesota, April 14, 1992
Steve Yzerman vs. Tampa Bay, April 8, 1993

**Most Shorthanded Goals, Period**
2 Lorne Ferguson vs. NY Rangers, Feb. 2, 1957
Shawn Burr vs. Minnesota, Jan. 9, 1990

## Winning Goals

**Most Winning Goals, Career**
121 Gordie Howe, 1946-47 to 1970-71

**Most Winning Goals, Season**
11 Sergei Fedorov, 1995-96

**Most Winning Goals by Defenseman, Season**
5 Red Kelly, 1949-50
Reed Larson, 1983-84

**Most Winning Goals, Rookie Season**
6 Alex Delvecchio, 1951-52

## Hat Tricks

**Most Games, Three or More Goals, Career**
19 Gordie Howe, 1946-47 to 1970-71

**Most Games, Three or More Goals, Season**
4 Frank Mahovlich, 1968-69

**Most Games, Four or More Goals, Career**
2 Mud Bruneteau, 1935-36 to 1945-46
Sergei Fedorov, 1990-91 to 1996-97

## Penalty Shots

**Most Penalty Shots Attempted, Career**
10 Ebbie Goodfellow, 1929-30 to 1942-43

**Most Penalty Shots Attempted, Season**
6 Ebbie Goodfellow, 1934-35

**Most Penalty Shots Converted, Career**
3 Steve Yzerman, 1983-84 to 1995-96

**Most Penalty Shots Converted, Season**
2 Steve Yzerman, 1991-92

## Assists

**Most Assists, Career**
1,023 Gordie Howe, 1946-47 to 1970-71

**Most Assists by Center, Career**
825 Alex Delvecchio, 1950-51 to 1973-74

**Most Assists by Right Wing, Career**
1,023 Gordie Howe, 1946-47 to 1970-71

**Most Assists by Left Wing, Career**
393    Ted Lindsay, 1944-45 to 1957-57, 1964-65

**Most Assists by Defenseman, Career**
382    Reed Larson, 1976-77 to 1985-86

**Most Assists by Goalie, Career**
15    Tim Cheveldae, 1988-89 to 1993-94

**Most Assists, Season**
90    Steve Yzerman, 1988-89

**Most Assists by Center, Season**
90    Steve Yzerman, 1988-89

**Most Assists by Right Wing, Season**
59    Gordie Howe, 1968-69

**Most Assists by Left Wing, Season**
55    Ted Lindsay, 1949-50
Ted Lindsay, 1955-56

**Most Assists by Defenseman, Season**
63    Paul Coffey, 1993-94

**Most Assists by Goalie, Season**
5    Tim Cheveldae, 1990-91

**Most Assists, Rookie Season**
49    Marcel Dionne, 1971-72
Nicklas Lidstrom, 1991-92

**Most Assists by Defenseman, Rookie Season**
49    Nicklas Lidstrom, 1991-92

**Most Assists, Game**
7    Billy Taylor vs. Chicago, March 16, 1947

**Most Assists by Defenseman, Game**
4    Several times. *Last:*
Paul Coffey vs. Vancouver, Jan. 24, 1995

**Most Assists, First NHL Game**
4    Dutch Reibel vs. New York Rangers, Oct. 8, 1953

**Most Assists, Period**
4    Joe Carveth vs. New York Rangers, Jan. 23, 1944

## Penalties

**Most Penalty Minutes, Career**
2,090    Bob Probert, 1985-86 to 1993-94

**Most Penalty Minutes, Season**
398    Bob Probert, 1987-88

**Most Penalty Minutes, Rookie Season**
302    Dennis Polonich, 1975-76

**Most Penalty Minutes, Game**
42    Joe Kocur vs. St. Louis Blues, Nov. 2, 1985

**Most Penalty Minutes, Period**
37    Joe Kocur vs. St. Louis Blues, Nov. 2, 1985

**Most Penalties, Game**
8    Dennis Polonich vs. Washington, March 24, 1976
Bob Probert vs. Buffalo, Dec. 23, 1987

**Most Penalties, Period**
6    Joe Kocur vs. St. Louis Blues, Nov. 2, 1985

# Goaltending
## Service
**Most Seasons**
14    Terry Sawchuk, 1949-50 to 1954-55, 1957-58 to
1963-64, 1968-69

**Most Games, Career**
734    Terry Sawchuk, 1949-50 to 1954-55, 1957-58 to
1963-64, 1968-69

**Most Games, Season**
72    Tim Cheveldae, 1991-92

**Most Games, Rookie Season**
70    Terry Sawchuk, 1950-51
Glenn Hall, 1955-56
Roger Crozier, 1964-65

## Wins
**Most Wins, Career**
352    Terry Sawchuk, 1949-50 to 1954-55, 1957-58 to
1963-64, 1968-69

**Most Wins, Season**
44    Terry Sawchuk, 1950-51
Terry Sawchuk, 1951-52

**Most Wins, Rookie Season**
44    Terry Sawchuk, 1950-51

**Most Consecutive Wins**
13    Chris Osgood, Jan. 30-March 20, 1996

## Goals-Against Average
**Lowest Goals-Against Average, Career (Minimum 100 Games)**
2.14    Glenn Hall, 1952-53, 1954-55 to 1955-56

**Lowest Goals-Against Average, Season**
1.43    Dolly Dolson, 1928-29

**Lowest Goals-Against Average, Rookie Season**
1.43    Dolly Dolson, 1928-29

## Shutouts
**Most Shutouts, Career**
85    Terry Sawchuk, 1949-50 to 1954-55, 1957-58 to
1963-64, 1968-69

**Most Shutouts, Season**
12    Terry Sawchuk, 1951-52
Terry Sawchuk, 1953-54
Terry Sawchuk, 1954-55
Glenn Hall, 1955-56

**Most Shutouts, Rookie Season**
11    Terry Sawchuk, 1950-51

**Most Consecutive Shutouts**
3    Terry Sawchuk, Nov. 7, 1954 vs. New York Rangers,
Nov. 11, 1954 vs. Toronto, Nov. 13, 1954 vs. Toronto
Glenn Hall, Dec. 11, 1955 vs. New York Rangers,
Dec. 15, 1955 vs. Toronto, Dec. 18, 1955 vs.
Montreal Canadiens
Jim Rutherford, Dec. 31, 1975 vs. Washington,
Jan. 3, 1976 vs. Toronto, Jan. 8, 1976 vs. Minnesota

# Team Records

## Points

**Most Points, Season**
131   1995-96
**Fewest Points, Season**
28   1926-27

## Games Won

**Most Games Won, Season**
62   1995-96
**Most Consecutive Games Won**
9   March 3-21, 1951
Feb. 27-March 20, 1955
March 3-22, 1996
**Most Consecutive Games Won From Start of Season**
6   Oct. 7-22, 1972
**Fewest Games Won, Season**
12   1926-27
1937-38
**Most Home Games Won, Season**
36   1995-96
**Most Consecutive Home Games Won**
14   Jan. 21-March 25, 1965
**Most Consecutive Home Games Won From Start of Season**
6   Oct. 14-Nov. 4, 1962
Oct. 10-26, 1990
**Fewest Home Games Won, Season**
6   1926-27
**Most Road Games Won, Season**
26   1995-96
**Most Consecutive Road Games Won**
7   March 25-April 14, 1995
**Most Consecutive Road Games Won From Start of Season**
4   Oct. 27-Nov. 12, 1949
Oct. 18-Nov. 3, 1951
**Fewest Road Games Won, Season**
3   1931-32
1980-81

## Games Lost

**Most Games Lost, Season**
57   1985-86
**Most Consecutive Games Lost**
14   Feb. 24-March 25, 1982
**Most Consecutive Games Lost From Start of Season**
5   Oct. 10-18, 1980
**Fewest Games Lost, Season**
11   1995

**Most Home Games Lost, Season**
26   1985-86
**Most Consecutive Home Games Lost**
7   Feb. 20-March 25, 1982
**Most Consecutive Home Games Lost From Start of Season**
3   Several times. *Last:* Oct. 6-20, 1982
**Fewest Home Games Lost, Season**
3   Several times. *Last:* 1995-96
**Most Road Games Lost, Season**
33   1976-77
**Most Consecutive Road Games Lost**
14   Oct. 19-Dec. 21, 1966
**Most Consecutive Road Games Lost From Start of Season**
14   Oct. 19-Dec. 21, 1966
**Fewest Road Games Lost, Season**
7   1951-52
1995

## Games Tied

**Most Games Tied, Season**
18   1952-53
1980-81
**Fewest Games Tied, Season**
4   1926-27
1966-67
1995
**Most Home Games Tied, Season**
10   1952-53
**Fewest Home Games Tied, Season**
0   1926-27
1990-91
**Most Road Games Tied, Season**
12   1959-60
**Fewest Road Games Tied, Season**
1   1941-42
1966-67
1995
**Most Scoreless Ties, Season**
3   1927-28
1952-53

## Unbeaten Streaks

**Most Consecutive Games Without a Loss**
15   Nov. 27-Dec. 28, 1952 (8 wins, 7 ties)
**Most Consecutive Games Without a Loss From Start of Season**
10   Oct. 11-Nov. 4, 1962 (8 wins, 2 ties)
**Most Consecutive Home Games Without a Loss**
18   Dec. 26, 1954-March 20, 1955 (13 wins, 5 ties)

**Most Consecutive Home Games Without a Loss From Start of Season**
17    Oct. 11-Dec. 25, 1956 (13 wins, 4 ties)

**Most Consecutive Road Games Without a Loss**
15    Oct. 18-Dec. 26, 1951 (11 wins, 4 ties)

**Most Consecutive Road Games Without a Loss From Start of Season**
15    Oct. 18-Dec. 26, 1951 (10 wins, 5 ties)

## Winless Streaks

**Most Consecutive Games Without a Win**
19    Feb. 26-April 3, 1977 (18 losses, 1 tie)

**Most Consecutive Games Without a Win From Start of Season**
10    Oct. 8-26, 1975 (7 losses, 3 ties)

**Most Consecutive Home Games Without a Win**
10    Dec. 11, 1985-Jan. 18, 1986 (9 losses, 1 tie)

**Most Consecutive Home Games Without a Win From Start of Season**
5    Oct. 8-25, 1975 (2 losses, 3 ties)
      Oct. 10-23, 1985 (1 loss, 4 ties)

**Most Consecutive Road Games Without a Win**
26    Dec. 15, 1976-April 3, 1977 (23 losses, 3 ties)

**Most Consecutive Road Games Without a Win From Start of Season**
19    Oct. 19, 1966-Jan. 14, 1967 (18 losses, 1 tie)

## Goals

**Most Goals, Season**
369    1992-93

**Fewest Goals, Season**
72    1928-29

**Most Goals, Game**
15    Jan. 23, 1944 vs. New York Rangers

**Most Goals, Period**
8    Jan. 23, 1944 vs. New York Rangers

## Power-Play Goals

**Most Power-Play Goals, Season**
113    1992-93

**Most Power-Play Goals, Game**
6    Nov. 5, 1942 vs. New York Rangers
     Nov. 22, 1952 vs. Chicago

**Most Power-Play Goals, Period**
4    Nov. 5, 1942 vs. New York Rangers

## Shorthanded Goals

**Most Shorthanded Goals, Season**
22    1993-94

**Most Shorthanded Goals, Game**
3    Several times. *Last:* March 22, 1996 vs. Colorado

**Most Shorthanded Goals, Period**
2    Several times. *Last:* Feb. 11, 1994 vs. Philadelphia

## Fastest Goals

**Fastest Two Goals**
0:07 apart    Nov. 5, 1936 vs. Toronto (S. Howe, Aurie)
              Nov. 25, 1987 vs. Winnipeg (Sharples, Ashton)

**Fastest Two Goals From Start of Game**
0:37 apart    Dec. 4, 1987 vs. Chicago (Higgins, Yzerman)

**Fastest Three Goals**
0:28 apart    Nov. 16, 1944 vs. Toronto (Jackson, Wochy, Grosso)

**Fastest Four Goals**
2:25 apart    Nov. 7, 1991 vs. St. Louis (Burr, Carson, Lidstrom, Ysebaert)

**Fastest Five Goals**
4:54 apart    Nov. 25, 1987 vs. Winnipeg (Gallant, Oates, Bridgman, Sharples, Ashton)

## Goals Allowed

**Most Goals Allowed, Season**
415    1985-86

**Fewest Goals Allowed, Season**
63    1928-29

**Most Goals Allowed, Game**
13    Jan. 2, 1971 vs. Toronto

## Power-Play Goals Allowed

**Most Power-Play Goals Allowed, Season**
111    1985-86

**Most Power-Play Goals Allowed, Game**
5    Feb. 1, 1987 vs. Buffalo
     Nov. 11, 1987 vs. Chicago
     Jan. 25, 1991 vs. St. Louis
     Dec. 9, 1992 vs. Toronto

**Most Power-Play Goals Allowed, Period**
3    Several times. *Last:* Nov. 25, 1992 vs. St. Louis

## Shorthanded Goals Allowed

**Most Shorthanded Goals Allowed, Season**
15    1984-85

**Most Shorthanded Goals Allowed, Game**
2    Several times. *Last:* Feb. 9, 1992 vs. New York Rangers

**Most Shorthanded Goals Allowed, Period**
2    Several times. *Last:* Feb. 9, 1992 vs. New York Rangers

## Shutouts

**Most Shutouts, Season**
13    1953-54

**Most Consecutive Shutouts**
3    Nov. 7, 11, 13, 1954 (vs. New York Rangers, Toronto, Toronto)
     Dec. 11, 15, 18, 1955 (vs. New York Rangers, Toronto, Montreal)
     Dec. 31, 1975, Jan. 3, 8, 1976 (vs. Washington, Toronto, Minnesota)

**Fewest Shutouts, Season**
0    1980-81
     1981-82
     1984-85

# Stanley Cup Playoffs: Individual Records

## Service

**Most Years in Playoffs**
19 Gordie Howe, 1947-58, 1960-61, 1963-66, 1970

**Most Consecutive Years in Playoffs**
13 Ted Lindsay, 1945-57

**Most Games, Career**
154 Gordie Howe, 1947-58, 1960-61, 1963-66, 1970

## Points

**Most Points, Career**
158 Gordie Howe, 1947-58, 1960-61, 1963-66, 1970

**Most Points by Defenseman, Career**
50 Paul Coffey, 1993-96

**Most Points, Playoff Year**
24 Sergei Fedorov, 1995

**Most Points by Defenseman, Playoff Year**
18 Paul Coffey, 1995

**Most Points by Rookie, Playoff Year**
9 Shawn Burr, 1987

**Most Points, Game**
5 Several times. *Last:*
Steve Yzerman, May 5, 1996 vs. St. Louis Blues

**Most Points by Defenseman, Game**
5 Eddie Bush, April 9, 1942 vs. Toronto

**Most Points, Period**
4 Carl Liscombe, March 26, 1942 vs. Mont. Canadiens

**Most Consecutive Games Scoring Point**
12 Gordie Howe, 1964

## Goals

**Most Goals, Career**
67 Gordie Howe, 1947-58, 1960-61, 1963-66, 1970

**Most Goals by Defenseman, Career**
16 Red Kelly, 1948-58

**Most Goals, Playoff Year**
10 Petr Klima, 1988

**Most Goals by Defenseman, Playoff Year**
6 Paul Coffey, 1995

**Most Goals by Rookie, Playoff Year**
7 Shawn Burr, 1987

**Most Goals, Game**
4 Carl Liscombe, April 3, 1945 vs. Boston
Ted Lindsay, April 5, 1955 vs. Montreal Canadiens

**Most Goals, Period**
3 Ted Lindsay, April 5, 1955 vs. Montreal Canadiens

**Most Consecutive Games Scoring Goal**
5 Gordie Howe, 1949
Ted Lindsay, 1952
Gordie Howe, 1964

## Fastest Goals

**Fastest Goal From Start of Game**
0:09 Gordie Howe, April 1, 1954 vs. Toronto

**Fastest Two Goals**
0:05 apart Norm Ullman, April 11, 1965 vs. Chicago

## Power-Play Goals

**Most Power-Play Goals, Career**
16 Gordie Howe, 1947-58, 1960-61, 1963-66, 1970
Dino Ciccarelli, 1993-96

**Most Power-Play Goals, Playoff Year**
6 Alex Delvecchio, 1955
Gordie Howe, 1955
Dino Ciccarelli, 1995
Dino Ciccarelli, 1996

**Most Power-Play Goals, Game**
3 Syd Howe, March 23, 1939 vs. Montreal Canadiens
Gordie Howe, April 10, 1955, vs. Mont. Canadiens
Dino Ciccarelli, April 29, 1993 vs. Toronto
Dino Ciccarelli, May 11, 1995 vs. Dallas

**Most Power-Play Goals, Period**
2 Syd Howe, March 23, 1939 vs. Montreal Canadiens
Floyd Smith, April 10, 1966 vs. Chicago
Dino Ciccarelli, April 29, 1993 vs. Toronto

## Shorthanded Goals

**Most Shorthanded Goals, Career**
4 Gordie Howe, 1947-58, 1960-61, 1963-66, 1970

**Most Shorthanded Goals, Playoff Year**
2 Sergei Fedorov, 1992
Paul Coffey, 1996

## Winning Goals

**Most Winning Goals, Career**
11 Gordie Howe, 1947-58, 1960-61, 1963-66, 1970

**Most Winning Goals, Playoff Year**
4 Petr Klima, 1988
Slava Kozlov, 1995

## Overtime Goals

**Most Overtime Goals, Career**
2 Mud Bruneteau, 1936-37, 1939-45
Syd Howe, 1936-37, 1939-45
Leo Reise, 1947-52
Ted Lindsay, 1945-57, 1965

**Most Overtime Goals, Playoff Year**
2 Leo Reise, 1950

## Hat Tricks

**Most Games, Three or More Goals, Career**
3   Norm Ullman, 1956-58, 1960-61, 1963-66
     Steve Yzerman, 1984-85, 1987-89, 1991-96

**Most Games, Three or More Goals, Playoff Year**
2   Norm Ullman, 1964
     Petr Klima, 1988

## Assists

**Most Assists, Career**
91   Gordie Howe, 1947-58, 1960-61, 1963-66, 1970

**Most Assists by Defenseman, Career**
36   Paul Coffey, 1993-96

**Most Assists, Playoff Year**
18   Sergei Fedorov, 1996

**Most Assists by Defenseman, Playoff Year**
12   Paul Coffey, 1995
     Niklas Lidstrom, 1995

**Most Assists by Rookie, Playoff Year**
5   Paul Woods, 1978
     Sergei Fedorov, 1991

**Most Assists, Game**
4   Several times. *Last:*
     Sergei Fedorov, May 23, 1996 vs. Colorado

**Ted Lindsay holds one of the seven Stanley Cups the Red Wings have won in their long history.**

**Most Assists by Defenseman, Game**
4   Eddie Bush, April 9, 1942 vs. Toronto

**Most Assists, Period**
3   Billy Taylor, March 29, 1947 vs. Toronto
     Alex Delvecchio, April 14, 1966 vs. Chicago
     Slava Kozlov, May 21, 1995 vs. San Jose

## Penalties

**Most Penalty Minutes, Career**
218   Gordie Howe, 1947-58, 1960-61, 1963-66, 1970

**Most Penalty Minutes, Playoff Year**
71   Joe Kocur, 1987

**Most Penalty Minutes, Game**
29   Randy McKay, April 12, 1991 vs. St. Louis

# Goaltending

## Service

**Most Years in Playoffs**
10   Terry Sawchuk, 1951-55, 1958, 1960-61, 1963-64

**Most Games, Career**
84   Terry Sawchuk, 1951-55, 1958, 1960-61, 1963-64

**Most Games, Playoff Year**
18   Mike Vernon, 1995

## Wins

**Most Wins, Career**
47   Terry Sawchuk, 1951-55, 1958, 1960-61, 1963-64

**Most Wins, Playoff Year**
12   Mike Vernon, 1995

**Most Consecutive Wins**
9   Terry Sawchuk, March 25, 1952-March 24, 1953

## Goals-Against Average

**Lowest Goals-Against Average, Career (Minimum 10 Games)**
1.28   Norm Smith, 1936-37

**Lowest Goals-Against Average, One Playoff Year**
0.62   Terry Sawchuk, 1952

## Shutouts

**Most Shutouts, Career**
11   Terry Sawchuk, 1951-55, 1958, 1960-61, 1963-64

**Most Shutouts, Playoff Year**
4   Terry Sawchuk, 1952

**Most Consecutive Shutouts**
3   Terry Sawchuk, April 13, 15, 1952 vs. Montreal,
     March 24, 1953 vs. Boston

**Longest Shutout Sequence, Playoff Year**
248:32   Norm Smith, 1936

**Longest Shutout Sequence, Game**
176:30   Norm Smith, March 24, 1936 vs.
          Montreal Maroons

# Stanley Cup Playoffs: Team Records

**Earliest Playoff Date**
March 19, 1929 vs. Toronto; 1940 vs. New York Americans;
1946 vs. Boston

**Latest Playoff Date**
June 24, 1995 vs. New Jersey

**Most Games Played, Playoff Year**
19   1996

**Most Consecutive Games Won, Playoff Year**
8   March 25-April 15, 1952
May 15-June 6, 1995

**Most Consecutive Games Lost, Playoff Year**
4   Several times. *Last:* June 17-24, 1995

**Longest Game**
176:30 March 24, 1936 vs. Montreal Maroons

**Most Goals, Game**
9   April 7, 1936 vs. Toronto
March 29, 1947 vs. Toronto

**Most Power-Play Goals, Game**
4   Several times. *Last:* April 23, 1996 vs. Winnipeg

**Most Power-Play Goals, Period**
3   April 11, 1978 vs. Atlanta

**Most Shorthanded Goals, Game**
2   April 5, 1936 vs. Toronto
April 29, 1993 vs. Toronto
April 19, 1996 vs. Winnipeg

**Fastest Two Goals**
0:05 apart   April 11, 1965 vs. Chicago (Ullman 2)

**Fastest Three Goals**
1:30 apart   March 29, 1947 vs. Toronto (J. Conacher,
R. Conacher, E. Bruneteau)

**Most Goals Allowed, Game**
9   April 14, 1942 vs. Toronto
April 10, 1985 vs. Chicago

**Most Power-Play Goals Allowed, Game**
4   March 28, 1963 vs. Chicago

**Most Shorthanded Goals Allowed, Game**
2   April 23, 1978 vs. Montreal Canadiens
April 11, 1989 vs. Chicago

**Most Penalty Minutes, Game**
152   April 12, 1991 vs. St. Louis

**Most Penalty Minutes, Period**
114   April 12, 1991 vs. St. Louis

**Goalie Roger Crozier, recipient of the 1966 Conn Smythe Award, outhustles the Blackhawks' Bobby Hull for the puck during that year's playoffs.**

# All-Time Roster

## A

Gerry Abel, C . . . . . . . . . . 1966-67
**Sid Abel, C-LW . . . . . . . . 1938-39 to 42-43;**
**1945-46 to 51-52**
Gene Achtymichuk, C . . . . 1957-58
Greg Adams, LW . . . . . . . . 1989-90
Micah Aivazoff, LW . . . . . . 1993-94
Gary Aldcorn, LW . . . . . . . 1959-60 to 60-61
Keith Allen, D . . . . . . . . . . 1953-54 to 54-55
Ralph Almas, G . . . . . . . . . 1946-47; 1952-53
Dave Amadio, D . . . . . . . . 1957-58
Dale Anderson, D . . . . . . . 1956-57
Earl Anderson, RW . . . . . . 1974-75
Ron Anderson, RW . . . . . . 1967-68 to 68-69
Tom Anderson, C . . . . . . . 1934-35
Al Arbour, D . . . . . . . . . . . 1953-54;
1955-56 to 57-58
Jack Arbour, D-LW . . . . . . 1926-27
Murray Armstrong, C . . . . . 1943-44 to 45-46
Brent Ashton, LW . . . . . . . 1986-87 to 87-88
Ossie Asmundson, RW . . . . 1934-35
Pierre Aubry, C-LW . . . . . . 1983-84 to 84-85
Larry Aurie, RW . . . . . . . . 1927-28 to 38-39

## B

Pete Babando, LW . . . . . . . 1949-50
Ace Bailey, LW . . . . . . . . . . 1972-73 to 73-74
Bob Bailey, RW . . . . . . . . . 1956-57 to 57-58
Doug Baldwin, D . . . . . . . . 1946-47
Doug Barkley, D . . . . . . . . 1962-63 to 65-66
Dave Barr, RW . . . . . . . . . 1986-87 to 90-91
John Barrett, D . . . . . . . . . 1980-81 to 85-86
**Marty Barry, C . . . . . . . . . 1935-36 to 38-39**
Hank Bassen, G . . . . . . . . . 1960-61 to 63-64;
1965-66 to 66-67
Frank Bathe, D . . . . . . . . . 1974-75 to 75-76
**Andy Bathgate, C-RW . . . . 1965-66 to 66-67**
Bob Baun, D . . . . . . . . . . . 1968-69 to 70-71
Sergei Bautin, D . . . . . . . . 1993-94
John (Red) Beattie, LW . . . . 1937-38
Clarence Behling, D . . . . . . 1940-41 to 42-43
Pete Bellefeuille, RW . . . . . 1926-27;
1928-29 to 29-30
Frank Bennett, C . . . . . . . . 1943-44
Gordon (Red) Berenson, C . 1970-71 to 74-75
Michel Bergeron, RW . . . . . 1974-75 to 77-78
Marc Bergevin, D . . . . . . . . 1995-96
Gary Bergman, D . . . . . . . . 1964-65 to 74-75
Thommie Bergman, D . . . . 1972-73 to 74-75;
1977-78 to 79-80
Fred Berry, C . . . . . . . . . . . 1976-77
Phil Besler, RW . . . . . . . . . 1938-39
Pete Bessone, D . . . . . . . . 1937-38
Allan Bester, G . . . . . . . . . 1990-91 to 91-92
Bill Beveridge, G . . . . . . . . 1929-30
Tim Bissett, C . . . . . . . . . . 1990-91
Steve Black, LW . . . . . . . . . 1949-50 to 50-51

Tom Bladon, D . . . . . . . . . 1980-81
Mike Blaisdell, RW . . . . . . 1980-81 to 82-83
Mike Bloom, LW . . . . . . . . 1974-75 to 76-77
John Blum, D . . . . . . . . . . 1988-89
Marc Boileau, C . . . . . . . . . 1961-62
Gilles Boisvert, G . . . . . . . . 1959-60
**Leo Boivin, D . . . . . . . . . . 1965-66 to 66-67**
Ivan Boldirev, C-LW . . . . . 1982-83 to 84-85
Dan Bolduc, RW . . . . . . . . 1978-79 to 79-80
Marcel Bonin, LW . . . . . . . 1952-53 to 54-55
Henry Boucha, LW . . . . . . 1971-72 to 73-74
Claude Bourque, G . . . . . . 1939-40
Scotty Bowman, D . . . . . . . 1934-35 to 39-40
Rick Bowness, RW . . . . . . . 1977-78
Irwin (Yank) Boyd, RW . . . . 1934-35
John Brenneman, LW . . . . . 1967-68
Carl Brewer, D . . . . . . . . . . 1969-70
Archie Briden, LW . . . . . . . 1926-27
Mel Bridgman, LW-C . . . . . 1986-87 to 87-88
Bernie Brophy, C . . . . . . . . 1928-29 to 29-30
Adam Brown, LW . . . . . . . 1941-42 to 43-44;
1945-46 to 46-47
Andy Brown, G . . . . . . . . . 1971-72 to 72-73
Arnie Brown, D . . . . . . . . . 1970-71 to 71-72
Connie Brown, C . . . . . . . . 1938-39 to 42-43
Doug Brown, RW-LW . . . . 1995 to 96-97
Gerry Brown, LW . . . . . . . 1941-42; 1945-46
Larry Brown, D . . . . . . . . . 1970-71
Stan Brown, D . . . . . . . . . 1927-28
Jeff Brubaker, C . . . . . . . . . 1988-89
Ed Bruneteau, RW . . . . . . 1941-42;
1943-44 to 48-49
Mud Bruneteau, RW . . . . . 1935-36 to 45-46
Bill Brydge, D . . . . . . . . . . 1928-29
**John Bucyk, LW . . . . . . . . 1955-56 to 56-57**
Tony Bukovich, LW . . . . . . 1943-44 to 44-45
Hy Buller, D . . . . . . . . . . . 1943-44 to 44-45
Charlie Burns, C . . . . . . . . 1958-59
Shawn Burr, C . . . . . . . . . . 1984-85 to 1995
Cummy Burton, LW . . . . . . 1955-56;
1957-58 to 58-59
Eddie Bush, D . . . . . . . . . . 1938-39; 1941-42
Walter Buswell, D . . . . . . . 1932-33 to 34-35

## C

Al Cameron, D . . . . . . . . . 1975-76 to 78-79
Craig Cameron, RW . . . . . . 1966-67
Colin Campbell, D . . . . . . . 1982-83 to 84-85
Terry Carkner, D . . . . . . . . 1993-94 to 95
Gene Carrigan, C . . . . . . . . 1932-33 to 33-34
Billy Carroll, C . . . . . . . . . 1985-86 to 86-87
Greg Carroll, C . . . . . . . . . 1978-79
Dwight Carruthers, D . . . . . 1965-66
Frank Carson, C-RW . . . . . 1931-32 to 33-34
Jimmy Carson, C . . . . . . . . 1989-90 to 92-93
Joe Carveth, RW-C . . . . . . 1940-41 to 45-46;
1949-50 to 50-51

Frank Cernik, LW . . . . . . . 1984-85
John Chabot, C . . . . . . . . . 1987-88 to 90-91
Milan Chalupa, D . . . . . . . 1984-85
Bob Champoux, G . . . . . . . 1963-64
Guy Charron, C-LW . . . . . . 1970-71 to 74-75
Lude Check, LW . . . . . . . . 1943-44
Real Chevrefils, LW . . . . . . 1955-56
Tim Cheveldae, G . . . . . . . 1988-89 to 93-94
Alain Chevrier, G . . . . . . . . 1990-91
Steve Chiasson, D . . . . . . . 1987-88 to 93-94
Dino Ciccarelli, RW . . . . . . 1992-93 to 95-96
Chris Cichocki, RW . . . . . . 1985-86 to 86-87
Rejean Cloutier, D . . . . . . . 1979-80 to 81-82
Roland Cloutier, C . . . . . . . 1977-78 to 78-79
Steve Coates, RW . . . . . . . 1976-77
Paul Coffey, D . . . . . . . . . . 1992-93 to 95-96
Bill Collins, RW . . . . . . . . . 1970-71 to 73-74
Brian Conacher, C . . . . . . . 1971-72
**Charlie Conacher, RW . . . . 1938-39**
Jim Conacher, LW . . . . . . . 1945-46 to 48-49
Roy Conacher, LW . . . . . . . 1946-47
**Alex Connell, G . . . . . . . . 1931-32**
Wayne Connelly, RW . . . . . 1968-69 to 70-71
Bob Connors, C . . . . . . . . . 1928-29 to 29-30
Bob Cook, RW . . . . . . . . . 1972-73
Carson Cooper, RW . . . . . . 1927-28 to 31-32
Norm Corcoran, RW . . . . . 1955-56
Murray Costello, C . . . . . . . 1955-56 to 56-57
Gerry Couture, RW . . . . . . 1944-45 to 50-51
Abbie Cox, G . . . . . . . . . . 1933-34
Danny Cox, LW . . . . . . . . . 1931-32
Bart Crashley, D . . . . . . . . 1965-66 to 68-69;
1974-75
Murray Craven, LW-C . . . . 1982-83 to 83-84
Bobby Crawford, C . . . . . . . 1982-83
Jim Creighton, C . . . . . . . . 1930-31 to 31-32
Troy Crowder, RW . . . . . . . 1991-92
Gary Croteau, LW . . . . . . . 1969-70
Doug Crossman, D . . . . . . 1990-91 to 91-92
Roger Crozier, G . . . . . . . . 1963-64 to 69-70
Wilf Cude, G . . . . . . . . . . . 1933-34
Barry Cullen, RW . . . . . . . 1959-60
Ray Cullen, C . . . . . . . . . . 1966-67
Jim Cummins, LW . . . . . . . 1991-92 to 92-93
Ian Cushenan, D . . . . . . . . 1963-64

## D

Frank Daley, D-LW . . . . . . 1928-29
Joe Daley, G . . . . . . . . . . . 1971-72
Mathieu Dandenault, RW-D 1995-96 to 96-97
Lorne Davis, RW . . . . . . . . 1954-55
Bob Davis, D . . . . . . . . . . . 1932-33
Mal Davis, RW . . . . . . . . . 1978-79 to 80-81
Billy Dea, LW . . . . . . . . . . 1956-57 to 57-58;
1969-70 to 70-71
Don Deacon, C . . . . . . . . . 1936-37;
1938-39 to 39-40

Nelson DeBenedet, LW . . . . 1973-74
Denis Dejordy, G . . . . . . . . 1972-73 to 73-74
Gilbert Delorme, D . . . . . . . 1986-87 to 88-89
**Alex Delvecchio, C-LW . . . 1950-51 to 73-74**
Al Dewsbury, D . . . . . . . . . 1946-47 to 47-48;
    1949-50
Per Djoos, D . . . . . . . . . . . 1990-91
Ed Diachuk, LW . . . . . . . . 1960-61
Bob Dillabough, LW . . . . . . 1961-62 to 64-65
Cecil Dilon, RW . . . . . . . . 1939-40
Bill Dineen, RW . . . . . . . . 1953-54 to 57-58
Peter Dineen, D . . . . . . . . 1989-90
Connie Dion, G . . . . . . . . 1943-44 to 44-45
**Marcel Dionne, C . . . . . . . 1971-72 to 74-75**
Gary Doak, D . . . . . . . . . 1965-66; 1972-73
Dolly Dolson, G . . . . . . . . 1928-29 to 30-31
Bobby Dollas, D . . . . . . . . 1990-91 to 92-93
Lloyd Doran, C . . . . . . . . . 1946-47
Lloyd (Red) Doran, D . . . . 1937-38
Ken Doraty, RW . . . . . . . . 1937-38
Kent Douglas, D . . . . . . . 1967-68 to 68-69
Les Douglas, C . . . . . . . . . 1940-41; 1942-43;
    1946-47
Dallas Drake, C-LW . . . . . . 1992-93 to 93-94
Kris Draper, C . . . . . . . . . 1993-94 to 96-97
Rene Drolet, RW . . . . . . . 1974-75
Clarence Drouillard, C. . . . . 1937-38
Gilles Dube, LW . . . . . . . . 1953-54
Ron Duguay, RW-C . . . . . . 1983-84 to 85-86
Lorne Duguid, LW . . . . . . 1934-35 to 35-36
Art Duncan, D . . . . . . . . . 1926-27
Blake Dunlop, C . . . . . . . . 1983-84

### E

Bruce Eakin, C . . . . . . . . . . 1985-86
Murray Eaves, C . . . . . . . . 1987-88; 1989-90
Tim Ecclestone, RW . . . . . 1970-71 to 73-74
Roy Edwards, G . . . . . . . . 1967-68 to 70-71;
    1972-73 to 73-74
Pat Egan, D . . . . . . . . . . . 1943-44
Gerry Ehman, RW . . . . . . . 1958-59
Bo Elik, LW . . . . . . . . . . . 1962-63
Darren Eliot, G . . . . . . . . . 1987-88
Hap Emms, LW . . . . . . . . 1931-32 to 33-34
Anders Eriksson, D . . . . . . 1995-96 to 96-97
Bob Errey, LW . . . . . . . . . 1995 to 96-97
Bob Essensa, G . . . . . . . . . 1993-94
Chris Evans, D . . . . . . . . . 1973-74
Stu Evans, D . . . . . . . . . . 1930-31;
    1932-33 to 33-34

### F

Bob Falkenberg, D . . . . . . . 1966-67 to 68-69;
    1970-71 to 71-72
Alex Faulkner, C . . . . . . . . 1962-63 to 63-64
Bernie Federko, C . . . . . . . 1989-90
Lorne Ferguson, LW . . . . . 1955-56 to 57-58
Sergei Fedorov, C-RW . . . . 1990-91 to 96-97
Brent Fedyk, RW . . . . . . . 1987-88 to 91-92
Mark Ferner, D . . . . . . . . . 1995
Slava Fetisov, D . . . . . . . . 1995 to 96-97

Guyle Fielder, C . . . . . . . . 1952-53; 1957-58
Tom Filmore, RW . . . . . . . 1930-31 to 31-32
Dunc Fisher, RW . . . . . . . . 1958-59
Joe Fisher, RW . . . . . . . . . 1939-40 to 42-43
Lee Fogolin, D . . . . . . . . . 1947-48 to 50-51
Rick Foley, D . . . . . . . . . . 1973-74
Mike Foligno, RW . . . . . . . 1979-80 to 81-82
Bill Folk, D . . . . . . . . . . . 1951-52 to 52-53
Len Fontaine, RW . . . . . . . 1972-73 to 73-74
Val Fonteyne, C-LW . . . . . 1959-60 to 62-63;
    1964-65 to 66-67
Dwight Foster, C . . . . . . . . 1982-83 to 85-86
Harry (Yip) Foster, D . . . . . 1933-34 to 34-35
**Frank Foyston, C . . . . . . . 1926-27 to 27-28**
Bobby Francis, C . . . . . . . . 1982-83
Jimmy Franks, G . . . . . . . . 1936-37 to 37-38;
    1943-44
Gord Fraser, D . . . . . . . . . 1927-28 to 28-29
**Frank Frederickson, C . . . . 1926-27; 1930-31**
Tim Friday, D . . . . . . . . . . 1985-86
Miroslav Frycer, RW . . . . . 1988-89
Robbie Ftorek, C . . . . . . . . 1972-73 to 73-74

### G

**Bill Gadsby, D . . . . . . . . . 1961-62 to 65-66**
Jody Gage, RW . . . . . . . . . 1980-81 to 81-82;
    1983-84
Art Gagne, RW . . . . . . . . . 1931-32
Dave Gagnon, G . . . . . . . . 1990-91
Johnny Gallagher, D . . . . . . 1932-33 to 33-34;
    1936-37
Gerard Gallant, LW . . . . . . 1984-85 to 92-93
George Gardner, G . . . . . . . 1965-66 to 67-68
Danny Gare, RW . . . . . . . . 1981-82 to 85-86
Johan Garpenlov, LW . . . . . 1990-91 to 91-92
Dave Gatherum, G . . . . . . . 1953-54
Fern Gauthier, RW . . . . . . . 1945-46 to 48-49
George Gee, C . . . . . . . . . 1948-49 to 50-51
**Ed Giacomin, G . . . . . . . . 1975-76 to 77-78**
Gus Giesebrecht, C . . . . . . 1938-39 to 41-42
Gilles Gilbert, G . . . . . . . . 1980-81 to 82-83
Art Giroux, RW . . . . . . . . . 1935-36
Larry Giroux, D . . . . . . . . . 1974-75 to 77-78
Lorry Gloeckner, D . . . . . . 1978-79
Fred Glover, RW . . . . . . . . 1948-49 to 51-52
Howie Glover, RW . . . . . . . 1960-61 to 61-62
Warren Godfrey, D . . . . . . . 1955-56 to 61-62;
    1963-64 to 67-68
Pete Goegan, D . . . . . . . . . 1957-58 to 66-67
Bob Goldham, D . . . . . . . . 1950-51 to 55-56
Leroy Goldsworthy, RW . . . 1930-31; 1932-33
**Ebbie Goodfellow, C-D . . . 1929-30 to 42-43**
Fred Gordon, RW . . . . . . . 1926-27
Ted Graham, D . . . . . . . . . 1933-34 to 34-35
Danny Grant, LW . . . . . . . 1974-75 to 77-78
Doug Grant, G . . . . . . . . . 1973-74 to 75-76
Leo Gravelle, RW . . . . . . . 1950-51
Adam Graves, C . . . . . . . . 1987-88 to 89-90
Gerry Gray, G . . . . . . . . . 1970-71
Harrison Gray, G . . . . . . . . 1963-64
Red Green, LW . . . . . . . . . 1928-29

Rick Green, D . . . . . . . . . 1990-91
Stu Grimson, LW . . . . . . . 1995 to 96-97
Lloyd Gross, LW . . . . . . . . 1933-34 to 34-35
Don Grosso, C . . . . . . . . . 1938-39; 1944-45
Danny Gruen, LW . . . . . . . 1972-73 to 73-74
Bep Guidolin, LW . . . . . . . 1947-48 to 48-49

### H

Marc Habscheid, C-RW . . . . 1989-90 to 90-91
Lloyd Haddon, D . . . . . . . . 1959-60
Gord Haidy, RW . . . . . . . . 1949-50
Slim Halderson, D . . . . . . . 1926-27
Len Haley, RW . . . . . . . . . 1959-60 to 60-61
Bob Halkidis, D . . . . . . . . 1993-94 to 95
**Glenn Hall, G . . . . . . . . . 1952-53;**
    **1954-55 to 55-56**
Murray Hall, C . . . . . . . . . 1964-65 to 66-67
Doug Halward, D . . . . . . . . 1986-87 to 88-89
Jean Hamel, D . . . . . . . . . 1973-74 to 80-81
Ted Hampson, C . . . . . . . . 1963-64 to 64-65;
    1966-67 to 67-68
Glen Hanlon, G . . . . . . . . 1986-87 to 90-91
Dave Hanson, D . . . . . . . . 1978-79
Emil Hanson, D . . . . . . . . 1932-33
Terry Harper, D . . . . . . . . . 1975-76 to 78-79
Billy Harris, C . . . . . . . . . 1965-66
Ron Harris, D . . . . . . . . . 1962-63 to 63-64;
    1968-69 to 71-72
Ted Harris, D . . . . . . . . . 1973-74
Gerry Hart, D . . . . . . . . . 1968-69 to 71-72
Harold Hart, LW . . . . . . . . 1926-27
Buster Harvey, RW . . . . . . 1975-76 to 76-77
**Doug Harvey, D . . . . . . . . 1966-67**
Ed Hatoum, RW . . . . . . . . 1968-69 to 69-70
**George Hay, C-LW . . . . . . 1927-28 to 33-34**
Jim Hay, D . . . . . . . . . . . 1952-53 to 54-55
Galen Head, RW . . . . . . . . 1967-68
Rich Healey, D . . . . . . . . . 1960-61
Paul Henderson, LW . . . . . 1962-63 to 67-68
Jack Hendrickson, D . . . . . 1957-58 to 58-59;
    1961-62
Jim Herberts, C . . . . . . . . 1928-29 to 29-30
Art Herchenratter, C . . . . . 1940-41
Bryan Hextall, C . . . . . . . . 1975-76
Glenn Hicks, LW . . . . . . . . 1979-80 to 80-81
Harold Hicks, D . . . . . . . . 1929-30 to 30-31
Tim Higgins, RW . . . . . . . . 1986-87 to 88-89
Dutch Hiller, LW . . . . . . . . 1941-42
Jim Hiller, LW . . . . . . . . . 1992-93
Larry Hillman, D . . . . . . . . 1954-55 to 56-57
John Hilworth, D . . . . . . . . 1977-78 to 79-80
Kevin Hodson, G . . . . . . . . 1995-96 to 96-97
Bill Hogaboam, C . . . . . . . 1972-73 to 75-76;
    1978-79 to 79-80
Ken Holland, G . . . . . . . . . 1983-84
Flash Hollett, D . . . . . . . . 1943-44 to 45-46
Bucky Hollingworth, D . . . . 1955-56 to 57-58
Chuck Holmes, RW . . . . . . 1958-59; 1961-62
**Hap Holmes, G . . . . . . . . 1926-27 to 27-28**
Tomas Holmstrom, LW . . . 1996-97
John Holota, C . . . . . . . . . 1942-43; 1945-46

Pete Horeck, RW-LW . . . . . 1946-47 to 48-49
Doug Houda, D . . . . . . . . . 1985-86;
　　　　　　　　　　　　　1987-88 to 90-91
**Gordie Howe, RW . . . . . . . 1946-47 to 70-71**
Mark Howe, D . . . . . . . . . 1992-93 to 95
**Syd Howe, C-LW . . . . . . . 1934-35 to 45-46**
Steve Hrymnak, D . . . . . . . 1952-53
Willie Huber, D . . . . . . . . . 1978-79 to 82-83
Ron Hudson, RW . . . . . . . . 1937-38; 1939-40
Brent Hughes, D . . . . . . . . 1973-74
Rusty Hughes, D . . . . . . . . 1929-30
Dennis Hull, LW . . . . . . . . 1977-78

## I

Miroslav Ihnacak, LW . . . . . 1988-89
Peter Ing, G . . . . . . . . . . . 1993-94
Earl Ingarfield, C-LW . . . . . 1980-81
Ron Ingram, D . . . . . . . . . 1963-64

## J

Hal Jackson, D . . . . . . . . . . 1940-41;
　　　　　　　　　　　　　1942-43 to 46-47
Lou Jankowski, RW . . . . . . 1950-51; 1952-53
Gary Jarrett, LW . . . . . . . . 1966-67 to 67-68
Pierre Jarry, LW . . . . . . . . . 1973-74 to 74-75
Larry Jeffrey, LW . . . . . . . . 1961-62 to 64-65
Bill Jennings, RW . . . . . . . . 1940-41 to 43-44
Al Jensen, G . . . . . . . . . . . 1980-81
Al Johnson, RW . . . . . . . . . 1960-61 to 62-63
Brian Johnson, RW . . . . . . 1983-84
Danny Johnson, C . . . . . . . 1971-72
Earl Johnson, C . . . . . . . . . 1953-54
Greg Johnson, C . . . . . . . . 1993-94 to 96-97
Larry Johnston, D . . . . . . . 1971-72 to 73-74
Ed Johnstone, RW . . . . . . . 1983-84;
　　　　　　　　　　　　　1985-86 to 86-87
Greg Joly, D . . . . . . . . . . . 1976-77 to 82-83
Buck Jones, D . . . . . . . . . . 1938-39 to 39-40;
　　　　　　　　　　　　　1941-42
Ed Joyal, C . . . . . . . . . . . 1962-63 to 64-65

## K

Francis (Red) Kane, D . . . . . 1943-44
Al Karlander, C-LW . . . . . . 1969-70 to 72-73
Jack Keating, LW . . . . . . . . 1938-39 to 39-40
**Duke Keats, C . . . . . . . . . 1926-27 to 27-28**
Dave Kelly, RW . . . . . . . . . 1976-77
**Leonard (Red) Kelly, D . . . 1947-48 to 59-60**
Pete Kelly, RW . . . . . . . . . 1935-36 to 38-39
Forbes Kennedy, C . . . . . . . 1957-58 to 59-60;
　　　　　　　　　　　　　1961-62
Sheldon Kennedy, RW . . . . 1989-90 to 93-94
Alan Kerr, RW . . . . . . . . . 1991-92
Brian Kilrea, LW . . . . . . . . 1957-58
Hec Kilrea, LW . . . . . . . . . 1931-32;
　　　　　　　　　　　　　1935-36 to 39-40
Ken Kilrea, C-LW . . . . . . . 1939-40 to 41-42;
　　　　　　　　　　　　　1943-44
Wally Kilrea, C . . . . . . . . . 1934-35 to 37-38
Kris King, RW . . . . . . . . . 1987-88 to 88-89
Scott King, G . . . . . . . . . . 1990-91 to 91-92

Mark Kirton, C . . . . . . . . . 1980-81 to 82-83
Kelly Kisio, C . . . . . . . . . . 1982-83 to 85-86
Hobie Kitchen, D . . . . . . . 1926-27
Petr Klima, LW . . . . . . . . . 1985-86 to 89-90
Joe Kocur, RW . . . . . . . . . 1984-85 to 90-91;
　　　　　　　　　　　　　1996-97
Steve Konroyd, D . . . . . . . 1992-93 to 93-94
Vladimir Konstantinov, D . . 1991-92 to 96-97
Jim Korn, D . . . . . . . . . . . 1979-80 to 81-82
Mike Korney, RW . . . . . . . 1973-74 to 75-76
Chris Kotsopoulos, D . . . . . 1989-90
Slava Kozlov, LW . . . . . . . . 1991-92 to 96-97
Dale Krentz, LW . . . . . . . . 1986-87 to 88-89
Jim Krulicki, LW . . . . . . . . 1970-71
Gord Kruppke, D . . . . . . . . 1990-91;
　　　　　　　　　　　　　1992-93 to 93-94
Mike Krushelnyski, LW-C . 1995
Dave Kryskow, LW . . . . . . . 1974-75
Mark Kumpel, RW . . . . . . . 1986-87 to 87-88

## L

Leo Labine, RW . . . . . . . . . 1960-61 to 61-62
Dan Labraaten, LW . . . . . . 1978-79 to 80-81
Randy Ladouceur, D . . . . . . 1982-83 to 86-87
Mark Laforest, G . . . . . . . . 1985-86 to 86-87
Claude Laforge, LW . . . . . . 1958-59;
　　　　　　　　　　　　　1960-61 to 61-62;
　　　　　　　　　　　　　1963-64 to 64-65
Roger Lafreniere, D . . . . . . 1962-63
Serge Lajeunesse, D . . . . . . 1970-71 to 72-73
Hec Lalande, C . . . . . . . . . 1957-58
Joe Lamb, LW . . . . . . . . . . 1937-38
Mark Lamb, C . . . . . . . . . . 1986-87
Lane Lambert, RW . . . . . . . 1983-84 to 85-86
Al Langlois, D . . . . . . . . . . 1963-64 to 64-65
Rick LaPointe, D . . . . . . . . 1975-76 to 76-77
Martin Lapointe, RW . . . . . 1991-92 to 96-97
Igor Larionov, C . . . . . . . . 1995-96 to 96-97
Reed Larson, D . . . . . . . . . 1976-77 to 85-86
Brain Lavender, LW . . . . . . 1972-73 to 73-74
Dan Lawson, RW . . . . . . . . 1967-68 to 68-69
Reggie Leach, RW . . . . . . . 1982-83
Jim Leavins, D . . . . . . . . . . 1985-86
Fernand Leblanc, RW . . . . 1976-77 to 78-79
JP Leblanc, C . . . . . . . . . . 1975-76 to 78-79
Rene Leclerc, RW . . . . . . . 1968-69; 1970-71
Claude Legris, G . . . . . . . . 1980-81 to 81-82
Real Lemieux, LW . . . . . . . 1966-67
Tony Leswick, RW . . . . . . . 1951-52 to 54-55;
　　　　　　　　　　　　　1957-58
Dave Lewis, D . . . . . . . . . . 1986-87 to 87-88
**Herbie Lewis, LW . . . . . . . 1928-29 to 38-39**
Nick Libett, LW . . . . . . . . . 1967-68 to 74-75;
　　　　　　　　　　　　　1976-77 to 78-79
Tony Licari, RW . . . . . . . . 1946-47
Nicklas Lidstrom, D . . . . . . 1991-92 to 96-97
**Ted Lindsay, LW . . . . . . . . 1944-45 to 56-57;
　　　　　　　　　　　　　1964-65**
Carl Liscombe, LW . . . . . . . 1937-38 to 45-46
Ed Litzenberger, RW . . . . . 1961-62
Bill Lochead, RW . . . . . . . 1974-75 to 78-79

Mark Lofthouse, RW . . . . . 1981-82 to 82-83
Claude Loiselle, C . . . . . . . 1981-82 to 85-86
Barry Long, D . . . . . . . . . . 1979-80
Clem Loughlin, D . . . . . . . 1926-27 to 27-28
Ron Low, G . . . . . . . . . . . 1977-78
Larry Lozinski, G . . . . . . . . 1980-81
Dave Lucas, D . . . . . . . . . . 1962-63
Don Luce, C . . . . . . . . . . . 1970-71
**Harry Lumley, G . . . . . . . . 1943-44 to 49-50**
Len Lunde, C-RW . . . . . . . 1958-59 to 61-62
Tord Lundstrom, LW . . . . . 1973-74
Pat Lundy, C . . . . . . . . . . . 1945-46 to 48-49
Chris Luongo, D . . . . . . . . 1990-91
George Lyle, LW . . . . . . . . 1979-80 to 81-82
Jack Lynch, D . . . . . . . . . . 1973-74 to 74-75
Vic Lynn, D . . . . . . . . . . . 1943-44

## M

Lowell MacDonald, RW . . . 1961-62 to 64-65
Parker MacDonald, LW . . . . 1960-61 to 66-67
Bruce MacGregor, RW . . . . 1960-61 to 70-71
Calum MacKay, LW . . . . . . 1946-47; 1948-49
Howard Mackie, RW . . . . . 1936-37 to 37-38
Paul MacLean, RW . . . . . . 1988-89
Rick MacLeish, LW . . . . . . 1983-84
Brian MacLellan, LW . . . . . 1991-92
John MacMillan, LW . . . . . 1963-64 to 64-65
**Frank Mahovlich, LW . . . . 1967-68 to 70-71**
Pete Mahovlich, C . . . . . . . 1965-66 to 68-69;
　　　　　　　　　　　　　1979-80 to 80-81
Mark Major, LW . . . . . . . . 1996-97
Steve Maltais, LW . . . . . . . 1993-94
Dan Maloney, LW . . . . . . . 1975-76 to 77-78
Kirk Maltby, RW . . . . . . . . 1995-96 to 96-97
Randy Manery, D . . . . . . . . 1970-71 to 71-72
Ken Mann, RW . . . . . . . . . 1975-76
Bob Manno, LW-D . . . . . . 1983-84 to 84-85
Lou Marcon, D . . . . . . . . . 1958-59 to 59-60;
　　　　　　　　　　　　　1962-63
Gus Marker, RW . . . . . . . . 1932-33 to 33-34
Brad Marsh, D . . . . . . . . . . 1990-91 to 91-92
Gary Marsh, LW . . . . . . . . 1967-68
Bert Marshall, D . . . . . . . . 1965-66 to 67-68
Clare Martin, D . . . . . . . . . 1949-50 to 50-51
Pit Martin, C . . . . . . . . . . 1961-62;
　　　　　　　　　　　　　1963-64 to 65-66
Don Martineau, RW . . . . . 1975-66 to 76-77
Steve Martinson, D . . . . . . 1987-88
Charlie Mason, RW . . . . . . 1938-39
Roland Matte, D . . . . . . . . 1929-30
Gary McAdam, RW . . . . . . 1980-81
Jud McAtee, LW . . . . . . . . 1943-44 to 44-45
Stan McCabe, LW . . . . . . . 1929-30 to 30-31
Doug McCraig, D . . . . . . . . 1941-42;
　　　　　　　　　　　　　1945-46 to 47-48
Rick McCann, C . . . . . . . . 1967-68 to 71-72;
　　　　　　　　　　　　　1974-75
Tom McCarthy, LW . . . . . . 1956-57 to 58-59
Darren McCarty, LW . . . . . 1993-94 to 96-97
Kevin McClelland, RW . . . . 1989-90 to 90-91
Bob McCord, D . . . . . . . . . 1965-66 to 67-68

Dale McCourt, C . . . . . . . . 1977-78 to 81-82
Bill McCreary, LW . . . . . . . 1957-58
Brad McCrimmon, D . . . . . 1990-91 to 92-93
Brian McCutcheon, LW . . . . 1974-75 to 76-77
Ab McDonald, LW . . . . . . . 1965-66 to 66-67;
    1971-72
Bucko McDonald, D . . . . . . 1934-35 to 38-39
Byron McDonald, LW . . . . . 1939-40; 1944-45
Al McDonough, RW . . . . . . 1977-78
Bill McDougall, C . . . . . . . . 1990-91
Pete McDuffe, G . . . . . . . . 1975-76
Mike McEwen, D . . . . . . . . 1985-86
Jim McFadden, C . . . . . . . . 1946-47 to 50-51
Bob McGill, D . . . . . . . . . . 1991-92
Tom McGratton, G . . . . . . . 1947-48
Bert McInenly, LW . . . . . . 1930-31 to 31-32
Doug McKay, LW . . . . . . . 1949-50
Randy McKay, RW . . . . . . 1988-89 to 90-91
Jack McIntyre, LW . . . . . . 1957-58 to 59-60
Walt McKechnie, C . . . . . . 1974-75 to 76-77;
    1981-82 to 82-83
Tony McKegney, RW . . . . . 1989-90
Don McKenney, LW . . . . . 1965-66
Bill McKenzie, G . . . . . . . . 1973-74 to 74-75
John McKenzie, RW . . . . . 1959-60 to 60-61
Andrew McKim, C . . . . . . . 1995
Rollie McLenahan, D . . . . 1945-46
Al McLeod, D . . . . . . . . . . 1973-74
Don McLeod, G . . . . . . . . 1970-71
Mike McMahon, D . . . . . . 1969-70
Max McNab, C . . . . . . . . . 1947-48 to 50-51
Billy McNeill, RW . . . . . . . 1956-57 to 59-60;
    1962-63 to 63-64
Stu McNeill, C . . . . . . . . . 1957-58 to 59-60
Basil McRae, LW . . . . . . . 1985-86 to 86-87
Chris McRae, LW . . . . . . . 1989-90
Pat McReavy, LW . . . . . . . 1941-42
Harry Meeking, LW . . . . . . 1926-27
Tom Mellor, D . . . . . . . . . 1973-74 to 74-75
Gerry Melnyk, C . . . . . . . . 1955-56;
    1959-60 to 60-61
Barry Melrose, D . . . . . . . 1983-84; 1985-86
Howie Menard, C . . . . . . . 1963-64
Glenn Merkosky, LW . . . . . 1985-86; 1989-90
Corrado Micalef, G . . . . . . 1981-82 to 85-86
Nick Mickoski, LW . . . . . . 1957-58 to 58-59
Hugh Millar, D . . . . . . . . . 1946-47
Greg Millen, G . . . . . . . . . 1991-92
Kevin Miller, RW . . . . . . . 1990-91 to 91-92
Perry Miller, D . . . . . . . . . 1977-78 to 80-81
Tom Miller, C . . . . . . . . . . 1970-71
Eddie Mio, G . . . . . . . . . . 1983-84 to 85-86
John Miszuk, D . . . . . . . . 1963-64
Bill Mitchell, D . . . . . . . . . 1963-64
John Mokosak, D . . . . . . . 1988-89 to 89-90
Ron Moffatt, LW . . . . . . . 1932-33 to 34-35
Gary Monahan, LW . . . . . . 1969-70
Hank Montieth, LW . . . . . 1968-69 to 70-71
Alfie Moore, G . . . . . . . . . 1939-40
Don Morrison, C . . . . . . . . 1947-48 to 48-49
Jim Morrison, D . . . . . . . . 1959-60

Rod Morrison, RW . . . . . . 1947-48
Dean Morton, D . . . . . . . . 1989-90
Gus Mortson, D . . . . . . . . 1958-59
Alex Motter, D . . . . . . . . . 1937-38 to 42-43
Johnny Mowers, G . . . . . . 1940-41 to 42-43;
    1946-47
Wayne Muloin, D . . . . . . . 1963-64
Don Murdoch, RW . . . . . . 1981-82
Brian Murphy, C . . . . . . . . 1974-75
Joe Murphy, C-RW . . . . . . 1986-87 to 89-90
Ron Murphy, LW . . . . . . . 1964-65 to 65-66
Ken Murray, D . . . . . . . . . 1972-73
Terry Murray, D . . . . . . . . 1976-77

## N

Jim Nahrgang, D . . . . . . . . 1974-75 to 76-77
Vaclav Nedomansky, C-RW . 1977-78 to 81-82
Rick Newell, D . . . . . . . . . 1972-73 to 73-74
John Newman, C . . . . . . . . 1930-31
Eddie Nicholson, D . . . . . . 1947-48
Jim Niekamp, D . . . . . . . . 1970-71 to 71-72
Jim Nill, RW . . . . . . . . . . 1987-88 to 89-90
**Reg Noble, D** . . . . . . . . . . **1927-28 to 32-33**
Ted Nolan, LW . . . . . . . . . 1981-82; 1983-84
Lee Norwood, D . . . . . . . . 1986-87 to 90-91
Hank Nowak, LW . . . . . . . 1974-75

## O

Adam Oates, C . . . . . . . . . 1985-86 to 88-89
Russ Oatman, LW . . . . . . . 1926-27
Mike O'Connell, D . . . . . . . 1985-86 to 89-90
Gerry Odrowski, D . . . . . . 1960-61 to 62-63
John Ogrodnick, LW . . . . . 1979-80 to 86-87;
    1992-93
Murray Oliver, C . . . . . . . . 1957-58;
    1959-60 to 60-61
Dennis Olson, LW . . . . . . . 1957-58
Jimmy Orlando, D . . . . . . . 1936-37 to 37-38;
    1939-40 to 42-43
Mark Osborne, LW . . . . . . 1981-82 to 82-83
Chris Osgood, G . . . . . . . . 1993-94 to 95-96

## P

Pete Palangio, LW . . . . . . . 1927-28
**Brad Park, D** . . . . . . . . . . . **1983-84 to 84-85**
Joe Paterson, LW . . . . . . . 1980-81 to 83-84
George Patterson, RW . . . . 1934-35
Butch Paul, C . . . . . . . . . . 1964-65
Marty Pavelich, LW . . . . . . 1947-48 to 56-57
Jim Pavese, D . . . . . . . . . 1987-88 to 88-89
Mark Pederson, LW . . . . . . 1993-94
Bert Peer, RW . . . . . . . . . 1939-40
Bob Perreault, G . . . . . . . . 1958-59
Jim Peters Jr, C . . . . . . . . . 1964-65 to 67-68
Jim Peters Sr, RW . . . . . . . 1949-50 to 50-51;
    1953-54
Brent Peterson, C . . . . . . . 1978-79 to 81-82
Gord Pettinger, C . . . . . . . 1933-34 to 37-38
Robert Picard, D . . . . . . . . 1989-90
Alex Pirus, RW . . . . . . . . . 1979-80
Rob Plumb, LW . . . . . . . . 1977-78 to 78-79

Nellie Podolsky, LW . . . . . 1948-49
**Bud Poile, RW** . . . . . . . . . **1948-49**
Don Poile, C-RW . . . . . . . . 1954-55; 1957-58
Dennis Polonich, RW . . . . 1974-75 to 80-81;
    1982-83
Poul Popiel, D . . . . . . . . . 1968-69 to 69-70
Marc Potvin, LW . . . . . . . . 1990-91 to 91-92
Dean Prentice, LW . . . . . . 1965-66 to 68-69
Noel Price, D . . . . . . . . . . 1961-62
Keith Primeau, C-LW . . . . . 1990-91 to 95-96
Bob Probert, LW-RW . . . . . 1985-86 to 93-94
Andre Pronovost, LW . . . . . 1962-63 to 64-65
**Marcel Pronovost, D** . . . . . **1949-50 to 64-65**
Metro Prystai, RW-C . . . . . 1950-51 to 57-58
Cliff Purpur, RW . . . . . . . . 1944-45
Chris Pusey, G . . . . . . . . . 1985-86
Jamie Pushor, D . . . . . . . . 1995-96 to 96-97
Nelson Pyatt, C . . . . . . . . 1973-74 to 74-75

## Q

**Bill Quackenbush, D** . . . . . **1942-43 to 48-49**

## R

Yves Racine, D . . . . . . . . . 1989-90 to 92-93
Clare Ragian, D . . . . . . . . 1950-51
Mike Ramsey, D . . . . . . . . 1995 to 95-96
Matt Ravlich, D . . . . . . . . . 1969-70
Marc Reaume, D . . . . . . . . 1959-60 to 60-61
Billy Reay, C . . . . . . . . . . 1943-44 to 44-45
Mickey Redmond, RW . . . . 1970-71 to 75-76
Earl (Dutch) Reibel, C . . . . . 1953-54 to 57-58
Gerry Reid, C . . . . . . . . . . 1948-49
Leo Reise, D . . . . . . . . . . 1946-47 to 51-52
Dave Richardson, LW . . . . . 1967-68
Terry Richardson, G . . . . . 1973-74 to 76-77
Steve Richmond, D . . . . . . 1985-86
Vincent Riendeau, G . . . . . 1991-92 to 93-94
Dennis Riggin, G . . . . . . . . 1959-60; 1962-63
Jim Riley, RW . . . . . . . . . 1926-27
Bob Ritchie, LW . . . . . . . . 1976-77 to 77-78
Wayne Rivers, RW . . . . . . 1961-62
John Ross Roach, G . . . . . . 1932-33 to 34-35
Phil Roberto, RW . . . . . . . 1974-75 to 75-76
Doug Roberts, RW . . . . . . 1965-66 to 67-68;
    1973-74 to 74-75
Earl Robertson, G . . . . . . . 1936-37
Fred Robertson, D . . . . . . . 1933-34
Torrie Robertson, LW . . . . 1988-89 to 89-90
Mike Robitaille, D . . . . . . . 1970-71
Desse Roche, RW . . . . . . . 1934-35
Earl Roche, LW . . . . . . . . 1934-35
Dave Rochefort, C . . . . . . . 1966-67
Leon Rochefort, RW . . . . . 1971-72 to 72-73
Harvey Rockburn, D . . . . . 1929-30 to 30-31
Dale Rolfe, D . . . . . . . . . . 1969-70 to 70-71
Rollie Rossignol, LW . . . . . 1943-44; 1945-46
Rolly Roulston, D . . . . . . . 1936-37
Bob Rouse, D . . . . . . . . . 1995 to 95-96
Tom Rowe, RW . . . . . . . . 1982-83
Bernie Ruelle, LW . . . . . . . 1943-44
Pat Rupp, G . . . . . . . . . . . 1963-64

Jimmy Rutherford, G ..... 1970-71;
1973-74 to 80-81;
1982-83

## S

Andre St Laurent, C ..... 1977-78 to 78-79;
1983-84
Sam St Laurent, G ....... 1986-87 to 89-90
Borje Salming, D ........ 1989-90
Barry Salovaara, D ...... 1974-75 to 75-76
Tomas Sandstrom, RW .... 1996-97
Ed Sanford, C .......... 1955-56
Bob Sauve, G ........... 1981-82
**Terry Sawchuk, G** ....... **1949-50 to 54-55;**
**1957-58 to 63-64;**
**1968-69**
Kevin Schamehorn, RW ... 1976-77; 1979-80
Jim Schoenfeld, D ....... 1981-82 to 82-83
Dwight Schofield, D ..... 1976-77
Enio Sclisizzi, LW ....... 1946-47 to 49-50;
1951-52
**Earl Seibert, D** .......... **1944-45 to 45-46**
Ric Seiling, RW ......... 1986-87
Brendan Shanahan, LW ... 1996-97
Daniel Shank, RW ....... 1989-90 to 90-91
Jeff Sharples, D ......... 1986-87 to 88-89
Doug Shedden, RW ...... 1985-86 to 86-87
Bobby Sheehan, C ....... 1976-77
Tim Sheehy, RW ........ 1977-78
Frank Sheppard, C ....... 1927-28
John Sheppard, LW ...... 1926-27 to 27-28
Ray Sheppard, RW ....... 1991-92 to 95-96
Gord Sherritt, D ......... 1943-44
John Sherf, LW ......... 1935-36 to 38-39;
1943-44
Jim Shires, LW .......... 1970-71
Steve Short, D .......... 1978-79
Gary Shuchuk, RW ...... 1990-91
Dave Silk, RW .......... 1984-85
Mike Sillinger, C ........ 1990-91 to 95
Cully Simon, D ......... 1942-43 to 44-45
Thain Simon, D......... 1946-47
Cliff Simpson, C......... 1946-47 to 47-48
Reg Sinclair, RW ........ 1952-53
**Darryl Sittler, C-LW** ..... **1984-85**
Bjorn Skaare, C ......... 1978-79
Glen Skov, C ........... 1949-50 to 54-55
Al Smith, G ............ 1971-72
Alex Smith, D .......... 1931-32
Brad Smith, RW......... 1980-81 to 84-85
Brian Smith, LW ........ 1957-58; 1960-61
Carl Smith, LW ......... 1943-44
Derek Smith, C ......... 1981-82 to 82-83
Floyd Smith, RW ........ 1962-63 to 67-68
Dalton (Nakina) Smith, LW. 1943-44
Normie Smith, G........ 1934-35 to 38-39;
1943-44 to 44-45
Rick Smith, D .......... 1980-81
Ted Snell, RW .......... 1974-75
Harold Snepts, D........ 1985-86 to 87-88

Sandy Snow, RW ........ 1968-69
Dennis Sobchuk, C ...... 1979-80
Ken Solheim, LW ....... 1982-83
Bob Solinger, LW........ 1959-60
Johnny Sorrell, LW ...... 1930-31 to 37-38
Fred Speck, C .......... 1968-69 to 69-70
Ted Speers, RW ......... 1985-86
Irv Spencer, D-LW....... 1963-64 to 65-66;
1967-68
Ron Stackhouse, D....... 1971-72 to 73-74
Ed Stankiewicz, LW...... 1953-54; 1955-56
Wilf Starr, C ........... 1933-34 to 35-36
Vic Stasiuk, RW-LW ..... 1950-51 to 54-55;
1960-61 to 62-63
Ray Staszak, RW ........ 1985-86
Frank Steele, LW ........ 1930-31
Greg Stefan, G ......... 1981-82 to 89-90
Pete Stemkowski, C ...... 1967-68 to 70-71
Blair Stewart, LW ....... 1973-74 to 74-75
Gaye Stewart, LW ....... 1950-51
**Jack Stewart, D** ......... **1938-39 to 42-43;**
**1945-46 to 49-50**
Gord Strate, D .......... 1956-57 to 58-59
Art Stratton, C .......... 1963-64
Herb Stuart, G .......... 1926-27
Barry Sullivan, RW ...... 1947-48
Bill Sutherland, LW ...... 1971-72

## T

John Taft, D ............ 1978-79
Jean-Guy Talbot, D ...... 1967-68
Chris Tancill, C ......... 1991-92 to 92-93
Billy Taylor, C .......... 1946-47
Ted Taylor, LW ......... 1966-67
Tim Taylor, LW ......... 1993-94 to 96-97
Harvey Teno, G ......... 1939-39
Larry Thibeault, LW ..... 1944-45
Billy Thompson, RW..... 1938-39; 1943-44
**Cecil (Tiny) Thompson, G . 1938-39 to 39-40**
Errol Thompson, LW ..... 1977-78 to 80-81
Jerry Toppazzini, RW..... 1955-56
Larry Trader, D ......... 1982-83; 1984-85
Percy Traub, D.......... 1927-28 to 28-29
Dave Trottier, LW ....... 1938-39
Joe Turner, G ........... 1941-42

## U

**Norm Ullman, C** ........ **1955-56 to 67-68**
Garry Unger, C.......... 1967-68 to 70-71

## V

Rogie Vachon, G......... 1978-79 to 79-80
Eric Vail, LW .......... 1981-82
Rick Vasko, D .......... 1979-80 to 80-81
Darren Veitch, D ........ 1985-86 to 87-88
Mike Vernon, G ......... 1995 to 95-96
Dennis Vial, D .......... 1990-91 to 92-93
Doug Volmer, RW ....... 1969-70 to 71-72
Carl Voss, C ........... 1932-33

## W

**Jack Walker, LW** ........ **1926-27 to 27-28**
Bob Wall, D          1964-65 to 66-67;
1971-72
Wes Walz, C ........... 1995-96
Aaron Ward, D ......... 1993-94;
1995-96 to 96-97
Eddie Wares, RW ....... 1937-38 to 42-43
Bryan Watson, D ....... 1965-66 to 66-67;
1973-74 to 76-77
Harry Watson, LW....... 1942-43; 1945-46
Jim Watson, D .......... 1963-64 to 65-66;
1967-68 to 69-70
Brian Watts, LW ........ 1975-76
Tom Webster, RW ....... 1970-71 to 71-72;
1979-80
**Cooney Weiland, C** ...... **1933-34 to 34-35**
Stan Weir, C ........... 1982-83
Carl Wetzel, G .......... 1964-65
Bob Whitelaw, D ........ 1940-41 to 41-42
Archie Wilder, LW....... 1940-41
Bob Wilkie, D .......... 1990-91
Burr Williams, D ........ 1933-34; 1936-37
Carl Williams, D ........ 1931-32
Dave (Tiger) Williams, LW. 1984-85
Fred Williams, C ........ 1976-77
Johnny Wilson, LW ...... 1949-50 to 54-55;
1957-58 to 58-59
Larry Wilson, C ......... 1949-50;
1951-52 to 52-53
Rick Wilson, D.......... 1976-77
Ross (Lefty) Wilson, G .... 1953-54
Murray Wing, D......... 1973-74
Eddie Wiseman, RW ..... 1932-33 to 35-36
Steve Wochy, C-RW ..... 1944-45; 1946-47
Benny Woit, D ......... 1950-51 to 54-55
Mike Wong, C .......... 1975-76
Paul Woods, LW......... 1977-78 to 83-84
Larry Wright, RW-C ..... 1977-78

## Y

Jason York, D .......... 1992-93 to 95
Doug Young, D ......... 1931-32 to 38-39
Howie Young, D......... 1960-61 to 62-63;
1966-67 to 67-68
Warren Young, LW ...... 1985-86
Paul Ysebaert, LW....... 1990-91 to 92-93
Steve Yzerman, C-LW .... 1983-84 to 96-97

## Z

Larry Zeidel, D ......... 1951-52 to 52-53
Ed Zeniuk, D ........... 1954-55
Rick Zombo, D ......... 1984-85 to 91-92
Rudy Zunich, D......... 1943-44

**Bold indicates member
of Pro Hockey Hall of Fame**

# Bibliography

Charles L. Coleman. *The Trail of the Stanley Cup* (Montreal: National Hockey League, 1976). (3 vol.)

David Cruise and Alison Griffiths. *Net Worth: Exploding the Myths of Pro Hockey* (New York: Penguin, 1992).

Dan Diamond (ed.). *The Official National Hockey League 75th Anniversary Commemorative Book* (Toronto: McClelland & Stewart, 1991).

Dan Diamond (ed.). *The Official National Hockey League Stanley Cup Centennial Book* (Buffalo: Firefly Books, 1992).

Dan Diamond (ed.). *Years of Glory, 1942-1967: The National Hockey League's Official Book of the Six-Team Era* (Toronto: McClelland & Stewart, 1994).

Stan Fischler. *The Fast-Flying Wings* (Englewood Cliffs, N.J.: Prentice-Hall, 1972).

Stan Fischler. *The Flakes of Winter* (Toronto: Warwick, 1992).

Stan Fischler. *Motor City Muscle: Gordie Howe, Terry Sawchuk, and the Championship Detroit Red Wings* (Toronto: Warwick, 1996).

Stan Fischler. *Those Were the Days* (New York: Dodd Mead, 1976).

Trent Frayne. *The Mad Men of Hockey* (Toronto: McClelland & Stewart, 1974).

Zander Hollander (ed.). *Inside Sports Hockey* [formerly *The Complete Encyclopedia of Ice Hockey*] (Detroit: Visible Ink Press, 1997).

Colleen and Gordie Howe and Charles Wilkins. *After the Applause* (Toronto: McClelland & Stewart, 1989).

Gordie Howe and Colleen Howe (with Tom DeLisle). *And . . . Howe!* (Traverse City, MI: Power Play Publications, 1995).

Dick Irvin. *The Habs: An Oral History of the Montreal Canadiens, 1940-1980* (Toronto: McClelland & Stewart, 1991).

D'Arcy Jenish. *The Stanley Cup: A Hundred Years of Hockey at Its Best* (Toronto: McClelland & Stewart, 1992).

Phil Loranger. *If They Played Hockey in Heaven: The Jack Adams Story* (Grosse Pointe Farms, MI: Marjoguyhen, 1976).

Roy MacSkimming. *Gordie: A Hockey Legend* (Vancouver: Greystone, 1994).

Don O'Reilly. *Mr. Hockey: The World of Gordie Howe* (New York: Henry Regnery Co., 1975).

Andrew Podnieks. *The Red Wings Book: The Most Complete Detroit Red Wings Fact Book Ever Published* (Toronto: ECW Press, 1996).

Jim Vipond. *Gordie Howe: Number 9* (Chicago: Follett, 1968).

Don Weekes. *Old-Time Hockey Trivia* (Vancouver: Greystone, 1995).

# Photo Credits